EDUCATING SEVERELY AND PROFOUNDLY HANDICAPPED STUDENTS

Contributors

Gary L. Adams

Mary Lou Caldwell

Janet W. Hill

Jeffrey Schilit

Les Sternberg

Ronald L. Taylor

Bonnie Utley

EDUCATING SEVERELY AND PROFOUNDLY HANDICAPPED STUDENTS

Les Sternberg

Gary L. Adams

Florida Atlantic University

AN ASPEN PUBLICATION®
Aspen Systems Corporation
Rockville, Maryland
London
1982

Library of Congress Cataloging in Publication Data

Main entry under title:
Educating severely and profoundly handicapped students.

Includes bibliographies and indexes.
1. Handicapped children—Education—Addresses,
essays, lectures. I. Sternberg, Les. II. Adams, Gary L.
LC4015.E37   371.9   82-4102
ISBN: 0-89443-695-3   AACR2

Publisher: John Marozsan
Editorial Director: R. Curtis Whitesel
Managing Editor: Margot Raphael
Editorial Services: Eileen Higgins
Printing and Manufacturing: Debbie Swarr

Library of Congress Catalog Card Number: 82-4102
ISBN: 0-89443-695-3

Printed in the United States of America

1 2 3 4 5

To *Stan* and *Ev*,
for their interest and encouragement.

L. S.

To *James* and *Nina*,
for their support through the years.

G. L. A.

And to *R. Curtis Whitesel*,
whose contribution and dedication can never be measured,
only admired.

Table of Contents

Preface... xi

Acknowledgments xiii

PART I—INTRODUCTION 1

Chapter   1—Perspectives on Educating Severely and Profoundly
            Handicapped Students 3
            Les Sternberg

            Defining the Population of Severely and Profoundly
            Handicapped.. 3
            Critical Training Concerns 5
            The Umbrella Model of Education 6
            Conclusion 9

PART II—ENVIRONMENTAL CONCERNS 11

Chapter   2—Establishing a Program for Severely and Profoundly
            Handicapped Students 13
            Jeffrey Schilit

            Problems and Past Practices 13
            Suggested Methods 14
            Conclusion 24

Chapter 3—Parent Involvement and Training................................... **27**
Les Sternberg and Mary Lou Caldwell

Problems and Past Practices 27
Suggested Methods 30
Conclusion 41

PART III—ASSESSMENT CONCERNS................................ **45**

Chapter 4—Assessment.. **47**
Ronald L. Taylor

Problem.. 47
Past Practices 47
Suggested Methods 52
Conclusion 92

PART IV—BEHAVIOR MANAGEMENT CONCERNS **95**

Chapter 5—Social Skills Training **97**
Gary L. Adams, Les Sternberg, and Ronald L. Taylor

Problems and Past Practices 97
Suggested Methods 105
Conclusion 128

PART V—CURRICULUM CONCERNS **133**

Chapter 6—Curriculum Development and Implementation................... **135**
Gary L. Adams

Problems and Past Practices 135
Suggested Methods 146
Conclusion 156

Chapter 7—Motor Skills and Adaptations............................. **163**
Bonnie Utley

Problems and Past Practices 163
Suggested Methods 164
Conclusion 204

Chapter 8—Communication Instruction **209**
Les Sternberg

    Problem.. 209
    Past Practices 209
    Suggested Methods 210
    Conclusion 238

Chapter 9—Independent Living Skills... **243**
Gary L. Adams

    Problem.. 243
    Past Practices and Suggested Methods........................ 243
    Conclusion 263

Chapter 10—Vocational Training... **269**
Janet W. Hill

    Problem.. 269
    Past Practices 275
    Suggested Methods 277
    Conclusion 309

   PART VI—SUMMARY... **313**

**Chapter 11—Future Directions in the Education of Severely and
                Profoundly Handicapped Students** **315**
Les Sternberg and Gary Adams

    A Future Look at the Environment................................ 315
    A Future Look at Assessment 317
    A Future Look at Behavior Management....................... 319
    A Future Look at Curriculum.. 320
    Conclusion 322

Appendix—Communication Programming Inventory **324**

Author Index... **339**

Subject Index **349**

Preface

The basic purpose of *Educating Severely and Profoundly Handicapped Students* is enlightenment. Education of the severely and profoundly handicapped is a relatively recent practice and, in order to avoid the trial-and-error experiences of instruction that predominated the early history of education of other types of handicapped individuals, it is imperative that systematic types of instructional practices be set forth. This book presents a global instructional view of severely and profoundly handicapped students yet focuses on specific concerns and strategies that must be dealt with in order that educational growth can be achieved.

This edited text has been designed so that there is continuity and consistency between and within each chapter. Each contributing author was requested to provide information within his or her area of expertise and to format the material within discrete topics. Therefore, each chapter (aside from the introductory and summary chapters) has been written to address four major concerns: problem, past practices, suggested methods, and conclusion. The *problem* has to do with various constraints or limitations that are presently in existence pertaining to the specific content emphasis of the chapter. *Past practices* outline techniques or strategies that have already been devised to address the problems. In the *suggested methods* section, each author has specified what he or she deems noteworthy in terms of preferred practice. The intent of the *conclusion* is to relate past practices to preferred methods and to provide an idea of what may be in store in the future.

If one were to attempt to identify a common thread that runs through this entire text, it would probably be situation-specific eclecticism. Various points of view have been presented and different approaches have been discussed and supported. Rather than looking upon these approaches as antithetical, the case has hopefully been made for the need, and commitment, to adjust all methods to the specific needs and problems of the individual handicapped student. This may necessitate the adoption of "conflicting" hypotheses, but if the point is to make progress, this form of adoption may be necessary.

Les Sternberg, Ph.D.
and
Gary L. Adams, Ph.D.
August 1982

Acknowledgments

Family support through the completion of an endeavor of this nature should never be taken for granted. Our children deserve special praise for their continual acceptance of the absence (oftentimes in mind only) of their fathers during the preparation of this book. A special debt of gratitude is felt for Jean Sternberg and Barbara Adams. Their support has been extraordinary.

Part I

Introduction

Chapter 1

Perspectives on Educating Severely and Profoundly Handicapped Students

Les Sternberg
Florida Atlantic University

DEFINING THE POPULATION OF SEVERELY AND PROFOUNDLY HANDICAPPED

Our society is in the midst of a shift toward increased emphasis on providing education for more severely disabled students. Given this shift, administrators, educators, and other individuals responsible for providing services have been faced with an interesting problem: how to define the target population. This has not been an easy task, especially given the divergent viewpoints and professional backgrounds of the individuals responsible for such decision making and the fact that definitions used by professionals typically reflect the type of classification scheme they support. In this case many individuals prefer etiological classifications (on the basis of chromosomal aberrations, for example). Others tend toward psychometric descriptions (such as a measured intelligence quotient of 20) or educational classifications (custodial mentally retarded, for example). More recently, behavioral descriptions (self-abuse, for example) have received attention. The result is one of two extremes: either the categorical labeling of students, which precludes consideration of their individual needs (as typified by the use of etiological, psychometric, or educational classifications), or the total individualization of students, which precludes consideration of shared characteristics with other students (as typified by the use of behavioral descriptions).

It should be obvious that any definition that is posited should reflect both the individual *and* group context of the student being considered. In this way, between-group differences (as, for example, between severely/profoundly handicapped and mildly/moderately handicapped) and within-group similarities and differences can be delineated.

A definition should not be developed only to assist educators in making administrative decisions (such as where to place the student for services delivery or under what category to place the student for state reimbursement).

3

A definition ought to provide direction in both assessment and programming practices. Given the fact that assessment is typically the first step in determining instructional alternatives, a definition should assist in specifying three basic conditions: (1) the eligibility of the student to qualify as a severely or profoundly handicapped student; (2) the general performance levels of that student; and (3) the competencies (specific strengths and weaknesses) of the student. A statement in regard to these conditions can be of invaluable assistance in determining the direction and content of an appropriate instructional program.

Specific problems are inherent in a number of definitions that have been drafted to describe the severely and/or profoundly handicapped. Justen (1976) has summarized a number of issues pertaining to these definitions. First, some of the definitions tend to be based on an exclusion principle. That is, if one's handicapping condition were of such a nature that he or she would be excluded from any currently operating special education instructional unit, then that individual would be defined as severely or profoundly handicapped. Second, if the definition specifies a category of handicapping condition (such as profound mental retardation), there is no distinction between a category for eligibility versus a category for specific services. This can lead to instructional decisions based solely on the individual's label rather than the individual's needs. Third, some definitions describe the severely or profoundly handicapped in terms of certain behaviors but do not put those behaviors into any type of developmental framework. Without including the developmental perspective, one may very well lose sight of expectations for the individual student. The behaviors observed may be developmentally appropriate and, in terms of the age of the student, may not constitute a severe or profound disability. Fourth, very few definitions provide information that is of educational significance. If a definition is present to assist in making instructional program and placement decisions, some description of educational parameters should be an integral part of that definition.

Given these criticisms, it is clear that a definition should have at a minimum the following components: (1) a statement that describes the behavioral domains that must be considered in making a diagnosis of a severe or profound handicapping condition; (2) a description of functional level within those behavioral domains that takes into account developmental concerns; (3) a statement reflecting the educational needs of the individual; and (4) if a label specification is mandated (as is the case in certain states), a label designation that is used only for the purpose of determining eligibility for services. The following is tendered as an adequate and acceptable definition of the severely and profoundly handicapped:

A severely or profoundly handicapped individual is one who (1) is eligible to receive educational services under one or more legally defined categories of handicapping condition; (2) exhibits severe developmental discrepancies in at least three of the following behavioral/content areas: motor/mobility, activities of daily living (self-help skills), communication, cognition, and social/emotional development; and (3) requires a self-contained educational structure with continuous monitoring and observation.

A *severe developmental discrepancy* is defined as one where the individual's current performance level of behavior is less than one-half of expectancy based on the individual's chronological age. However, a developmental age ceiling of six years per behavioral/content area is imposed (that is, if an individual is functioning at or above a six-year developmental level within an area, the individual would not be considered to have a severe developmental discrepancy within that area regardless of chronological age). *Self-contained educational structures* are classrooms where the total educational needs of the individual are met by specially trained personnel. These structures may be found within the full range of environments, from segregated facilities like state schools to public schools.

The above-stated definition and the preceding points of clarification represent a compilation of ideas presented in other definitions and classification schemes (Haring, 1978; Justen, 1976). In order for an individual to be defined as severely or profoundly handicapped, that individual would have to meet all three criteria specified in the definition. Although restrictive in nature, the definition will aid in understanding the target focus of this text.

CRITICAL TRAINING CONCERNS

Compared with the educational situation of the mildly and moderately handicapped, provision of educational services for the severely and profoundly handicapped represents a relatively recent endeavor. Unfortunately, in many respects, the education that is currently being provided for severely and profoundly handicapped students is very similar to what was available during the infancy stage of education for the mildly and moderately handicapped. During that time, the handicapped student's needs were broken down into separate fragments (such as academic and behavioral control needs), and education and/or treatment to meet these needs were accomplished under an isolated training model. If the student had a reading problem and an out-of-seat problem, for example, the two were treated as completely separate entities. Techniques that emphasized the isolated qualities of these problems were used. This ensured the continuation of an instructional practice that did not allow for the integration of strategies based on the integrated quality of student needs. As the years progressed and research data began to prove the worth of the integrated instructional model, dramatic and beneficial changes were wrought in the area of education of the mildly and moderately handicapped.

Even though the needs of the severely and profoundly handicapped are considerably different from those of the more mildly impaired, it should stand to reason that their needs and the corresponding educational techniques to address those needs ought to be looked upon from an integrated point of view. In order to accomplish this, it is paramount that personnel responsible for providing education for the severely and profoundly handicapped look at the complete picture. The entire ecology of this population must be analyzed and addressed.

THE UMBRELLA MODEL OF EDUCATION

There are a number of interacting components which, when combined, will constitute the educational arena for severely and profoundly handicapped students. These components can be placed within a structure that describes them in terms of their *level of consideration*. This structure is termed the *vertical umbrella model* (Sedlak & Sternberg, 1978; see Figure 1-1). Within multiple "umbrellas," specific components and areas are addressed in a supraordinate to subordinate fashion. The overriding umbrella is the handicapped individual's environment. This is represented by the handicapped individual's home and school setting and by the people who provide services within those situations (administrators, parents, teachers, etc.). Below this umbrella, one would find another dealing with assessment procedures that should be used with the severely or profoundly handicapped student. The placement of this umbrella below the environmental umbrella indicates that assessment must take into account the environmental constraints imposed upon the handicapped student. The third umbrella is devoted to management or behavior control. Its position dictates that direction in management techniques should stem from assessment data and that behavior control must be considered within the context of the handicapped individual's environment. The last umbrella deals with curriculum designs and skill development. Inherent in its placement are consideration of skill instruction within the context of the behavioral needs of the handicapped individual, education that is based on assessment information, and instruction that relates to the total environment in which the individual finds himself or herself.

The order of these umbrellas does not dictate an order of importance. What we have is a model for viewing the education of the severely and profoundly handicapped from an integrated point of view rather than from an approach that addresses educational needs in a piecemeal fashion. The umbrella model also provides an organizational framework within which topics addressing the

Figure 1-1 The Vertical Umbrella Model of Educational Concerns

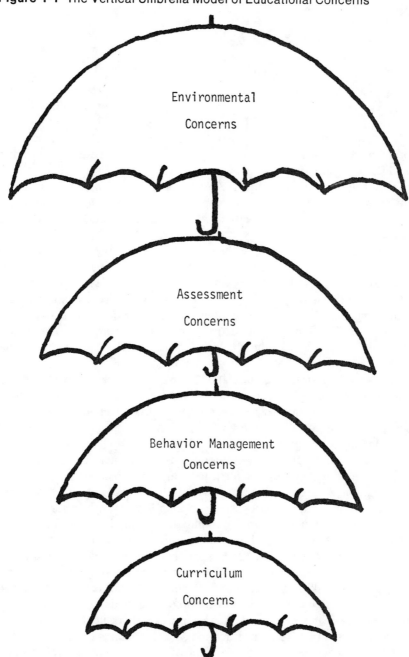

educational needs of the severely and profoundly handicapped can be presented and discussed.

Content within the Umbrella Model

Various components related to educational practices may be described within each of the programmatic umbrellas. Material presented in this text has been arranged so that each umbrella area of concern is addressed in a comprehensive fashion. Chapters 2 and 3 deal with variables directly affecting the type of educational environment that will be established for the severely or profoundly handicapped student. Chapter 2 considers the establishment of an ecologically sound systems approach for providing public school education for this target population. Chapter 3 provides information related to parent involvement and training, with emphasis on a model system for parent participation in the education of severely and profoundly handicapped students.

Concerns related to the assessment of the severely and profoundly handicapped are presented in Chapter 4. Here, specific statistical concerns are addressed, coupled with coverage of current assessment procedures and instrumentation that may be appropriate for use with severely and profoundly handicapped students. Since one major purpose of assessment is the generation of educational goals and objectives, a pragmatic approach is presented for determining which procedure or instrument to select in the assessment process.

Chapter 5 presents material related to the behavior management umbrella. Social skills training is discussed within the framework of three interrelated components: systematic observation procedures, techniques for changing social behaviors, and validation strategies for determining the effectiveness of behavior change programs.

The curriculum umbrella is represented by Chapters 6 through 10. In Chapter 6, different designs for curriculum development and classroom organization are presented. General skill techniques that cross different content emphases are also discussed. Chapter 7 deals with motor aspects of severe and profound handicapping conditions. Emphasis is placed on relating motor adaptations (such as different handling techniques) not only to motor skill development but also other curricular areas (different positioning strategies for developing attending behavior, for example). In Chapter 8, communication skill development is considered. Here, communication skills are separated from language skills with procedures to develop both discussed. Independent living skills training comprises the content of Chapter 9. Included within this area is instruction in the development of self-help skills. In Chapter 10, components related to vocational programming are presented.

A step-by-step procedure for implementing a vocational program for the severely and profoundly handicapped draws the discussion of curriculum concerns to a close.

Chapter 11 provides a summary of the information that has been presented in the text. Taking the current state of the art in the education of severely and profoundly handicapped students, this chapter looks at anticipated and hoped for future directions in services delivery for this population and makes a strong call for continued research in the field.

CONCLUSION

The population of severely and profoundly handicapped students represents a rather small percentage of all those considered handicapped. This low incidence factor has led some to believe that provision of educational services to this population may not be worthwhile or cost effective. However, the real issue should not be whether we should provide services but rather how the services can be made more worthwhile and more cost effective. Historically, this has been a question that has permeated all of special education, and to draw the line now in terms of severely and profoundly handicapped students is ludicrous. Greene (1981) describes the direction of educational research and the role of educational researchers. However, what is being said has considerable pertinence to the above issue as well as the state of special education in general.

> Detachment will not do. . . . And there ought to be mutual respect, regard for each one's "competence and integrity." If we cannot listen to each other with consideration, our house will not be "ethically in order"; indeed, the house may fall. (p. 6)

REFERENCES

Greene, M. Response to a predecessor. *Educational Researcher,* 1981, *10*(3), 5–6.

Haring, N.G. The severely handicapped. In N.G. Haring (Ed.), *Behavior of exceptional children.* Columbus, Ohio: Charles E. Merrill, 1978.

Justen, J.E. Who are the severely handicapped?: A problem in definition. *AAESPH Review,* 1976, *1*(5), 1–12.

Sedlak, R., & Sternberg, L. A teacher training program for the severely/profoundly retarded. *Journal for Special Educators of the Mentally Retarded,* 1978, *14*(3), 193–196.

Environmental Concerns

Chapter 2

Establishing a Program for Severely and Profoundly Handicapped Students

Jeffrey Schilit
Florida Atlantic University

PROBLEM AND PAST PRACTICES

For years, school systems have been responding to the educational needs of the mildly and moderately handicapped populations. Very few school systems, however, have developed and funded comprehensive programs for the severely and profoundly handicapped segments of their society (Sontag, Burke, & York, 1976).

With the passage and adoption of P.L. 94-142, the concept of "zero reject" has added new dimensions to the role and scope of the public school administrator in relation to providing direct and indirect services to the severely and profoundly handicapped school age population. Brown, Branston, Hamre-Nietupski, Johnson, Wilcox, and Gruenewald (1979) have reported that the primary educational approach utilized by the public school sector has been segregated, self-contained classrooms or programs located within state or private institutions. Yet, according to Stetson (1979), in meeting the mandate set forth in P.L. 94-142 to provide the most appropriate educational setting in the least restrictive environment, increasing numbers of severely and profoundly handicapped individuals are finding themselves back in their home community and in the public schools.

The primary question that must be raised is, are the public school systems adequately equipped to meet the challenge that the severely and profoundly handicapped bring in addition to their handicapping condition? Concerns that must be addressed in order to establish a positive, viable, and multifaceted program for the severely and profoundly handicapped relate to such matters as administrative theory, physical facilities and architectural barrier removal, transportation, staffing needs and multidisciplinary involvement, advisory boards, staff and student preparation, and placement procedures/least restrictive environment. Each of these topics will be discussed in this chapter to facilitate understanding of how the development and continuation of programs for the severely and profoundly handicapped must proceed.

SUGGESTED METHODS

Numerous administrative tasks need to be explored prior to the establishment of any program for the severely and profoundly handicapped.

Administrative Theory

There are educational administrators, and there are educational leaders. The educational administrator strives to maintain a smooth running operation and is not much of a risk taker. The educational leader seeks innovation and ways in which to maximize output from various instructional situations without risking educational priorities. If a program is to be developed for the severely and profoundly handicapped, an educational leader will be needed. This assumption is predicated on the belief that new and original theories will be needed to provide the type and range of services requisite for the population under discussion.

Administrators must realize that traditional administrative theories, either in special education or regular education administration, may not appropriately serve the severely and profoundly handicapped. As Reynolds and Birch (1977) point out,

> The administrative arrangements for special education in most schools of the nation well into the 1960's and even into the 1970's, in many places, can be described in terms of the "two box" theory. From this point of view, in local school buildings there are two types of classrooms (regular and special), two general classes of children (regular class children and exceptional children), and two sets of teachers (regular education and special education). In effect, two separate school systems are operated, each with its own supervisory staff and funding system. (p. 30)

In order to allow for public school integration of the more severely disabled, it should be obvious that this administrative operational theory must be replaced by school systems and individuals planning to establish new and functional programs for severely and profoundly handicapped individuals.

Historically, theories of special education administration have evolved out of general educational administrative theories or theories related to societal concepts. Weber's bureaucratic model (1947), McGregor's Theory X and Theory Y motivational theory (1960), Burello and Sage's social system theory

(1979), and Hersey and Blanchard's situational leadership theory (1977) have all been implemented and have met with success as administrative theories for special education. Perhaps Burello's and Sage's theory most closely encompasses the performance roles of the administrator working with severely and profoundly handicapped students—change agent, advocate, and when necessary, adversary.

Culbertson (1979) reviewed many theories applied in special and general educational administration and indicated that much of the theoretical movement has, perhaps, outlived its usefulness in today's educational society. He holds that what is now needed is a "theory of practice" that would inform the educational leadership of the "is" and "ought" aspects of both the school and the society. According to Howe (1981), "Considering the prevailing uncertainties about the usefulness of theory, as well as its most appropriate methods of inquiry, a theory of special education administration might be fraught with even more problems. The best approach may be for special education administrators to join with general administrators in a continuing effort to build a more useful theory of practice" (p. 11).

Physical Facilities and Architectural Barrier Removal

The physical facilities required for the severely and profoundly handicapped may be considerably different from those needed by nonhandicapped students or those with mild or moderate handicapping conditions. As such, special considerations must be kept in mind when establishing a program. In addition to criteria established by P.L. 94-142, close attention must be given to P.L. 93-112, the Vocational Rehabilitation Act, as amended in Section 504 in 1978. Subpart C: Program Accessibility of Section 504 prohibits exclusion of qualified handicapped persons from educational programs or activities due to facilities that are inaccessible or unusable. Therefore, when establishing a program for the severely and profoundly handicapped, the physical facility should be of primary concern and not an afterthought. Without prior planning, the entire educational process could be negated.

When considering the physical facilities appropriate for the severely and profoundly handicapped, three general concerns must be kept in mind (Rogers, Grigsby, Welch, Garton, & Greenwood, 1979). These are (1) the accessibility of program and services, (2) the usability of the facilities, and (3) the facilitative qualities of the structure and the design of the environment. In order to resolve whether or not these concepts have been fully explored and remedies proposed, certain key areas must be addressed. The first deals with the nature of the population. What types of handicapped individuals and handicapping conditions will be served? Will ambulation or sensory impairment be a consideration? What will the age of the students be and how will they be grouped? The second relates to location. How will the facilities for the severely and profoundly handicapped relate to other parts of the building and to the outdoor areas? Will programming take place on one or more floors? In one or more buildings? Third, capacity of current operation must be considered. The number of potential students will dictate the answers to many of the preceding questions. Fourth, proposed instructional activities should be outlined. A determination of the regularly scheduled uses of each space in the facility must be made. "Consideration of these four areas will provide not only information related to program accessibility and utility but also information related to ways in which instruction can be facilitated" (Rogers et al., 1979, p. 49).

Information relative to physical facilities and the removal of architectural barriers can be found in the following documents:

The American National Standards Institute. *American National Standards Specifications for Making Buildings and Facilities Accessible to, and Usable by, the Physically Handicapped.* New York: Author, 1979.

United States Architectural and Transportation Barriers Compliance Board. *A Guidebook to: The Minimum Federal Guidelines and Requirements for Accessible Design.* Washington, D.C.: Author, 1981.

Transportation

Traditional modes of transportation will be, in all probability, inappropriate for many of the severely and profoundly handicapped. Alternate and innovative transportation schemes must be established. While literature abounds related to transporting exceptional students as outlined in P.L. 94-142, there is a paucity of literature pertaining to transportation concerns of severely and profoundly handicapped individuals. Stetson (1979) and Sontag, Burke, and York (1976) briefly address this pressing problem, focusing on two major aspects: the student and the mode of transportation.

As the service base of school districts increases and as education of exceptional individuals is more and more incorporated into the basic services of the rural school district, transportation becomes increasingly more important. As more severely and profoundly handicapped individuals are served by the school system, the range of handicapping conditions will increase. Therefore, specific student-oriented concerns must be explored related to transportation.

The amount of time a student must spend being transported should be evaluated with respect to the degree of his or her handicapping condition. The distance traveled by the severely and profoundly handicapped student should be as minimal and direct as possible. To this extent, bus travel may be precluded. Therefore, alternative modes of transportation should be explored, including taxicabs, minivans, and car pooling.

Another consideration must be the handicapping condition itself. This will dictate the type of physical accommodation necessary within the transporting vehicle. Determination must be made as to how many students will be wheelchair bound and how many, if any, will be stretcher bound. This information will assist in determining which methods of transportation are viable and which must be excluded.

Finally, when establishing a transportation program for the severely and profoundly handicapped, sufficient funds must be set aside to cover the transportation needs of the students. This could amount to a sizable part of any operating budget. Therefore, preplanning is a requirement that cannot and should not be avoided.

The various modes of transportation will depend on many factors (proximity of school to home, type of handicapping condition, etc.). The importance of the vehicle itself, while critical, should not be placed above that of the driver of the vehicle. Care should be taken to train the driver of the severely and profoundly handicapped student in emergency medical techniques, positioning, use and care of bracing apparatus, and other pertinent information needed to best serve the student during the transportation period of the school day. *Transportation of the Handicapped: A Survey of State Education Agency Transportation Directors* (1981), a publication of the National Association of State Directors of Special Education, provides invaluable information on this subject.

Staffing Needs and Multidisciplinary Involvement

The traditional staffing patterns usually found within a school system will most likely not be sufficient for or compatible with the needs of the severely and profoundly handicapped. Therefore, a reorganization of the administrative and teaching table of organization will be required. This reorganization or redefinition of positions will extend from the school board of education to the building maintenance staff and include volunteers and parents. In other words, everyone involved with the education of severely and profoundly handicapped students must be trained and acquainted with the various needs of this population.

To achieve the desired staffing needs and arrangements within a multidisciplinary approach, the school system should recognize that the position of Assistant Superintendent for Special Education must be established. After reviewing numerous tables of organization, Howe (1981) has indicated that this position is missing in most school systems and that the attempt to develop such a position has not been very successful. Staffing and team development usually fall within the scope of responsibility of the local administrator or the building principal.

While multidisciplinary teams are not new to the educational arena, they are now mandated for special education by P.L. 94-142. Whether this mandate will result in better educational programming for the severely and profoundly handicapped has yet to be determined. If used effectively, multidisciplinary teams should benefit the handicapped in three major areas: instruction, diagnosis, and service delivery.

What must be avoided at all cost when establishing a multidisciplinary team is a power struggle for the leadership and control of the team. While a leader of the team must emerge and help to establish goals and objectives, caution must be exercised that special interest groups such as parents, psychologists, or teachers are not allowed to dominate and subvert the intent of the team. The problem can be a very serious one. Landau and Gerken (1979) indicated that building administrators preferred that the school psychologist be the leader of the team. Yet Waters (1973) reported that the school psychologist preferred the role of a consultant on the team. Teachers supported the findings of Waters but also indicated that they should have the major role on the multidisciplinary team (Landau & Gerken, 1979). However, who the team leader is should not be the main concern. How he or she merges the strengths of all the team members to best serve the severely and profoundly handicapped is primary to the role and scope of the multidisciplinary team.

Rogers et al. (1979) have identified five basic goals and objectives related to the operation of an effective multidisciplinary team. The first objective is establishing the need for the team. An assessment should be conducted to ensure the need for the team and to assist in determination of its composition. Upon completion and analysis of the needs assessment, a statement of intent should be developed that describes the goals, objectives, procedures, timelines, responsibilities, expected outcomes, and priorities of service delivery for each member of the team and for the team as a whole.

The second objective is establishing the program data base. The team should review all documents that contain information about agencies and/or programs currently providing services to the severely and profoundly handicapped in the area. Once the agencies and programs are identified, methods for integrating their services within the school system should be implemented.

The third objective is identifying the planning target. This involves ensuring that all components necessary for the full delivery of services are available as needed for the handicapped population.

The fourth objective is establishing interagency provisions. The members of the multidisciplinary team must resolve three basic areas of possible disagreement:

> specification of inter-program *responsibilities* (e.g., which program provides which services, services which children, definition of case management process, etc.), specification of *cost* absorption, sharing or reimbursement (e.g., first dollar/last dollar responsibility, joint use of equipment, facilities, etc.), and specification of *procedures* to be used in delivering services (e.g., provisions for case management, assignments, preparation of cooperative individual plans). (Rogers et al., 1979, p. 161)

The final objective is ensuring collaboration in service delivery. This entails designing the team in such a way that member cooperation in implementation of direct services is guaranteed. Inherent in this objective are proper and complete information dissemination, training, and continuous updating of all relevant factors pertaining to each handicapped student's case.

Advisory Board

A point that must be stated without equivocation is that an advisory board is just that: advisory. This should be explained in detail to those members chosen to serve on the board. Though the advisory board may be asked to assist in the formulation of policy, procedures, services, and programs, its recommendations must be evaluated in light of the school board's administrative and operational policies and guidelines.

The advisory board should not be developed or put together in a cavalier manner. It must have a definite role in the provision of services to the severely and profoundly handicapped. Therefore, the composition of the board must reflect the goals and objectives of the program that have been formulated.

The proverb "too many chefs spoil the broth" should be kept in mind when determining the size and composition of the advisory board. Still, there should be representation on the board from the following populations: administration, teaching staff, ancillary service staff, medicine, university training programs, community programs, parents, local government, and local business. The school system must recognize that if it selects and charges an advisory board to assist in the development of comprehensive services for the severely and profoundly handicapped, and requests that members contribute to the decision-making process, then it must also recognize that this group of individuals has as much to contribute as the school professionals.

Staff Preparation

Stainback, Stainback, and Maurer (1976) forecast that as more state and local school systems mandated education programs for the severely and profoundly handicapped, there would be a substantial demand for teachers for this population. Indeed, the prophecy has come true. Wilcox (1977) cautions that because of the high demand for services for the severely and profoundly handicapped, conditions now exist that might be counterproductive to the movement and gains achieved on behalf of this population. In the area of staff preparation, she raises two major concerns that must be addressed:

> The first problem is that school districts may be forced to respond to pressure by hiring and staffing classrooms with personnel who are *willing*, rather than *trained* or *qualified*, to work with the severely handicapped. . . . A second danger arising from current pressures to serve the severely and profoundly impaired is that history may repeat itself. We may find that teachers' colleges respond to training needs in the field in terms of quantity, rather than quality. (p. 418)

The first problem addressed by Wilcox relates to the axiom in special education that it is better not to organize and develop a special classroom if a competent and qualified teacher cannot be found. However, the demand for services and current litigation have forced many school districts to ignore this axiom. If this practice is carried out in a large-scale manner, the outcome will be failure of the schools to meet the overall needs of the severely and profoundly handicapped. Teachers trained to work with the mildly or moderately handicapped may not readily adapt to the major training needs of the more severely handicapped. Additional staff development and training may be beneficial. Sontag, Burke, and York (1973) indicated that there was a direct relationship between the degree of the handicapping condition and the competence of the teacher. Their contention was that the greater the degree of the handicap, the greater and more precise were the training skills needed by the staff.

Wilcox's second concern is directly tied into the first. That is, teacher training institutions should not simply prepare their graduates for existing positions that are in demand in the public sector (such as those positions dealing with the mildly/moderately disabled). If this occurs, what will evolve are teachers who are ill-equipped to meet the demands of severely and profoundly handicapped students in the schools.

There are two primary approaches to staff preparation. One is preservice education and the other is inservice education. Preservice programs have greater control over prospective teachers and typically can provide a more structured learning sequence. There are many good special education teachers already in the schools, however, who have the skills and abilities to adapt and become outstanding teachers of the severely and profoundly handicapped if comprehensive inservice education is provided. Regardless of whether preservice or inservice training is the mode of staff preparation, each participant must acquire a basic set of skills and be able to translate these skills into programmatic operation based on the needs expressed by the severely and profoundly handicapped students placed under his or her care and direction.

Rogers et al. (1979) have devised the Professional and Support Staff Needs Assessment Survey as an example of an outline of effective staff preparation and development. It can be utilized with pre- or inservice regular or special educators, administrators, support staff, and parents. Seven major areas are covered: general knowledge and role responsibility, assessment, educational programming, evaluation and monitoring, interpersonal skills, administration and management, and special educators as resource individuals.

Integration: Nonhandicapped Students and Regular Educators

Nonhandicapped students' acceptance of the severely and profoundly handicapped is an important facet in the effort to successfully include these individuals in the public sector. Smith and Smith (1978) state that the practice of including the severely and profoundly handicapped in the school system has become a highly visible trend. However, without direct intervention on the part of special education, the nonhandicapped student's attitude about the handicapped or handicapping conditions will in all likelihood not change (Gottlieb, 1980).

Ottman (1981) indicates that in order to assist the nonhandicapped student to deal with and accept the severely and profoundly handicapped, the special educator must first deal with the regular educator. This might take the form of recommendations for adapting lessons, materials, and facilities to be used with the handicapped individual within the regular education setting, or discussion of the social and educational interactive needs of the severely and profoundly handicapped. Ottman states that a more direct approach might be to make special presentations to nonhandicapped students and then be available to answer questions that might arise.

Hamre-Nietupski and Nietupski (1981) offer a different suggestion. They recommend a hands-on approach to increase positive interaction between nonhandicapped students and severely and profoundly handicapped individuals. For example, in relation to school jobs and activities they suggest that nonhandicapped students can serve as tutors to handicapped students to help them acquire certain necessary skills needed to do simple, routine tasks (collating a school newspaper, for example). They also contend that properly trained high school students have the skills and abilities to serve as information disseminators to their peers concerning aspects of severe and profound handicapping conditions. This information could effect positive changes in attitudes.

Preparation of regular educators to deal with severely and profoundly handicapped students should also be a preservice training concern (Flynn, Gacka, & Sundeen, 1978). Unfortunately, the current effort is being directed toward familiarizing prospective regular educators with only the mildly and moderately handicapped, that is, those handicapping conditions that lend themselves more to a mainstreaming option. Hamre-Nietupski and Nietupski (1981) have, therefore, opted for a continuous, on-site type of inservice attempt. They have outlined a number of methods that can be utilized to prepare regular teaching faculty to work effectively with the severely and profoundly handicapped. These methods range from actual inservice training sessions on integration efforts to sensitization procedures that can be built into regular education curricula. Permeating their entire approach is the emphasis on visibility of the severely and profoundly handicapped student within the public school.

> The integration of severely handicapped students into regular schools requires a great deal of time and energy on the part of many individuals. To provide severely handicapped students with an educational environment that truly approaches being less restrictive requires *ongoing systematic efforts*. . . . Such efforts must include faculty and student use of several formal and informal methods on a longitudinal basis. Such efforts, carried out by those who are enthusiastic about present and future possibilities for integration, can help to insure that severely handicapped students are not only physically present but also an *integral* part of the regular public schools they attend.[1] (Hamre-Nietupski & Nietupski, 1981, p. 39)

Placement/Due Process/Least Restrictive Environment

The concepts of placement, due process, and least restrictive environment are intertwined in relation to the establishment of programs for the severely and profoundly handicapped. The zero reject concept of P.L. 94–142 implies that no handicapped individual may be excluded from an appropriate public education regardless of the severity of the handicapping condition. Therefore, this population must go through the same placement process as an individual identified as mildly handicapped. Abeson, Bolick, and Hass (1976) have described the following sequence of events:

1. referral by teacher or parent
2. notification to parent of intent to evaluate student
3. receipt of notification by parent
4. receipt by education agency of parental permission to evaluate student
5. scheduling of evaluation
6. notification to parent of scheduled evaluation
7. completion of evaluation
8. report of results and recommendation for educational programming
9. input by parent into program/placement options
10. receipt of parental permission to institute program/placement
11. placement of student in appropriate instructional environment
12. review of placement
13. development of subsequent recommendations (such as continued placement and change in placement)

Howe (1981) reports as follows on due process: "Central concepts of due process as it relates to this law (P.L. 94–142) are interpretations of the words *consent* and *notice*. State and local education agencies are currently struggling with issues such as what constitutes a reasonable amount of time for notice, and the meaning of *informed consent*" (p. 20). Of equal, if not greater, concern are the findings of Saunders and Sultana (1980), which indicate that neither special educators, regular educators, nor other professionals involved in the education of the handicapped had a thorough understanding of what due process was or how it related to the education of the handicapped.

Turnbull (1978) has succinctly pared down the concept of due process for the handicapped into six points, which revolve around the basic notions of consent and notice regarding placement. The six points are as follows:

1. Before any preplacement evaluation is conducted, parental consent must be obtained.
2. All relevant records related to the identification, evaluation, and educational placement of a student may be examined by that student's parents.
3. Parents may request an independent evaluation be conducted on their child and have that evaluation be considered by the school system in determining their child's appropriate program and placement.
4. Before initiating or changing any identification, evaluation, or educational placement of a student, the parents must receive written notification of intent to do so.
5. The State Education Agency must ensure that a student's legal rights are fully protected in the event that his or her parents are unknown, unavailable, or that he or she is a ward of the state.

6. In the event that parents (including guardian or surrogate) or local education agency see a problem in a child's identification, evaluation, placement, and/or program, the parents (including guardian or surrogate) and local education agency may initiate a due process hearing to present their complaints for the purpose of adjudication.

The interaction of placement and due process procedures will hopefully ensure that the student will receive an appropriate educational program within the least restrictive environment. P.L. 94–142 defines least restrictive environment as "... to the *maximum extent appropriate,* handicapped children, including children in public or private institutions or other care facilities, are *educated with children who are not handicapped,* and that special education classes, separate schooling or other *removal* of handicapped children from the regular educational environment occurs *only when the nature or severity of the handicap* is such that education in regular classes with the use of *supplemental aids and services* cannot be achieved satisfactorily" (P.L. 94–142, 1975, s 121a.550 (b) (1) (2)). In essence, then, the concept of least restrictive environment necessitates that the school system provide itself with options for serving the handicapped. These options should constitute a continuum of services and instructional environments. As Howe states, "Many of the past abuses that led to legal action can be traced to a lack of available options" (1981, p. 19). The determination of the least restrictive environment is the culmination of interactive efforts between school and agency personnel and parents, all desirous of providing optimal educational experiences to the severely or profoundly handicapped student.

CONCLUSION

"At last this nation has committed itself to the education and development of *all* of its children and youth. One hopes sincerely that this commitment is intense, long term, and sincere. History tells us that others, dedicated and learned, have made similar commitments which did not endure" (Smith & Smith, 1978, p. 478). When a system sets out to establish a program for the severely and profoundly handicapped, it must take into account the concerns and issues raised within this chapter: past practices, administrative theory, physical facilities, removal of architectural barriers, transportation, staffing needs, multidisciplinary involvement, advisory boards, staff preparation, nonhandicapped student preparation, training of regular teachers, placement, due process, and least restrictive environments.

We must study the past practices that have been employed in the education of the severely and profoundly handicapped and learn from our mistakes. If we do not, we will surely repeat those mistakes under the guise of new names; and the commitment noted by Smith and Smith will not endure or will not grow in magnitude, and the programs established for the severely and profoundly handicapped will disappear as those in the past have done.

REFERENCES

Abeson, A., Bolick, N., & Hass, J. *A primer on due process.* Reston, Va.: The Council for Exceptional Children, 1976.

Brown, L., Branston, M., Hamre-Nietupski, S., Johnson, J., Wilcox, B., & Gruenewald, L. A rationale for comprehensive longitudinal interactions between severely handicapped students and non-handicapped students and other citizens. *AAESPH Review,* 1979, *4,* 3–14.

Burello, L.C., & Sage, D.D. *Leadership and change in special education.* Englewood Cliffs, N.J.: Prentice-Hall, 1979.

Culbertson, J. *Some key epistemological questions about a "theory of practice."* Presentation at a symposium of the American Educational Research Association, San Francisco, April 1979.

Flynn, J.R., Gacka, R., & Sundeen, D.A. Are classroom teachers prepared for mainstreaming? *Phi Delta Kappan,* 1978, *59,* 562.

Gottlieb, J. Improving attitudes toward retarded children by using group discussion. *Exceptional Children,* 1980, *47*(2), 106–111.

Hamre-Nietupski, S., & Nietupski, J. Integral involvement of severely handicapped students within the regular public schools. *The Journal of the Association for the Severely Handicapped,* 1981, *6*(2), 30–39.

Hersey, P., & Blanchard, K. *Management of organizational behavior: Utilizing human resources* (3rd ed.). Englewood Cliffs, N.J.: Prentice-Hall, 1977.

Howe, C.E. *Administration of special education.* Denver, Colo.: Love Publishing Company, 1981.

Landau, S.E., & Gerken, K.C. Requiem for the testing role? The perceptions of administrators vs. teachers. *School Psychology Digest,* 1979, *8*(2), 202–206.

McGregor, D. *The human side of enterprise.* New York: McGraw-Hill, 1960.

National Association of State Directors of Special Education. *Transportation of the handicapped. A survey of state education agency transportation directors.* Washington, D.C.: Author, 1981.

Ottman, R.A. Before a handicapped student enters the classroom: What the special educator can do. *Teaching Exceptional Children,* 1981, *14*(1), 41–43.

Reynolds, M.C., & Birch, J.W. *Teaching exceptional children in all America's schools.* Reston, Va.: The Council for Exceptional Children, 1977.

Rogers, P., Grigsby, C., Welch, C., Garton, H., & Greenwood, J. *Providing educational services to severely handicapped students in regular school.* King of Prussia, Pa.: The National Learning Resource Center, 1979.

Saunders, M.K., & Sultana, Q. Professionals' knowledge of educational due process. *Exceptional Children,* 1980, *46*(7), 559–561.

Smith, D.D., & Smith, J.O. Trends. In M.E. Snell (Ed.), *Systematic instruction of the moderately and severely handicapped.* Columbus, Ohio: Charles E. Merrill, 1978.

Sontag, E., Burke, P.J., & York, R. Considerations for serving the severely handicapped in the public schools. *Education and Training of the Mentally Retarded,* 1973, *8,* 20–26.

Sontag, E., Burke, P.J., & York, R. Considerations for serving the severely handicapped in the public schools. In R.M. Anderson and J.G. Greer (Eds.), *Educating the severely and profoundly handicapped.* Baltimore: University Park Press, 1976.

Stainback, S., Stainback, W., & Maurer, S. Training teachers for the severely and profoundly handicapped: A new frontier. *Exceptional Children,* 1976, *42,* 203–210.

Stetson, F.E. *Critical administrative factors which facilitate the successful inclusion of severely handicapped students in the least restrictive environment.* Annandale, Va.: JWK International Corp., 1979.

The American National Standards Institute. *American National Standards specifications for making buildings and facilities accessible to, and usable by, the physically handicapped.* New York: Author, 1979.

Turnbull, A.P. Parent-professional interactions. In M.E. Snell (Ed.), *Systematic instruction of the moderately and severely handicapped.* Columbus, Ohio: Charles E. Merrill, 1978.

United States Architectural and Transportation Barriers Compliance Board. *A guidebook to: The minimum federal guidelines and requirements for accessible design.* Washington, D.C.: Author, 1981.

Waters, L.G. School psychologists as perceived by school personnel: Support for a consultant model. *Journal of School Psychology,* 1973, *11*(1), 40–46.

Weber, M. *The theory of social and economic organization.* New York: Free Press, 1947.

Wilcox, B. A competency-based approach to preparing teachers for the severely and profoundly handicapped: Perspective I. In E. Sontag, J. Smith, & N. Certo (Eds.), *Educational programming for the severely and profoundly handicapped.* Reston, Va.: The Council for Exceptional Children, 1977.

REFERENCE NOTE

1. Reprinted from "Integral involvement of severely handicapped students within the regular public schools," by S. Hamre-Nietupski and J. Nietupski from the *Journal of the Association for the Severely Handicapped* 6(2): 30–39, 1981, © 1981.

Chapter 3

Parent Involvement and Training[*]

Les Sternberg and Mary Lou Caldwell
Florida Atlantic University

PROBLEM AND PAST PRACTICES

Parent involvement in the education of handicapped students has become not only a quasi-legal requirement (P.L. 94-142 mandates participation of a parent or parents in the development of the individualized educational program) but also a necessity if one is to expect generalization of skills between the home and school environment. An active type of involvement is preferred and it is the job of educators and parents alike to establish procedures that will guarantee that a close relationship between parents and school exists (Kean, 1975). The purpose of this relationship is two-way communication so that necessary behavioral and instructional changes may be wrought.

Various model intervention programs have been established with accompanying parent involvement training components. The need is especially obvious in infant and preschool programs, where it has been shown that parent application of instructional technologies can aid in the improvement of certain developmental deficits (Bereiter & Engelmann, 1966; Karnes, Wollersheim, Stoneburner, Hodgins, & Teska, 1968). Moreover, improvement has been not only in relation to student-centered variables, but family adjustment problems have been ameliorated as well, with corresponding facilitation toward normalization (Baker & Heifetz, 1976; Brophy, 1970; Denhoff & Hyman, 1976; Haynes, 1976; Wiegerink & Parrish, 1976).

Although the need for parent involvement should be obvious, certain variables tend to play a predominant role as to whether or not effective parent

*All exhibits are reprinted from W. B. Stephens, L. Sternberg, and S. Jenkins. *Programs for severely/profoundly mentally retarded children and youth: Final report.* Dallas: University of Texas at Dallas, Project SPICY, 1980. Funded by the Department of Education, Office of Special Education and Rehabilitation Services, Contract No. 300-77-0254.

participation will be realized. First is the barrier that historically has been erected between parents and educators. On the one hand, many educators have assumed that because of their professional training they are the only educational experts. This attitude has forced many parents to abandon any hope that they might provide some type of enlightenment to educational staff. On the other hand, parents are not merely the innocent pawns of the instructional system. Often, they either are unwilling to accept educational advice or they demand educational practices that may be beyond the scope of those that are offered by a school system. The barrier of one-way communication and negative interactions must be broken if there is to be any possibility of establishing a viable parent involvement program (Turnbull, 1978).

A second variable that directly affects the realization of parent involvement is the type of parent involvement training model that is utilized. Depending upon the intent and direction of parent participation, different models of involvement have been developed. Jenkins, Stephens, and Sternberg (1980) have summarized a number of different approaches that have involved parents in education decision making. In the *individualized home intervention model,* a home trainer typically trains the parents, siblings, and handicapped student at home. This model has most often been used in conjunction with infant and preschool programs (Quick, Little, & Campbell, 1974; Shearer & Shearer, 1973). With this approach, the trainer becomes sensitive to the problems that permeate the at-home situation. Also, programming emphases involve the ecological constraints and demands of the home. However, scheduling of visitations may become a problem since all visits and subsequent training must be arranged around the work schedules of the parents. As is often the case, training may have to take place during the evening, and this might negate coordination with the at-school instructional program.

The *continuous group training model* (Bricker & Bricker, 1976, 1977; Turnbull, Strickland, & Goldstein, 1978) uses ongoing training sessions that are conducted in the school. The content of the training usually involves educational or behavioral aspects that are common to all of the handicapped students within the group. This type of model helps to support parent-to-parent interaction and the inherent emotional support system that evolves. Of import is the likelihood that parents will discover that others share common problems and attitudes regarding their handicapped son or daughter. Unfortunately, certain logistical problems develop in implementing this model, including obtaining babysitting services and arranging transportation to and from the training site.

A variation of the preceding approach is the *restrictive group training model* (Baker & Heifetz, 1976; Huber & Lynch, 1978). Here, a limited number of sessions are conducted (usually in school) to address the specific needs of each individual student. Again, group meetings are used and parents are made aware of the needs of other students and their families. However, the same logistical problems are inherent, and, in addition, parents may find it difficult to prioritize their specific training needs, especially when exposed to needs voiced by other parents. For example, a parent may desire training in fostering communication skills with his or her handicapped son or daughter. However, when he or she notices that other parents are focusing on behavioral training (training in social skills, for example), that parent may feel compelled to ask for training in that lower prioritized area. This problem is merely a reflection of the self-consciousness that may develop as a result of the utilization of this type of parent involvement model.

Hayden and Haring (1976) and Wiegerink and Parrish (1976) employ a *classroom involvement model.* In this approach, parents assist teachers within the classroom. An extremely strong aspect of this type of participation is the fact that parents are able to see, first hand, the educational emphases (including strategies and techniques) that are being used in the school setting. There is ample opportunity for parents to practice instructional procedures so that they may more easily extend those procedures into the home environment. It should be obvious that a major purpose of the classroom involvement model is to provide coordination, continuity, and consistency between the school instructional program and the carryover program in the home. However, one major drawback to this type of approach is that parents who work or who have other commitments may not be able to participate.

Tawney (1977) and Tawney, Aeschleman, Deaton, and Donaldson (1979) make use of the *telecommunication training model.* In this approach, parents receive mediated instructional packages that explain how best to teach their handicapped child at home. Also emphasized is the establishment of a telecommunications system with the teacher to address the day-to-day variance that the parents may find in the learning or behavioral repertoire of the students. This type of model is especially applicable to students whose primary handicapping condition prevents them from inclusion in the classroom (those with profound neuromuscular deficits or serious health problems, for example). With the utilization of this model, the student is assured of receiving an appropriate educational program even though at-school attendance is not possible. Unfortunately, this exclusion from school does negate the possibility of the student receiving appropriate and beneficial peer interactions. Also, the overall responsibility of educational services delivery rests with the parents, whose brief respite from the student during school hours is now eliminated.

In the *center-based training model* (Watson & Bassinger, 1974; Fredericks, Baldwin, & Grove, 1976), parent involvement and training take place both in home and in school. This system is especially suited for handicapped students whose maladaptive behaviors are of such a serious nature that in-school attendance is not presently possible. Parents are exposed to the requirements of the classroom within which their child will subsequently be placed. Parent training is conducted in both settings to indicate to the parents how more adaptive behaviors may be developed and brought under the natural environmental controls of both the school and home. This allows for the necessary coordination between the school-based educational program and related requirements of the home environment. However, this individualized approach may foster parental feelings of isolation and, again, while the student is receiving training at home, the parents do not receive the respite that is normally afforded parents of children who are in school.

SUGGESTED METHODS

Jenkins et al. (1980) concluded that four critical components should be included in any parent involvement training model that is used with severely and profoundly handicapped students. They would combine the strengths and address many of the weaknesses found in the other models described. The components are

- Training provided in the home so that parents and other family members can begin to use techniques to foster educational and behavioral changes under the control of at-home environmental stimuli
- Training provided within a group format that emphasizes common educational and behavioral concerns of all parents and family members
- Mandatory in-school attendance for the handicapped student so that parent respite is afforded
- Coordination of the school- and home-based educational/behavioral program so that consistency and continuity of instructional emphases are ensured.

What is important is that the above components be developed within a single operational model. Although all previously described parent training models do train parents, training is accomplished through a teacher (trainer)-to-parent training paradigm. What is being advocated here is a *parent-as-parent trainer model.*

One of the main reasons for enlisting the services of parents of handicapped children to supply training to other parents is that of sensitivity. In order to deliver appropriate services that meet the needs of the handicapped student's parents and family, the professional would have to comprehend the entire dynamics of the home situation. A typical scenario might find the parents displaying their frustration to the parent trainer concerning their inability to control some type of aberrant behavior being displayed by their handicapped child. A usual response by the professional might be "I understand what you're going through." Unfortunately, this understanding is rarely the case. An individual who has not personally experienced the frustration and hardships of dealing with a severely or profoundly handicapped student within a family setting and environment can never truly comprehend the feelings and attitudes that develop among family members. The sensitivity that is necessary can often be brought to the situation by another parent of a severely or profoundly handicapped student.

A second reason for using parents as parent trainers is communication. Although the population of severely and profoundly handicapped students is rather heterogeneous, commonalities of concerns do exist. With the similarity of role between the parent trainer and parent in the proposed model (both are parents of severely or profoundly handicapped students), the likelihood of communication between the two is enhanced. No longer can the parent say, "How do you know this technique will work with my child?" for the parent trainer has used the strategy with his or her own handicapped son or daughter and understands the at-home variables that will be detrimental or beneficial to the success of the program.

One should not assume that model parent involvement programs that do use professionals as trainers automatically have inherent communication problems. However, as Roos (1977) has pointed out, many of the interactions between parent and professional have proven to be counterproductive in the past and have led to the establishment of negative stereotypes. A number of authorities have, therefore, drawn attention to the viability of developing parent-as-parent trainer systems (Gordon, 1977; Morton, 1978; Schultz, 1978; Levitt & Cohen, 1976).

A Model Parent-as-Parent Trainer System

Stephens, Ferrara, and Jenkins (1979) have designed and implemented a noteworthy parent-as-parent trainer system for severely and profoundly handicapped students. In their design, two key personnel roles are mandated: a parent training coordinator and the parent trainer. The parent training coordinator is basically responsible for administering and supervising for effective parent participation. This individual should have a background in special education with special emphasis on working with parents, siblings, and surrogate parents of severely and profoundly handicapped students. Organizational and administrative ability is required. The parent training coordinator should be very familiar with all supportive agencies that may play a role in the education of the handicapped student. Knowledge of the referral process for these agencies is also mandated.

The parent trainer is specifically responsible for training other parents. In order to be considered as a parent trainer, the parent must have a handicapped child enrolled in the school program serving severely and profoundly handicapped students. Since much of the training will take place in other parents' homes, the parent trainer must have available transportation. The attitude of the parent trainer toward both the benefit of training and the role of professionals in aiding the design of that training must be positive. Given the fact that other parents will be relying on the parent trainer for training directives, the parent trainer must be able to express some leadership capabilities without appearing overly domineering. To gain the necessary expertise in training other parents, the parent trainer must be able to participate in joint training sessions with members of the educational staff. This training will later assist the parent trainer in coordinating the school program with the home program.

The working relationship between the parent training coordinator and the parent trainer must be positive and open. Direction and information must be given within a two-way communication mode. Although the parent training coordinator does administer the program, such administration relies heavily on the constant feedback from the parent trainer. Given this type of relationship, it is paramount that the parent training coordinator have the final say in the selection of parent trainers.

Implementation of the Model

Once the parent training coordinator has been identified, permission for parent participation should be acquired. This will require a home visit where the coordinator will explain the design of the model to the parents. Also included at this time is the administration of a parent needs survey or interview that will identify the prioritized training needs of the parents. An example of a parent needs survey may be found in Exhibit 3-1.

The next step involves the selection and training of the parent trainers. The educational background of potential trainers is not a crucial variable for selection. However, any training that is attempted must take into account the capabilities of each parent trainer for acquiring and mastering the content of the training. This training may take various forms. With generic content that will encompass all potential students (such as behavior change, activities of daily living), group training can be conducted by professionals having expertise within those content areas. For individual student concerns, the

Exhibit 3-1 Parent Training Needs Survey

> In order to help us plan sessions which will be of maximum benefit to you we are asking that you rate the following topics as they related to your handicapped child using #1 to indicate that topic you think would be of most help to you and so on down the line with #13 being that area you think is of least importance or relevance. Please feel free to add any topics we may have overlooked in the space provided at the bottom of the page.
>
> Information on child development   _____
>
> Training in behavior management   _____
>
> Understanding educational assessment   _____
>
> Implementing educational carryover in the home   _____
>
> Evaluating education progress   _____
>
> Handling feelings   _____
>
> Coping with family stress   _____
>
> Managing brothers and sisters of the handicapped child   _____
>
> Planning for sex education   _____
>
> Planning for your child's future   _____
>
> Legal rights of the handicapped   _____
>
> Selecting toys and clothing   _____
>
> Locating and utilizing community resources   _____
>
>
> Other:

training can be done by the parent training coordinator and/or the student's teacher. Much of the group training of the parent trainers would probably be accomplished on a restricted time basis, generally at the initial stages of implementation, whereas the individualized training would occur on an ongoing basis.

During the initial training period for the parent trainers, the parent training coordinator should begin to consider the assignments of different families to individual parent trainers. Various factors must be taken into account. Proximity between the parties must be considered so that transportation time is minimal. Personological variables, such as age of the participants, and economic and social background, should be considered only in regard to the

Exhibit 3-2 Policy on Home Visits

1. Make an appointment at least 3 days in advance for the first home meeting.

2. After the initial home interview, make a regular schedule for your visits. Be sure that each person knows when you will be there. Try to arrange a time and day that most of the family will be available, but when there will not be too many distractions.

3. Be sure to be on time for home visits and remember you are a guest.

4. Occasionally, due to unexpected circumstances, parents will be too busy or otherwise unable to talk with you. It is difficult, uncomfortable, and unproductive to try to visit in such situations, so set an appointment for another day and quickly excuse yourself.

5. Be informal but avoid being too casual.

6. Compliment the home. Notice and sincerely praise family pictures, pets, garden, or whatever is appropriate. The main idea is to be sincere.

7. Avoid filling out forms during a visit. Use the time to learn about or work with the child and his family. After the meeting make notes or fill out the forms.

8. Do not smoke unless the parents invite you to smoke or they smoke first.

9. Wear comfortable but attractive clothes. In working with the child you may need to do activities on the floor.

10. Listen to what the parents have to say. Remember that they have spent more time with their child than anyone so they probably know more about him/her than anyone else.

11. Be aware of non-verbal communication such as tone of voice, body language, and general attitude.

12. Be diplomatic and supportive. Do not be argumentative, authoritarian, condescending, or judgmental.

13. Remember the purpose for your visit and do not "chase rabbits" but do not appear hurried.

14. Plan what you want to cover in advance by establishing and writing down clear goals. Assemble any materials you might need.

15. In presenting specific activities for them to do with their child, show, tell, and let them do. Give them a list of the steps in each activity for them to follow after you are gone.

16. In working with the parents and child, try to arrange for a place in the home where there will not be too many distractions. It is very difficult to attend to the task when there is a program on TV that is more interesting.

Exhibit 3-2 continued

17. Include anyone in the household who may do the activity with the child, especially brothers and sisters, when you are doing training sessions.

18. Be aware of the language level and level of understanding of those with whom you are dealing. Deal with each person on his/her own level but don't be solicitous.

19. Be positive in your approach.

20. Recognize your own limitations and make referrals when appropriate.

21. On return visits, remember the behavior management principles and provide positive reinforcement (praise) to the family members for the work they have done with the child.

possible effect they may have on participation. Of paramount importance is matching the parent trainers and families in such a way that two-way communication is ensured and necessary training information can be presented in an understandable and acceptable fashion.

It is extremely important that all parent trainers be made aware of necessary policies and procedures that must be followed in any home training session. These reminders should be presented in written format and hopefully such a device will decrease the possibility of any future parent participation problems. A copy of a policy statement for home visits can be found in Exhibit 3-2.

At this point in the implementation process, the parent training coordinator and parent trainer conduct an introductory parent visit. This is done for a number of reasons. First, it is important to assure the parents that what was described during the initial permission-to-participate visit is being started. Second, the parents are introduced to the principal members of the training team. Third, the visit gives the parent training coordinator the opportunity to discover whether there are any interaction problems between the family and parent trainer. It may be that anticipated problems can be dealt with through coordinator and trainer consultation or through reassignment.

The parent training coordinator must now begin coordinating anticipated home training activities with the student's school-based program. This requires that the coordinator begin to interact at length with the professional educational staff, including the student's teacher, paraprofessionals, and any related services personnel (physical therapist, occupational therapist, speech clinician, etc.) who may be supplying services to the student. Since parent trainer assignments have already been made, it is necessary at this time to include the parent trainer in any implementation discussions. This is not to say that parents, if available, should not be participating in this segment of program development. On the contrary, although the purpose of this coordination effort is home extension training, it still should be looked upon as a required component of the student's individualized educational program (IEP). Under these circumstances, parent participation is extremely important. However, in the event that the parents are not available, the parent training coordinator can serve in the role of student/parent advocate and use the information from the parent needs assessment (or interview) to guarantee that parent home training concerns are dealt with in the home training program. A home education plan is then drafted (see Exhibit 3-3).

Once an initial home training program has been designed, the parent training coordinator supervises the parent trainer at an initial home training session. Here, the parent trainer actually carries out a training session with the parents and, if available, other family members. The parent training coordinator serves basically as a consultant to answer any questions that either the trainer, parents, or other family members may have. At the end of this session, the next home visit is planned and scheduled. At this time (and for all future home visits) a home visit plan is drafted. Exhibit 3-4 shows a home visit plan form. It is appropriate at this time to draft some preliminary guidelines to remind parents and family members of behaviors they can display that will aid in the improvement of the student's educational and behavioral repertoire. A suggested list of principles may be found in Exhibit 3-5.

It is at this point that the parent training coordinator removes himself or herself from a continuous, on-site supervisory role. In the future, however, occasional visits to the home are conducted with the parent trainer.

The parent trainer now assumes almost total responsibility for direct services delivery to the parents regarding the home extension of the student's individualized educational program. This is not to say that the parent training coordinator does not continue to supply necessary information. A cyclical feedback model is incorporated so that all parties continue to be aware of the

---

Exhibit 3-3 Home Education Plan

Child _____ School/Teacher _____

Address _____ Parent _____

Home Trainer _____

| | | | Date | Date |
| Identified Needs | Source | Strategy | Begun | Completed |

Exhibit 3-4 Home Visit Plan

```
Child's Name _____ Date Scheduled _____

Parent's Name _____ Time Scheduled _____

Address _____ School _____

Phone # _____ Teacher _____

1.  Objective of visit:




2.  Activities to do to meet the objective:




3.  Materials needed:
```

direction and nature of training. This is accomplished through the use of a home visit evaluation system. Each further home visit conducted by the parent trainer is evaluated by both the parents and the trainer. Two separate devices are used to collect this information. In the parent evaluation (see Exhibit 3-6), specific questions are asked regarding the information that was presented and demonstrated and the overall rating of the session. The intent of this evaluation is to determine the quality of the training as perceived by the parents. In the parent trainer evaluation (see Exhibit 3-7), parent and family receptivity to training is assessed. Both of these evaluations are then discussed during home visit reports made by the parent trainer to the parent training coordinator. The results obtained by these evaluations are used in planning further home visits and in making any necessary adjustments in the overall intent of the home training. In the event that anticipated changes may affect the school-based program, a general IEP planning meeting may be called to make the needed adjustments.

As specified earlier, a necessary component of the parent-as-parent trainer model is the use of group meetings. These meetings are usually scheduled after each family has had at least one supervised home training visit with the parent

Exhibit 3-5 Guidelines for Parents

1. Praise your child's successes and the things s/he does correctly, no matter how small. Praise includes physical affection - pats and hugs - as well as words.

2. Correct your child indirectly whenever possible by showing him how to do things correctly. For example, rather than correcting the way your child says something by saying, "That's wrong. Say it this way," you should say correctly what your child tried to say.

3. Speak clearly in a normal voice. It does not help to speak to the immature child in "baby talk" or to shout at the hearing impaired child.

4. Whenever possible use more than one approach by talking to your child about the things around him/her and by letting him/her touch, taste, and smell things. The use of all the senses is especially important for children with problems because one or more senses may be impaired.

5. Be consistent in what you say and do and in the rules your child is to follow.

6. Give your child physical love and support. Young children, particularly those with problems, may not understand words alone.

7. Provide a variety of experiences, showing and explaining things as much as possible.

8. When one way of helping your child learn does not work, try other ways.

9. Talk with your child informally throughout the day as you would with a friend. Set aside small amounts of time of 5 to 15 minutes and teach an activity when both you and your child are relaxed, not rushed.

10. At all times, speak to and treat your child with the same courtesy and consideration you would give your friends.

training coordinator and parent trainer. Arranging these group meetings is no easy task. It is the responsibility of the parent trainer to determine potential dates, times, and locations by requesting this information from each family. Schedule conflicts will have to be dealt with. Once each meeting has been scheduled, it is again the responsibility of the parent trainer to inform the parents of the meeting and to make sure that all logistical problems involving their attendance (for example, transportation and babysitting services) are handled. Generally, the topics of presentation or discussion at the group meetings will be decided on by the group. This information can be gleaned from the original parent needs survey or from material obtained from the home education plan or home evaluation forms.

Exhibit 3-6 Home Training Session Evaluation

Child/Children's Names _____ Date _____

Parent/Guardian's Name _____

1. What topic(s) did you discuss during the home training
    session?

2. Was the session helpful to you?

3. What new ideas did you get from the session?

4. What additional information do you need about the topic of
    this session?

5. In what other areas do you need help?

6. What is your overall rating of this particular training
    session?

    Circle the answer - Poor

                         Below Average

                         Average

                         Above Average

                         Excellent

Validation of the Parent-as-Parent Trainer Model

Stephens, Sternberg, and Jenkins (1980) have presented preliminary data related to the validation of a parent-as-parent trainer model that was used with parents of severely and profoundly handicapped students. Their findings are as follows:

- In terms of at-home training, 80 percent of the ratings made by parents of the quality of home demonstrations were above average to excellent.

Exhibit 3-7 Home Visit Record

Child's Name _____ Date of Visit _____

Parent(s) _____Time: Arrive _____Leave_____

School _____ Teacher _____

Signature of Home Trainer _____

1. Purpose of visit:

   Did you achieve this purpose?

2. What household members were present?

3. What activities were demonstrated? How long did it take?

4. How did the family respond to your visit?

5. Describe any problems you feel affect the well being of

   this family.

6. Notes for future visits, follow-up plans.

7. Questions:

8. Referrals made:

9. Materials, equipment, and books left in the home:

10. Was there indication previous suggestions have been used?

    What suggestions?

11. Comments on visit.

- Given a random sample of two home visit reports drawn from the file of each student included in the program, 80 percent of home training assignments being implemented by the parents or other family members were being conducted effectively.
- In terms of improved interactions between parent and handicapped child, a pre/post testing design using the *Fels Parent Behavior Rating Scale* (Baldwin, Kalhorn, & Breese, 1950) was employed to assess changes in parent behavior. Results indicated that the greatest positive change occurred in variables having to do with parental warmth and objectivity

regarding the handicapped child. Also positively affected was the overall adjustment of the parents to the student, especially in regard to the parents' approach to child discipline and training.

- In terms of content preferred by parents in either home- or group-based training, that content dealing with behavior management received the highest priority. This was followed by the need for instruction in implementing home education, planning for the handicapped student's future, and understanding educational assessment.

- Although group meetings were rated highly, the data indicate that only a small percentage of parents participated in the group meetings. This may be a function of the emphasis that the parents placed on the content received during home visits. Crucial content concerns of material presented in group format could be dealt with during at-home training.

CONCLUSION

A number of different types of parent training involvement models have been described in this chapter. Each contributes important variables that help to determine the success of any parent participation program. The parent-as-parent trainer model has been discussed as a system that can alleviate many of the problems inherent in other approaches. Perhaps most important is the fact that it recognizes that parents and parenting constitute critical aspects of successful programming. Although the parent-as-parent trainer model has been advocated, this should not be inferred as a statement of exclusion. Parent participation is so crucial to the effectiveness and success of education of severely and profoundly handicapped students that the operation of any validated model is better than the operation of no model.

REFERENCES

Baker, B.L., & Heifetz, L.J. The Read Project: Teaching manuals for parents of retarded children. In T.D. Tjossem (Ed.), *Intervention strategies for high risk infants and young children.* Baltimore: University Park Press, 1976.

Baldwin, A.L., Kalhorn, J., & Breese, F.H. The appraisal of parent behavior. *Psychological Monographs,* 1950, *63,* 4.

Bereiter, C., & Engelmann, S. *Teaching disadvantaged children in the preschool.* Englewood Cliffs, N.J.: Prentice-Hall, 1966.

Bricker, W.A., & Bricker, D.D. A developmentally integrated approach to early intervention. *Education and Training of the Mentally Retarded,* 1977, *12,* 100–108.

Bricker, W.A., & Bricker, D.D. The infant, toddler, and preschool research intervention project. In T.D. Tjossem (Ed.), *Intervention strategies for high risk infants and young children.* Baltimore: University Park Press, 1976.

Brophy, J.E. Mothers as teachers of their own preschool children: The influence of socio-economic status and task structure on teaching capacity. *Child Development*, 1970, *41*, 79–94.

Denhoff, E., & Hyman, I. Parent programs for developmental management. In T.D. Tjossem (Ed.), *Intervention strategies for high risk infants and young children*. Baltimore: University Park Press, 1976.

Fredericks, B., Baldwin, J., & Grove, D.A. A home-center based parent training model. In D. L. Lillie & P. L. Trohanis (Eds.), *Teaching parents to teach*. New York: Walker, 1976.

Gordon, I. Parent education and parent involvement. *Childhood Education*, 1977, *54*, (2), 71–78.

Hayden, A.H., & Haring, N.G. Early intervention for high risk infants and young children: Programs for Down's syndrome children. In T.D. Tjossem (Ed.), *Intervention strategies for high risk infants and young children*. Baltimore: University Park Press, 1976.

Haynes, V.B. The national collaborative infant project. In T.D. Tjossem (Ed.), *Intervention strategies for high risk infants and young children*. Baltimore: University Park Press, 1976.

Huber, H., & Lynch, F. Teaching behavioral skills to parents. *Children Today*, 1978, *7*, (1), 8–10.

Jenkins, S., Stephens, W.B., & Sternberg, L. The use of parents as parent trainers of handicapped children. *Education and Training of the Mentally Retarded*, 1980, *15*, 256–263.

Karnes, M.B., Wollersheim, J.P., Stoneburner, R.L., Hodgins, A.S., & Teska, J.A. An evaluation of two preschool programs for disadvantaged children: A traditional and a highly experimental school. *Exceptional Children*, 1968, *34*, 667–676.

Kean, J. Successful integration: The parent's role. *Exceptional Parent*, 1975, (5), 5, 35–40.

Levitt, E., & Cohen, S. Educating parents of children with special needs—approaches and issues. *Young Children*, 1976, *31*, (4), 263–272.

Morton, K. Identifying the enemy—A parent's complaint. In A.P. Turnbull & H.R. Turnbull III (Eds.), *Parents speak out*. Columbus, Ohio: Charles E. Merrill, 1978.

Quick, A.D., Little, T.L., & Campbell, A.A. *Project MEMPHIS: Enhancing developmental progress in preschool exceptional children*. Belmont, Calif.: Fearon, 1974.

Roos, P. A parent's view of what public education should accomplish. In E. Sontag, J. Smith, & N. Certo (Eds.), *Educational programming for the severely and profoundly handicapped*. Reston, Va.: The Council for Exceptional Children, Division on Mental Retardation, 1977.

Schultz, J. The parent-professional conflict. In A.P. Turnbull & H.R. Turnbull III (Eds.), *Parents speak out*. Columbus, Ohio: Charles E. Merrill, 1978.

Shearer, D.E., & Shearer, M.S. The Portage project: A model for early childhood education. *Exceptional Children*, 1973, *39*, 210–217.

Stephens, W.B., Ferrara, D.M., & Jenkins, S. *Programs for severely/profoundly mentally retarded children and youth: Annual report*. Dallas: University of Texas at Dallas, Project SPICY, 1979.

Stephens, W.B., Sternberg, L., & Jenkins, S. *Programs for severely/profoundly mentally retarded children and youth: Final report*. Dallas: University of Texas at Dallas, Project SPICY, 1980.

Tawney, J.W. Educating severely handicapped children and their parents through telecommunications. In N.G. Haring & L.J. Brown (Eds.), *Teaching the severely handicapped: Volume II*. New York: Grune & Stratton, 1977.

Tawney, J.W., Aeschleman, S.R., Deaton, S.L., & Donaldson, R.M. Using telecommunications to instruct rural severely handicapped children. *Exceptional Children*, 1979, *46*, 118–125.

Turnbull, A.P. Parent-professional interactions. In M.E. Snell (Ed.), *Systematic instruction of the moderately and severely handicapped*. Columbus, Ohio: Charles E. Merrill, 1978.

Turnbull, A.P., Strickland, B., & Goldstein, S. Training professionals and parents in developing and implementing the IEP. *Education and Training of the Mentally Retarded*, 1978, *13*, 414–423.

Watson, L.S., & Bassinger, J.F. Parent training technology: A potential service delivery system. *Mental Retardation*, 1974, *12*, 3–10.

Wiegerink, R., & Parrish, V. A parent-implemented school program. In D.L. Lillie & P.L. Trohanis (Eds.), *Teaching parents to teach*. New York: Walker, 1976.

Assessment Concerns

Chapter 4

Assessment

Ronald L. Taylor
Florida Atlantic University

PROBLEM

Timothy is a twelve-year-old boy who has been classified as profoundly handicapped as a result of "congenital encephalopathy." He is nonverbal, nonambulatory and has a very restricted range of motion. Timothy has been referred to you for evaluation to determine his cognitive potential and to establish educational objectives. Where do you begin? What instruments should you use? To what extent can you adapt the tests or testing environment and still consider the results valid and reliable? These questions and many more are usually raised when assessment of severely and profoundly handicapped individuals is discussed.

PAST PRACTICES

Assessment of this population has been and still is a multidisciplinary endeavor. Usually included on the evaluation team are a physician, physical therapist, speech therapist, social worker, psychologist, and teacher. In some instances, other specialists might also be involved. The physician will often be the first person to identify the severely or profoundly handicapped child. This is accomplished through medical diagnosis using neurological, biochemical, or other appropriate instruments, as well as a comprehensive medical history. The physician might also initially administer vision and hearing tests to check sensory acuity. The physical therapist will usually perform an in-depth analysis of the child's motor skills. This information can aid in the development of programs for establishing appropriate positioning and therapy, as well as designing necessary adaptive equipment. The speech/communication therapist will evaluate prelanguage, language, speech, and prespeech areas. Results from this evaluation could be used to develop a speech or language therapy program or to help initiate a nonverbal communication system. The social worker might evaluate the home situation in areas that are outside the realm of the educational setting. The psychologist is primarily responsible for establishing eligibility requirements, and the teacher is primarily responsible for developing and monitoring educational programs. In an ideal situation, the psychologist and teacher will work together, integrating their information with that from other team members.

At best, the assessment of this population is difficult, frustrating, and often a seemingly impossible task. The purpose of this chapter, however, is not simply to discuss the difficulties of assessing severely and profoundly handicapped individuals. Rather, the intent is to present tests and testing procedures that have been used with this population, to offer constructive criticism of these attempts, and to propose a realistic, pragmatic model to follow.

Assessment: An Overview

Assessment involves the collection of information about an individual. Assessment procedures can include interviews, case histories, work samples, and observation. Usually, however, assessment involves the use of some type of instrument (scales, surveys, or tests). *Norm-referenced* tests compare an individual's score with others who have taken the test. The reference group to which the scores are compared is called the standardization sample or standardization population. Usually, raw scores (number of items passed) are converted to one of a variety of derived scores (scores that compare the individual's performance with those of a group of known demographic variables). Common derived scores are age equivalents, grade equivalents, percentiles, scaled scores, and stanines. A *criterion-referenced* test does not allow the direct comparison of a person's performance with that of other individuals. This type of test measures a person's mastery of content and typically is more concerned with *what* an individual can and cannot do as opposed to *how much* he or she can do compared with others of the same sex, age, socioeconomic status, and the like.

Cone and Hawkins (1977) differentiate between descriptive and prescriptive assessment instruments. A *descriptive* test identifies problem areas, evaluates student progress, and offers an overall assessment of a student's strengths and weaknesses. A *prescriptive* test yields more precise information that relates specifically to educational objectives.

Two important qualities that all tests must have are reliability and validity. *Reliability* refers to the consistency or dependency of a test. The most common type of reliability, test-retest, measures the degree to which a test will yield the same or similar results if it is administered to the same population more than once. Other types of reliability are split-half, which measures the internal consistency of a test, and alternate form, which measures how similar scores are when a test has an equivalent form, such as form A and B of an instrument, both of which measure the same thing.

Validity of a test refers to the degree to which a test measures what it is supposed to measure. For instance, does an intelligence test really measure "intelligence" or does it measure something else? There are several types of validity: criterion-related, content, and construct. Both reliability and validity are usually stated in terms of correlation coefficients. Correlation coefficients range from -1.00 (perfect negative correlation) to $+1.00$ (perfect positive correlation) and are expressed by a two-decimal number, such as .68, .92 or .57. The closer to $+1.00$, the higher the validity or reliability. For example, to determine the test-retest reliability of a test, it would be administered twice to a group of subjects. The two scores for each subject would then be correlated. The resulting coefficient would be an indication of how consistent the test is over time. Usually, a correlation of .60 is considered the minimum acceptable reliability coefficient. Similarly, to establish criterion-related validity of an instrument, it would be administered along with another test (the criterion measure) to a group of students. Scores from the two tests would be correlated to yield the validity coefficient. Again, at least a .60 correlation should be reported. It is also important to remember that in determining criterion-related validity, the criterion measure itself must be valid.

For norm-referenced tests, another technical characteristic is important: the standardization population on which the test is based. The standardization sample should be both sufficiently large and representative. The characteristics (sex, socioeconomic status, intellectual level, and the like) of the individuals of the sample are also extremely important since scores are compared with their performance on the same test. For instance, if a person scored at the 50th percentile on a test that was normed on nonhandicapped children of average intelligence, his or her performance would be quite different from that of a child who scored at the 50th percentile on a test standardized on deaf-blind, severely retarded children.

The technical characteristics of many tests used with severely and profoundly handicapped students are inadequate. Cicchetti and Sparrow (1981) indicate that many of these instruments do not contain enough items to differentiate among lower functioning individuals. They also indicate that most scales for this population have deficient reliability and validity estimates, and that many of the norm-referenced tests and criterion-referenced tests do not have reported reliability and validity data in the manuals. This fact makes it difficult to determine their technical adequacy.

Procedures for Assessing Severely and Profoundly Handicapped Students

The area of assessment of severely and profoundly handicapped individuals did not receive serious attention until the mid 1970s. This attention, in part, was due to the legal mandate specified in Public Law 94-142. There are six principles mentioned in P.L. 94-142 that elaborate on the basic premise of a right to a free and appropriate education for *all* handicapped children. One of these principles, the nondiscriminatory evaluation section, contains six parts that specifically address the issue of assessment. Those are as follows:

1. Tests and other evaluation materials a) are provided and administered in the child's native language or other dominant mode of communication, unless it is clearly not feasible to do so; b) have been validated for the specific purpose for which they are used; and c) are administered by trained personnel in conformance with the instructions provided by the producer.
2. Tests and other evaluation materials include those that are tailored to assess specific areas of educational need and not merely those that are designed to provide a single general I.Q.
3. Tests are selected and administered so as best to ensure that when a test is administered to a child with impaired sensory, manual, or speaking skills, the test accurately reflects the child's aptitude or achievement level or whatever other factors the test purports to measure, rather than reflecting the child's impaired sensory, manual, or speaking skills (except where those skills are the factors that the test purports to measure).
4. No single procedure is used as the sole criterion for determining an appropriate educational program for a child.
5. The evaluation is made by a multidisciplinary team or group of persons, including at least one teacher or other specialist with knowledge in the area of the suspected disability.
6. The child is assessed in all areas related to the suspected disability, including, where appropriate, health, vision, hearing, social and emotional status, general intelligence, academic performance, communication status, and motor abilities. (*Federal Register,* pp. 42496–97)

Prior to the passage of P.L. 94-142, the few attempts to assess severely and profoundly handicapped students were usually limited to the modification and administration of infant intelligence scales. Theoretically, this procedure was followed because the "functioning level" of severely and profoundly handicapped children is similar to chronologically younger children. Tests such as the *Bayley Scales of Infant Development* (Bayley, 1969) and the *Cattell Infant Intelligence Test* (Cattell, 1950) were used. Unfortunately, this practice violates basic assessment principles. Most notably, the tests are usually administered to a population that is outside of the age range for which the test was intended. Thus, the norms are rendered useless. At best, a rough developmental level is given. However, most infant scales consist of items in the areas of sensorimotor development, fine motor skills, and beginning language skills. The developmental level yielded depends on the number of items passed in all of the combined areas. Because of the relatively high incidence of sensory and motor problems in the severely and profoundly handicapped population, this approach is inconsistent with the principles stated in P.L. 94-142. More specifically, the section that requires that "the test accurately reflects the child's aptitude or achievement level or whatever other factors the test purports to measure, rather than reflecting the child's impaired sensory, manual, or speaking skills" is violated.

Another assessment approach is the use of other types of tests, both norm-referenced and criterion-referenced, that were designed for "normal" children but have items appropriate for handicapped students. These include certain adaptive behavior scales, behavior checklists, and development scales. A number of these instruments will be discussed later in this chapter.

Other attempts at assessment have included the adaptation of test items of existing instruments, the use of response-fair tests, and the use of tests designed for and standardized on handicapped individuals (Salvia & Ysseldyke, 1981).

Adaptation of Test Items

Adaptation of existing instruments (usually norm-referenced) can be accomplished by changing the mode of presentation, eliminating or modifying certain test items, or changing the scoring procedures. In changing the mode of presentation, one might give instructions through the subject's dominant mode of communication. For instance, sign language might be used with deaf students. Another change of presentation might involve the use of verbal cues or physical prompts that are indicated in the test manual. It might also be necessary for the subject to change the mode of response. For instance, on an instrument requiring a pointing response, a severely spastic cerebral palsied student might need to use adaptive equipment such as a head pointer or to respond in a nonpointing mode. It is important in assessing this population to determine how a student communicates a functional yes/no response. If you are able to discriminate the yes and no response, many tests can be adapted to accommodate a yes/no format. If a standardized test is used, however, these modifications violate the "standard" format and thus invalidate the results.

Eliminating or modifying test items also violates the standardization procedures. Usually, a derived score cannot be obtained and the results can be used only informally. The modification of scoring procedures involves prorating or extrapolating test scores when the individual's performance is outside of those included in the standardization.

Response-Fair Tests

The use of response-fair tests involves the careful selection of instruments that minimize the child's handicaps when measuring aptitude or determining educational objectives. This approach is consistent with P.L. 94-142. It should be noted, however, that the use of this approach depends on the initial reason for assessment. There are many times when you might *want to measure* the "degree of handicap." For instance, you might want to find out the amount of motor control a child has in order to initiate the most effective program for self-help skills. Whatever the purpose for assessment might be, it is extremely important for persons involved in assessment to be aware, for each instrument, of the prerequisite skills necessary for a student simply to perceive the instructions and to give a response.

Tests Designed for Severely and Profoundly Handicapped Individuals

More and more tests are being developed specifically for the severely and profoundly handicapped population. Both norm-referenced and criterion-referenced instruments are currently on the market. One must remember, however, that when a norm-referenced test is used, the scores must be compared with those of the standardization sample. In other words, if a test is normed on a severely or profoundly handicapped population, a person's score on the test is compared with scores of that population. There are times when this is advantageous, as in program development or program evaluation, and other times when it is disadvantageous, as with classification.

SUGGESTED METHODS

There are currently over 200 instruments being used to evaluate severely and profoundly handicapped individuals. Many of these, however, are nothing more than checklists or sequential lists of behavior. Others have been standardized but are deficient in terms of validity, reliability, and representation of the norms. Also, many of the tests used with this population include a large number of items. This is done to increase the sensitivity to the small changes in behavior usually found. Typically, a task analytic model is followed in which sequential behavioral steps are measured.

Most norm-referenced tests for this population are adaptive behavior scales. *Adaptive behavior* is a difficult term to define and measure, but is nonetheless receiving a good deal of attention in the area of special education. The American Association on Mental Deficiency (AAMD) includes a deficit in adaptive behavior as one of the criteria for the classification of mental retardation. The AAMD gives as examples of adaptive behavior such areas as sensorimotor, communication, self-help, and socialization skills. These skills are concerned with an individual's ability to adapt to the social and cultural demands of the environment. Most of the criterion-referenced instruments used for this population are developmental scales. In addition, although either type can be used for a variety of purposes, norm-referenced tests are often *descriptive* and criterion-referenced tests *prescriptive*.

The tests described in this section were chosen because of their present popularity and past usage, and in some cases their future potential. The tests will be classified according to type (norm-referenced or criterion-referenced), purpose (descriptive or prescriptive), and target population (handicapped or nonhandicapped). Table 4-1 summarizes this information.

AAMD Adaptive Behavior Scale (Nihira, Foster, Shellhaas, & Leland, 1975)
Type: Norm-referenced
Purpose: Descriptive
Target Population: Handicapped (all levels of mentally retarded individuals)

The *American Association on Mental Deficiency Adaptive Behavior Scale* (ABS) is an individually administered rating scale used with mentally retarded, emotionally maladjusted, and other handicapped individuals. Norms are provided for individuals ages 3–69. Adaptive behavior as measured by this instrument refers to "the effectiveness of an individual in coping with the natural and social demands of his or her environment" (p. 5). According to the authors, the ABS can be used for identifying areas of deficiency in individuals under different situations, comparing ratings of different evaluators, providing a means of communication among professionals, stimulating research, and facilitating administrative decisions.

The ABS consists of two parts. Part One deals primarily with personal independence in daily living skills. Part Two is concerned with the measurement of maladaptive behavior. For both parts, information is collected by one of three methods. The first method is first person assessment. This is used when the evaluator is thoroughly familiar with the person who is being evaluated. The second method is third party assessment. In this approach, the evaluator asks other individuals, such as a teacher, parent, or ward attendant, about each item on the scale. This is usually a very time-consuming endeavor. The last method is the interview. The evaluator using this approach asks more

Table 4-1 Tests Frequently Used with the Severely and Profoundly Handicapped

Name of Test	Type	Purpose	Intended Population
A.A.M.D. Adaptive Behavior Scale	Norm-referenced	Descriptive	Mentally retarded
Balthazar Scales	Norm-Referenced	Prescriptive	Severely and Pro- foundly handicapped
Behavior Character- istics Progression	Criterion- Referenced	Prescriptive	Handicapped and non-handicapped
Brigance Inventory of Early Development	Criterion-Refer- enced (some norma- tive information included	Prescriptive	Non-handicapped
Cain-Levine Social Competency Scale	Norm-Referenced	Descriptive	Trainable Mentally Retarded
Callier Azusa	Criterion- Referenced	Prescriptive	Multiply handi- capped deaf-blind
Camelot Behavioral Checklist	Norm-Referenced	Descriptive/ Prescriptive	Handicapped
Empirically Based Training Assessment	Criterion- referenced	Prescriptive	Mentally retarded
Learning Accomplish- ment Profile	Criterion- referenced	Prescriptive	Handicapped and non-handicapped

Table 4-1 continued

Name of Test	Type	Purpose	Target Population
Project Memphis	Criterion-referenced	Descriptive/Prescriptive	Preschool handicapped
Pennsylvania Training Model	Criterion-referenced	Descriptive/Prescriptive	Severely handicapped
TARC	Norm-referenced	Descriptive	Severely handicapped
Vineland Social Maturity Scale	Norm-referenced	Descriptive	Non-handicapped
Vulpé Assessment Battery	Criterion-referenced	Prescriptive	Handicapped and non-handicapped

open-ended questions ("Tell me about your child's toileting skills."), and completes the scale based on the information obtained during the interview.

Part One and Part Two

Part One includes ten domains measuring the degree of independence in daily living skills. Each item in a given domain is scored in one of five ways. For some items, there is a breakdown of skills on a dependent-independent continuum. The examiner determines which behavioral description best fits the individual being evaluated. For the other items, a list of behaviors is provided and the examiner must check all that apply. Descriptions of the ten domains of Part One are as follows:

Independent Functioning (21 items): Includes eating, toilet use, cleanliness, appearance, care of clothing, dressing and undressing, travel, and general independent functioning.
Physical Development (6 items): Includes items measuring sensory (vision and hearing) and motor (gross and fine) abilities.
Economic Activity (4 items): Measures money handling, budgeting, and shopping skills.

Language Development (9 items): Includes measures of language reception and expression plus two items concerning social language development (such as conversational behavior).

Numbers and Time (3 items): Measures a person's ability to understand and manipulate numbers and to understand time concepts.

Domestic Activity (6 items): Includes items concerning meal preparation and cleaning skills.

Vocational Activity (3 items): Measures work habits and job performance.

Self-Direction (5 items): Measures an individual's initiative, perseverance, and use of leisure time.

Responsibility (2 items): Measures an individual's dependability.

Socialization (7 items): Includes measures of cooperation, consideration for others, and social maturity.

Part Two was designed specifically to measure the degree of an individual's maladaptive behavior. There are 14 domains, though the last domain, "Use of Medications," is not really a measure of maladaptive behavior. For each item in a given domain there are a number of behaviors listed. The examiners must determine if each behavior occurs frequently (scored a 2), occasionally (scored a 1), or not at all (not scored). Unfortunately, no guidelines are provided that operationally define "frequently" and "occasionally." The 14 domains are summarized below.

Violent and Destructive Behavior (5 items): Includes such items as "threatens or does physical violence" and "damages personal property."

Antisocial Behavior (6 items): Includes such items as "bosses and manipulates others," "is inconsiderate of others," and "uses angry language."

Rebellious Behavior (6 items): Includes measures of impudence, resistance to instructions, and absenteeism.

Untrustworthy Behavior (2 items): Measures lying, cheating, and stealing behavior.

Withdrawal (3 items): Includes measures of inactivity and shyness.

Stereotyped Behavior and Odd Mannerisms (2 items): Measures stereotypic and repetitive behavior.

Inappropriate Interpersonal Mannerisms (1 item): Includes behavior such as "kisses or licks others."

Unacceptable Vocal Habits (1 item): Includes behavior such as "giggles hysterically."

Unacceptable or Eccentric Habits (4 items): Includes items such as "has unacceptable oral habits" and "removes or tears off own clothing."

Self-Abusive Behavior (1 item): Includes behavior such as "bites or cuts self."

Hyperactive Tendencies (1 item): Includes behavior such as "talks excessively."

Sexually Aberrant Behavior (4 items): Measures such behaviors as masturbation in inappropriate settings and indecent exposure.

Psychological Disturbances (7 items): Includes items such as "reacts poorly to criticism," "demands excessive attention or praise," and "has hypochondriacal tendencies."

Use of Medications (1 item): Indicates the degree to which an individual uses prescribed medications.

Interpretation of Scores

Each item on the ABS is scored using one of the three methods previously mentioned. Each item in a given domain is summed to obtain a raw score for that domain. On Part One, it is also possible to obtain a raw score for various subdomains. The domain raw scores can then be transformed into percentile ranks, which are then plotted on the Profile Summary to provide a visual representation of the individual's adaptive behavior functioning.

Technical Characteristics

The ABS was standardized on 4,014 mentally retarded persons in residential settings. The subjects represented all levels of retardation. The ABS was administered to 133 residents at three training schools to obtain reliability data. Each subject was rated independently by two staff members and the scores correlated. For Part One, the correlation coefficients ranged from .71 (*Self-Direction*) to .93 (*Physical Development*), with a mean coefficient of .86. The correlations for Part Two were considerably lower, ranging from .37 (*Unacceptable Vocal Habits*) to .77 (*Use of Medications*), with a mean coefficient of .57. Validity studies of the ABS are generally lacking.

Summary

The ABS has received a tremendous amount of attention in recent years. Much of the research on the ABS has constructively criticized its scoring system. Most notably, the rather subjective scoring format, particularly for Part Two, has been noted. In addition, Part Two has low reliability and does not take into account the severity of the maladaptive behavior in the scoring system (Taylor, Warren, & Slocumb, 1979). The ABS does not have enough items that measure lower level skills to be considered an effective tool with the severely and profoundly handicapped population. This instrument along with the Vineland (to be discussed) has been used primarily for classification purposes.

Balthazar Scales of Adaptive Behavior (Balthazar, 1976)
Type: Norm-referenced
Purpose: Prescriptive
Target Population: Severely and profoundly retarded
   The *Balthazar Scales of Adaptive Behavior* (BSAB) consist of two sections designed for assessing severely and profoundly retarded individuals. Section One is called the Scales of Functional Independence and Section Two is termed the Scales of Social Adaptation. The first section deals with self-help skills such as eating, dressing, and toileting. Section Two deals with coping behaviors such as play activities and verbal communication. Unlike most adaptive behavior measures, information for the BSAB is collected via direct observation rather than from interviews. Another feature of the BSAB is two separate scoring systems for each section, one for the professional supervisor and one for the rater technician.

Scales of Functional Independence

   The Eating Scale consists of five specific behaviors (or classes) further broken down into sequential steps used as test items. The classes are dependent feeding (9 items), finger feeds (9 items), spoon usage (13 items), fork usage (13 items), and drinking (13 items). For each item, the examiner must determine how many times out of a possible ten trials the subject did or could do each behavior. For instance, for the item "drinks from cup independently," the examiner would estimate how many times out of ten the subject manipulated the cup with no direct assistance with one or both hands. In addition to the five classes, there is also a supplementary eating checklist that includes items pertaining to rate of eating, knife usage, etc. This part is not scored, however. Throughout the administration of the Eating Scale, the examiner is not allowed to initiate or respond to the subject's behavior.

   The Dressing Scale measures the degree of independence a subject has in dressing and undressing. Several articles of clothing are used including shoes, socks, briefs, T-shirt/undershirt, regular shirt or blouse, pants, skirts, and dresses. The examiner must observe the person putting on and taking off each relevant article of clothing and rate him or her on a 0 (no participation) to 6 (independent, perfect performance) scale.

The Toileting Scales, unlike the rest of the BSAB, use an interview and questionnaire format. There is both a daytime questionnaire and nighttime supplementary sheet.

Scales of Social Adaptation

Scales of Social Adaptation measure an individual's self-directedness and sociability. Unadaptive Self-Directed Behavior includes five items: failure to respond, stereotypy and posturing, repetitive verbalization and isolated smiling or laughing, inappropriate self-directed behavior, and disorderly nonsocial behavior. Unadaptive Interpersonal Behavior includes inappropriate contact with others and aggression or withdrawal. Adaptive Self-Directed Behaviors consists of exploratory searching activities, recreational activities, and self-interest or self-regard. Adaptive Interpersonal Behaviors deals with the area of fundamental social behaviors, such as precommunication, social vocalization, and gesturing. Verbal Communication includes areas of nonfunctional, repetitious, or inarticulate verbalization as well as articulate, meaningful speech. Play Activities measures an individual's ability to manipulate objects and engage in playful activity. Response to Instructions measures the individual's cooperativeness and willingness to follow "instructions checklist" items. This is simply a checklist of behaviors that might interfere with the rating process for the other items.

Interpretation of Scores

Scores from Sections One and Two of the BSAB are interpreted in different ways. Section One yields percentile tables for each of the Scales of Functional Independence. The author suggests that these percentile tables be used as guidelines and not as strict normative information. Section Two yields information that is *not* standardized. This section includes a tally sheet that measures each item in terms of frequency on a one-minute interval basis. There is also a scoring summary sheet included. Data from Section Two (as well as Section One) are used informally for program development and program evaluation. Scoring of the BSAB, for the most part, is tedious and overly complicated.

Technical Characteristics

The BSAB was standardized through observational studies that began in 1964 and continued to 1971. The population included 451 ambulant institutional severely or profoundly retarded residents from Wisconsin, although the manual notes that additional studies were conducted in other states as well as European sites. The age range of the sample was 5–57, with a median age of 17.27.

Reliability and Validity

For Section One of the BSAB, no reliability or validity data are presented. The author suggests that these be established by the person using the instrument for finer instructional purposes. Section Two reports interrater reliability data from two studies. The percentage of agreement is extremely variable and is based on a limited sample size.

Summary

While the BSAB can technically be considered a standardized test, it is best not to use it in this manner. The author continually downplays the normative aspects of the test and stresses its use for program development and evaluation. Section One does include a sequence of behaviors that could easily be considered objectives in developing individual educational plans.

Behavioral Characteristics Progression (1973)
Type: Criterion-referenced
Purpose: Prescriptive
Target Population: Handicapped students

The *Behavioral Characteristics Progression* (BCP) is a nonstandardized continuum of behaviors in chart form that contains 2,400 observable traits referred to as *behavioral characteristics*. Ages and labels are not used and behavioral characteristics are grouped into criterion-referenced categories called *strands*.

This tool was intended to assist teachers of exceptional children to structure the teaching of the various areas they are asked to cover into a more coherent and manageable sequence. Particular care was taken to address the self-help, emotional, and more practically oriented academic skills that are commonly needed by the special education student. Although the BCP does get into some "higher functioning" areas, many of the strands are appropriate for severely and profoundly handicapped individuals.

As an assessment tool, the BCP provides the teacher with a comprehensive chart of pupil behaviors to aid in identifying which characteristics pupils display and which they do not. As an *instructional* tool, the BCP assists the teacher in developing individualized and appropriate learner objectives for each student. As a *communication* tool, the BCP offers a historical recording device that can be used throughout the education of students to indicate their progress.

Strands 1–22 deal with self-help skills. Strands 23–45 include items related to social, academic, and recreational skills, and strands 46–56 involve skills specifically designed for blind, deaf, and orthopedically handicapped individuals. The evaluator should choose the strand or strands that are most appropriate for the person being evaluated. This process is facilitated by using the *identifying behaviors* associated with each strand as a checklist to determine and prioritize the most appropriate strands. (Exhibit 4-1 shows an example of the identifying behaviors and associated behavioral characteristics of part of the Dressing Strand.)

Interpretation of Scores

For each student, the strands selected are placed in an individual record booklet. A baseline for each strand is determined by measuring the behavioral characteristics. The behavioral characteristics are scored by the use of the following system: (−) behavior not displayed, (1/2) behavior exhibited, but less than the recommended 75 percent required incidence level, ( ) behavior displayed at the 75 percent level with no assistance, (H) physical handicap prevents demonstration of behavior, or (E) the equipment/materials are not available that are necessary for the behavior to occur. From this information, objectives can be delineated and monitored. Booklets of instructional suggestions that are correlated with the strands are also available.

Summary

The BCP is a comprehensive criterion-referenced instrument. Although it is designed for individuals with a wide range of abilities, there are a number of items concerned with lower level skills. One potential disadvantage of the test is that it could be cumbersome if the number of strands is not limited. Another disadvantage is that there are not enough items within each strand.

Brigance Diagnostic Inventory of Early Development (Brigance, 1978)
Type: Criterion-referenced
Purpose: Prescriptive
Target Population: Nonhandicapped
The *Brigance Inventory of Early Development* was designed for use with individuals below the developmental level of seven years. It can be used to identify strengths and weaknesses, to determine instructional objectives, and to indicate the developmental level of the individual. It can also be used as an ongoing evaluation system to monitor progress. The test is not normed in the traditional sense. The test items were cross-referenced with texts and other tests to determine developmental age equivalents.

Content Areas Assessed

Eleven areas are measured on the Brigance, although not all are relevant for the severely and profoundly handicapped population. Included in these 11 areas are 98 skill sequences. Descriptions of the 11 areas are as follows:

Exhibit 4-1 Sample Page from the Behavioral Characteristics Progression

DRESSING

IDENTIFYING BEHAVIORS:

Requires assistance in dressing ● Buttons, snaps, zips ineffectively ● Misaligns
buttons ● Ties hard knot instead of bow ● Changes clothing infrequently ● Neglects
to use protective clothing according to weather

Date of observation _____	1	2	3	4	5	6
1.0 Cooperates passively when being dressed . . .						
2.0 Moves limbs to aid in dressing (e.g., holds out foot for shoe, arm for sleeve).						
3.0 Assists in getting dressed by passing or holding clothing.						
4.0 Identifies own clothing						
5.0 Partially closes one of the three front fasteners (e.g., pushes button halfway into hole, zips halfway up or pushes snaps to-gether)						
6.0 Pulls t-shirt, undershirt and other pullover garments down over chest after head and arms put in by adult						
7.0 Puts one arm into sleeve of t-shirt and pulls over chest.						
8.0 Puts both arms into sleeves of t-shirt and pulls over chest						
9.0 Pulls t-shirt down over head, puts arms in sleeves and pulls over chest.						
10.0 Places head into neckhole and puts t-shirt on completely						
11.0 Closes one of three front fasteners - either buttons, zips or snaps.						
12.0 Pulls pants, briefs, and other pull-down garments up from hips to waist after pants pulled up to that point by adult.						
13.0 Pulls pants up from knees to waist.						
14.0 Pulls pants up from ankles to waist						

Source: Reprinted from the *Behavior Characteristics Progression* with permission of VORT Corporation, © 1973.

Preambulatory Motor Skills and Behaviors (77 items): Includes 4 skill sequences: supine position, prone position, sitting position, and standing position.

Gross Motor Skills and Behaviors (115 items): Includes 13 skill sequences beginning with standing, walking, and climbing stairs and ending with ball bouncing, rhythm, and wheel toys.

Fine Motor Skills and Behaviors (102 items): Includes 9 skill sequences, such as general manipulative skills, puzzle assembling, prehandwriting skills, copying designs, and painting.

Self-Help Skills (126 items): Includes 11 skill sequences, such as feeding/ eating skills, undressing, dressing, toileting, grooming, and household chores.

Pre-Speech (34 items): Includes 3 skill sequences: receptive language, pre-speech gestures, and pre-speech vocalization.

Speech and Language (162 items): Includes 10 skill sequences, such as syntax, social speech, picture vocabulary, articulation, and sentence memory.

General Knowledge and Comprehension (275 items): Includes 13 skill sequences, such as knowledge of body parts, colors, time concepts, classifying, telling use of objects, and knowing where to go for service.

Readiness (208 items): Measures 5 areas: response to and experience with books, visual discrimination, reciting alphabet, and matching, identifying, and naming upper case and lower case letters.

Reading (118 items plus 4 reading lists): Includes 11 skill sequences, such as auditory discrimination, initial consonants with pictures, short vowel sounds, long vowel sounds, and reading level.

Manuscript Writing (125 items): Measures 7 areas, including printing upper and lower case letters sequentially and from dictation and printing simple sentences.

Basic Math (open-ended number of items): Assesses 12 skill sequences, such as number concepts, rote counting, numeral comprehension, addition combinations, subtraction combinations, recognition of money, and time concepts.

Interpretation of Scores

Exhibit 4-2 shows the format for administrating and scoring the Brigance. Most notable are the objectives that are spelled out for the student's performance. These are designed for use with individual educational plans. There are also developmental age equivalents assigned to certain items to give a rough estimate of the student's ability level.

Exhibit 4-2 Administration and Scoring Format for The Brigance Inventory of Early Development

MODEL OF FORMAT FOR AN ASSESSMENT PROCEDURE WITH A CHILD PAGE

1. **SKILL:** A general statement of the skill being assessed. When appropriate, the skill sequence in the *Developmental Record Book* is also listed.

2. **DEVELOPMENTAL AGE NOTATION:** The numbers preceding a sequence indicate the year and month the child usually begins to learn or master that skill. Those following indicate when mastery is usually accomplished. Example: for [4-7], read 4 years and 7 months developmental age.

   In addition, the developmental ages are explained or discussed in a separate note where necessary.

3. **DEVELOPMENTAL RECORD BOOK:** The page on which this skill is listed in the *Developmental Record Book*.

4. **ASSESSMENT METHODS:** The means recommended for assessing.

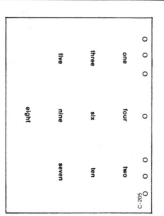

CHILD PAGE
(Oriented for the child facing the examiner.)

NOTES ON CHILD PAGE:

a. You have the publisher's permission to reproduce the child pages in the *Inventory* for non-profit educational purposes.

b. Some child pages have been designed for copying and cutting so you can present items individually.

c. Screen part of the page if the child finds a whole page visually confusing.

d. You may cover the child's page with acetate to prevent soiling and to make it possible to use an acetate marker.

e. All child pages are designated with a "C" preceding the number, which corresponds to the facing examiner page.

5. **MATERIALS:** Materials which are needed for the assessment.

6. **DISCONTINUE:** Indicates the number of items the child may fail before you discontinue the assessment of skills in this sequence.

7. **TIME:** Time limits suggested for the child's response.

8. **ACCURACY:** Explanation of scoring criteria.

9. **DIRECTIONS:** The recommended directions for assessing the skills sequence. Recommended phrasing of instructions or questions is clearly labeled, indented and printed in bold face type.

10. **OBJECTIVE:** The objective for the skills being assessed is stated, and is a valuable resource for developing individualized education programs (IEP's).

11. **REFERENCES:** the numbers listed correspond to the sources used to establish and validate the skill sequences and developmental ages. References are found in the *Bibliography* on page 246-7.

12. **NOTES:** Helpful notes on observations, resources or diagnosing are listed here.

13. Examiner's page number.

14. Skill assessed.

15. The first letter, "I," indicates the section, where all basic reading skills are located.

16. This number indicates the ninth of the skills sequenced in the basic reading section of the *Inventory*.

EXAMINER PAGE

Exhibit 4-2 continued

DIRECTIONS FOR RECORDING RESULTS AND IDENTIFYING OBJECTIVES

COLOR-CODING: Record assessment data in the *Developmental Record Book (DRB)* by using a color-code to develop an on-going, graphic, specific and easily interpreted record. Color-coding consists of using different-colored pencils or pens to identify the skills and objectives at each time of evaluation. As indicated on page 1 of the *DRB*, record the assessment in pencil. Use a blue pen to identify objectives for the second instructional period and to record data for that assessment. Use a red pen for the third assessment. *(See the illustration on page viii and/or "Recording Procedures and Color-Code" on page 1 of the DRB.)*

CIRCLE SKILLS DEMONSTRATED: The recording system is not time-consuming. Designate each skill the child masters by circling the skill or its number in the skill sequence found in the *DRB*. Use a colored pencil or pen as explained above. Do not mark skills attempted but not achieved.

If the child does not perform a skill, do not circle it. However, it may be helpful to make some notation for later reference and/or indicate that the skill was assessed. You may wish to underline the skill or make a notation before it, such as no, to indicate the skill was not performed. *(See item i on page viii for an illustration.)*

For various reasons, some skills will be skipped or omitted. It may be well to make a notation, such as DNA to indicate you did not administer the assessment procedures for the skill. *(See item b and notations before skills l—6 on page viii.)*

NOTES: Space is provided in the *Developmental Record Book* for your notes, observations, types of response, or other information.

GRAPH: Some skill sequences in the *DRB* have a horizontal bar graph underneath them so the developmental age can be graphed in an

appropriate color. This is optional. *(See items d and e on page viii for explanations and illustration.)*

UNDERLINE OBJECTIVES WITH COLOR TO BE USED FOR THE NEXT ASSESSMENT: Following the assessment of skills in a skills sequence, use the recorded information as baseline data in developing an individualized education program (IEP). The skills immediately following those mastered, and which have been circled in the skill sequence in the *DRB*, are the logical skills to be developed during the next instructional period—providing disabilities do not impose limitations.

These instructional objectives or skills are identified by underlining them or their numbers in the sequence. Use a pen of the color designated for recording the next assessment. *(See skills 13 and 14 in the illustration on page viii.)*

INTERPRET THE RECORD: After the color code described above has been used to develop a record such as the one illustrated on page xii, it can be interpreted easily. Following the color code, one can interpret the record to determine:

1. the child's performance level when first assessed,
2. the progress (skills mastered) since the first assessment, and
3. the objectives the teacher or others hope to accomplish/achieve during the next instructional period.

For example, the record on page viii would be interpreted as follows:
a. The child performed skills 7-10 when he/she entered the program in September;
b. has achieved skills 11 and 12 between September and February, and
c. the teacher anticipates he/she will master skills 13—14 by May 15, 1980.

Source: Brigance® Inventory of Early Development, © 1978.

Summary

The *Brigance Inventory of Early Development* is a comprehensive test measuring 11 major skill areas. The test should not be given in its entirety. Rather, the evaluator should choose the most appropriate areas to measure. The developmental age equivalents yielded should be considered only as estimates. The test is not norm-referenced in the traditional sense. There are no reliability data mentioned in the manual.

Cain-Levine Social Competency Scale (Cain, Levine, & Elzey, 1977)
Type: Norm-referenced
Purpose: Descriptive
Target Population: Trainable mentally retarded

The *Cain-Levine Social Competency Scale* is an individually administered instrument designed for use with trainable mentally retarded children ages 5–13. The authors define social competency as "the development of learned skills which ultimately permits the child to achieve self-sufficiency and socially contributory behaviors" (p. 2). The instrument consists of 44 items divided into four subscales. The information is collected via an interview of someone who is familiar with the child. Each item has four or five behavioral descriptions or levels that measure varying degrees of independence. The examiner must decide at which level to place a child for each item on the basis of the interview. Descriptions of each subscale are found below.

Self-Help (14 items): Measures motor or manipulative ability, including such skills as dressing, brushing teeth, and cleaning up spilled liquids.

Initiative (10 items): Measures ability to be self-directed and independent, including items such as "initiates dressing" or "hangs up clothes."

Social Skills (10 items): Measures ability to relate appropriately with other individuals, including items such as setting the table and going on errands.

Communication (10 items): Measures the degree to which a child can express himself or herself, including his or her needs and concerns, the use of language, and the ability to relate objects to action.

Interpretations of the Results

After the examiner determines the level (from 1 to 4 or 5) for each item, they are totaled for each subscale. For the self-help subscale, there are additional points given depending on the age and sex of the child. These four scores can then be converted to percentile ranks. In addition, the total raw score can be converted to a percentile rank. Note that the Cain-Levine offers information relative to trainable mentally retarded children. In other words, a percentile rank of 64 would indicate the child's relative performance compared with other trainable level children.

Technical Characteristics

The standardization sample included 716 trainable mentally retarded children from ages 5–0 to 13–11. The children (414 boys, 302 girls) were all from California. Parents' educational level, income, and occupational level were reported in the manual. The income and occupational levels of the parents were lower than the national average.

Both split-half and test-retest reliability coefficients were computed. Split-half reliability was determined for each subscale as well as the total test for each sex and separate age group. For the self-help subscale the correlations ranged from .65 to .86. The ranges for the initiative, social skills, and communication subscales and total scores were .62–.86, .50–.73, .84–.95, and .75–.91, respectively. Test-retest reliability was determined from retesting 35 sample subjects after a three-week period. The correlations ranged from .88 (social skills subscale) to .98 (total score). These high correlations have to be weighed against the small sample size.

There is no mention of validity studies. The authors do give their rationale behind initial item selection and state that the criterion for accepting an item into the final instrument was at best 70 percent agreement among a group of judges. The scale went through three revisions before its present form.

Summary

The Cain-Levine has a limited number of items for programming purposes. The small standardization sample and lack of validity limit its effectiveness as a classification instrument. Note that the percentiles yielded by the Cain-Levine compare an individual's score to a trainable mentally retarded population.

Callier-Azusa Scale (Stillman, 1978)
Type: Criterion-referenced
Purpose: Descriptive/prescriptive
Target Population: Multiply handicapped
The *Callier-Azusa Scale* is an individually administered instrument designed to assess the developmental level of deaf-blind and severely or profoundly handicapped children. The scale is comprised of 18 subscales in five major areas. The *Callier-Azusa Scale* is designed to be administered by teachers or other individuals who are thoroughly familiar with the child. The author states that the child should be observed for at least two weeks, and preferably in a classroom setting. The age range for the scale is from birth

through approximately nine years old. Descriptions of each major area are as follows:

Motor Development: Includes the subscales of postural control (18 steps), locomotion (17 steps), fine motor skills (20 steps), and visual motor (21 steps).

Perceptual Development: Includes the subscales of visual development (15 steps), auditory development (6 steps), and tactile development (13 steps).

Daily Living Skills: Includes the subscales of undressing and dressing (16 items), personal hygiene (13 steps), feeding skills (16 steps), and toileting (13 steps).

Cognition, Communication, and Language: Includes the subscales of cognitive development (21 steps), receptive communication (18 steps), expressive communication (20 steps), and development of speech (10 steps).

Social Development: Includes the subscales of interaction with adults (16 steps), interactions with peers (17 steps), and interactions with environment (10 steps).

Note: The items referred to are actually sequential steps measuring the particular developmental milestone of each subscale. In some cases, the step is further broken down into as many as five separate items.

Interpretation of Scores

In order to give a child credit for a particular step, he or she must attain all the behaviors described in all items within that step. If a behavior is emerging, occurs only infrequently, or occurs only after prompting or in specific situations, credit is not given. Some items in the scale are starred (*). These items can be omitted if "a child cannot be expected to exhibit behavior because of a specific sensory or motor deficit" (p. 4). To score the scale, the steps in each subscale that are exhibited by the child are noted (a certain format for scoring is discussed in the manual). Each subscale score can be converted to a "rough" age equivalency. The author notes, however, that the behavior sequences for a child, not the age norms, provide the most important information.

Summary

The Callier-Azusa is one of a few scales that is specifically designed to use with individuals with sensory and/or motor deficits. There are also a number of items designed for lower functioning individuals. The test should be used for the determination of strengths and weaknesses and educational objectives rather than an individual's developmental level.

Camelot Behavioral Checklist (Foster, 1974)
Type: Norm-referenced
Purpose: Descriptive/prescriptive
Target Population: Handicapped

The *Camelot Behavioral Checklist* was developed to help identify teaching and training objectives and to aid in the classification of an individual based on those objectives. The Camelot consists of 399 behaviors grouped into 40 subdomains. These 40 subdomains are further grouped into 10 domains. The Camelot can be completed in one of three ways: from memory by one person, from memory by a number of persons, or through direct observation. For each item the evaluator scores a "+" if the individual can perform the behavior and a "−" if he or she needs training in producing the behavior. The following are descriptions of the domains:

Self-Help (8 subdomains, 59 items): Includes items describing eating, dressing, toileting, and bathing and grooming behaviors.

Physical Development (6 subdomains, 41 items): Includes measures of balance, walking, posture, movement, and sensory development.

Home Duties (6 subdomains, 74 items): Measures typical responsible behaviors such as cooking, housecleaning, yard care, and care of clothing.

Vocational Behavior (2 subdomains, 37 items): Measures job and work related skills.

Economic Behavior (3 subdomains, 26 items): Includes measures of shopping skills, money handling, and use of credit.

Independent Travel (2 subdomains, 19 items): Measures transportation and travel skills.

Numerical Skills (2 subdomains, 24 items): Includes items measuring arithmetic skills and concept of time.

Communication Skills (5 subdomains, 55 items): Measures the areas of receptive and expressive language, reading, writing, and telephone skills.

Social Behaviors (3 subdomains, 35 items): Includes such areas as participation with groups and interaction with others.

Responsibility (3 subdomains, 19 items): Measures social responsibility, response to emergencies, and security.

Interpretation of Scores

Scores on the Camelot are analyzed in two ways: with an item profile and a score profile. For the item profile, the 40 subdomains are listed on a sheet with the corresponding item numbers listed under each column. The item numbers are arranged from the least difficult through the most difficult. All the items that were given a "+" are circled on the item profile sheet. This allows the examiner to identify the specific behaviors that the individual can and cannot do. The subdomain scores can then be summed to yield domain scores as well as a score for the overall checklist. These scores can be plotted on the score profile (see Exhibit 4-3). This profile sheet also gives information regarding percentile ranking.

Technical Information

Six hundred and twenty-four subjects were included in the standardization sample. They were subdivided into four groups based on "functioning level," the percentage of the 399 items a person could pass. Thus, there were 156 subjects in the top quarter, 156 in the upper middle quarter, 156 in the lower middle quarter, and 156 in the lower quarter. The 399 items were then administered to the four groups to determine the percentages of subjects that could successfully pass each item. All of these percentages are described in the manual.

Reliability and Validity

Interrater reliability was computed by administering the Camelot to 50 residents in a state hospital and training center. Two teams of staff members rated each resident. The resulting correlation coefficients ranged from .69 (Social Behavior Domain) to .98 (Communication Skill Domain). The reliability coefficient for the total Camelot checklist was .93.

Concurrent validity (the manual refers to it as "construct validity") was determined by correlating the Camelot with seven measures of adaptive behavior and general intelligence. The validity coefficients ranged from .33 (with the *Leiter International Performance Scale*) to .86 (with the *Stanford-Binet Intelligence Scale*).

Summary

The Camelot is an easy instrument to administer and score and gives a rough idea of strengths and weaknesses. Although the Camelot has been used for classification purposes, it really should be thought of more as a screening instrument that initially identifies teaching objectives. A skill acquisition program bibliography is available that identifies instructional programs addressing the various behavioral objectives. Many of the items on the Camelot are only appropriate with higher functioning students.

Empirically Based Training Assessment (Adams, 1981)
Type: Criterion-referenced
Purpose: Prescriptive
Target Population: Mildly to profoundly handicapped

Exhibit 4-3 Score Profile from the Camelot Behavioral Checklist

Circle Domain Score Totals from Item Profile   Name_____   ID_____

Percentile: Percentage of the test population with scores equal to or lower than corresponding tabled score.

Percentile	Self Help	Physical Development	Home Duties	Vocational Behaviors	Economic Behaviors	Independent Travel	Numerical Skills	Communication Skills	Social Behaviors	Responsibility	Camelot Adaptive Behavior	Percentile
100	67	41	64	34	14	13	24	25	32	15	298	100
99	65		63	33	10		22	17	28	12	294	99
98			57	28	9	12	21	16	27		279	98
97	64		55	26	8		20	13	25	10	276	97
96	63		53	24		11	19	12			272	96
95	62		50	23	7		18	11	24		267	95
94			48	20	6	10	17	8		9	257	94
93	61	40			5		16	6	23	8	254	93
92				19	4	9		5			246	92
91		39	47	18		8	16	4	22	7	241	91
90	60		46		3		15	3	21		231	90
89	59		45	17			14	2		6	226	89
88			44	16		7		1	20		221	88
87		38	42	14	2	6	13	0	19		216	87
86	58		41	13						L	210	86
85			40	11			12		18		208	85
84	57	37	39		1						204	84
83			36				5		17		199	83
82	56	36	35	10			4			4	188	82
81	55		31	9					16		179	81
80			29	8			9				172	80
79	54		28								166	79
78		35	26	7			8			3	162	78
77				6							158	77
76	52	34	24				7		15		153	76
75	51		20	5	0		6		14		150	75
74	50		19								146	74
73	49	33							13		140	73
72				18			5				135	72
71				16	4				12		133	71
70	47	32		15			4				131	70
69	46				3						129	69
68				13			2		11	2	125	68
67	44	31		12							124	67
66											121	66
65	43			11	2				10		119	65
64		30					2				117	64
63				10							114	63
62	42						1				112	62
61	41		29						9		110	61
60	40										108	60
59	39										105	59
58											104	58
57	38		28	8	1						103	57
56						1			8		99	56
55	37		27	7				0			98	55
54	35		26								96	54
53										1	94	53
52	34										93	52
51	33										90	51
50	32		25	6					7		87	50
49				5							85	49
48	31										83	48
47	30										81	47
46	29		24	4	0				6		78	46
45	28		23								77	45
44											76	44
43	27		22								73	43
42	26										71	42
41	25										69	41
40			21	3		0					68	40
39			20						5		66	39
38	24										63	38
37	23										62	37
36				2							60	36
35	22		19						4		58	35
34	21									0	55	34
33											53	33
32	20		18						3		52	32
31	19		17	1							49	31
30	18		16								47	30
29			15								44	29
28	17										41	28
27											39	27
26	15		14								37	26
25			13	0							35	25
24	14										34	24
23									2		32	23
22			12								30	22
21			11								29	21
20	13		10								27	20
19	12										25	19
18											24	18
17	11		9						1		23	17
16			8								21	16
15			7								20	15
14	10										19	14
13	9		6								18	13
12			5						0		15	12
11	8		4								13	11
10	7										12	10
9			3									9
8	6											8
7	5										11	7
6											10	6
5			2								9	5
4	4	3									8	4
3	3	2									7	3
2	2	1										2
1	1		1									1
0	0	0	0								0	0
	I	II	III	IV	V	VI	VII	VIII	IX	X	Total	

CAMELOT BEHAVIORAL CHECKLIST SCORE PROFILE

Copyright Camelot Behavioral Systems 1974

Source: Reprinted from the Camelot Behavioral Checklist by R. Foster with permission of Camelot Behavioral Systems, © 1974.

The *Empirically Based Training Assessment* (EBTA) is an individually administered instrument designed for use with mildly to profoundly retarded individuals. The EBTA was developed as a comprehensive measure of adaptive skills that could be used for developing specific training programs. The test is administered by someone who is familiar with the student and his or her behavior. The instrument uses a "mixed testing procedure" approach where most items are completed from memory (over 90 percent) and others from direct behavioral observation. The inclusion of items and their method of evaluation were accomplished through a series of controlled experimental studies. The sequence of items was based on the percentage of institutional subjects that passed the various items during field testing. After the items were selected, interrater reliability was determined. Items completed from memory with less than 90 percent interrater agreement were designated as requiring direct testing or behavioral observation. The EBTA also gives a criterion for each test item to decrease the subjectivity inherent in many tests.

The EBTA includes approximately 550 items grouped into seven major sections. Descriptions of the major sections are found below.

Self-Help Skills (153 items): Includes such items as toileting, eating, dressing, and grooming.

Home Living Skills (135 items): Includes items measuring the use and cleaning of some appliances and utensils typically found in various rooms in the home.

Independent Living Skills (81 items): Includes such skill areas as health and safety, telephone skills, economic skills, and vocational skills.

Social Skills (52 items): Measures self-awareness, interaction skills, and leisure skills.

Sensory and Motor Skills (50 items): Measures the areas of sensory awareness and discrimination, motor skills, and sports related motor skills.

Language Skills (30 items): Measures both receptive and expressive language.

Academic Skills (31 items): Measures math, reading, and writing skills.

Summary

The EBTA was developed through rigorous experimental testing, and the sequencing of items was empirically based. The criterion statement for each item greatly increases its reliability (established at 99 percent agreement). The author is currently standardizing the instrument and creating a matching curriculum and computer-based individual educational plan. One limitation of the EBTA for severely and profoundly handicapped students is that many of the items are too difficult.

Learning Accomplishment Profile (Sanford, 1974)
Type: Criterion-referenced
Purpose: Prescriptive
Target Population: Young handicapped

The *Learning Accomplishment Profile* (LAP) is an individually administered criterion-referenced test used with handicapped individuals up to the developmental age of six years. The LAP uses a task analytic model to offer a hierarchy of sequential skills. The LAP is specifically designed to help the teacher identify behavioral objectives and to evaluate the student's progress with respect to those objectives. The items on the LAP were chosen from existing developmental and intellectual scales.

There are six areas measured on the LAP. In each area the items are sequential. In addition, there are checklists that allow precise measurement of a number of skill areas. Descriptions of the six areas are as follows:

Gross Motor (37 items): Items range from "sits without support" and "pulls self to stand" to "jumps from height of 12 inches landing on toes only."

Fine Motor (47 items): Measures general fine motor skills such as "transfers cube hand-to-hand" and writing skills such as "scribbles spontaneously" and "copies circle."

Social Skills (38 items): Items range from "smiles spontaneously" and "reaches for familiar persons" to "gets along in small groups" and "conforms to adult ideas."

Self-Help (38 items): Measures the general areas of eating, dressing, and toileting.

Cognitive (35 items): Items range from "fetches or carries familiar objects" and "uses names of familiar objects" to "can tell how a crayon and pencil are the same and how they are different" and "understands numbers up to ten."

Language Development (53 items): Items range from "makes small, throaty noises" and "responds to bell" to "speaks fluently and correctly except for confusions of s, f, and th" and "asks meaning of abstract words."

Interpretation of Scores

For each item on the LAP, a developmental age equivalent is given. There are many times when different numbers of items are given for different developmental ages. Also, the increments are not always consistent. For instance, the items in the gross motor section are given for 5, 8, 11, 12, 14, 21, 24, 30, 36, 36–48, 48–60, 56, and 60–72 months. On the record sheet there are places to put comments and the date of achievement for each item. There is also a separate booklet of learning activities that correspond to the LAP items.

Summary

The LAP is an individually administered criterion-referenced instrument. It is appropriate for individuals up to the developmental age of six years. Generally speaking, there are too few items at the lower ranges to be effective for programming the more severely and profoundly handicapped students. There is also some question about the sequence of items in each area. Finally, many of the items, particularly at the upper levels, are rather subjective and would tend to decrease its reliability. The LAP is, however, a comprehensive instrument that might help in the areas of programming and accountability with certain types (less handicapped) of students. There is also an Early LAP (for children birth to 36 months) and a LAP Diagnostic edition. Thus, a LAP total evaluation system is available.

Project MEMPHIS (Quick, Little, & Campbell, 1974)
Type: Criterion-referenced
Purpose: Descriptive/prescriptive
Target Population: Preschool handicapped
As a part of *Project MEMPHIS* (acronym for Memphis Educational Model Providing Handicapped Infant Services), a three-step developmental-educational evaluation and program evaluation is provided. The assessment model includes the MEMPHIS Comprehensive Developmental Scale, the Developmental Skill Assignment Record, and the Continuous Record for Educational-Developmental Gain.

MEMPHIS Comprehensive Developmental Scale

The MEMPHIS Comprehensive Developmental Scale assesses developmental skills in five areas. It is designed for preschool exceptional children between birth and age five. Information for the scale can be gathered through either direct observation (by someone who is familiar with the child) or interview. The scale gives only rough estimates of developmental levels and should be considered more of a screening and programming instrument rather than a diagnostic device.

There are a total of 260 items on the Comprehensive Developmental Scale. Each of the items in the various subscales is correlated with developmental age levels and is therefore presented in sequential fashion. Descriptions of the five areas are as follows:

> *Personal-Social Skills* (60 items): Includes such items as "drinks from glass or cup unassisted" (18-month developmental age), "dries hands well" (33-month developmental age), and "distinguishes front from back of clothes" (51-month developmental age).
>
> *Gross Motor Skills* (40 items): Includes such items as "rolls over to side from back position" (3-month developmental age), "stands on one leg momentarily" (30-month developmental age), and "walks distances on tiptoe or skips alternating feet" (60-month developmental age).
>
> *Fine Motor Skills* (40 items): Includes such items as "good grasp and release are present" (12-month developmental age) and "copies a cross from an example" (51-month developmental age).
>
> *Language Skills* (60 items): Includes such items as "imitates words" (12-month developmental age), "knows last name and sex" (33-month developmental age), and "repeats a five-word sentence" (51-month developmental age).
>
> *Perceptual-Cognitive Skills* (60 items): Includes such items as "responds to bye-bye" (9-month developmental age), "counts two objects" (30-month developmental age), and "recognizes and names common coins" (60-month developmental age).

Scoring

An item is considered passed if it is regularly a part of the child's behavioral repertoire. Each item administered (you discontinue testing after six consecutive failures) is marked either passed or failed. The raw score is simply the total number of items passed. There is a raw score for each subscale. This raw score is converted to a developmental age. Each developmental age can then be plotted on a profile available in the scale.

Developmental Skill Assignment Record

The Developmental Skill Assignment Record helps the teacher plan individual programs. Based on the results of the Comprehensive Developmental Scale, skills to be taught for a particular child are identified and placed on the Developmental Skill Assignment Record. A description of each skill, including criteria for passing the skill, must then be made by the teacher. In addition, an estimated time period for programming a child on the pinpointed skills is recorded. This section simply provides a standard format for prioritizing educational objectives and offers a guideline for meeting those objectives.

Continuous Record for Educational-Developmental Gain

The Continuous Record for Educational-Developmental Gain assists a teacher in keeping ongoing records of the skills identified on the Developmental Skill Assignment Record. There are five pages (one for each subscale). Each page allows for the evaluation of a total of four skills. Information on the Continuous Record includes date evaluated, a pass or fail category, and a quality category. The quality category involves the recording of the degree of competence with which a child demonstrates a skill. There is also a completion record on the cover sheet that summarizes the number of skills assigned from each subscale, the number mastered, and the percent mastered.

Summary

The assessment section of *Project MEMPHIS* offers a systematic and accountable method for evaluating preschool handicapped children. One criticism, however, is that the skills on the Comprehensive Developmental Scale are not well defined and require some degree of subjectivity.

Pennsylvania Training Model Individual Assessment Guide (Somerton-Fair & Turner, 1979)
Type: Criterion-referenced
Purpose: Descriptive/prescriptive
Target Population: Severely and profoundly handicapped
The *Pennsylvania Training Model* was developed to meet the educational requirements of the severely and profoundly handicapped population. In addition to a Curriculum Assessment Guide, which serves as a gross screening instrument in several behavioral domains, there are sections on Developmental Taxonomies and Skill Observation Strategies. Also included is an Individual Prescription Planning Sheet.

Curriculum Assessment Guide

The purpose of this section is to provide information in four areas: (1) how an individual receives and expresses information; (2) how an individual moves about in his or her environment; (3) how an individual socializes; and (4) how an individual processes and retains information. There are 70 items broken down into 14 skill areas, each 14 containing five major behavioral items representing the range considered "traditional" among the severely and profoundly handicapped population. Information for the assessment is usually obtained through direct observation. There are well-defined criteria for each item. Descriptions of each skill area are as follows:

Tactile Skills: Items range from "responds to tactile stimulation" to "ability to discriminate objects."

Auditory Skills: Items range from "reacts positively or negatively to loud noise" to "changes activity with change of sound."

Visual Skills: Items range from "responds to light" to "identifies familiar objects through sight."

Gross Motor Skills: Items range from "holds head in prone position" to "brings self to standing position."

Fine Motor Skills: Items range from "claps hands" to "strings beads."

Feeding and Drinking Skills: Items range from "swallows when stimulated externally" to "eats independently using spoon."

Toilet Training Skills: Items range from "retains urine for one hour" to "toilets independently."

Dressing and Undressing Skills: Items range from "takes sock off" to "buttons."

Washing and Bathing Skills: Items range from "attempts to wash with washcloth" to "washes and dries self independently."

Nasal Hygiene Skills: Items range from "wipes nose" to "cleans nose independently."

Oral Hygiene Skills: Items range from "opens mouth for toothbrushing" to "brushes teeth independently."

Communication Skills: Items range from "responds to 'look at me' " to "spontaneously verbalizes."

Perceptual-Cognitive Skills: Items range from "lifts cups to obtain object underneath" to "copies circle."

Social Interaction Skills: Items range from "smiles in response to facial expression of others" to "takes turns."

Each item in the Curriculum Assessment Guide can be scored in one of four ways. Depending on the item, the number of days the task was presented, the number of trials to reach criterion, the total time spent on the item, or the total number of correct responses can be recorded. This information can be used as a rough guide for identifying areas to consider for educational programming, and to give an indication of the modality strengths and weaknesses and motivational factors pertinent for each individual educational plan.

Developmental Taxonomies

The Developmental Taxonomies section was developed to give detailed sequences of behaviors in each of the previously mentioned 14 skill areas.

These behavioral sequences are intended to assist the teacher/trainer in determining the appropriate curriculum by giving a much more detailed breakdown of the skill areas. For instance, the gross motor area is broken down into 43 behaviors. The feeding and drinking area is broken down into 80 behaviors, and the toileting area is broken down into 43 behaviors. For each behavior in the sequence, an individual can be scored in one of six ways. An "O" is given if the behavior was observed. An "X" is given if the behavior was not observed. A "U" is given if the behavior was unknown (unable to be observed). If applicable, a "P" (physical prompt), "G" (gestural prompt), or "V" (verbal prompt) is specified if it was necessary to initiate the child's behavior.

Skill Observation Strategies

The Skill Observation Strategies section of the *Pennsylvania Training Model* was developed to incorporate the information from the Curriculum Assessment Guide and the Developmental Taxonomies sections into functional lesson plans. This information gives the teacher/trainer instructional suggestions after developmental pinpoints (skill area and specific behaviors) have been identified.

Individual Prescriptive Planning Sheet

The Individual Prescriptive Planning Sheet provides for the systematic planning of the student's curriculum (see Exhibit 4-4). Included are antecedents (preparation procedures necessary prior to teacher intervention), the behavior itself (including definitions of correct and incorrect behavior), the consequences given by the teacher of both correct and incorrect behaviors, and the criteria necessary to master a particular behavioral item.

Summary

The *Pennsylvania Training Model Individual Assessment Guide* has many positive characteristics, including well-defined test items and a means of translating assessment information into functional educational plans.

TARC Assessment System (Sailor & Mix, 1975)
Type: Norm-referenced
Purpose: Descriptive
Target Population: Severely handicapped

The TARC (so called because of its development with the Topeka Association for Retarded Citizens) is a behavioral assessment system designed for use with severely handicapped children. The authors state that the TARC provides a quick assessment that stresses observable behavior characteristics

Exhibit 4-4 Individual Prescriptive Planning Sheet from the Pennsylvania Training Model

Student's Name _____ Date _____ Area Involved _____ Terminal Objective _____ Educator _____

ANTECEDENTS (GIVENS)		BEHAVIOR		CONSEQUENCES		CRITERIA	COMMENTS
Preparation	Procedures	Correct	Error	Correct	Error		
1) Mash food. 2) Place food in yellow bowl. 3) Place Dennis' therapy spoon in bowl. 4) Place Dennis in chair with feet & side support. 5) Place chair at lunch table with no other children present. 6) Instructor should sit to Dennis' right side.	1) Place Dennis' right hand around handle of spoon. 2) Instructor should place her right hand over Dennis' right hand. 3) Instructor's left hand supporting right elbow. 4) Guide Dennis' hand to scoop small amount of food from bowl. 5) Direct full spoon to mouth. 6) Give verbal command "eat your food". 7) Instructor should withdraw spoon from Dennis' mouth & guide his hand & spoon back to bowl.	1) Dennis takes food from spoon with lips.	1) More than half the food is left on the spoon.	1) Pat on left shoulder paired with "Dennis eats nicely". 1:1	1) Ignore unsuccessful trial. 1:1	8 out of 10 correct trials for 3 consecutive days.	

Source: Reprinted from the Pennsylvania Training Model by E. Somerton-Fair & K. Turner with permission from the Pennsylvania Department of Education, © 1979.

and can be used for a number of purposes including the demonstration of accountability, development of instructional objectives and goals, and the evaluation of instructional programs. It is not meant to be used for in-depth comprehensive assessment purposes. The TARC includes an inventory that provides scores in five areas and a profile sheet to graphically represent the child's strengths and weaknesses. Descriptions of the five areas are found below.

Self-Help Skills (10 items): Includes such behaviors as toileting, washing, eating, and dressing. For each item a continuum of behavior descriptions is given. The examiner circles the one statement that best describes the child's behavior (scaled item).

Motor Skills (5 items): Includes small muscle coordination, large motor coordination, and preacademic skills. For two of the items (involvement in fine motor activities and involvement in gross motor activities) the format is the same as the self-help section. For the other three items, a number of behavioral descriptions that are not mutually exclusive are scored as either applicable or not applicable (categorical items).

Communication Skills (3 items): Includes the receptive language, expressive language, and preacademic communication areas. Receptive and expressive language items are scored with the scaled method and the preacademic communication item uses the categorical scoring approach.

Social Skills (8 items): Includes such areas as following directions, emotional control, peer and adult interaction, and individual and group behavior. These are all scaled items. There is also a preacademic skill categorical item.

Interpretation of Results

It is recommended that the rater make his or her judgment on scoring an item after a minimum of three weeks of observation. After completing the inventory the raw scores can be computed for each section. The maximum raw score is 50 for the self-help skills, 61 for motor skills, 38 for communication skills, 45 for social skills, and 194 for the total. It is also possible to obtain raw scores for subsections (such as small muscle coordination, large motor coordination, and preacademic skills for the motor skills section). These scores can be placed on the profile sheet (see Exhibit 4-5). The scores in the columns represent the raw scores for each subsection and section. The numbers (0–100) on the left and right axes are standard scores with a mean of 50 and a standard deviation of 20. For instance, a total self-help score of 38 and a total communication score of 19 would both be considered "average" in comparison to the standardization population.

Exhibit 4-5 Profile Sheet from the TARC Assessment System (Standard Scores*)

PROFILE SHEET

STANDARD SCORES*

NAME _____
(or identification number)

CLASS OR UNIT _____

RATED BY _____

DATE _____

*Standard scores here are adjusted so that the mean score is 50 and the standard deviation is 20.

Categories: SELF-HELP (TOILETING, WASHING, EATING, CLOTHING, TOTAL), MOTOR (SMALL MUSCLE, LARGE MUSCLE, PRE-ACADEMIC, TOTAL), COMMUNICATION (RECEPTIVE, EXPRESSIVE, PRE-ACADEMIC, TOTAL), SOCIAL (BEHAVIOR, PRE-ACADEMIC, TOTAL), RAW TOTAL

Source: Reprinted from the *TARC Assessment System* by W. Sailor and B. Mix with permission of H & H Enterprises, © 1975.

Technical Characteristics

The TARC was standardized on 283 severely handicapped children ages 3–16. This population included children who were primarily considered mentally retarded, though some were labeled autistic, cerebral palsied, perceptually handicapped, or learning disabled. The authors state, however, that the level of retardation was consistent with moderate-to-profound levels.

Sixty-six children from the standardization sample were assessed by two professionals to establish interrater reliability. Those correlations ranged from .59 (self-help) to .85 (total). Test-retest data were collected for the same 66 children six months later. The authors state that all the correlations were .80 or greater. No validity data were presented in the manual, though the authors stated that a longitudinal study was underway to establish predictive validity.

Summary

The TARC should be used for screening purposes only. There is some question about the makeup of the standardization population. Although the sample was called "severely handicapped," there is apparently quite a heterogeneous group of students included. The rather large standard deviation of 20 (with a mean of 50) indicates considerable variability of scores. Most important, the validity of the TARC has not been established. There is a computer retrieval system available that matches the items to various curriculum materials.

Vineland Social Maturity Scale (Doll, 1965)
Type: Norm-referenced
Purpose: Descriptive
Target Population: Nonhandicapped
The *Vineland Social Maturity Scale* (VSMS) is the oldest and most widely researched instrument dealing with the area of adaptive behavior. The scale, according to the author, is used to provide a schedule of normal development on which to base growth or change, a measure of individual differences, an index of developmental variations in certain types of individuals, a measure of improvement following treatment or training, and a schedule to review developmental histories from a research point of view. The scale is used with individuals from birth to 30 years of age. The information is obtained via an interview with someone who is thoroughly familiar with the person being evaluated. There are 117 items that fall into eight categories, which are arranged in terms of "normal average life progression." No separate category scores are obtained. Descriptions of the eight categories are as follows:

Self-Help General (14 items): Includes such behaviors as "rolls over," "asks to go to toilet," and "tells time to quarter hour."

Self-Help Eating (12 items): Includes items such as "drinks from cup or glass assisted," "eats with spoon," and "cares for self at table."

Self-Help Dressing (13 items): Includes items such as "pulls off socks," "washes face unassisted," and "bathes self unaided."

Locomotion (10 items): Items range from "moves about on floor" to "goes to distant points alone."

Occupation (22 items): Includes items such as "initiates own play activities," "helps at little household tasks," "does simple creative work," and "performs expert or professional work."

Communication (15 items): Includes behaviors such as "imitates sounds," "writes occasional short letters," and "follows current events."

Self-Direction (14 items): Items range from "is trusted with money" to "purchases for others."

Socialization (17 items): Includes items such as "reaches for familiar persons," "plays with other children," "contributes to social welfare," and "promotes civic progress."

Note: Each item is operationally defined, though not in depth.

Interpretation of Results

The manual presents five possible scores that can be assigned to each item. It is the evaluator's responsibility to determine if the subject routinely performs the behavior, formerly performed the behavior but no longer has the opportunity, has had no opportunity to perform the behavior, performs the behavior occasionally, or does not perform the behavior. The total score can be converted to an age equivalent using interpolation of the age scores provided on the record sheet. This technique allows the conversion of a raw score to both a social age and a social quotient (social age divided by chronological age $\times$ 100 = SQ).

Technical Characteristics

A total of 620 subjects (ten "normal" subjects for each sex at each year from birth to 30) were included in the standardization sample. The norms presented were from the original 1936 edition of the VSMS.

Test-retest reliability data were obtained on a sample of 250 of the original subjects after a time interval of 1.7 to 1.9 years. This population tended to be younger and with slightly higher social quotients. The reported correlation coefficient between the social ages of the subjects between the two testings was .98, though the correlation between social quotients was only .57.

In a recent study, Roszkowski (1980) investigated the concurrent validity of the VSMS using the *Adaptive Behavior Scale* (ABS) as the criterion measure. He reported a .79 correlation between the VSMS total score and ABS Part One score and only a .11 correlation between the VSMS total score and the ABS Part Two score. The lower correlation with the ABS Part Two is not surprising given the difference in types of items measured by this part.

Summary

The Vineland is definitely in need of revision. There are too few items and many are outdated. The standardization sample was small. Further, the reliability and validity of the instrument has not been sufficiently established. There is a revised edition currently being developed and is scheduled for publication in 1983.

Vulpé Assessment Battery (Vulpé, 1979)
Type: Criterion-referenced
Purpose: Prescriptive
Target Population: Handicapped and nonhandicapped

The *Vulpé Assessment Battery* is a developmentally based system for measuring behaviors of children ages birth to six years. Information from the Vulpé can be used to determine an appropriate specific teaching approach, to indicate program goals and objectives, and to provide an accountability system for individual programs. The Vulpé is sequentially based in a number of developmental skill areas and the author states that it is applicable to all children, including multihandicapped, at-risk, and normal. She further states that the battery is extremely comprehensive, individualized, and competency oriented. The Vulpé is divided into various developmental skill areas or sections, and further divided into subskill areas or subsections. There is also an appendix that includes a developmental reflex test and functional tests of muscle strength, motor planning, and balance.

There are eight skill areas included in the *Vulpé Assessment Battery*. Many of the items appear in more than one section. In order to eliminate the need to administer an item more than once, those which are included in more than one section are cross-referenced on the assessment form. In addition, all the equipment necessary and the instructions for administering each item are included on the record form. Descriptions of the skill areas are as follows:

Basic Senses and Functions (16 items): Measures the central nervous system functions considered important in performing basic activities. Includes the areas of vision, hearing, olfaction, balance, muscle strength, range of motion, and reflex status.
Gross Motor Behaviors (206 items): Includes items that measure such behaviors as standing, jumping, lying down, sitting, kneeling, skipping, and running.

Fine Motor Behaviors (177 items): Includes items concerned with behaviors of small muscle movements such as eye coordination, eye-hand coordination, reaching, manipulation, and use of toys and utensils.

Language Behaviors (241 items): Divided into two subsections. The Auditory Expressive Language subsection (160 items) includes items ranging from vocalizing noises to saying one-word sentences to using free expression. The Auditory Receptive Language subsection (81 items) ranges from hearing sounds in the environment to comprehending full sentences.

Cognitive Processes and Specific Concepts (245 items): Divided into 13 subsections. The first, Object Concepts (17 items), measures a child's understanding of objects from a developmental (for example, Piagetian) framework. The second subsection, Body Concepts (32 items), includes information regarding self-image and knowledge of body parts. The next subsection, Color Concepts (9 items), includes items ranging from matching and sorting to naming and discriminating colors. The Shape Concept subsection (22 items) includes items that require a child to identify shapes and discriminate three-dimensional objects and parts of objects. The Size Concepts subsection (6 items) includes items measuring the understanding of such concepts as "bigger," "longer," and "shorter." The Space Concepts subsection (36 items) includes items related to the child's understanding of relationships of his or her own body to objects in space and the abstract understanding of space not directly related to self. The Time Concepts subsection (16 items) includes items measuring a child's understanding of events occurring in the immediate, present time as well as more abstract concepts of past and future. The Amount and Number Concepts subsection (22 items) includes counting and understanding quantitative concepts. The Visual Memory subsection (12 items) includes items requiring a child to use rote memory and more complex sequential memory. The Auditory Discrimination subsection (12 items) requires a child to discriminate consonants, words, sounds, and tones. The Auditory Attention, Comprehension, and Memory subsection (25 items) includes items such as "follows one-step command," "repeats four words," "follows three-step command," and "repeats four digits." The Cause/Effect or Means/End Behavior subsection (12 items) includes items such as "understands relationship of adult's presence to being lifted" and "uses parts of objects for specific purposes." The Categorizing/Combining Scheme subsection (24 items) includes items requiring a child to integrate information and to organize it into meaningful thoughts and actions.

Organization of Behavior (79 items): Divided into four parts. The Attention and Goal Orientation section (18 items) is concerned with the ability of the child to orient and react to sensory stimuli, and to selectively attend, focus, and maintain attention. The Internal Control to Environmental Limits section (20 items) includes recognition of boundaries or behavioral limits within the environment and the desire and ability to control behaviors in order to function effectively within the environment. The Problem Solving and Learning Patterns section (17 items) includes items measuring a child's ability to react appropriately to the environment, to imitate others, and to solve problems of different complexity. The Dependence/Independence section (24 items) measures a child's behavior along a dependence/independence continuum.

Activities of Daily Living: Includes subsections on feeding (47 items), dressing (32 items), social interaction (48 items), playing (50 items), sleeping (16 items), toileting (17 items), and grooming (12 items). The items in this section are similar to those in most adaptive behavior scales measuring daily living skills.

Assessment of Environment: This section is somewhat unique for a developmental skill instrument such as the Vulpé. It measures the interaction of the child and the environment to discover whether the child's physical and emotional needs are met by the physical environment. There are also items that measure the characteristics and knowledge level of the "primary caregiver."

Interpretation of Scores

Each item on the Vulpé is scored in one of seven ways. A *no* score is given if the child has no apparent interest or motivation to participate or cannot attend to the task. An *attention* score is given when a child shows any interest to any part of the activity but does not actively participate because of physical incapacity or insufficient attention. A *physical assistance* score is used if a child actively participates in the activity when the task or environment is modified. A *social-emotional assistance* score is used when the child is given more feedback, reinforcement, or reassurance in order to participate in the task. A *verbal assistance* score is given when the child's performance changes if verbal cues are given or the instructions repeated. An *independent* score is given when the child succeeds with no assistance within familiar surroundings. Finally, a *transfer* score is given when a child can perform tasks of similar complexity in different environments.

These scores can be marked directly on the Performance Analysis/Developmental Assessment scoring pad (see Exhibit 4-6). In addition, comments about a child's performance can be included. Age levels are provided for the items but they represent gross indicators and should be used only to determine relative strengths and weaknesses.

Summary

The Vulpé offers a very comprehensive assessment of developmental skills of children aged birth to six years. Its comprehensiveness, in fact, might be

Exhibit 4-6 Scoring Sheet from the Vulpé Assessment Battery

VULPE ASSESSMENT BATTERY * SCORING PAD

PERFORMANCE ANALYSIS/DEVELOPMENTAL ASSESSMENT

Name: . . . . Birthdate: . . . .

Developmental Area: . . . .

Date: . . . . Manual page: . . . .

SCALE SCORE	COMMENTS
	INFORMATION PROCESSING AND ACTIVITY ANALYSIS

No	Attention	Phys. Assis.	Soc./Emot. Assis.	Verbal Assis.	Independent	Transfer	1. Analyse activities consider-ing component parts of each and relationship to: Basic Senses & Functions Organizational Behaviors Cognitive Processes & Specific Concepts Auditory Language Gross & Fine Motor	2. Information Processing Consider: Input Integration Feedback Assimilation Output
1	2	3	4	5	6	7		

Activity (Item number)

2 3 4 5 6 7

Activity (Item number)

1 2 3 4 5 6 7

Activity (Item number)

1 2 3 4 5 6 7

Activity (Item number)

1 2 3 4 5 6 7

Activity (Item number)

1 2 3 4 5 6 7

©NIMR, 1977 For use with the Vulpé Assessment Battery, by Shirley German Vulpé. NIMR, 4700 Keele St., Downsview, Ont. Canada M3J1P3

considered one of its drawbacks. It takes time to administer and score all the appropriate items using the Vulpé system. The results, however, are more meaningful than those yielded from most developmental tests, particularly for educational programming purposes. Another limitation is the fact that there are relatively few items in certain subsections.

A Model of Assessment: Choosing the Best Instrument

There are indeed a number of instruments available to the teacher/ specialist for assessing severely and profoundly handicapped students. The question of "which test do I use?" is a very important one. Before this question is answered, however, a more fundamental one must first be addressed. That is "what is the purpose for the assessment?" (Taylor, in press). Figure 4-1 presents a model for assessing severely and profoundly handicapped individuals that includes many of the potential purposes.

Screening

Screening is a procedural term that has multiple meanings. It can be, for instance, a process through which one identifies the presence of a handicap, or it can represent a method through which a rough profile of a student's strengths and weaknesses is obtained. The first type of screening is usually initiated by members of the assessment team other than the teacher. The teacher, however, is actively involved in the second type of screening. Of the instruments previously discussed, two would be appropriate for screening a student's strengths and weaknesses to identify programmatic goals. Those are the *Camelot Behavioral Checklist* and the *TARC Assessment System*. Both of these instruments are relatively simple to administer and easy to score. Thus, they do not take a tremendous amount of time on the part of the teacher. They are also norm-referenced so that scores could be used, if so desired, for comparison purposes. Results from these tests are used to generate an idea of general program goals and objectives, not specific instructional objectives.

Figure 4-1 Model for Assessing Severely and Profoundly Handicapped Individuals

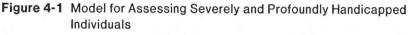
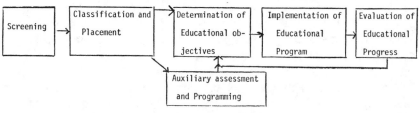

Classification and Potential Placements

Although a student might have a medical diagnosis prior to receiving educational programming, eligibility requirements for special education must also be met. This is accomplished through the administration of instruments that establish an educational need as well as determining the most appropriate "label" to assign the student to receive the most appropriate program. For severely and profoundly handicapped students, some type of adaptive behavior scale is usually administered as part of the battery to determine the label and the potential placements. The *AAMD Adaptive Behavior Scale* and the Vineland have been used for this purpose. These instruments are not sensitive enough for determining specific objectives; rather they compare an individual's general adaptive behavior level with others. Thus, degrees of handicap can be determined. The Cain-Levine is also a general norm-referenced adaptive behavior scale. Though it is sometimes used to help classify and place students, it is more appropriately used to document individual progress. Its limitation as a classification tool is due to the fact that it was standardized on a trainable mentally retarded population. Scores on the test are thus compared to the typical trainable level individual and not to the typical "nonhandicapped" person.

Determination of Educational Objectives

For the teacher of the severely and profoundly handicapped, the determination of educational objectives is probably the most important purpose of assessment. Nine of the fifteen instruments discussed in this chapter are primarily used for this purpose. In order to help the teacher choose the best instrument, these nine tests will be further divided into four categories: tests designed for special populations, comprehensive tests requiring preselection, comprehensive tests without preselection, and assessment systems.

Two tests were specifically designed for special populations. The *Balthazar Scales* were standardized using severely and profoundly mentally retarded individuals. As a result, compared with most other instruments, there are fewer areas measured (functional independence and social adaptation) with more items in each area. The *Callier-Azusa Scale* was designed for use with deaf-blind and severely or profoundly handicapped children. The scoring system thus allows the omission of certain items if a child has a sensory or motor deficit. The *Behavior Characteristics Progression* also includes some areas that are designed for deaf, blind and/or orthopedically handicapped individuals, although these areas comprise only about 20 percent of the total test.

Several tests are extremely comprehensive, requiring the examiner to administer only portions or certain areas. This requires either that the examiner is familiar enough with the student to know the priority areas of assessment or that screening measures are obtained to determine the target areas. The *Vulpé Assessment Battery* measures eight major areas and includes approximately 6,000 items. The Vulpé also has a rather detailed scoring system that further necessitates the need for limiting the number of items. The *Behavior Characteristics Progression* includes 56 behavior strands that contain 2,400 behavior characteristics (items). The *Brigance Diagnostic Inventory of Early Development* measures eleven areas and contains approximately 1,200 items. For all of these tests, the amount of usable information is largely dependent on the ability of the examiner to determine and prioritize assessment need areas.

There are also comprehensive tests that are usually administered in their entirety. The *Learning Accomplishment Profile* and the *Empirically Based Training Assessment* are examples of this type. Both tests are sequentially based and measure a number of developmental and skill areas. Although the tests are designed to be given in their entirety, there will typically be some areas that are inappropriate for the severely and profoundly handicapped and, therefore, not administered.

Finally, there are some tests used for determination of educational objectives that are actually assessment systems. The *Pennsylvania Training Model* includes a Curriculum Assessment Guide that serves as a screening instrument in a number of skill areas as well as a Developmental Taxonomies section to give detailed behavior sequences for each of the skill areas. The *Pennsylvania Training Model* also includes a Skill Observation Strategies section to aid in the development of functional educational programs and an Individual Prescriptive Planning Sheet section to monitor the program. *Project MEMPHIS* includes a Comprehensive Developmental Scale that measures five areas, a Developmental Skill Assignment Record to help prioritize objectives, and a Continuous Record for Educational-Developmental Gain.

Auxiliary Assessment and Programming

This step of the assessment model involves the development and integration of programs from the other members of the assessment team. For instance, the physical therapist, speech therapist, and social worker might develop specific programs that are integrated with the teacher's information in the student's overall educational program.

Implementation of Educational Program

A total educational program involves the integration of all the assessment data to develop the most appropriate program. Included in the program are such factors as general program goals, specific program objectives, personnel involved, adaptive equipment (if needed), and criteria for successfully meeting the program objectives.

Evaluation of Educational Program

The evaluation of an educational program is, in reality, nothing more than the evaluation of the student's progress toward attainment of objectives. Typically, documentation of this progress is accomplished through pre-, post-, or continuous evaluation. Usually, the instrument used to establish the objectives is also used to test progress related to those objectives. Certain instruments, however, deserve additional comment. The *Adaptive Behavior Scale* and the Vineland, because they are norm-referenced, are sometimes used to measure global progress usually on an annual basis. Typically, however, because of their lack of sensitivity with severely and profoundly handicapped students, little if any progress is documented. The *Brigance Diagnostic Inventory of Early Development* includes a means of establishing criteria for successful completion of the objectives that are identified. The *Pennsylvania Training Model* and *Project MEMPHIS* both include a system of accountability to measure progress.

CONCLUSION

This chapter has summarized the past practices, reviewed the current practices, and offered a pragmatic model to follow in determining the most appropriate instruments to use in the assessment process. It is imperative that in the future new tests for this population be developed and older tests be improved. The lack of adequate technical characteristics of many currently available instruments makes the difficult task of assessing severely and profoundly handicapped individuals even more difficult.

Finally, the importance of knowing what test to use in a given situation cannot be minimized. The model discussed in this chapter emphasizes the importance of carefully designating the purpose for assessment.

REFERENCES

Adams, G.L. *Empirically Based Training Assessment.* Unpublished manuscript, 1981.

Balthazar, E. *Balthazar Scales of Adaptive Behavior.* Palo Alto, Calif.: Consulting Psychologists Press, 1976.

Bayley, N. *Bayley Scales of Infant Development.* Atlanta: The Psychological Corporation, 1969.

Behavior Characteristics Progression. Palo Alto, Calif.: VORT Corporation, 1973.

Brigance, A. *Brigance Diagnostic Inventory of Early Development.* North Billerica, Mass.: Curriculum Associates, 1978.

Cain, L., Levine, S., & Elzey, F. *Cain-Levine Social Competency Scale.* Palo Alto, Calif.: Consulting Psychologists Press, 1977.

Cattell, P. *Cattell Infant Intelligence Scale.* Atlanta: The Psychological Corporation, 1950.

Cicchetti, D.V., & Sparrow, S.S. *Some recent research on adaptive behavior scales: Toward resolving some methodologic issues.* Paper presented at the 105th meeting of the American Association on Mental Deficiency, Detroit, Mich., May 1981.

Cone, J., & Hawkins, R. *Behavioral assessment: New directions in clinical psychology.* New York: Brunner/Mazel, 1977.

Doll, E. *Vineland Social Maturity Scale.* Circle Pines, Minn.: American Guidance Service, 1965.

Federal Register. Washington, D.C.: U. S. Government Printing Office, August 23, 1977.

Foster, R. *Camelot Behavioral Checklist.* Lawrence, Kans.: Camelot Behavioral Systems, 1974.

Nihira, K., Foster, R., Shellhaas, M., & Leland, H. *AAMD Adaptive Behavior Scale.* Washington, D.C.: American Association on Mental Deficiency, 1975.

Quick, A., Little, T., & Campbell, A. *Project MEMPHIS: Memphis Comprehensive Development Scales.* Belmont, Calif.: Fearon, 1974.

Roszkowski, M. Concurrent validity of *The Adaptive Behavior Scale* as assessed by *The Vineland Social Maturity Scale. American Journal on Mental Deficiency,* 1980, *85,* 86–89.

Sailor, W., & Mix, B. *TARC Assessment System.* Lawrence, Kans.: H and H Enterprises, 1975.

Salvia, J., & Ysseldyke, J. *Assessment in special and remedial education* (2nd ed.). Boston: Houghton Mifflin, 1981.

Sanford, A. *Learning Accomplishment Profile.* Winston-Salem, N.C.: Kaplan Press, 1974.

Somerton-Fair, E., & Turner, K. *Pennsylvania Training Model.* Harrisburg, Pa.: Pennsylvania Department of Education, 1979.

Stillman, R. *Callier-Azusa Scale.* Dallas, University of Texas at Dallas, Callier Center for Communication Disorders, 1978.

Taylor, R.L. *Assessment procedures in special education.* Englewood, N.J.: Prentice-Hall, in press.

Taylor, R., Warren, S., & Slocumb, P. Categorizing behavior in terms of severity: Considerations for Part Two of *The Adaptive Behavior Scale. American Journal of Mental Deficiency,* 1979, *83,* 411–414.

Vulpé, S.G. *Vulpé Assessment Battery.* Toronto, Canada: National Institute on Mental Retardation, 1979.

Part IV

Behavior Management Concerns

Chapter 5

Social Skills Training*

Gary L. Adams, Les Sternberg, and Ronald L. Taylor
Florida Atlantic University

PROBLEMS AND PAST PRACTICES

One of the major deficiencies of severely and profoundly handicapped students is the poor quality of their social behavior. Teachers are responsible for improving that behavior. Unfortunately, many teachers are often unsuccessful. Some teachers seem to rely only on verbal admonishments and others use techniques they have read and heard about during teacher or inservice training. A major problem is that teachers do not systematically apply a specific intervention and they do not collect data to evaluate if what they are doing actually works. In this section, some of the behavioral techniques will be explained. The review of the literature will be limited to studies containing profoundly to moderately retarded or disturbed persons. The majority of the research was conducted in either a school or an institutional setting. To improve readability the word "student" will be used, even to describe older institutionalized persons, because it is assumed that they are or could be in a teaching situation.

Reinforcement Concerns

Several concepts need to be explained before social skill training procedures can be understood. It is important to differentiate between two terms that are often confused: "rewards" and "reinforcers." Many people use the terms interchangeably. Rewards are "something given in return for good or,

---

*Sections of this chapter are reprinted or adapted from "A review of single subject methodologies in applied settings," by R. L. Taylor and G. L. Adams from *Journal of Applied Behavioral Science,* 1982, *18*(1), 95–103, with permission from JAI Press, Inc., Greenwich, Connecticut.

sometimes, evil, or for service or merit" (*Webster's New World Dictionary,* 1976). Reinforcement is "an increase in the frequency of a response when the response is immediately followed by a particular consequence" (Kazdin, 1975, p. 257). An item that is often thought of as a reward may not necessarily be reinforcing to a particular student. The decision about whether or not some reward is reinforcing is based on observations of the targeted student. If you give the student a piece of carrot every time the student is sitting in his or her chair and the amount of in-chair behavior does not increase, then carrots are not reinforcing to that student at that time.

It might be expected that people could fairly easily guess what items or events are reinforcing to severely and profoundly handicapped students. Adams (1981) found that this expectation was unjustified; teachers and special education university students were unable to successfully estimate the difference in training progress for severely and profoundly handicapped students under two reinforcement conditions: paired social praise and edible items and social praise only.

The procedure to evaluate what a severely and profoundly handicapped student finds reinforcing is called a *reinforcer sampling.* Authors have described different procedures to evaluate what reinforcers an individual student prefers. One procedure is to place the student in front of many items, such as different edible items and toys, and see which items the student selects first, second, third, etc. Another procedure is to create a forced choice situation (Teaching Research Staff, 1979). Two items are placed in front of the student and the observer notices which item the student selects. Then the selected item and a new item are presented. This procedure is continued until there is a ranked order evaluation of different possible reinforcers.

Several types of reinforcers can be used. *Primary reinforcers* refer to items or events that satisfy bodily needs, such as hunger and thirst. For example, candy has been used to reinforce correct responses (Guralnick & Kravik, 1973; Locke, 1969). Teachers have often rejected the use of primary reinforcers, especially edible items, on ethical grounds. Their argument is that by giving edible items the teacher is bribing the student to perform correctly (see O'Leary, Poulos, & Devine, 1972, for a discussion on this topic). Unfortunately, the teacher who blindly rejects the use of edible items may be hurting the student. Some students may perform better when given edible items that are paired with social praise for correct responding (Adams, 1981).

Social reinforcers include social praise ("Good, David, you sat down when I asked you to."), hugs and other forms of affection, and facial expressions of approval (smiles). Social reinforcers, unlike edible and other types of primary reinforcers that meet physical needs, are learned responses. Kazdin (1975) has noted several advantages of social reinforcers: (1) they are easy to administer and, unlike edible items, do not have the problem of delivery; (2)

social reinforcers can be delivered without disrupting the ongoing activity of the student; (3) social praise is a generalized conditioned reinforcer, which means that it can be used with other reinforcers and in multiple settings (giving praise in a sheltered workshop and in a classroom, for example); and (4) social praise is a natural response by many teachers to good behavior by students.

Token reinforcement is the use of items such as money, token chips, and trading stamps that have no intrinsic value but can be traded for backup reinforcers (such as food). Tokens are also conditioned reinforcers in that they are exchanged for other items. They do not have value by themselves but for their worth in trade. Probably the clearest example of token reinforcement is the employee who works at an acceptable performance level for 40 hours in exchange for a paycheck (a token). The paycheck may then be exchanged for money (more tokens), which in turn is exchanged for items that fulfill needs directly or indirectly (food, a movie, rent, etc.).

Research has shown that severely and profoundly handicapped students can learn to use the somewhat abstract tokens to exchange for food and privileges (Ayllon & Azrin, 1968; Lent, 1968). The difficult part of using tokens for severely and profoundly handicapped students is that they must learn the relationship of the exchange process. Smith and Snell (1978) have suggested the following procedure to teach severely and profoundly handicapped students this relationship:

1. A behavior or class of behaviors, easily performed by the individual, is selected (e.g., imitation of movements, following simple commands—"Show me the baby," "Comb your hair," "Look at me").
2. A choice of known back-up reinforcers (arranged on a tray or cupcake pan), a token container (one-pound coffee can), and a uniform set of at least 30 tokens (poker chips, washers, checkers, etc.) are readied at a training table.
3. The individual is requested to perform the behavior and:
   A. is reinforced immediately following the behavior with a single token placed into the individual's hand and with enthusiastic praise.
   B. prompted if the behavior is forthcoming, and then is reinforced with a token and praise immediately following the behavior.
4. Immediately, the trainer holds out a hand to collect the token (with prompting if necessary) and presents the reinforcer tray from which the individual is prompted to select one reinforcer.
5. This cycle—request for the behavior, praise and token reinforce-

ment, and immediate exchange—is repeated until the individual, without any prompts, shows evidence of making an association between tokens and token exchange. For example, an individual may reach for the tokens after a response as an attempt to "speed up" the exchange process. The exchange schedule is increased gradually from one token to an accumulation of four or five tokens before exchange.

6. While remaining at four or five tokens the token container is introduced to facilitate the collection and exchange process. Tokens are then dropped into the can by the teacher and the individual is shown how to lift and empty the contents during exchange time.

7. The exchange ratio is increased gradually over the remainder of the token training session, which should not last beyond 15 to 20 minutes.

8. At this point, tokens may be used during actual teaching sessions as the method of reinforcement. Initially, a brief review (a few ·immediate or low ratio exchanges) may be necessary to remind the individual of the tokens' exchange value (p. 78).

Kazdin (1975) described several advantages of using tokens: (1) they can often maintain behavior at higher rates than other social reinforcement; (2) if an activity is used as a reinforcer (two minutes of playing with toys, for example), tokens can be used and then the activity (the backup reinforcer) can be given when it is convenient and thus the training process is not interrupted; and (3) many backup reinforcers can be used in exchange for tokens. (This is an advantage over using a single reinforcer because often the student will get tired of that item or event.) The major disadvantage of the use of tokens is that the token exchange process may be above the intellectual capacity of some severely and profoundly handicapped students (see Kazdin, 1977, for a review of the research on token economies).

Another important reinforcement procedure utilizes the *Premack principle*. The definition of the Premack principle is "For any pair of activities, the more probable one will reinforce the less probable one" (Bandura, 1969, p. 222). To simplify this concept, the Premack principle has often been called "Grandma's rule," which equals "Herman, first eat your squash (a low probability event) and then you get your ice cream (a high probability event)." The advantage of using the Premack principle in the training setting is that it is easy to use because it simply requires the sequencing of events. For example, teachers of moderately retarded or disturbed students could schedule classes in half-hour time periods. Approximately 25 minutes of school work are assigned and it is explained to the students that if they complete the work early, the students get extra play time. However, if a student malingers there will be no play time left and the slow students will have to go on to the next assigned activity.

Differential Reinforcement Procedures

After taking a baseline to evaluate the present level of performance, one of four differential reinforcement procedures can be used. For example, suppose that a student yells an average of 37 times an hour. The teacher can use a *differential reinforcement of low rates* (DRL) program in which the student is given a token whenever he or she yells less than 37 times within the hour. As time goes by, the teacher would use a continually lower criterion of yells. The inverse process is the use of *differential reinforcement of high rates* (DRH). For example, if the baseline shows that a student approaches a peer only one time per minute, the teacher may use differential reinforcement of high rates and give a token if the student approaches a peer more than one time a minute. Like DRL, the criterion is then modified until the student reaches an acceptable level.

Teachers have also used a *differential reinforcement of other behavior* (DRO) procedure. In this case the student is reinforced if he or she is doing any behavior except the target behavior. For example, if the target behavior was hitting and the student does not hit anyone during a 15-minute time period, the teacher reinforces the student. One of the disadvantages of this procedure is that the teacher is continually attending to the inappropriate behavior. Or, the student may also be displaying another behavior (spitting, for example) and yet the student would be reinforced only for not hitting (Sulzer-Azaroff & Mayer, 1977). The result is that the spitting may be reinforced and inadvertently increased. Because of this problem, a better procedure is to reinforce alternative behavior (Alt-R). Instead of reinforcing the student for not displaying the target behavior, the teacher selects an alternative behavior for the student. For example, if the student hits his or her head ten times per minute, the teacher may present games or other activities and then reinforce the student for playing without hitting. The hitting is, therefore, ignored. For examples of the application of differential reinforcement procedures to vocational training, see Chapter 10.

Response Cost

Response cost refers to the "removal of previously awarded or earned reinforcers for the purpose of reducing behavior that is considered deviant or inappropriate" (Walker, 1979, p. 124). With a severely and profoundly handicapped population, response cost procedures have usually been used with token economies. Most of the research on this procedure has been conducted with mildly handicapped students (see, for example, Hundert, 1976; Phillips, 1968; Walker, Hops, & Fiegenbaum, 1976), and there is no strong proof that response cost (taking away tokens) is an effective procedure with severely and profoundly handicapped students.

Timeout

Timeout is the removal of the student from a positive environment. When the target behavior is displayed, the student is moved from a positive to a neutral environment. This procedure has been shown to be effective in reducing some behavior problems, such as aggressive behavior (Noll & Simpson, 1979; Vukelich & Hake, 1971).

Overcorrection

Overcorrection is a procedure whereby the student is required to display a behavior repetitively as a consequence for exhibiting an inappropriate behavior. The overcorrection procedure contains two components: *restitution* and *positive practice*. During the restitution phase, the student is trained to restore the environment that he or she has disrupted by returning it to a better than original condition. Then during the positive practice phase the student intensively practices the appropriate behavior. There are certain characteristics of the overcorrection procedure (Foxx & Azrin, 1972):

- The overcorrection procedure must be directly related to the misbehavior.
- The overcorrection procedure must immediately follow each episode of misbehavior.
- The overcorrection procedure should be extended in duration (at least 30 minutes, except for self-stimulatory behaviors).
- The student should be actively involved without pausing.
- No positive reinforcement should be given during the procedure and the teacher should remain neutral in tone.

The requirement that the overcorrection must be related to the misbehavior by using a topographically similar behavior (for example, hitting would require an overcorrection program involving the hands) has not been supported by further research. Several researchers have shown that topographically dissimilar overcorrection programs (such as a hand overcorrection for kicking) are successful (Epstein, Doke, Sajwaj, Sorrel, & Rimmer, 1974; Roberts, Iwata, McSween, & Desmond, 1979). Carey and Bucher (1981) have probably done the most careful and thorough analysis of the overcorrection components. They compared the suppressive effects of restitution, positive practice of topographically similar behavior, and positive practice of topographically dissimilar behavior. All three practices were approximately equal in suppressing inappropriate behavior. Topographically similar overcorrection, however, was the most effective in teaching a new behavior.

Overcorrection has been used for various behavior problems: self-stimulation, household orderliness training for disturbing the placement of objects, social reassurance (apology) training for frightening other people, and quiet training (bed rest) for agitation. A review of some of the research on overcorrection will follow.

Attention Training

Many severely and profoundly handicapped students avoid eye contact with the result that they do not hear directions and become off-task. For this reason, eye contact training is often the first step in training programs (Kozloff, 1973; Risley and Wolf, 1967). A common practice is to give social praise and edibles for progressively longer durations of eye contact. Foxx (1977) compared this practice to a combination of overcorrection, social praise, and edible items on three resistant autistic and retarded students. Social praise and edibles were given for eye contact, but if the student did not respond to the verbal prompt, overcorrection was used. The results of this comparison showed that the students attended 90 percent of the time under the combination training condition and never exceeded 55 percent of the time under the social praise and edibles condition.

Self-Stimulatory Behavior Reduction

Self-stimulatory behaviors are highly repetitive motor behaviors that seem to have no apparent purpose. Observations of institutionalized mentally retarded clients show that the majority display at least one type of self-stimulatory behavior (Berkson & Davenport, 1962). Research has shown that students who display self-stimulatory behavior interact less with their environment and thus do not learn (Lovaas, Litrownik, & Mann, 1971). A review of past research of reducing self-stimulatory behaviors shows there has been only minor success (see, for example, Guess & Rutherford, 1967). Enduring suppression of self-stimulation has been accomplished by the systematic application of pain (Lovaas, Schaeffer, & Simmons, 1965), but the use of pain lacks public acceptance (Kazdin, 1980).

The restitution component of overcorrection has not been used for self-stimulatory behaviors because the environment is not disrupted. The positive practice process requires the student to "move the body-part used in his self-stimulation only under instructions rather than being self-directed, the form of the movement being opposed to the original stereotype with repeated changes of posture" (Azrin, Kaplan, & Foxx, 1973, p. 243).

Azrin, Kaplin, and Foxx (1973) studied nine institutionalized students who had high rates of self-stimulatory behaviors. During baseline, the average rate of self-stimulation was 75 percent. A positive reinforcement intervention resulted in a small improvement. On the first day of the positive practice intervention there was a two-thirds reduction of self-stimulation and after one week there was an 85 percent reduction for eight of the nine students. A three-month followup showed a 90 percent decrease for all students. Other research (such as that of Epstein et al., 1974; Foxx & Azrin, 1973) has shown that not only is there a decrease in self-stimulatory behavior but also there is an increase in appropriate behavior. This finding gives further support for the viability of positive practice.

Disruptive Behavior

Foxx and Azrin (1972) used overcorrection on one severely brain-damaged and two profoundly retarded institutionalized students who had histories of physical assault, tantruming, and property damage. Social disapproval, timeout, and simple correction had little effect. Overcorrection sessions were scheduled for at least 30 minutes for every misbehavior. Overcorrection had an immediate effect; however, when staff members shortened a session (ran it for less than 30 minutes), the rate of misbehavior on the following day was either static or increased.

In another study (Webster & Azrin, 1973), the researchers required a two-hour bedrest overcorrection period for eight disruptive students. After each disruptive episode, the student had to go to his or her bed, disrobe, and practice relaxing. There was a 90 percent reduction by the fourth day. Follow-up showed that only one student was above a near zero level of disruptive behaviors 84 days later, and at the tenth month the disruptions had dropped 97 percent. The authors believe that bedrest overcorrection was successful because (1) relaxation quieted all of the residents; (2) it provided an acceptable alternative to disruption; (3) it had a modeling effect on other students; and (4) the procedure also had a timeout effect. Another interesting note was that staff preferred overcorrection over timeout by a 4 to 1 ratio. Klinge, Thrasher, and Myers (1975) replicated the study. Originally, most of the staff members predicted that overcorrection would not work because the student would enjoy isolating himself. Only these staff members were involved in the study. Overcorrection, again, was successful.

Other Behavior Problems

Overcorrection has been used to decrease other maladaptive behaviors that are often seen in institutional settings. Azrin and Wesolowski (1974) used a simple correction procedure for food stealing. The stealer had to obtain additional food items from the serving area for the offended person. After three days, there were no incidents of food stealing. Azrin and Wesolowski (1975) described a program to reduce a high rate of floor sprawling. A program of intensive positive reinforcement was ineffective, but positive practice was successful. Foxx (1976) compared an overcorrection with a timeout procedure to stop public disrobing. Under the timeout condition, the student was still undressing an average of five times a day, but the overcorrection program successfully eliminated the behavior. Foxx and Martin (1975) were successful in stopping four students with high rates of scavenging (eating feces, trash, cigarette butts, etc.), and Polvinale and Lutzker (1980) were able to decrease assaultive and inappropriate sexual behavior. In both studies, overcorrection procedures were implemented.

Summary

The preceding section has discussed several techniques that have been proven to be effective in social skills training. Again, the problem is that too often teachers do not implement them systematically. In the next section, a pragmatic approach to systematizing social skills training will be presented.

SUGGESTED METHODS

Most textbooks on educating severely and profoundly handicapped students explain a wide variety of behavioral procedures that have been successfully used on certain behaviors. A major problem with this approach is that practitioners may still not know which procedure should be attempted first. A different approach will be used in this chapter. Rather than being presented in isolation, they will be explained within a behavioral guidelines format.

Behavior change programs must pass two criteria. First, the least restrictive (intensive) behavioral intervention should be the first one used in the possible sequence of interventions. Too often, teachers when confronted by a student who displays high rates of aversive behaviors, such as hitting others or spitting, overreact and initiate a possibly overly intrusive procedure (as with overcorrection) as a first program. The second criterion is that the proposed behavioral intervention be acceptable by community and legal standards. For example, the application of electric shock would probably stop a student's inappropriate yelling in the classroom almost immediately, but it would not be an acceptable first behavioral intervention.

To protect both students and teachers, it is important to create specific behavioral guidelines that are based on these two criteria. School districts, community-based training programs (such as group homes), and institutions tend to create behavioral guidelines that are vague. Instead, behavioral guidelines should be explicit so that the public can understand that the least intrusive program will be used first, that the program will be monitored, and that changes in programs will be based on the students' data and not subjective decisions. Also, teachers and other instructional staff should be able to use the behavioral guidelines as a training manual with explanations of the acceptable behavioral interventions. If the school district or other administrative unit has not established behavioral guidelines, the school or possibly the teacher should create behavioral guidelines so that parents and other community members can clearly understand what behavioral interventions will be implemented in the classroom.

The behavioral guidelines established by the National Association for Retarded Citizens (NARC) in 1976 are excellent examples to follow. Besides being explicit, the NARC behavioral guidelines include an oversight committee (the Committee for Legal and Ethical Protection) that approves behavioral programs. Members should be from the community and not from the administrative unit, such as school district personnel. By using parents, psychologists, and physicians, there is a higher probability that any decision will be acceptable by community standards. Once the sequence of behavioral interventions is selected and written into behavioral guidelines, the main responsibilities of the committee are to ensure that the guidelines have indeed been followed (that the data collection system for a student was correctly administered, for example) and to evaluate the quality of behavioral interventions, especially any that include the introduction of aversive stimuli.

The following is a modified version of the NARC behavioral guidelines. The intent is to explain the types of behavioral programs that teachers should use and the sequence of their proposed use.

Step 1: Define Target Behavior, Conduct Baseline, and Design Evaluation

The teacher needs to clearly define the student's target behavior and select the correct observation strategy. All observation strategies require that the behaviors targeted for change be carefully defined in observable terms and be discrete. The following example, which is too often heard in teachers' lounges, shows the problem of not using behavioral terms—"I can't do anything with Herman. Of course, he is 'hyperactive.' " The person hearing that statement may visualize a student who is constantly out of his seat and hitting other children when actually the teacher who made the statement is describing a student who begins to bang the object placed on the table in front of him or her on the table after sitting alone with nothing to do for five minutes.

To ensure that there is clarity, an imprecise term like "hyperactive" must be replaced by specific observable behaviors that the student displays. The selected target behavior must also be discrete (have a starting and ending point). The determination of what is then one episode of the target behavior is made by the teacher. Depending on the rate and intensity of the target behavior, the teacher may count five rapid yells as one yell episode or as five separate yell episodes. The important point is the amount of time allowed between occurrences. Counting every occurrence of high rate behaviors may be extremely difficult. Instead, the teacher may choose to define an episode as an observable occurrence of the target behavior (which may last five seconds) with a pause of a certain length (say, ten seconds) before another occurrence (which may last fourteen seconds). This process is basically a tradeoff in efficiency.

To ensure that a behavior is clearly defined, the teacher and another person, such as an aide, should observe the student at the same time. This is called an *interrater reliability check*. There are two important reasons why interrater reliability checks should be conducted. First, reliability checks assist in the initial phase of defining the target behaviors because two people can evaluate what the attributes of the specified behavior are. Second, when only one observer, such as the teacher, is used, there is the possibility of *observer drift*. This problem occurs when the observer slowly begins to redefine the target behavior (drift from the original definition), with the result being that the data show an increase or decrease in behavior when actually there may be no change. There will be more discussion of reliability later in this chapter.

The following section will focus on four of the most commonly used observation strategies and accompanying reliability checks. Observational data should be taken during *baseline* (the phases without active intervention) and during the intervention phases to ensure that the proposed behavioral intervention program is successful. The specific strengths and weaknesses of each observation strategy will be discussed.

Event Sampling

In an event sampling procedure, the observer counts the number of times the student displays a specific target behavior. This is also called taking a *frequency*. Event sampling is especially useful with low rate behaviors that are discrete. If teachers are tracking only one or two target behaviors, a golf counter or tally sheet as shown in Exhibit 5-1 is easy to use. Event sampling can be used when the teacher wishes to observe the same behavior or multiple behaviors of more than one student. The number of behaviors and students that can be recorded depends on the types of targeted behaviors.

If the teacher does not use consistent observation time periods, an inaccurate picture of a student's behavior can occur. For example, a student may

Exhibit 5-1 An Event Sampling Data Collection Sheet

Student's Name _____

Date _____

Observer _____

Target Behavior (must be observable) _____

_____

_____

MON	TUE	WED	THU	FRI

NOTES:

show ten occurrences of a negative target behavior on Day 1 and 20 occurrences on Day 2. This leaves the impression that the student's behavior is getting worse. If observation on Day 1 was for fifteen minutes and observation on Day 2 was for thirty minutes, there is obviously no difference in the frequency per fifteen minutes (or *rate*). For this reason, the teacher must use a consistent time period, which can be transformed to a rate per session.

$$\text{Rate} = \frac{\text{Number of events}}{\text{Specified number of minutes or hours}}$$

Notice that this formula does not mandate that one can observe for only a specific number of minutes. It requires only that all observations be converted to a standard amount of time.

Example of Event Sampling. O'Brien, Bugle, and Azrin (1972) attempted to modify the self-feeding behavior of a six-year-old profoundly retarded girl. A correct self-feeding response was defined as the child taking food from a bowl with the spoon held right side up by the handle and bringing the food to her mouth without spilling. An observer was present at each meal during the baseline and training periods to record the behaviors by counting each occurrence of that specific behavior.

Duration Measure

Another observation strategy that can be used with severely and profoundly handicapped students is duration measure. Here, the observer determines how long the target behavior occurs. Duration measure mandates that the observer accurately determine the amount of time per session that the student is exhibiting the target behavior. Exhibit 5-2 shows a duration data sheet. Again, a rate (percent duration) per session can be used.

$$\text{Rate} = \frac{\text{Total time behavior is exhibited}}{\text{Total number of minutes in the session}} \times 100$$

In this procedure the observer must use a stopwatch that can monitor continuous time (push for start, push for stop, push for start, etc.). The major drawback of this observational strategy is that it requires constant attention. Most teachers are able to observe only a single student and a single target behavior. However, a well-trained observer may resort to the use of multiple watches.

Example of Duration Measure. Whitman, Mercurio, and Caponigri (1970) observed four severely retarded children during classroom situations for the purpose of determining the frequency and duration of social responses to other pupils. Desired social responses were those that required cooperation with other children (a block-passing task among three children; a ball-rolling task, etc.). An observer rated the number and duration (length of time) of social responses in which subjects participated in free play during the baseline period.

Momentary Time Sampling

Momentary time sampling is another frequently used observation strategy. It involves observing and recording behaviors at specific points in time (such as every ten seconds). The observer looks at the subject at these specific points and records (usually with a plus or minus) whether the target behavior is or is

Exhibit 5-2 A Duration Measure Data Collection Sheet

Student's Name _____

Date _____

Observer _____

Target Behavior (must be observable) _____

_____

_____

DATE	OBSERVATION TIME START	OBSERVATION TIME STOP	OBSERVATION TOTAL TIME	# OF MINUTES OF TARGET BEHAVIOR

IF MULTIPLE OBSERVATIONS PER DATE:

    TOTAL OBSERVATION TIME: _____

    TOTAL TIME OF TARGET BEHAVIOR: _____

NOTES:

not exhibited. Exhibit 5-3 shows a time sampling data sheet. With this data sheet the observer looks up every tenth second and checks whether the target behavior has occurred (+) or not occurred (−). The formula for calculating the rate (percentage of time periods) containing the targeted behavior is as follows:

$$\text{Rate} = \frac{\text{Number of time intervals with occurrences } (+\text{'s})}{\text{Total number of intervals}} \times 100$$

The time sampling technique is excellent for observing the same behavior of more than one child. The observer merely delineates beforehand the rotation

Exhibit 5-3 A Time Sampling Data Collection Sheet

```
Student's Name _____

Date _____

Observer _____

Target Behavior (must be observable) _____

_____

_____


    + = target behavior occurring

    - = target behavior absent


    Time Start        10      20      30      40      50      60
```

	10	20	30	40	50	60
	+ −	+ −	+ −	+ −	+ −	+ −
	+ −	+ −	+ −	+ −	+ −	+ −
	+ −	+ −	+ −	+ −	+ −	+ −
	+ −	+ −	+ −	+ −	+ −	+ −
	+ −	+ −	+ −	+ −	+ −	+ −
	+ −	+ −	+ −	+ −	+ −	+ −

```
NOTES:
```

of attention. For example, the observer may watch one student for five minutes at ten-second intervals and then rotate to another student. Also, multiple behaviors can be observed. A major disadvantage of the momentary time sampling procedure is that it does require constant surveillance.

Example of Momentary Time Sampling. Nelson, Cone, and Hanson (1975) investigated modeling and physical guidance as two alternative procedures to modify utensil use in 24 profoundly retarded males. Correct utensil behavior was defined as gripping the utensil (knife, fork, and spoon) correctly and using the utensil with an appropriate food. Three observers observed the subjects, one for each group of eight subjects. Every 7.5 seconds the observer was cued (by tape recorded voice) to look at an individual subject and record whether or not the behavior was being exhibited.

Interval Time Sampling

Interval time sampling is similar to momentary time sampling. Instead of observing whether or not a target behavior occurs at a specific point in time, the teacher observes whether the behavior occurs during any part of the time interval. For example, if the time interval is fifteen seconds and the target behavior is head slapping, one episode of head slapping during the fifteen-second interval is marked as having occurred.

The decision as to whether to use a momentary or interval time sampling procedure depends on the target behavior. For example, it is difficult to use momentary time sampling when the target behavior is self-stimulation (nonpurposeful motor activity). Observers often cannot tell in a split second if the motor activity is purposeful (the student is reaching for a toy) or nonpurposeful (the student reaches out and then flaps his or her hand). In this case, an interval time sampling procedure is superior.

As far as recording observations, the same type of recording sheets used in the time sampling approach can be employed. However, one must remember that the seconds on the top of the time sampling recording sheets are points in time and not intervals of time. The momentary and interval time sampling procedures should not be used when the target behavior occurs infrequently (that is, if the target behavior occurs only two or three times a week). For infrequent behaviors, event sampling is superior.

> *Example of Interval Time Sampling.* Pendergrass (1972) used timeout from positive reinforcement to reduce specific inappropriate behaviors of two severely retarded children. The behaviors focused upon were those that showed persistent high rates (banging toys, throwing books on floor, biting own hands and lips, continuous jerking movements of the body, etc.). Observations were made in the classroom during baseline and training phases. A tape recorded sound would cue the observer for alternating periods of twenty seconds (observation interval) and ten seconds (recording interval). At the observation cue, the observer would observe the subject for twenty seconds and determine if one or more of the high rate behaviors occurred during that interval.

Determining Interrater Reliability

Interrater reliability checks are a necessary part of any behavior change program. One reason for conducting interrater reliability checks is to initially ensure a clear, precise definition of the target behavior. The other major reason is to ensure that observer drift does not occur (that is, that changes in data are the result of student changes and not redefinition of the target behavior by the observer). For this reason, reliability checks should be conducted in all phases of the intervention program from baseline to followup probes taken after the active intervention phase.

Each observational strategy has its own formula for determining interrater reliability. All are based on a percentage of agreement. Usually, if there is not at least 85 percent agreement on the part of two observers observing the same target behavior, then revisions must be made in the definition of the target behavior.

After two observers have counted the occurrences of a specific target behavior during one session using an event sampling procedure, they should compare their results by slotting in their numbers in the following formula:

$$\frac{\text{Smaller number of occurrences of behavior}}{\text{Larger number of occurrences of behavior}} \times 100 = \frac{\text{Interrater}}{\text{Reliability}}$$

For example, if one observer counted nine occurrences of verbalization in a five-minute interval and the other observer counted ten occurrences of verbalization, the interrater reliability would be 90 percent ($9/10 \times 100 = 90$). The formula for interrater reliability for the duration observational strategy is very similar. Instead of the number of occurrences, the length of time that each observer recorded is used.

For momentary and interval time sampling, after two observers have recorded the target behaviors on the recording sheets, it is possible to compare the sheets in terms of points in time (momentary time sampling) or intervals of time (interval time sampling). Just adding the number of +'s is not an acceptable practice. The following simplified example will show the problem. Observer 1 could mark +'s in the first five time periods and −'s in the next five time periods and Observer 2 could mark just the opposite pattern. Both scores would be 5, or 100 percent agreement. Of course, there is no agreement. To obtain an interrater reliability check, therefore, the following formula is used:

$$\frac{\text{Total number of agreements}}{\text{Total number of agreements and disagreements}} \times 100 = \frac{\text{Interrater}}{\text{Reliability}}$$

Validation of Intervention Programs

With the knowledge of how to observe student behavior, the next step is to evaluate intervention programs when they are introduced. As we have seen, teachers in the past often selected programs based on research by persons called "researchers." This research was usually conducted on groups of institutionalized residents in a laboratory setting with a task that was often superficial with regard to real world needs of severely and profoundly handicapped students. Over the last decade, with the development of single subject designs, the us (teachers)-them (researchers) dichotomy has grown less pronounced. Both groups are interested in creating interventions that work. Brooks and Baumeister (1977), for example, emphasized the continued need for research studies demonstrating "ecological validity," that is, experimental research aimed toward more meaningful and socially relevant goals. This new emphasis on clinical efficacy has led to the development and refinement of a number of experimental methodologies designed to measure the effects of specific intervention programs in a systematic fashion. These methodologies are concerned with controlling and accounting for the variables that affect *individual* rather than *group* behavior.

In this section the advantages and disadvantages of single subject methodology will be explained. Single subject designs fall into four major categories: reversal, multiple baseline, changing criterion, and multielement.

In applied settings, teachers have often collected preintervention or baseline data and then introduced an intervention (an AB design) as an attempt to measure the effectiveness of the intervention. Like a before-after group design (Campbell & Stanley, 1966), the AB design does not allow for any statements about causality because the student may have changed without an intervention. A *reversal design* (such as an ABAB design), however, allows for statements of causality. After getting a stable baseline (Phase A), an intervention is introduced (Phase B). To show that the intervention caused the improvement in behavior, the baseline procedure is reintroduced. If the behavior returns to the original baseline rate, this would suggest that the behavior was under the control of the intervention. If no change occurs under the return to baseline phase, then other variables probably caused the improvement under Phase B. Usually Phase B is then reintroduced, not only to increase the plausibility of the explanation for the change in behavior, but also because the continued improvement of the student is important in applied settings.

The following example shows the usefulness of this design. The problem was to increase work productivity of a mentally retarded woman in a sheltered workshop. She was often off-task and did not spend much time at her job of sanding wood. An observer viewed the student on a daily basis and the baseline (Phase A) showed that she was not working the majority of the time (see Figure 5-1). Because of her poor performance, an intervention was designed and implemented. When she was sanding, she was praised by the trainer and after every five praises was given a sip of coffee (Phase B). The observational data showed that there was a rapid increase in on-task behavior. There may have been other explanations for this change in behavior, such as a

Figure 5-1 An Example of a Reversal Design

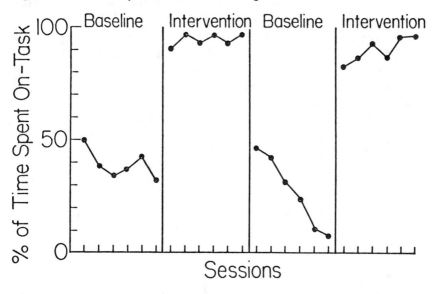

new trainer in the room or a change in the home environment. To show that the intervention caused the improvement, the baseline was reintroduced, and the trainer stopped his praise for on-task behavior and his rewards of coffee (Phase A). Figure 5-1 shows that the client's on-task behavior plummeted. The reintroduction of the intervention (Phase B) had an immediate impact of improving on-task behavior.

The above example of a reversal design involves one active intervention (Phase B). Other reversal designs are possible. A major consideration when designing studies with multiple interventions is that only one variable can be changed at a time and that the phases must be compared with each other directly. For example, suppose one chooses to compare two interventions (B and C) to see which is better. An ABAC intervention would not be useful because the two interventions are not compared directly. A better design to answer this question is an ABACBC design, in which the two interventions can be compared (Hersen & Barlow, 1976).

One problem in using reversal designs is that it is not always clinically desirable for individuals to return to their baseline behavior. For instance, if a program was initiated in which a retarded student was successfully taught to sight-read words, it would not be likely, and certainly not desirable, that he or she would "lose the skill" after the intervention was removed. In a more extreme case, once an intervention has been used to suppress head-banging behavior, it would be somewhat dangerous to discontinue the intervention (that is, return to baseline) to merely prove the effectiveness of the procedure. Another validation technique must be used.

The *multiple baseline design* (Baer, Wolf, & Risley, 1968) avoids many of the limitations of the reversal design. There are three major variations of this design: *multiple baseline across behaviors, across individuals, and across situations.* In the multiple baseline across behaviors design, baseline data are collected on two or more behaviors. The intervention condition is then put into effect for one of the behaviors, while baseline conditions continue for the other or others. Each behavior can be introduced systematically to the intervention condition and should theoretically change only during that condition. The advantage of this design comes from the premise that the experimental condition, and not any extraneous variable, is responsible for the change in behavior. Assume, for instance, that a teacher was interested in determining the effects of two reinforcement programs (social versus tangible) on the development of self-help skills. The two specific behaviors (such as the number of sips from a cup without spilling and the percentage of time the student indicates the need for toileting) would first be identified and defined. Next, baseline conditions would be collected for each behavior. After baseline conditions stabilize, the social reinforcement system could be initiated for the drinking but not the toileting behavior. Theoretically, if the reinforcement system is effective, it will increase only the drinking behavior. Later, the tangible reinforcement could be used to increase the drinking behavior, while the social reinforcement system is initiated with the toileting behavior. Finally, the tangible reinforcement system could be used with the toileting behavior.

Figure 5-2 illustrates this example of a multiple baseline across behaviors design. In this example, social reinforcement was shown to be the more effective procedure. Used for either the drinking or toileting behavior, social reinforcement increased the behavior. The baseline conditions for both behaviors were fairly stable, and the tangible reinforcement condition decreased both drinking and toileting behaviors. The power of this design lies in the fact that the increase in behavior was present only during the social reinforcement condition regardless of what condition was in effect for the other behavior. This eliminates many sources of extraneous variables. Several caveats should be considered when using this design, however. First, and foremost, the behaviors chosen must not be interdependent. If a change in one behavior affects the rate or frequency of the other, results will most likely be biased. For instance, in the previous example, if the number of urinations had been chosen as the toileting behavior, there could have been a definite interaction with the drinking behavior. A second consideration is the choice of which behavior to consequate (be introduced to the intervention condition)

Figure 5-2 An Example of a Multiple Baseline across Behaviors Design

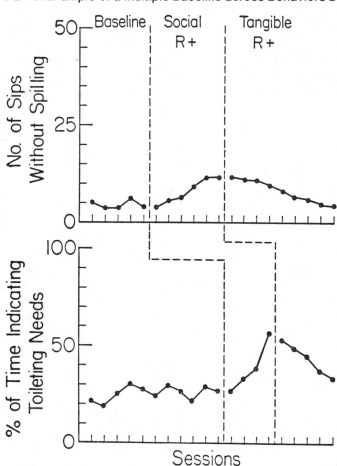

first. Because the first behavior is experimentally manipulated for a longer time, clinical goals should be prioritized to be consistent with the design.

In the multiple baseline across individuals design, baseline data are collected on the *same* behavior for two or more individuals. The teacher then systematically introduces the intervention program to each individual one at a time, maintaining baseline conditions until that point. Again, the idea is to demonstrate that the intervention was responsible for the behavior change. For example, if a teacher was interested in studying the effects of modeling on verbal output in an institutional setting, three students could be chosen who have a low amount of verbal output. Preferably, these students would not have interpersonal contact, so that a change in one subject's behavior would not affect the others'. The teacher could observe each student and collect data until the baselines stabilized. Next, the experimental modeling condition could be initiated with one student while baseline conditions continued for the other two students. The second student would then enter the intervention condition while the third student was still in baseline. Finally, the third student would receive the intervention. Figure 5-3 graphically shows this design.

Great care must be taken that the behavior of one student does not affect the behavior of the others. Another concern of this design is that intervention is being temporarily withheld from some of the students. It is therefore imperative that the teacher select the students and behaviors carefully.

The third type of multiple baseline design is across situations. In this design, data are collected for a behavior for one or more students in two or more different settings or situations. An intervention is then initiated for the behavior in one situation but not the others. The program is then conducted for the behaviors in the other settings. For example, to determine the effects of a timeout procedure on a particular student's self-stimulatory behavior, a baseline would be collected in a number of settings (at home, in physical therapy, and in the classroom, for example). The timeout procedure would first be initiated only in the home situation. Next it would be initiated during physical therapy, and finally during classroom time. If the timeout procedure itself is responsible for any change in behavior, the behavior should change only when the program is in effect. Figure 5-4 shows this design.

The *changing criterion design* involves collecting baseline data and then gradually requiring improvement in behavior until the terminal goal is reached. Figure 5-5 presents an example of this type of design. A student banged his head against the wall an average of 31 times a day during the baseline condition. His teacher decided to reduce the student's head banging by four instances per step. His criterion was two out of three days being at or below the prior criterion level before going to the next criterion level. When he was successful at a criterion level, his reinforcer (a bottle of soda) was given. His first criterion level was 27 head-banging incidents (31 − 4) per day. On the first two days, he was below the criterion level, so he was given a bottle of soda and his criterion level was changed to 23 (27 − 4) per day. On the next two out of three days, he met criterion, so his criterion level was moved to 19 per day. At this criterion level it took him five days before two of the last three days produced a graduation to the next criterion level. The teacher continued to use this program until the subject had stopped head banging completely.

A major advantage of the changing criterion design is its flexibility. The goal, of course, is to improve behavior. If the teacher decides on steps that are too large and the student continually does not reach criterion, smaller steps

Figure 5-3 An Example of a Multiple Baseline across Individuals Design

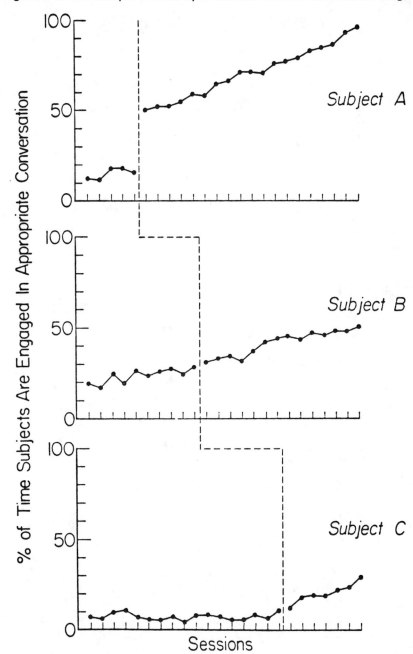

Figure 5-4 An Example of a Multiple Baseline across Situations Design

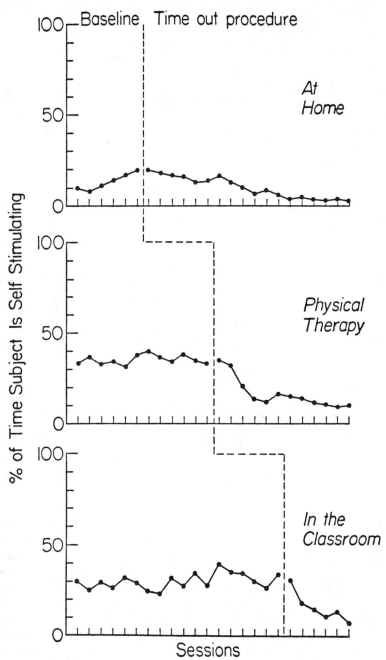

Figure 5-5 An Example of a Changing Criterion Design

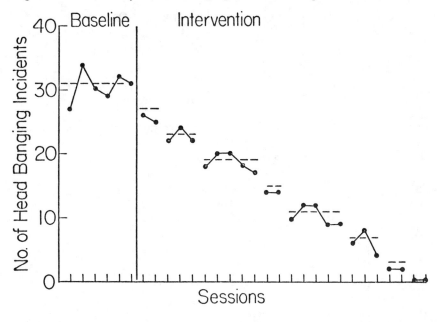

are introduced until the student is consistently reaching criterion and is, therefore, successful.

This design is often used in applied settings, though there is a major flaw in its use for purely experimental reasons. The problem is that there is no proof of causality.

The *multielement design,* unlike other single subject designs that use phases, intersperses baseline and intervention or multiple interventions throughout the program. Each of the separate conditions is alternated (within each session or between sessions) until a distinct pattern of superiority is displayed. For example, in a sheltered workshop setting the teacher may want to compare the current practice of a noncontingent coffee break (baseline) with a contingent coffee break based on job performance. On a preselected random basis, the targeted student would receive a noncontingent coffee break or a contingent coffee break. Each day a teacher observes the student at six-second intervals for five minutes every hour and records whether or not he or she is working. Figure 5-6 shows the results of this study. The contingent coffee break consistently resulted in more production.

Sulzer-Azaroff and Mayer (1977) have mentioned six advantages for the multielement design: (1) multiple independent variables can be studied; (2) variables can be studied that have a likelihood of not being reversed; (3) rapid

Figure 5-6 An Example of a Multielement Design

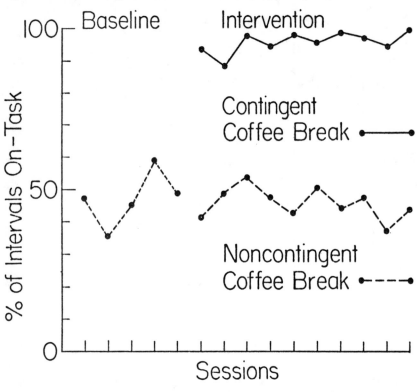

differential effects can occur, which reduces the overall time of the program; (4) the problem of an unstable baseline is reduced; (5) it is more acceptable to human services personnel; and (6) it minimizes the problem of confounding when one intervention follows another intervention. Because of these advantages, the multielement design is becoming increasingly popular. One disadvantage is that since the interventions are presented simultaneously, it is necessary that the student be able to discriminate among the various interventions.

Step 2: Evaluate Data across Multiple Time Periods and Introduce Environmental Adaptations

Often an analysis of the student's data across multiple time periods will show times when the student displays inappropriate rates of the target behavior. By using another observer, such as an aide, the chances of finding the antecedents that increase the probability of the inappropriate behavior occurring are more favorable. The resolution of many behavior problems may stop at this point. Mild changes, such as adding more activities while other students are in individualized training programs or telling the speech therapist that he or she is accidentally reinforcing the student's inappropriate behavior, may be all that is needed. Antecedent analysis of this type can easily lead to improvements in classroom management and physical structure (see Hart and Risley, 1976, for an example). Antecedent analysis seems like such a common-sense approach that we might expect that most teachers would be conducting ongoing antecedent analyses. In actual practice, it is rare for this to occur. Instead, teachers tend to start with very intrusive (and negative) interventions with or without taking baseline. Probably the main reason why the antecedent analysis is not conducted is because teachers may be defensive about finding possible deficiencies in their classrooms. They prefer to conduct consequent interventions aimed at what they perceive to be misbehaving students.

When the antecedent adaptations are introduced, the same observation strategy as was used during baseline is continued. Three possible events can occur. (1) The antecedent adaptation may be sufficient to improve the student's behavior and the observations will continue until it appears that the antecedent adaptation has a long-term effect. (2) The antecedent adaptation may have some positive effect but it is not sufficient. During the data-collection process, however, other antecedent adaptations may be noted and systematically introduced until the behavior problems are resolved. (3) Or the antecedent adaptations may be insufficient to significantly improve the student's behavior. If no significant improvement is made (even after multiple attempts at antecedent adaptations), then the teacher should move to Step 3.

Step 3: Implement a Positive Reinforcement Procedure

Knowledge of *reinforcement schedules* is important to the success of positive reinforcement programs. There are four schedules of reinforcement; two are time based and two are response based. A *fixed-interval* schedule means that the student is reinforced at a set interval of time, such as every two minutes. The main problem with this reinforcement schedule is that students begin to realize there will be a time gap before the reinforcer will be delivered. The result is that there is a deterioration of behavior immediately after the reinforcement exchange and then improved behavior around the reinforcement time period. For another example, if the teacher sets off a kitchen timer at five-minute intervals and reinforces the student with raisins if the student is in his or her chair and not running around the room when the timer goes off, probably the student will begin to get out of his or her chair right after being reinforced and then spend more time in his or her chair when the next five minutes are up. This problem can be alleviated by switching to a *variable-interval* schedule of reinforcement. Thus, instead of reinforcing every five minutes, the teacher can reinforce on the *average* of every five minutes; the timer is set at one minute, then six minutes, then four minutes, and then nine minutes. Teachers must be careful and not begin to use a predictable pattern. This variable interval reinforcement schedule leads to a more consistent behavior pattern because the student cannot predict when the timer will ring and when he or she would possibly be reinforced. Once the student begins to perform consistently, the reinforcement schedule is then learned; that is, changing the average time interval from five minutes to an average of every ten minutes and then, after consistent acceptable performance, changing the interval to an average of every fifteen minutes.

Some behaviors are not conducive to time-based reinforcement programs. Suppose a teacher wants to teach a student to stand on command ("Alice, stand up."). It would not make sense to use a time-based reinforcement schedule because the teacher wants to reinforce the student when she performs the behavior. For this example, it would be better to reinforce the student every time she responds correctly. This is an example of a *fixed-ratio* schedule. The practice of reinforcing every correct response is an excellent one to help initiate a new response (such as reinforcing a nonverbal student every time he or she makes a babbling sound). Once the student begins to consistently respond correctly, the teacher should change the fixed ratio of one correct response resulting in the presentation of a reinforcer. After the student is consistently responding correctly, the fixed-ratio schedule is changed to a *variable-ratio* schedule where the student is reinforced after the completion of varying numbers of correct responses. Again, as in the variable-interval schedule, reinforcement is delivered based on the display of an *average* (in this case, average *number* of responses).

One way to ensure that positive reinforcement programs include an acceptable level of reinforcement is to require documentation. For example, in dealing with reducing a student's out-of-chair behavior, the teacher and other staff members are required to reinforce the student a specified number of times per time period. The teacher would wear a golf counter and tally the number of reinforcement exchanges. While this is better than not reinforcing the student, the main flaw with this program is that often teachers forget to evenly space the reinforcing episodes across the time period. One helpful technique is to use a kitchen timer as a reminder. For example, if the behavior intervention program states that the teacher will attempt to reinforce the student for in-chair behavior 12 times per hour, then the teacher would use a variable interval schedule and set the timer so that it will ring *on the average* of every five minutes. If the student is in his or her chair when the timer rings, he or she is reinforced. The advantages of this program are that it is easy to run (especially if an electronic alarm watch is used), the student does not know when the timer will ring, and the possible reinforcement exchanges are evenly distributed throughout the time period.

If the initial program is successful, then the reinforcement schedule is *learned.* With success, the time interval or number of responses for reinforcement is increased. Using the previous example, the time interval might be changed from an interval of five minutes to ten minutes. This process is continued until the need for a systematic program is no longer present. Of course, the student will continue to receive social praise for improved behavior.

Considerations for Removing Positive Reinforcement

The process by which appropriate social behaviors (such as following directions) are created and maintained through the use of contingent positive reinforcement is the same for inappropriate social behaviors (such as hitting others). Often by giving attention to the very behaviors that they are trying to eliminate, teachers reinforce and increase the rates of those behaviors. A common example of this problem is when teachers want to have the students sitting in chairs. When a child gets out of his or her chair, the teacher tells him or her to sit down. If there is not a high level of reinforcement for other appropriate social behaviors, the result will probably be an increase of out-of-chair behavior because the students learn that they can get attention (a type of reinforcement) by getting out of their chairs. There are several examples of this problem in the literature (Herbert, Pinkston, Hayden, Sajwaj, Pinkston, Cordua, & Jackson, 1973; Thomas, Becker, & Armstrong, 1968). One way to stop the inappropriate behavior is just to stop reinforcing the target behavior. This process of witholding reinforcement is called *extinction.* Extinction has been shown to be effective (Hart, Allen, Buell, Harris, & Wolf, 1964; Wolf, Risley, & Mees, 1964). For example, a student may discover that he or she can control a teacher's behavior by hitting his or her head on the nearest wall. By saying "No, don't hit your head on the wall," the teacher may be giving the attention needed to maintain that behavior. If the teacher stops attending to (reinforcing) the head-banging behavior, the teacher should expect an immediate *increase* in head banging. The reason for this pattern is simple: the student has a history of being reinforced for the inappropriate behavior so he or she will probably increase the rate and intensity of the head banging to see if the teacher will "give in" and attend to the behavior.

Possibly because the explanation of extinction is at the beginning of most behavior modification texts and appears to be such an easy procedure, many teachers rely on this procedure. The major problem is that extinction is often hard to implement in an applied setting. For example, the staff at a residential facility suggested conducting an extinction program on a student who screamed during mealtime. After taking baseline, the staff members said they would begin to ignore the student's screaming. After one week, the data showed no change in the number of screams per meal. However, during the half-hour lunch period, 43 episodes of attention were observed. Some staff members simply could not ignore the increasingly louder yells and went over to quiet down the student or made facial expressions that gave attention. Other students were the main source of reinforcement. They disliked sitting next to the noisy student so they would attempt to get her to keep quiet.

Teachers must realize that they are not the only possible source of reinforcement and that peers can have a great influence on a student. In an open environment, like a classroom, the teacher's attempts to ignore a student are negated by the student's classmates. Furthermore, by not consequating inappropriate behavior, the target student with possibly higher rates of inappropriate behavior may actually be acting as a model for other students and so the rates of inappropriate behaviors of other students will increase.

Issues in Using Positive Reinforcement

There are two major problems in implementing behavior change programs based only on positive reinforcement. One, the inability to ignore the inappropriate behavior, has already been mentioned. The other problem is that teachers simply may not provide the needed positive reinforcement. Although they may state that they will reinforce the student for not displaying the inappropriate behavior (DRO), or that they will reinforce other incompatible appropriate behavior (Alt-R), often teachers forget. The result is that the student does not improve and more restrictive programs are initiated.

In the event that a well-designed and documented positive reinforcement program is unsuccessful, one should, if possible, attempt another positive reinforcement behavior intervention. The other possibility is to go to Step 4.

Step 4: Implement Contingent Education Procedures

Contingent education procedures are meant to interrupt a student's pattern of inappropriate activities and teach appropriate social behavior. Any of the following three procedures can be used (the decision as to which to select is based on previous interventions).

Contingent Observation

Contingent observation is a mild form of timeout from a positive environment. The purpose of this program is for the student to sit back and observe the appropriate behavior of his or her peers. During this time, the teacher reinforces the peers for their appropriate social behavior. When the student regains composure, he or she returns to the group. If the student refuses to gain self-control, he or she is taken to a timeout area away from the other students.

The teacher must remember that timeout is only effective if a positive environment exists. One method to improve the chances of having a positive environment is to use the timer game mentioned earlier in this chapter. By setting the timer to go off at variable intervals and then reinforcing those students who are in the group (not in contingent observation or timeout), the effectiveness of contingent observation can be enhanced.

Educational Fine

Educational fines are used within a token economy system. They are a type of response cost in which the student is penalized for displaying inappropriate behavior. For example, a teacher wants to reduce a student's hitting so the teacher gives tokens for behaviors that are incompatible with the inappropriate behavior (such as approaching a peer without making threatening gestures and talking softly without disturbing others). If, however, the student hits someone, then the student is fined a specific number of tokens. The teacher tells the student what the misbehavior is and how the student can earn back a portion of the fine by returning to displaying appropriate behavior.

Overcorrection

The intent of the overcorrection procedure is for the student to learn to take responsibility for his or her actions. If there has been no environmental disruption, a positive practice procedure can be used. Otherwise, an overcorrection procedure employing restitution and positive practice is used, as explained earlier in this chapter.

Step 5: Implement Aversive Procedures

The need to use aversive procedures should be infrequent. Most behavior problems can be solved by using procedures that were described in the previous steps. Some students, however, are so self-abusive or noncompliant that aversive programs may be needed. It is the responsibility of the teacher and the Committee on Legal and Ethical Protection to design and implement aversive programs if that appears to be the only way to improve the student's behavior. To avoid this responsibility and continue to use only protective devices (such as restraints), rather than trying to improve the student's behavior, may not be in the student's best interest. It is especially important that the Committee on Legal and Ethical Protection authorize and supervise the implementation of any aversive programs.

For some students the aversive procedures will be based on a *compliance training* situation where the student must follow the teacher's requests. Typically, a compliance training model involves administering an aversive consequence, such as a loud noise or physical insult, after a noncompliant behavior and immediately reinforcing the occurrence of the compliant response. The purpose of compliance training is, therefore, to increase specific behaviors. Getting compliance is important because, as Russo, Cataldo, and Cushing (1981) showed, compliance training has a positive effect even on behaviors that do not receive intervention.

Negative reinforcement procedures are used when an aversive situation is created and the student must escape to be reinforced. For example, a student may avoid eye contact even after the teacher has used other procedures to get the student to look at the teacher (reinforcing eye contact with candy, for example). A negative reinforcement procedure may be selected in which the student's head is held until he or she gives eye contact. This response is negatively reinforced by the release of the head and should also be positively reinforced (as with a piece of candy). In the next training trial, the probability is that there will be an increase in student eye contact because the student will want to avoid prolonged head holding.

Unlike compliance training and negative reinforcement procedures in which there is an increase in behavior, *punishment* procedures are used when there is a need to decrease a behavior. Usually, the target behavior (self-mutilation, severe aggression, etc.) is dangerous to the student or to others. For example, the occurrence of a self-abusive behavior has been decreased by the systematic use of a water mist (Dorsey, Iwata, Ong, & McSween, 1980), aromatic ammonia (Tanner & Zeiler, 1975), and shock (Lovaas & Simmons, 1969). It is important to remember that, as in compliance training and negative reinforcement, behavioral intervention programs using punishment procedures should also include a positive reinforcement component.

CONCLUSION

Teachers often use behavior change techniques in a reactive manner; they wait until a student's behavior irritates them and then they try to do something about it. Probably one of the most exciting new approaches to increasing the appropriate behavior of severely and profoundly handicapped students is the use of social skills training curricula. Rather than reacting to student behavior problems when they reach high levels, teachers and others can use these programs to train social skills as if they were any other skills (such as self-help behaviors). For example, Matson and Adkins (1980) used a series of ten scenes that were placed on an audiotape to train three students. Each scene presented a situation. A sample situation follows: the tape would say "You can get along better with people if you say nice things. You might say something nice about their appearance." Then the student would be prompted by "Can you say something nice about someone?" The trainer provided instructions, feedback, modeling, and role-playing opportunities. Correct responses were socially reinforced and uncorrected responses were shaped through feedback ("That's better, but . . ."). Client observations were taken in a different room. The results showed improvements in verbal behavior in the different setting.

Other social skills training programs are in the pilot stage and have yet to be thoroughly tested (see, for example, Carney, Clobuciar, Corley, Wilcox, Bigler, Fleisher, Pany, & Turner, 1977) or are limited in scope (Matson, 1979; Matson & Adkins, 1980; Matson & Zeiss, 1979). They represent, however, an important trend in meeting the social skills training needs of the severely and profoundly handicapped. It is hoped that the trend will continue.

REFERENCES

Adams, G.L. The importance of reinforcer sampling before initiating training. *Journal for Special Educators,* 1981, *22,* 188–198.

Ayllon, T., & Azrin, N.H. *The token economy: A motivational system for therapy and rehabilitation.* New York: Appleton-Century-Crofts, 1968.

Azrin, N.H., Kaplan, S.J., & Foxx, R.M. Autism reversal: Eliminating stereotyped self-stimulation of retarded individuals. *American Journal of Mental Deficiency,* 1973, *78,* 241–248.

Azrin, N.H., & Wesolowski, M.D. Theft reversal: An overcorrection procedure for eliminating stealing by retarded persons. *Journal of Applied Behavior Analysis,* 1974, *7,* 577–581.

Azrin, N.H., & Wesolowski, M.D. The use of positive practice to eliminate persistent floor sprawling by profoundly retarded persons. *Behavior Therapy,* 1975, *6,* 627–631.

Baer, D.M., Wolf, M.M., & Risley, T.R. Some current dimensions of applied behavior analysis. *Journal of Applied Behavior Analysis,* 1968, *1,* 91–97.

Bandura, A. *Principles of behavior modification.* New York: Holt, Rinehart, & Winston, 1969.

Berkson, G., & Davenport, R.K. Stereotyped movements in mental defectives: I. Initial survey. *American Journal of Mental Deficiency,* 1962, *66,* 849–852.

Brooks, P., & Baumeister, A. A plea for consideration of ecological validity in the experimental psychology of mental retardation: A guest editorial. *American Journal of Mental Deficiency,* 1977, *81,* 407–416.

Campbell, D.T., & Stanley, J.C. *Experimental and quasi-experimental designs for research.* Chicago: Rand-McNally, 1966.

Carey, R.G., & Bucher, B. Identifying the educative and suppressive effects of positive practice and restitutional overcorrection. *Journal of Applied Behavior Analysis,* 1981, *14*(1), 71–80.

Carney, I., Clobuciar, G., Corley, E., Wilcox, B., Bigler, J., Fleisher, L., Pany, D., & Turner, P. Social interaction in severely handicapped students: Training basic social skills and social acceptability. In B. Wilcox, F. Kohl, & T. Vogelsberg (Eds.), *The severely and profoundly handicapped child.* Springfield: Illinois Office of Education, 1977.

Dorsey, M.F., Iwata, B.A., Ong, P., & McSween, T.E. Treatment of self-injurious behavior using a water mist: Initial response suppression and generalization. *Journal of Applied Behavior Analysis,* 1980, *13,* 343–354.

Epstein, L.H., Doke, L.A., Sajwaj, T.E., Sorrel, S., & Rimmer, B. Generality and side effects of overcorrection. *Journal of Applied Behavior Analysis,* 1974, *7,* 385–390.

Foxx, R.M. The use of overcorrection to eliminate the public disrobing (stripping) of retarded women. *Behaviour Research and Therapy,* 1976, *14,* 53–61.

Foxx, R.M. Attention training: The use of overcorrection avoidance to increase the eye contact of autistic and retarded children. *Journal of Applied Behavior Analysis,* 1977, *10,* 489–499.

Foxx, R.M., & Azrin, N.H. Restitution: A method of eliminating aggressive-disruptive behavior of retarded and brain damaged patients. *Behaviour Research and Therapy,* 1972, *10,* 15–27.

Foxx, R.M., & Azrin, N.H. The elimination of autistic self-stimulatory behavior by overcorrection. *Journal of Applied Behavior Analysis,* 1973, *6,* 1–14.

Foxx, R.M., & Martin, E.D. Overcorrection as an effective treatment of the scavenging behaviors of coprophagy and pica. *Behaviour Research and Therapy,* 1975, *13,* 153–162.

Guess, D., & Rutherford, G. Experimental attempts to reduce stereotyping among blind retardates. *American Journal of Mental Deficiency,* 1967, *71,* 984–986.

Guralnick, M.J., & Kravik, M.A. Reinforcement procedures and social behavior in a group context with severely retarded children. *Psychological Reports,* 1973, *32,* 295–301.

Hart, B.M., Allen, K.E., Buell, J.S., Harris, F.R., & Wolf, M.M. Effects of social reinforcement on operant crying. *Journal of Experimental Child Psychology,* 1964, *1,* 145–153.

Hart, B., & Risley, T. Environmental programming: Implications for the severely handicapped. In H.J. Prehm & S.J. Deitz (Eds.), *Early intervention for the severely handicapped: Programming and accountability.* Eugene: University of Oregon, College of Education, 1976.

Herbert, E.W., Pinkston, E., Hayden, M., Sajwaj, T., Pinkston, S., Cordua, G., & Jackson, C. Adverse effects of differential parental attention. *Journal of Applied Behavior Analysis,* 1973, *6,* 15–30.

Hersen, M., & Barlow, D.H. *Single case experimental design.* New York: Pergamon, 1976.

Hundert, J. The effectiveness of reinforcement, response, cost, and mixed programs on classroom behaviors. *Journal of Applied Behavior Analysis,* 1976, *9,* 107.

Kazdin, A.E. *Behavior modification in applied settings.* Homewood, Ill.: Dorsey, 1975.

Kazdin, A.E. *The token economy: A review and evaluation.* New York: Plenum, 1977.

Kazdin, A.E. Acceptability of alternative treatments for deviant child behavior. *Journal of Applied Behavior Analysis,* 1980, *13,* 259–273.

Klinge, V., Thrasher, P., & Myers, S. Use of bedrest overcorrection in a chronic schizophrenic. *Journal of Behavior Therapy and Experimental Psychiatry,* 1975, *6,* 69–73.

Kozloff, M.A. *Reaching the autistic child.* Champaign, Ill.: Research Press, 1973.

Lent, J.R. Mimosa cottage: Experiment in hope. *Psychology Today,* 1968, *2,* 51–58.

Locke, B. Verbal conditioning with retarded subjects: Establishment or reinstatement of effective reinforcement consequences. *American Journal of Mental Deficiency,* 1969, *73,* 621–626.

Lovaas, O.I., Litrownik, A., & Mann, R. Response latencies to auditory stimuli in autistic children engaged in self-stimulatory behavior. *Behaviour Research and Therapy,* 1971, *9,* 39–49.

Lovaas, O.I., Schaeffer, B., & Simmons, J.Q. Experimental studies in childhood schizophrenia: Building social behavior in autistic children by the use of electric shock. *Journal of Experimental Research in Personality,* 1965, *1,* 99–109.

Lovaas, O.I., & Simmons, J.Q. Manipulation of self-destruction in three retarded children. *Journal of Applied Behavior Analysis,* 1969, *2,* 143–157.

Matson, J.L. Decreasing inappropriate verbalizations of a moderately retarded adult by a staff assisted self-control program. *Australian Journal of Mental Retardation,* 1979, *5,* 242–245.

Matson, J.L., & Adkins, J. A self-instruction social skills training program for mentally retarded persons. *Mental Retardation,* 1980, *18,* 245–248.

Matson, J.L., & Zeiss, R.A. The buddy system: A method of generalized reduction of inappropriate interpersonal behavior of retarded psychotic patients. *British Journal of Social and Clinical Psychology,* 1979, *18,* 401–405.

National Association for Retarded Citizens. *Guidelines for the use of behavioral procedures in state programs for retarded persons.* Arlington, Tex.: National Association for Retarded Citizens, 1976.

Nelson, G.L., Cone, J.D., & Hanson, C.R. Training correct utensil use in retarded children: Modeling vs. physical guidance. *American Journal of Mental Deficiency,* 1975, *80,* 114–122.

Noll, M.B., & Simpson, R.L. The effects of physical time-out on the aggressive behaviors of a severely emotionally disturbed child in a public school setting. *AAESPH Review,* 1979, *4,* 399–406.

O'Brien, F., Bugle, C., & Azrin, N.H. Training and maintaining a retarded child's proper eating. *Journal of Applied Behavior Analysis,* 1972, *5,* 67–72.

O'Leary, K.D., Poulos, R.W., & Devine, V.T. Tangible reinforcers: Bonuses or bribes. *Journal of Consulting and Clinical Psychology,* 1972, *38,* 1–8.

Pendergrass, V.E. Timeout from positive reinforcement following persistent, high-rate behavior in retardates. *Journal of Applied Behavior Analysis,* 1972, *5,* 85–91.

Phillips, E.L. Achievement place: Token reinforcement procedures in a home style rehabilitation setting for "predelinquent" boys. *Journal of Applied Behavior Analysis,* 1968, *1,* 213–223.

Polvinale, R.A., & Lutzker, J.R. Elimination of assaultive and inappropriate sexual behavior by reinforcement and social-restitution. *Mental Retardation,* 1980, *18,* 27–30.

Risley, T., & Wolf, M. Establishing functional speech in echolalic children. *Behaviour Research and Therapy,* 1967, *5,* 73–88.

Roberts, P., Iwata, B.A., McSween, T.E., & Desmond, E.F. An analysis of overcorrection movements. *American Journal of Mental Deficiency,* 1979, *83,* 588–594.

Russo, D.C., Cataldo, M.F., & Cushing, P.J. Compliance training and behavioral covariation in the treatment of multiple behavior problems. *Journal of Applied Behavior Analysis,* 1981, *14,* 209–222.

Smith, D.D., & Snell, M.E. Intervention strategies. In M.E. Snell (Ed.), *Systematic instruction of the moderately and severely handicapped.* Columbus, Ohio: Charles E. Merrill, 1978.

Sulzer-Azaroff, B., & Mayer, G.R. *Applying behavior analysis procedures with children and youth.* New York: Holt, Rinehart & Winston, 1977.

Tanner, B.A., & Zeiler, M. Punishment of self-injurious behavior using aromatic ammonia as the aversive stimulus. *Journal of Applied Behavior Analysis,* 1975, *8,* 53–57.

Teaching Research Staff. *A data based classroom for the moderately and severely handicapped* (rev. ed.). Monmouth, Oreg.: Instructional Development, 1979.

Thomas, D.R., Becker, W.C., & Armstrong, M. Production and elimination of disruptive classroom behavior by systematically varying teacher's behavior. *Journal of Applied Behavior Analysis,* 1968, *1,* 35–45.

Vukelich, R., & Hake, D.F. Reduction of dangerously aggressive behavior in a severely retarded resident through a combination of positive reinforcement procedures. *Journal of Applied Behavior Analysis,* 1971, *4,* 215–225.

Walker, H.M. *The acting-out child: Coping with classroom disruption.* Boston: Allyn & Bacon, 1979.

Walker, H.M., Hops, H., & Fiegenbaum, E. Deviant classroom behavior as a function of combinations of social and token reinforcement and cost contingency. *Behavior Therapy,* 1976, *7,* 76–88.

Webster's New World Dictionary (2nd ed.). Cleveland: William Collins & World, 1976.

Webster, D.R., & Azrin, N.H. Required relaxation: A method of inhibiting agitative-disruptive behavior of retardates. *Behaviour Research and Therapy,* 1973, *11,* 67–78.

Whitman, T.L., Mercurio, S.R., & Caponigri, V. Development of social responses in two severely retarded children. *Journal of Applied Behavior Analysis,* 1970, *3,* 133–138.

Wolf, M.M., Risley, T., & Mees, H. Application of operant conditioning procedures to the behavior problems of an autistic child. *Behaviour Research and Therapy,* 1964, *1,* 305–312.

Part V

Curriculum Concerns

Chapter 6

Curriculum Development and Implementation

Gary L. Adams
Florida Atlantic University

PROBLEMS AND PAST PRACTICES

In the past, it was believed that severely and profoundly handicapped students could not learn. The "training" was either a watered-down traditional nursery school approach or just custodial care. Demonstrated success in training this population has only recently been apparent, such training typically falling under one of two operational curriculum models for use with severely and profoundly handicapped students. Each model has its own set of assumptions and underlying principles. Although the models are not necessarily mutually exclusive, proponents of each model have historically attempted to find fault with the general hypotheses tendered in the alternative model.

The Developmental Model

In the developmental model, normal child development is used as the key to determining what and when to teach certain behaviors to a severely or profoundly handicapped student. The basic principle is that if one knows the sequence and average age of attainment of certain skills within the normal population, then one has the information necessary to determine appropriate instructional targets and sequences of future targets for a handicapped student. This principle is based on a number of hypotheses (Haring & Bricker, 1976). These are that (1) all behavior develops from simple to complex; (2) all complex behavior results from coordination of simpler components; and (3) all behavioral growth is hierarchical in nature (that is, certain behaviors are acquired before others). The selection of targets is based, therefore, on the *developmental* functioning level of the student rather than on the student's chronological age. Obviously, given the definition of severely and profoundly handicapped, this age of developmental functioning will usually be considera-

135

bly lower than the chronological age. A number of available curricula have been designed using the developmental model (see, for example, Teaching Research Staff, 1979; Wabash Center for the Mentally Retarded, 1977).

The basic assumption of the developmental model is that all individuals, regardless of handicap, follow the same sequence of skill or behavior acquisition. A related assumption is that the general developmental age of attainment of these skills remains the same for all individuals. Unfortunately, given the heterogeneity of the population of the severely and profoundly handicapped, these assumptions have never been validated with this group. A related problem is whether normal developmental patterns and sequences of performance ought to dictate that severely and profoundly handicapped students follow the same patterns and sequences in an instructional setting (Hogg, 1975). The validity of such a practice has also not been proven.

The Criteria of Ultimate Functioning Model

In the criteria of ultimate functioning model (Brown, Nietupski, & Hamre-Nietupski, 1976), target behaviors are selected based on their potential for impacting the student's life in terms of his or her independent functioning within the community. These targeted independent functioning skills (or skills leading toward more independent functioning) are based on the current and future demands of society in general.

The basic assumption of the criteria of ultimate functioning approach is that all acquired skills must have some immediate and future relevance to the expected role of the student within his or her natural environment. A related assumption is that instruction must take into account the myriad environmental cues to which a student must respond in order that all behaviors in need of generalization are generalized (Brown et al., 1976; Brooks & Baumeister, 1977).

A number of basic problems become obvious if one opts for the use of the criteria of ultimate functioning model. The first has to do with severity of handicap. In the case of a student whose profound handicapping condition may severely limit his or her expectations of independent functioning, a functional model of curriculum (that is, one geared toward anticipated community functioning) *may* not be appropriate. In this student's case, future functioning may be almost total dependence on some person or group in the community. A second problem involves the age of the student. For very young severely or profoundly handicapped students, it may be difficult to define future "required" behaviors. By the time the behaviors are acquired, they may not be applicable to community environments. These problems do not negate the possibility of implementing a criteria of ultimate functioning model with either very young or profoundly handicapped students. However, this curriculum model has not been validated with these two subgroups of severely and profoundly handicapped students.

Instructional Implementation

The curriculum model structures the educational environment. The next consideration is instructional implementation. The importance of quality instruction is reflected in the similarity of shape of learning curves of normal and retarded persons (that is, graphs showing the amount of time it takes to master specific tasks). The main difference in the curves is the length of time required for retarded persons to gain initial acquisition. As a rule, the retarded group takes longer to begin to show an increase in rate of performance. One of the teacher's main responsibilities is to decrease the length of time it takes before learning occurs.

Task Analysis

One of the major breakthroughs in educating severely and profoundly handicapped students has been the use of *task analysis*. A task analysis is the breaking down of a target behavior into small steps. Just as a nonhandicapped student learns a skill such as shoe tying by requiring first simple and then complex responses, the same basic process is used for educating severely and profoundly handicapped students. The major difference is the demand for precision. For example, a parent may need only to show a nonhandicapped child how to comb his or her hair, and the teacher may need only a five-step program to teach the same behavior to a mildly handicapped student. A severely and profoundly handicapped student, however, would probably require a much more detailed task analysis, increased number of steps and differences between steps, to acquire and master the same behavior.

Shaping and Chaining

There are two major processes that are integrated into task analysis development. Because of cognitive or motor deficits, severely and profoundly handicapped students make gradual progress; they simply cannot learn the entire behavior in one training session. The teacher *shapes* the behavior by reinforcing successive approximations of the behavior. For example, if the target behavior is to have the student pick up a block on the cue "Susan, pick up the block," the teacher could reinforce the student for touching the object. Over time, the student will learn the steps from touching the block to picking up the block and thus the target behavior of picking up is shaped through reinforcement. This process is no different from the way that any new skill is learned. The difference for the severely or profoundly handicapped student lies in the complexity of the behavior and the intensity of the prompts (instruction) that are required.

Severely and profoundly handicapped students learn by acquiring one step of a task analysis at a time until all of the steps are learned. This process is called *chaining*. For example, at first only one behavior (step) may be required before the student is reinforced. Then the teacher requires an increasing number of steps until the reinforcer can be given. There are several types of chaining:

- *Forward chaining.* The steps in the target behavior are taught from the first occurring behavior to the last.
- *Backward chaining.* The steps in the target behavior are taught from the last occurring behavior to the first.
- *Reverse chaining.* Similar to backward chaining; however, the student is physically assisted through all of the steps he or she cannot do and then instruction is started.

Exhibit 6-1 shows a simple task analysis for handwashing. This task analysis is written using forward chaining, with the first step being the logical first step

Exhibit 6-1 A Task Analysis for Handwashing

```
         Forward Chained Simplified Handwashing Program

Steps                          Behaviors

  1          Student walks to sink.
  2          Student turns on water.
  3          Student feels the water and adjusts water temperature.
  4          Student wets hands and applies soap.
  5          Student rubs hands together.
  6          Student rinses off soap and turns off the water.
  7          Student pulls out paper towel and dries hands.
  8          Student discards paper towel in garbage can.


    Backward or Reversed Chained Simplified Handwashing Program

Steps                          Behaviors

  1          Student discards paper towel in garbage can.
  2          Student pulls out paper towel and dries hands.
  3          Student rinses off soap and turns off the water.
  4          Student rubs hands together.
  5          Student wets hands and applies soap.
  6          Student feels the water and adjusts water temperature.
  7          Student turns on water.
  8          Student walks to sink.
```

when hands are washed. The step sequence would be inverted in a backward chaining process, with the first step of the task analysis being the last step in the previous sequence (Step 8 in the forward chaining program). Reverse chaining is like backward chaining except instead of starting the training session at the current step, the teacher physically assists the child through the other steps and then begins training (Teaching Research Staff, 1979). For example, if the student was on Step 3 in this program, the teacher would assist the student by physically guiding the student's hands through Steps 8 through 4 and then begin training at Step 3.

There has been very little research on which chaining sequence is superior. Popovich (1981) suggests that all task analyses should be written based on backward chaining. Some curriculum authors rely on forward chaining (see, for example, Henderson & McDonald, 1973), while others use forward and backward chaining (Staff of the Teaching Research Infant and Child Center, 1980). Empirical research by Walls, Zane, and Ellis (1981) found no significant difference in skill acquisition rates between forward and backward chaining procedures.

Fading

In addition to the shaping and chaining that are implicit in task analysis development, the teacher uses two types of *fading* in training. The first type of fading is used in the prompt process. For example, initially the student may require a verbal cue and physical assistance on a particular step to promote success. As the student begins to respond independently, the teacher may fade the use of physical assistance so that only the verbal cue is given. The other type of fading is the fading of reinforcing consequences. At first the teacher may want to ensure responding by giving an edible item while offering verbal praise. Again, when the responding is consistent, the teacher will fade the use of edible items so that only social praise is given.

Prompts

Once the starting point on the task analysis is discovered, the teacher must shape the correct behavior through the use of prompts. A prompt is an event that helps initiate a response (Kazdin, 1975). These prompts include verbal cues ("David, button your shirt."), modeling, gestures, and physical assistance. Also, prompts can be combined (a verbal cue, for example, while gesturing). Prompted or self-initiated responses are reinforced, usually with social praise, which may be paired with primary reinforcers (items or events that satisfy bodily needs). This reinforcement process increases the probability that students will continue to respond correctly. When the student begins to display a consistent pattern of correct responding, the teacher begins to fade the use of artificial prompts.

The use of *verbal prompts* seems natural because teachers often want students to follow their commands. Several researchers have relied on verbal prompts (Kazdin & Erickson, 1975; Striefel & Wetherby, 1973; Whitman, Zakaras, & Chardos, 1971). Minge and Ball (1967) taught six profoundly retarded females dressing and undressing skills using verbal directions, which were sometimes paired with gestures and light physical assistance. Lemke and Mitchell (1972) increased appropriate spoon use with a 12-year-old retarded male by using verbal and gestural prompts. Gold and Barclay (1973) conducted a study in which they stated that they were comparing a verbal cue to a no verbal cue condition in teaching a bicycle brake assembly task. They found that mentally retarded students learned faster and with better retention when a verbal cue was given. Actually, there is some question as to whether there was a valid no verbal cue condition. The procedure in this study was to state "Michael, flat side up. Try another way" if the student was in the verbal cue condition and to state "Michael, try another way" if the student was in the no verbal cue condition. However, since the phrase "try another way" is a type of verbal cue, it appears as if this study was comparing two verbal cue conditions. Close, Irvin, Prehm, and Taylor (1978), in a later study, compared the same two verbal prompts and found no statistically significant difference between the two conditions.

Verbal prompts have often been used as a part of a prompt sequence. For example, a sequence of prompts in the Project MORE program (Lent, 1975) is given if the student responds incorrectly or does not respond. First, a verbal prompt is given, then a gestural prompt, then a modeling of the correct behavior, and finally, the student is physically assisted through the correct behavior. Burleigh and Marholin (1977), however, found that verbal prompts acted as distractors to institutionalized mentally retarded students in their study. Previous research by Zigler (see Zigler & Balla, 1977, for a review) has shown that because of the high level of social deprivation in institutional settings, retarded students are more susceptible to the effects of social reinforcement by staff members (such as teachers). Verbal prompts, a possible source of social reinforcement, may act as a distractor because students look at the source of the verbal prompt (the teacher) and look away from the task.

Modeling is the demonstration of a part or all of the target behavior. The student is expected to perform the behavior that he or she has observed. Modeling may be done by a teacher or peer. O'Brien and Azrin (1972) used modeling in a study in which eating skills were taught. Modeling has also been used to train toileting (Azrin & Foxx, 1971), toothbrushing (Horner & Keilitz, 1975), and feeding (Nelson, Cone, & Hanson, 1975). Although there is some indication that modeling may be less effective with severely and profoundly retarded students (Bry & Nawas, 1972), no research comparing the effects of modeling on mildly versus profoundly handicapped students has been conducted.

The findings of research comparing verbal prompts with modeling have been inconsistent. Rosenthal and Kellogg (1973) found that modeling using silent demonstration was superior to verbal prompts. Altman, Talkington, and Cleland (1972) did not find any differences between verbal instruction and modeling. The discrepancy in findings may be due to the task involved. Yoder and Forehand (1974) found that modeling alone was sufficient to improve performance on simple tasks, but verbal prompts when added to modeling improved performance on complex tasks. It should be noted, however, that their study used mildly handicapped students.

Physical prompts are those where physical assistance is used in guiding the student through the target behavior, not doing the target behavior for the student (Snell, 1978). This type of prompt has been used extensively in self-help training. For example, toothbrushing programs have included physical assistance (Abramson & Wunderlich, 1972; Horner & Keilitz, 1975). Hamilton, Allen, Stephens, and Duvall (1969) used physical assistance in training 41 retarded females to use sanitary napkins. Close, Irvin, Prehm, and Taylor (1978) found that physical assistance in the form of positive practice was successful in increasing the rate of skill acquisition. By having retarded students practice the correct response five times, the researchers found that students made faster progress than if they were given a verbal or gestural prompt.

Comparative Research

Walls, Ellis, Zane, and Vanderpoel (1979) compared the following prompt conditions on a vocational task: verbal prompts, modeling, physical guidance, and a combination. The results showed that verbal prompts resulted in significantly lower performance. The combination of verbal, modeling, and physical assistance prompts was superior, but not significantly different from either the modeling or physical assistance conditions.

The previously cited research was based on external prompts given by a teacher. Another approach is to use *within-stimulus prompts*, in which the stimulus (task) is exaggerated. An example of the use of a within-stimulus prompt for teaching a coat zipping skill would be to place colored tape on each side of the coat opening to assist in lining up the two sides before zipping. Most of the research on this topic has involved autistic students learning cognitive tasks. Studies comparing external to within-stimulus prompts have consistently shown more success using within-stimulus prompts (Arick & Krug, 1978; Schreibman, 1975; Wolfe & Cuvo, 1978). This research suggests that within-stimulus prompts can be a valuable training technique.

Considering the importance of the topic, it is suprising that there is so little research on prompting. Most research has noted only that a certain prompt sequence has been used to train a specific skill. Most of the research has only examined prompts in isolation, and not prompt sequences. There are two major approaches to prompt sequence development. In one approach, the teacher uses one type of prompt throughout the steps of the task analysis and then changes to another type of prompt. This type of prompt sequence usually starts with a restrictive prompt (physical assistance) and goes to a less restrictive prompt (gestures). The other approach uses one type of prompt on a particular step and if it fails goes to another, and more restrictive, prompt. For example, Lent (1975) suggests using a sequence of more restrictive prompts if the student fails to respond or responds incorrectly. The prompt sequence is as follows: the teacher gives a verbal cue, the teacher gestures, the teacher models the correct response, and the teacher physically assists the student through the target response.

Glendenning, Adams, and Sternberg (1981) compared the number of correct responses of moderately to severely retarded students on a vocational task under three prompt sequences. The first prompt sequence was verbal cue, gesture, model, and full physical assistance. The second prompt sequence was verbal cue and full physical assistance, verbal cue and light physical assistance, verbal cue and gesture, and verbal cue. The third prompt sequence included full physical assistance, moderate physical assistance, light physical assistance, and gesture. All of the students were trained under the three prompt sequence conditions. One prompt per session was used. The results of this study indicated that the second prompt sequence was superior. The verbal prompt when given at the beginning of the prompt sequence (the first prompt sequence) leads to a much lower probability of self-initiated responding than when the verbal prompt is at the end of the sequence (the second prompt sequence).

Unlike the previous study in which one prompt per session was given, a study by Walls, Crist, Sienicki, and Grant (1981) compared three prompt sequences in which the lack of a response led to movement through the prompt hierarchy per session. For example, if the student did not respond to the first prompt after 15 seconds, the second prompt was given. The three prompt sequences were (1) physical assistance, model, and verbal; (2) verbal, model, and physical assistance; and (3) full physical assistance, partial physical as- sistance, and slight physical assistance. Also, the study compared the responses of moderately and mildly retarded students. The results of the study showed that although there was a significant difference between moderately and mildly retarded groups, there was no difference between the three prompt sequences for either group. It should be obvious that much more research is needed beyond these preliminary studies.

Reinforcement

Many types of reinforcers have been used in training. Research pertaining to their effectiveness is conflicting. Some studies have shown that handicapped students acquire skills at a significantly higher rate when they are socially reinforced (Ellis & Distefano, 1959; Gray & Kasteler, 1969). However, other research has shown that performance under social reinforcement is worse for institutionalized students, who, as mentioned earlier, may find social praise distracting (Harter, 1967; Harter, Brown, & Zigler, 1971). Also, social praise when given to some students with behavior problems has resulted in a deterioration of behavior (Herbert, Pinkston, Hayden, Sajwaj, Pinkston, Cordua, & Jackson, 1973; Wahler, 1969; Wahler, Winkel, Peterson, & Morrison, 1965).

The findings of research comparing social and primary reinforcers have also been conflicting. Some studies have favored social reinforcers (Gardner & Brandl, 1967; Smith, 1972) and others have favored primary reinforcers (Guralnick & Kravik, 1973; Tramontana, 1972). In actual practice, comparisons between primary and social reinforcers have little value, because primary reinforcers are usually not given without social reinforcement. The two types of reinforcement are usually paired with the expectation that the primary reinforcer will be faded out and the new behavior will come under the control of social reinforcement. There has been little research comparing paired reinforcement with social reinforcement for severely and profoundly handicapped students. McReynolds (1970) found that a four-year-old brain-damaged child made better language progress with verbal approval and ice cream than with only verbal approval. Adams (1981a), however, found no significant difference between paired edible reinforcement and social praise versus social praise only on the self-help skills acquisition of institutionalized retarded students. It should be noted that two students who had histories of training progress under paired reinforcement made no progress when they were assigned to the social praise only group. Because of the increased influence of social praise in institutional settings (Zigler & Balla, 1977), the addition of edible reinforcers to social praise may not add a significant level of reinforcing power. This result may not be the same for noninstitutionalized students.

At first glance, a study by Koop, Martin, Yu, and Suthons (1980) appears to contradict the Adams (1981a) study. They compared a minimal social reinforcement condition with an enriched social and edible reinforcement condition and found that the paired reinforcement condition was superior. The difference may be due to the difference in definition of conditions. Under the minimal social reinforcement condition in the Koop et al. (1980) study, the trainer avoided eye contact and gave only a "good" statement. The students under the enriched reinforcement condition received varied, and possibly more enthusiastic, praise (such as "good job" and "super") and edibles. The differences that were noted between the two experimental conditions in the two studies may have been due to the differences in the variety and quality of the social praise and the trainers' rapport during the session.

Measurement of Progress

Another key component of instructional implementation is the measurement of behavior change (Cooper, 1981; White & Haring, 1980). Exhibit 6-2 shows a sample data sheet for daily ten-trial sessions. Behavior change on a task analysis is shown by movement through the steps until the student can

Exhibit 6-2 A Sample Data Sheet for Daily Ten-Trial Sessions

DATA SHEET

Student's Name _____

First day of the week _____

Program _____Handwashing_____

			Trials									
Day	Step	Reinforcer	1	2	3	4	5	6	7	8	9	10
Mon												
Tue												
Wed												
Thu												
Fri												

Comments _____
_____
_____
_____
_____

perform the target behavior independently. The graduation from one step to the next has usually been made when the student reaches a certain criterion and responds correctly on a specific percentage of trials (80 percent, for example—eight of ten trials correct). Several possible criteria have been used in training; for example, 80 percent or 90 percent on two successive sessions. A search of the literature shows no research on which criterion facilitates acquisition and long-term retention of a skill.

After the training data have been collected, they should be graphed so that training progress can be visualized. Exhibit 6-3 shows a cumulative graphing process in which the student's latest step at the end of the week is recorded. The handwashing program that is graphed has eight steps. The baseline

Exhibit 6-3 A Cumulative Graphing of Steps for Handwashing Sessions

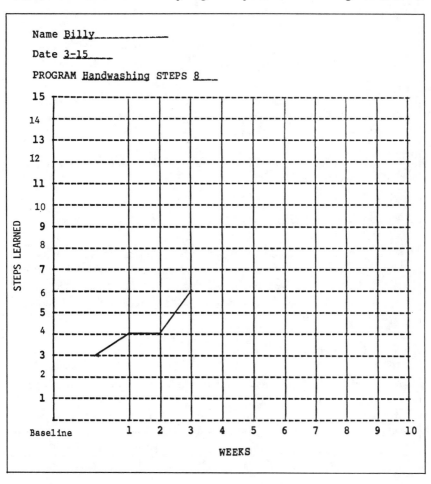

Name Billy

Date 3-15

PROGRAM Handwashing STEPS 8

showed that the student started at Step 3. During the next week, he gained one step and was on Step 4. Then he made no progress during the next week and stayed on Step 4. He made two step graduations during the third week. By graphing the obtained data, one can get a clearer picture of implementation success or failure.

Summary

Unfortunately, the implementation tenets and suggestions of the preceding section are evidently not being followed and used by many teachers of the severely and profoundly handicapped. A recent survey by The Association for the Severely Handicapped ("Say It Ain't So," 1981) showed that the quality of the current teaching of severely and profoundly handicapped students is at a very elementary level. The results of the survey were as follows:

- Of the teachers surveyed 20.3 percent did not provide daily training.
- Only half of the teachers surveyed had aims for their instructional programs.
- Less than half of the teachers had rules to change training steps.
- Less than half of the teachers evaluated progress on all of the students' programs.

It is hoped that this situation will be ameliorated through future research and more effective dissemination efforts.

SUGGESTED METHODS

Creating an acceptable educational program involves many issues. Unfortunately, most curriculum developers and educational supervisors, with few exceptions, have emphasized the need for conducting only individualized, data-based training. Larger issues, such as generalization and maintenance of acquired skills, have not been stressed.

Structure of the Learning Environment

The creation of a learning environment requires many decisions by teachers. One of the first involves the physical layout of the educational setting. By systematically evaluating furniture placement and work practices, teachers can reduce possible behavior problems and the amount of time and effort in searching for educational materials (Hart & Risley, 1976). For example, when teachers are unorganized and frequently used training materials are placed on a shelf across the room, the extra effort results in a tired teacher by midday.

Beyond the physical environment, the teacher must decide on the mixture of individual and group instruction. In the past, teachers have relied almost entirely on an individualized training format. The rationale for this decision is that severely and profoundly handicapped students need one-to-one attention. Favell, Favell, and McGimsey (1978) have shown that severely and profoundly retarded students can be trained in small groups. One of the main benefits of group training is that it is more efficient and cost effective. Koegel and Rincover (1974), however, found that autistic students became inattentive in a normal group classroom situation. When the students were trained on an individualized basis and then systematically transferred to work in small groups, they were able to adapt to a group training situation. Because of cost effectiveness, teachers should attempt to conduct group training *when possible* and evaluate if students are making progress that is comparable to success under individualized instruction.

The next decision is to select the number and length of training sessions. A considerable number of training models suggest using one daily ten-trial training session per skill. For example, each student may have four or five training programs with one ten-trial session conducted on each program daily. There have been two major alternatives to this procedure in recent years. Guess and associates in a series of articles (Brown, Holvoet, Guess, & Mulligan, 1980; Holvoet, Guess, Mulligan, & Brown, 1980; Mulligan, Guess, Holvoet, & Brown, 1980) have suggested the use of distributed training with more sessions having only a few trials per session (such as five sessions with two trials per session) instead of massed practice with only one ten-trial session per day. This approach is based on previous research primarily on nonhandicapped persons showing the advantages of distributed practice over massed practice (see, for example, Chasey, 1976; Dent & Johnson, 1964).

The other alternative is based on the research of Azrin. Rather than using multiple training programs of short duration each day, Azrin has developed intensive training programs for toileting (Foxx & Azrin, 1973), eating (Azrin & Armstrong, 1973), and dressing (Azrin, Schaeffer, & Wesolowski, 1976). Only one type of behavior is taught at a time and usually the training sessions last for the majority of the day. This approach has been adapted for the school setting (Trott, 1977). Although both of the above approaches appear promising and are being used in the field, there have been no systematic comparisons of different training session lengths.

After the previous two decisions concerning individualized versus group training and the length of the training sessions are made, the next decision is the development of staff and student schedules. The need for staff and student scheduling is evident in a number of research studies. Berkson and Davenport

(1962) demonstrated that a large percentage of student time is spent engaged in isolated, antisocial behavior. Wright, Abbas, and Meredith (1974) found that the extent of time staff members interact in a positive manner toward retarded adults is .001 percent. In the classroom setting, the problem is compounded by teachers and aides who walk across the classroom without interacting with students and without reinforcing positive behaviors.

There have been several successful attempts to improve staff-student interaction by improving management structuring. For example, Greene, Willis, Levey, and Bailey (1978) found that staff members in an institutional setting showed inconsistent program implementation. When programming data were publicly displayed, there was an increase in implementation. Burg, Reid, and Lattimore (1979) found that by having institutional staff self-record the frequency of their student interactions, the rate of those interactions increased significantly. Other research has shown that staff-student interaction can be improved through the use of feedback (Panyan, Boozer, & Morris, 1970), tokens (Pommer & Streedbeck, 1974), contingent days off (Iwata, Bailey, Brown, Foshee, & Alpern, 1976), and role-playing staff-student interaction during inservice training (Adams, Tallon, & Rimell, 1980).

To improve the probability of staff-student interaction and to improve program accountability, students and training staff (such as teacher, aides, and volunteers) should operate on a schedule. The problem from lack of scheduling is seen in many classrooms, where one or possibly two students are involved in individualized instruction with the teacher and others (such as aides) while the other students are sitting in chairs or lying on the floor either doing nothing or engaging in antisocial behavior. When creating an instructional schedule, the teacher must remember that *all* students should be involved in some type of educational activity. Rather than have all training personnel doing individualized instruction, they should be assigned activities for both individual and group training.

The use of *activity areas* (Teaching Research Staff, 1979) is a good example of what the other students should be doing while classmates are involved in individualized instruction. Classroom schedules are based on the assumption that teaching personnel will attempt to involve students in ongoing activities and not let the students isolate themselves. The activity area contains a staff member and all of the students who are not involved in individualized instruction. There are two main purposes to the activity area. First, it is a holding area for students who are not in individualized instruction (LeLaurin & Risley, 1972). The activity area is an ongoing program and when a certain student is needed for individualized instruction, he or she is removed. After the training session, the student is returned to the activity area. The second purpose of the activity area is that it is a place where activities can be introduced that are matched to the students' individualized instruction, thus improving the chances of rapid acquisition and generalization of skills. For example, a student may be having trouble with taking off a toothpaste cap during his or her individualized toothbrushing program. One of the tasks during the activity area time can be practicing unscrewing progressively smaller containers. In some cases, tasks can be structured so that two or more students can positively interact during task completion.

Program Selection and Implementation

Training programs should be based on the identified needs from the student's Individualized Educational Program (IEP). Turnbull, Strickland, & Brantley (1978) and Lovitt (1980) provide examples of a model for developing and implementing the IEP. A major part of the IEP process is the selection of the appropriate assessment instruments because proper selection can simplify both the writing and implementation of the IEP. (See Chapter 4 for a review of assessment concerns and procedures.) Because of the lower functioning level of the severely and profoundly handicapped students, tests of adaptive behavior are usually the main source of information. When deciding which of the over 200 adaptive behavior tests to use as a basis for program selection, the teacher must look for several key variables. First, the test should be in a format that leads to an efficient test/teach process. For example, the *AAMD Adaptive Behavior Scale* (Nihira, Foster, Shellhaas, & Leland, 1975) is a difficult test to use for program selection because some of the test items include multiple behaviors. If the teacher reads that the student cannot wash and dry self with help in the Bathing subdomain, it may mean that the student (1) can wash, but not dry with help; (2) can dry, but not wash with help; or (3) cannot wash or dry with help. Further testing is needed to get a clearer picture of the child's capabilities.

Beyond the issue of reliability and validity, teachers should be aware of several characteristics of tests that improve the quality of the test/teach process so that the test results can be used to select teaching programs. First, test items should describe behaviors that are specific and observable. Second, the teacher should consider the scope of the test and select a test that includes enough items applicable for the severely and profoundly handicapped population. Finally, the sequence of the test times is important if it is used as a basis for IEP program selection. Some tests have no particular sequence (for example, the *AAMD Adaptive Behavior Scale,* but most are based on a developmental or an empirical sequence. The developmental sequence of test items is based on the developmental pattern of normal children. One example of this type of test is the *Developmental Pinpoints* (Cohen, Gross, & Haring, 1976). Empirical sequencing is created by testing a large number of handicapped students and then placing the items in sequence from the first (the item that the highest percentage of students could do) to the last (the item that the fewest students could do). Other examples of this sequence are the *Empirically Based Training Assessment* (Adams, 1981b), and the *Camelot Behavioral Checklist* (Foster, 1974).

Too often, teachers do not ask parents and guardians for information during the adaptive behavior testing process. Not only should parents and guardians be providing information, but also they should be *independently* selecting training priorities based on the adaptive behavior testing. The school setting appears to shape program selection. Because they are in school, teachers seem to select many irrelevant items that have been used in traditional academic programs and these programs have no direct relationship to the student's future (putting pegs in a pegboard, for example). Parents seem to select programs that are required to meet the child's daily needs (such as toilet training). Program selection through discussion between parents and teachers leads to more appropriate programming.

A satisfactory test/teach process is enhanced by creating matching curricula for a selected test. In this process, every test item (such as "can wash face with wash cloth") has a matching task analysis. Another approach is basically the reverse of the test/teach process using an established test. Curriculum developers create a curriculum and then use the list of task analyses as a test. Several curriculum authors have used this second approach (see, for example, Popovich, 1981; Tawney, Knapp, O'Reilly, & Pratt, 1979; Teaching Research Staff, 1979). Although this approach is popular, it should be remembered that the list of training programs, when administered as a test, may lack important characteristics of an acceptable test (that is, it may have poor interrater reliability and validity). Teachers should be aware of the problem with this second approach.

After target behaviors are selected in the IEP process, the next step is to ensure consistent implementation of training programs. The basic problem is figuring out how many target programs should be established for each student so that all of the programs are conducted daily. The selection of too many programs leads to inconsistency (a particular program may be conducted only twice a week, for example) with the result being no progress. The selection of too few programs leads to the teaching staff finishing early and having nothing to do. Granted that there will be scheduling conflicts during the school week, the staff of the Teaching Research Infant and Child Center (1980) probably has one of the better procedures for empirically determining a satisfactory number of programs. At the end of the school week, the percentage of scheduled programs that were actually conducted should be around 90 percent. Programs are added or deleted to ensure this level of consistency.

The educational programs for severely and profoundly handicapped students must be carefully designed. Nonhandicapped or mildly handicapped students often show progress in spite of poor teaching techniques. Errors by the teacher are compensated for by the higher cognitive level of the student. For example, even though the teacher presents a poorly organized lecture on the multiplication tables, the mildly handicapped student may be able to figure out the underlying concept. Severely and profoundly handicapped students rarely have the ability to compensate for inadequate teaching (Williams, Brown, & Certo, 1975). For this reason, task analyses must be precise and clearly written. Although the process of writing task analyses seems easy, it is a very difficult skill. Some teachers prefer to use one or more of the commercial curricula that are available, but there have been complaints about the quality of these curricula (see, for example, Smith & Smith, 1978). Many of the curricula seem to be written for mildly handicapped students. The steps are unclear and large (that is, containing many behaviors). The result is that severely and profoundly handicapped students do not make progress.

An alternative approach is one in which the teacher writes a task analysis that includes adaptations for each individual student. Unfortunately, most teachers who write task analyses seem to overestimate their skills. A major problem is that the task analysis writer is not "intimately familiar" with the task (Gold & Pomerantz, 1978). The teacher tries to write the task analysis without going through the physical motions of the task. For example, the teacher tries to visualize the steps in brushing teeth, but the result is that a step is left out (for example, turning off the faucet). By going through the physical motions, a teacher may find alternative ways to train a particular skill.

What is truly needed, however, is an empirically validated curriculum that has been field tested. Realistically, this approach is probably beyond the energies of most teachers, who lack the time and the number of students to validate the large number of task analyses in a curriculum. Of the published curricula writers, Tawney et al. (1979) appear to be the only curriculum developers who have conducted large-scale field testing. An alternative may be to have a school district or state department of education create a field-tested curriculum. Within this framework, Cuvo (1978) has suggested a process to ensure the designing of quality task analyses. In some cases, an expert can be observed (such as a custodian for a bathroom cleaning program), but for other programs (such as crossing a street), teachers or aides can be videotaped doing the behavior. Then two or more people should independently write the task analysis for the targeted behavior. Pilot performance of the task analysis with handicapped students should be videotaped and then the task analysis can be modified, if necessary. Cuvo and his associates have shown this approach to be successful in a series of skill training studies (Cronin & Cuvo, 1979; Cuvo, Jacobi, & Sipko, 1981; Johnson & Cuvo, 1981). School districts would have the resources to (1) create the task analyses through writing teams; (2) collect the task analyses and place them in a central distribution center (possibly using a word-processing system for storage and retrieval); (3) collect data on the programs; and (4) evaluate the success of the task analyses through computer analyses. For example, the computer analyses would include the average number of days it takes students to progress through each step on every task analysis. When a particular step shows an extended period of time for completion, the task analysis is rewritten and the new task analysis would be distributed for further field testing. Using a word-processing system, this revision and distribution program would be greatly simplified.

Several features improve the quality of task analyses. One of the key features of using a task analysis is that it provides the opportunity for improved communication between trainers because others (such as an aide) can tell what should be done in training. For this reason, teachers need to write precise and descriptive steps so that trainers can visualize what should be done. One of the easiest ways to improve communication is to have the teacher illustrate each of the important steps. Unfortunately, most teachers do not have the time nor the artistic skills to do the illustrations. Again, this problem reinforces the need for a school district or state approach to curriculum design and validation.

Being more precise and descriptive would probably lead to an increase in the number of steps in a task analysis because there would be a reduction of steps that include multiple behaviors. Besides the improved clarity, the increased number of steps produces a higher probability of reinforcing students. When steps are large and contain multiple behaviors, students are not reinforced at an acceptable rate and do not show progress. For example, the student may be doing one of the two behaviors in the step correctly, but the end result is that the student's total response is corrected and often the student is kept on the same step for long periods of time. With smaller, tightly written steps, the probability of making a correct response to a step that includes only one behavior is higher, with the result that the student responds correctly and is reinforced. The difference between these two approaches is often shown in the students' resistance to entering the instructional situation. Teachers complain that students throw temper tantrums when they are told that it is time for training. A major reason for this resistance is that training becomes associated with failure (obviously, not the intent of training).

The Instructional Process

Two procedures must occur before actual teaching is started. First, the teacher must know what is reinforcing to the student by conducting a reinforcer sampling. A study by Ferrari and Harris (1981) showed how important this procedure is. They found major differences in reinforcer preferences across students. Also, they found that sensory stimuli (strobe light, vibration, and music) were as effective as traditional edibles and social reinforcers. Reinforcer preferences are not constant; they change over time. Egel (1981) compared varied with constant types of reinforcers and found better performance when the reinforcer was varied. Under the constant reinforcer condition, there was a deterioration in performance over time.

Second, the teacher must check to see whether the student knows any of the steps on the task analysis. There is no reason to start the student at the beginning of the task analysis if he or she already knows some of the steps. A baseline is the process of discovering where to begin training. One of the most popular baseline procedures is used in the Teaching Research Model (Teaching Research Staff, 1979). Two sessions on two days are conducted. Baseline is taken by starting at the last step in the task analysis and then the cue is given. The teacher provides two opportunities (trials) on that step. If the student cannot perform the behavior, the teacher moves back to the next to the last step and uses the previous procedure. This process is continued until the student can perform one of the steps. To ensure that the correct starting point is discovered, another session on the second day is conducted. The advantage of using sessions on two days is that the teacher can note differences in performance. Students, especially those who have just been moved from a more restrictive setting (such as an institution), may show differences across sessions because they may never have had the opportunity to display the target behavior. If the two baseline starting points are different, further baseline sessions can be conducted until a starting point is selected.

One of the main errors in student instruction is that teachers do not make data-based training decisions. Although most teacher training programs have emphasized the need for making data-based decisions, The Association for the Severely Handicapped survey (1981) showed that less than half of the teachers were doing so. White and Liberty (1976) have noted how hard it is to evaluate progress after looking at a stack of data sheets. Training decisions should be made on a daily basis. Unfortunately, most program models have only vague guidelines about what the teacher should do when a student is not making progress.

The Boulder Training Model (Rimell, Stagg, Hanson, Zeeck, Moore, Van Haecke, & Langworthy, 1977), which is an adaptation of the Teaching Research Model (Teaching Research Staff, 1979), has created some formal updating rules in the event that student progress is not being made:

1. After one session without meeting the criterion, stay on the current step.
2. After two sessions without meeting the criterion, change the reinforcer.

3. After three sessions without meeting the criterion, use one of the following techniques:
   —Divide the step into multiple steps
   —Add a physical assistance prompt
   —Add a gesture to a verbal prompt
   —Add praise or touch to shape approximations
4. If no success, use another technique in Step 3 (this process may need to be done several times).
5. If no success, conduct another baseline and reinitiate training process.

Because of these rules, the graphing of data is optional; it is assumed that the teacher will continually be making program changes based on the updating rules.

Probably the most sophisticated measurement system has been described by Haring, Liberty, and White (1980). This approach was first used on mildly handicapped students. Student data were placed on semilogarithmic graph paper and decision rules were used for making program changes. By analyzing the training data of severely and profoundly handicapped students, several response patterns were discovered. The findings support the need for empirical validation of programming techniques. For example, it was found that the common technique of moving back to a prerequisite skill when there was no training progress, which has been suggested by several curriculum authors, was successful only 5.8 percent of the time. However, when data-based decision rules were followed, success was achieved two-thirds of the time. Compliance with the rules, when compared with teacher decisions, resulted in a higher percentage of success. Again, this suggests the problem of making intuitive decisions about training programs. For a thorough explanation of the data-based decision rules, see Haring, Liberty, and White (1980).

Generalization and Maintenance Training

Acquiring new skills is important but teachers must look beyond the initial acquisition phase. There are probably two reasons why teachers do not check to ensure that the skill has been maintained. First, the student may be promoted to another teacher during the next school year and not be available for evaluation of skill maintenance. Second, the teacher may simply avoid the possible bad news that the student can no longer demonstrate the behavioral competency. The reality is that over half of the skills acquired by severely and profoundly handicapped students are not maintained even six months later (Sage, 1980). This means that a lot of teacher effort is being wasted.

There are several procedures to improve generalization and maintenance of skill acquisition. Most training programs have been based on an external person, such as a teacher, controlling the severely and profoundly handicapped student's behavior. Often it is assumed that because of a deficit in cognitive functioning, the student requires external support. There are several studies based on self-control techniques that show gains by mildly handicapped students (see, for example, Bolstad & Johnson, 1972; Bornstein, Bellack, & Hersen, 1977; Turkewitz, O'Leary, & Ironsmith, 1975). One of the major advantages of this approach is the reliance on the student to maintain the behavioral change without some external person being present (Williams, Hamre-Nietupski, Pumpian, McDaniel Marx, & Wheeler, 1978).

Matson, Marchetti, and Adkins (1980) used self-control techniques that they described as an "independence-training procedure." This approach was compared with a traditional operant training and a control procedure. Seventy-five institutionalized severely and profoundly handicapped students were randomly assigned to one of the three procedures. Baselines showed that the students had low rates of nightstand cleanliness and showering. Students in the operant group received five training sessions per week using traditional methods of verbal and modeling prompts, which were faded with social and tangible reinforcement for correct responses. The training progress was charted. The same daily training was used for the independence-training group, except on Friday, when they received a feedback session. During the feedback session, the students were asked about their progress. Honesty and accuracy were praised. If a low rate of progress was made, the teacher asked for suggestions to improve behavior and emphasized the need for the students to be responsible for their own behavior. If progress was made, a star was given. The control group did not receive instruction on either skill. The training program lasted six weeks and a followup probe was taken eight weeks later.

The results showed that students in the independence-training group made significantly more progress than students in the traditional operant group or the control group. This study indicates the possibility of using self-control procedures in which severely and profoundly handicapped students monitor their own behavior.

The probability of generalization and maintenance can also be increased by adding extra steps to the task analysis. First, there should be a process for fading the use of artificial reinforcers, if they are used, so that the behavior comes under the control of social praise. It is surprising to note how few curricula mention ways to decrease the use of edibles. After the student has acquired the target behavior with the student being reinforced with paired social praise and edibles, then extra steps are added so that the student must perform the behavior with progressively fewer trials being reinforced with edibles until the use of edibles has been completely faded.

Next, generalization training should be conducted. Again, extra steps should be added so that the student performs the target behavior across settings, across teachers, across language prompts, and across materials. Granted, these extra steps take more time because the student must learn, for example, to zip not only his red coat but also his blue and yellow coat, but the result is that the probability of continued performance is increased. After this generalization phase, maintenance probes (that is, conducting a baseline) should be taken at regular intervals (one week later, two weeks later, and then one, two, and three months later). If the student fails the probe (baseline) by less than 100 percent correct across settings, teachers, language prompts, or materials, the training program is reintroduced.

CONCLUSION

Although it was once thought that severely and profoundly handicapped students were unteachable, now there are many examples of successful training. There are still very few studies that indicate what are the components of successful instruction. As Wehman (1979) noted, few studies describe the interaction of variables such as institutionalization of the student, age, sex, and different training procedures. The lack of research on prompt sequences, an important training variable, is a prime example of the "best guess" approach to education.

Creating a successful learning environment requires careful planning. The teacher should not rely just on the research of others, but must systematically evaluate various instructional components by conducting his or her own research studies. The goal is that weak or counterproductive components are eliminated from the educational process. Severely and profoundly handicapped students have enough problems without teachers creating instructional roadblocks by using intuitive programming methods.

REFERENCES

Abramson, E.E., & Wunderlich, R.A. Dental hygiene training for retardates: An application of behavioral techniques. *Mental Retardation,* 1972, *10*(3), 6–8.

Adams, G.L. The importance of reinforcer sampling before initiating training. *Journal for Special Educators,* 1981a, *22,* 188–198.

Adams, G.L. *Empirically Based Training Assessment.* Unpublished manuscript, 1981b. Florida Atlantic University, Department of Exceptional Student Education.

Adams, G.L., Tallon, R.J., & Rimell, P. A comparison of lecture versus role-playing in the training of the use of positive reinforcement. *Journal of Organizational Behavior Management,* 1980, *2,* 205–212.

Altman, R., Talkington, L., & Cleland, C.C. Relative effectiveness of modeling and verbal instruction on severe retardates' gross motor performance. *Psychological Reports,* 1972, *31,* 695–698.

Arick, J.R., & Krug, D.A. Autistic children: A study of learning characteristics of programming needs. *American Journal of Mental Deficiency, 1978, 83,* 200–202.

Azrin, N.H., & Armstrong, P.M. The "mini-meal"—A method for teaching eating skills to the profoundly retarded. *Mental Retardation, 1973, 11*(1), 9–11.

Azrin, N.H., & Foxx, R.M. A rapid method of toilet training the institutionalized retarded. *Journal of Applied Behavior Analysis, 1971, 4,* 89–99.

Azrin, N.H., Schaeffer, R.M., & Wesolowski, M.D. A rapid method of teaching profoundly retarded persons to dress by a reinforcement-guidance method. *Mental Retardation, 1976, 14*(6), 29–33.

Berkson, G., & Davenport, R.K. Stereotyped movements in mental defectives: I. Initial survey. *American Journal of Mental Deficiency, 1962, 66,* 849–852.

Bolstad, O.D., & Johnson, S.M. Self-regulation in the modification of disruptive classroom behavior. *Journal of Applied Behavior Analysis, 1972, 5,* 443–454.

Bornstein, M.R., Bellack, A.S., & Hersen, M. Social skills training for unassertive children: A multiple-baseline analysis. *Journal of Applied Behavior Analysis, 1977, 10,* 183–195.

Brooks, P., & Baumeister, A. A plea for consideration of ecological validity in the experimental psychology of mental retardation: A guest editorial. *American Journal of Mental Deficiency, 1977, 81,* 407–416.

Brown, F., Holvoet, J., Guess, D., & Mulligan, M. The individualized curriculum sequencing model (III): Small group instruction. *Journal of The Association for the Severely Handicapped, 1980, 5,* 352–367.

Brown, L., Nietupski, J., & Hamre-Nietupski, S. Criterion of ultimate functioning. In M.A. Thomas (Ed.), *Hey don't forget about me.* Reston, Va.: The Council for Exceptional Children, 1976.

Bry, P.M., & Nawas, M.M. Is reinforcement necessary for the development of a generalized imitation operant in severely and profoundly retarded children? *American Journal of Mental Deficiency, 1972, 76,* 658–667.

Burg, M.M., Reid, D.H., & Lattimore, J. Use of a self-recording and supervision program to change institutional staff behavior. *Journal of Applied Behavior Analysis, 1979, 12,* 363–375.

Burleigh, R.A., & Marholin, D. Don't shoot until you see the whites of his eyes—An analysis of the adverse side effects of verbal prompts. *Behavior Modification, 1977, 1,* 109–122.

Chasey, W.C. Distribution of practice, learning and retention. *Perceptual and Motor Skills, 1976, 43,* 159–164.

Close, D.W., Irvin, L.K., Prehm, H.J., & Taylor, V.E. Systematic correction procedures in vocational skill training of severely retarded individuals. *American Journal of Mental Deficiency, 1978, 83,* 270–275.

Cohen, M.A., Gross, P.J., & Haring, N.G. Developmental pinpoints. In N.G. Haring & L.J. Brown (Eds.), *Teaching the severely handicapped.* New York: Grune & Stratton, 1976.

Cooper, J.O. *Measuring behavior* (2nd ed.). Columbus, Ohio: Charles E. Merrill, 1981.

Cronin, K.A., & Cuvo, A.J. Teaching mending skills to mentally retarded adolescents. *Journal of Applied Behavior Analysis, 1979, 12,* 401–406.

Cuvo, A.J. Validating task analyses of community living skills. *Vocational Evaluation and Work Adjustment Bulletin, 1978, 11,* 13–21.

Cuvo, A.J., Jacobi, L., & Sipko, R. Teaching laundry skills to mentally retarded students. *Education and Training of the Mentally Retarded, 1981, 16,* 54–64.

Dent, H., & Johnson, R. The effects of massed versus distributed practice on the learning of organic familial defectives. *American Journal of Mental Deficiency, 1964, 68,* 533–536.

Egel, A.L. Reinforcer variation: Implications for motivating developmentally disabled children. *Journal of Applied Behavior Analysis,* 1981, *14,* 345–350.

Ellis, N.R., & Distefano, M.K. Effects of verbal urging and praise upon rotary pursuit performance in mental defectives. *American Journal of Mental Deficiency,* 1959, *64,* 486–490.

Favell, J.E., Favell, J.E., & McGimsey, J.F. Relative effectiveness and efficiency of group vs. individual training of severely retarded persons. *American Journal of Mental Deficiency,* 1978, *83,* 104–109.

Ferrari, M., & Harris, S.L. The limits and motivating potential of sensory stimuli as reinforcers for autistic children. *Journal of Applied Behavior Analysis,* 1981, *14,* 339–343.

Foster, R.W. *Camelot Behavioral Checklist.* Lawrence, Kans.: Camelot Behavioral Systems, 1974.

Foxx, R.M., & Azrin, N.H. Dry pants: A rapid method of toilet training children. *Behaviour Research & Therapy,* 1973, *11,* 435–442.

Gardner, W.I., & Brandl, C. Reinforcement conditions and incidental learning in mentally retarded adolescents. *American Journal of Mental Deficiency,* 1967, *72,* 215–219.

Glendenning, N., Adams, G.L., & Sternberg, L. *A comparison of prompt sequences.* Manuscript submitted for publication, 1981.

Gold, M., & Barclay, C. The learning of difficult visual discriminations by the moderately and severely retarded. *Mental Retardation,* 1973, *11,* 9–11.

Gold, M.W., & Pomerantz, D.J. Issues in prevocational training. In M.E. Snell (Ed.), *Systematic instruction of the moderately and severely handicapped.* Columbus, Ohio: Charles E. Merrill, 1978.

Gray, R.M., & Kasteler, J.M. The effects of social reinforcement and training on institutionalized mentally retarded children. *American Journal of Mental Deficiency,* 1969, *74*(1), 50–56.

Greene, B.F., Willis, B.S., Levey, R., & Bailey, J.S. Measuring client gains from staff-implemented programs. *Journal of Applied Behavior Analysis,* 1978, *11,* 395–412.

Guralnick, M.J., & Kravik, M.A. Reinforcement procedures and social behavior in a group context with severely retarded children. *Psychological Reports,* 1973, *32,* 215–219.

Hamilton, J., Allen, P., Stephens, L., & Duvall, E. Training mentally retarded females to use sanitary napkins. *Mental Retardation,* 1969, *7*(1), 40–43.

Haring, N.G., & Bricker, D. Overview of comprehensive services for the severely/profoundly handicapped. In N.G. Haring & L.J. Brown (Eds.), *Teaching the severely handicapped.* New York: Grune & Stratton, 1976.

Haring, N.G., Liberty, K.A., & White, O.R. Rules for data-based strategy decisions in instructional programs: Current research and instructional implications. In W. Sailor, B. Wilcox, & L. Brown (Eds.), *Methods of instruction for severely handicapped students.* Baltimore: Paul H. Brookes, 1980.

Hart, B., & Risley, T. Environmental programming: Implications for the severely handicapped. In H.J. Prehm & S.J. Deitz (Eds.), *Early intervention for the severely handicapped: Programming and accountability.* Eugene: University of Oregon, College of Education, 1976.

Harter, S. Mental age, IQ, and motivational factors in the discrimination learning set performance of normal and retarded children. *Journal of Experimental Child Psychology,* 1967, *5,* 123–141.

Harter, S., Brown, L., & Zigler, E. The discrimination learning of normal and retarded children as a function of penalty conditions and etiology of the retarded. *Child Development,* 1971, *42,* 517–536.

Henderson, S., & McDonald, M. *Step-by-step dressing: A handbook for teaching the retarded to dress.* Champaign, Ill.: Suburban Publications, 1973.

Herbert, E.W., Pinkston, E., Hayden, M., Sajwaj, T., Pinkston, S., Cordua, G., & Jackson, C. Adverse effects of differential parental attention. *Journal of Applied Behavior Analysis,* 1973, *6,* 15–30.

Hogg, J. Normative development and educational program planning for severely educationally subnormal children. In C.C. Kiennan & F.P. Woodford (Eds.), *Behavior modification with the severely retarded.* Amsterdam: Associate Scientific Publishers, 1975.

Holvoet, J., Guess, D., Mulligan, M., & Brown, F. The individualized curriculum sequencing model (II): A teaching strategy for severely handicapped students. *Journal of the Association for the Severely Handicapped,* 1980, *5,* 337–351.

Horner, R.D., & Keilitz, I. Training mentally retarded adolescents to brush their teeth. *Journal of Applied Behavior Analysis,* 1975, *8,* 301–309.

Iwata, B.A., Bailey, J.S., Brown, K.M., Foshee, T.J., & Alpern, M.A. A performance-based lottery to improve residential care and training by institutional staff. *Journal of Applied Behavior Analysis,* 1976, *9,* 417–432.

Johnson, B.F., & Cuvo, A.J. Teaching mentally retarded adults to cook. *Behavior Modification,* 1981, *5,* 187–202.

Kazdin, A.E. *Behavior modification in applied settings.* Homewood, Ill.: Dorsey, 1975.

Kazdin, A.E., & Erickson, L.M. Developing responsiveness to instructions in severely and profoundly retarded residents. *Journal of Behavior Therapy and Experimental Psychiatry,* 1975, *6,* 17–21.

Koegel, R.L., & Rincover, A. Treatment of psychotic children in the classroom environment: I. Learning in a large group. *Journal of Applied Behavior Analysis,* 1974, *7,* 45–59.

Koop, S., Martin, G., Yu, D., & Suthons, E. Comparison of two reinforcement strategies in vocational-skill training of mentally retarded persons. *American Journal of Mental Deficiency,* 1980, *84,* 616–626.

LeLaurin, K., & Risley, T.R. The organization of day-care environments: "Zone" versus "man to man" staff assignments. *Journal of Applied Behavior Analysis,* 1972, *5,* 225–232.

Lemke, H., & Mitchell, R.D. Controlling the behavior of a profoundly retarded child. *American Journal of Occupational Therapy,* 1972, *26,* 261–264.

Lent, J.R. Teaching daily living skills. In J.M. Kauffman & J.S. Payne (Eds.), *Mental retardation: Introduction and personal perspectives.* Columbus, Ohio: Charles E. Merrill, 1975.

Lovitt, T. *Writing & implementing an IEP: A step-by-step plan.* Belmont, Calif.: Pitman Learning, 1980.

Matson, J.L., Marchetti, A., & Adkins, J.A. Comparison of operant- and independence-training procedures for mentally retarded adults. *American Journal of Mental Deficiency,* 1980, *84,* 487–494.

McReynolds, L.V. Reinforcement procedures for establishing and maintaining echoic speech by a non-verbal child. In F.L. Girardeau & J.E. Spradlin (Eds.), *A functional approach to speech and language.* Washington, D.C.: American Speech and Hearing Association, 1970.

Minge, M.R., & Ball, T.S. Teaching of self-help skills to profoundly retarded patients. *American Journal of Mental Deficiency,* 1967, *71,* 864–868.

Mulligan, M., Guess, D., Holvoet, J., & Brown, F. The individualized curriculum sequencing model (I): Implications from research on massed, distributed, or spaced trial training. *Journal of The Association for the Severely Handicapped,* 1980, *5,* 325–336.

Nelson, G.L., Cone, J.D., & Hanson, C.R. Training correct utensil use in retarded children: Modeling vs. physical guidance. *American Journal of Mental Deficiency,* 1975, *80,* 114–122.

Nihira, K., Foster, R., Shellhaas, M., & Leland, H. *AAMD Adaptive Behavior Scale* (rev. ed.). Washington, D.C.: American Association of Mental Deficiency, 1975.

O'Brien, F., & Azrin, N.H. Developing proper mealtime behaviors of the institutionalized retarded. *Journal of Applied Behavior Analysis,* 1972, *5,* 389–399.

Panyan, M., Boozer, H., & Morris, N. Feedback to attendants as a reinforcer for applying operant techniques. *Journal of Applied Behavior Analysis,* 1970, *3,* 1–4.

Pommer, D.A., & Streedbeck, D. Motivating staff performance in an operant learning program for children. *Journal of Applied Behavior Analysis,* 1974, *7,* 217–221.

Popovich, D. *Effective educational and behavioral programming for severely and profoundly handicapped students.* Baltimore: Paul H. Brookes, 1981.

Rimell, P., Stagg, M.M., Hanson, A., Zeeck, J., Moore, J., VanHaecke, D., & Langworthy, R. *The Boulder training model.* Boulder, Mont.: Boulder River School and Hospital, 1977.

Rosenthal, T.L., & Kellogg, J.S. Demonstration versus instruction in concept attainment by mental retardates. *Behaviour Research and Therapy,* 1973, *11,* 299–302.

Sage, H.M. Stimulus generalization among institutionalized mentally retarded persons: An analysis of the effect of subject variables across a variety of skills acquired through operant techniques. *Dissertation Abstracts International,* 1980, *40*(11-A), 5799.

Say it ain't so. *The Association for the Severely Handicapped Newsletter,* 1981, *7*(9), 1.

Schreibman, L. Effects of within-stimulus and extra-stimulus prompting on discrimination learning in autistic children. *Journal of Applied Behavior Analysis,* 1975, *8,* 91–112.

Smith, D.D., & Smith, J.O. Trends. In M.E. Snell (Ed.), *Systematic instruction of the moderately and severely handicapped.* Columbus, Ohio: Charles E. Merrill, 1978.

Smith, P.J. Effects of various reinforcement conditions on acquisitions of motor verbal performance by noninstitutionalized pre-academic trainable mentally retardates. *Dissertation Abstracts International,* 1972, *32*(11-A), 6254–6255.

Snell, M.E. (Ed.). *Systematic instruction of the moderately and severely handicapped.* Columbus, Ohio: Charles E. Merrill, 1978.

Staff of the Teaching Research Infant and Child Center. *The Teaching Research curriculum for moderately and severely handicapped: Self-help and cognitive.* Springfield, Ill.: Charles C. Thomas, 1980.

Striefel, S., & Wetherby, B. Instruction-following behavior of a retarded child and its controlling stimuli. *Journal of Applied Behavior Analysis,* 1973, *6,* 663–670.

Tawney, J.W., Knapp, D.S., O'Reilly, C.D., & Pratt, S.S. *Programmed environments curriculum.* Columbus, Ohio: Charles E. Merrill, 1979.

Teaching Research Staff. *The teaching research curriculum for moderately and severely handicapped* (rev. ed.). Monmouth, Oreg.: Instructional Development, 1979.

Tramontana, J. Social versus edible rewards as a function of intellectual level and socioeconomic class. *American Journal of Mental Deficiency,* 1972, *77,* 33–38.

Trott, M.C. Application of Foxx and Azrin toilet training for the retarded in a school program. *Education and Training of the Mentally Retarded,* 1977, *12,* 336–338.

Turkewitz, H., O'Leary, K.D., & Ironsmith, M. Producing generalization of appropriate behavior through self-control. *Journal of Consulting and Clinical Psychology,* 1975, *43,* 577–583.

Turnbull, A.P., Strickland, B.B., & Brantley, J.C. *Developing and implementing individualized education programs.* Columbus, Ohio: Charles E. Merrill, 1978.

Wabash Center for the Mentally Retarded. *Guide to early developmental training.* Boston: Allyn & Bacon, 1977.

Wahler, R.G. Setting generality: Some specific and general effects of child behavior therapy. *Journal of Applied Behavior Analysis,* 1969, *2,* 239–246.

Wahler, R.G., Winkel, G.H., Peterson, R.G., & Morrison, D.C. Mothers as behavior therapists for their own children. *Behaviour Research and Therapy,* 1965, *3,* 113–124.

Walls, R.T., Crist, K., Sienicki, D.A., & Grant, L. Prompting sequences in teaching independent living skills. *Mental Retardation,* 1981, *19,* 243–246.

Walls, R.T., Ellis, W.D., Zane, T., & Vanderpoel, S.J. Tactile, auditory, and visual prompting in teaching complex assembly tasks. *Education and Training of the Mentally Retarded,* 1979, *14,* 120–130.

Walls, R.T., Zane, T., & Ellis, W.D. Forward and backward chaining, and whole task methods: Training assembly tasks in vocational rehabilitation. *Behavior Modification,* 1981, *5,* 61–74.

Wehman, P. *Curriculum design for the severely and profoundly handicapped.* New York: Human Sciences Press, 1979.

White, O.R., & Haring, N.G. *Exceptional teaching* (2nd ed.). Columbus, Ohio: Charles E. Merrill, 1980.

White, O.R., & Liberty, K.A. Behavioral assessment and precise educational measurement. In N.G. Haring & R.L. Schiefelbusch (Eds.), *Teaching special children.* New York: McGraw-Hill, 1976.

Whitman, T.L., Zakaras, M., & Chardos, S. Effects of reinforcement and guidance procedures on instruction-following behavior of severely retarded children. *Journal of Applied Behavior Analysis,* 1971, *4,* 283–290.

Williams, W., Brown, L., & Certo, N. *Components of instructional programs for severely handicapped students.* Paper presented at the Conference on Education of Severely and Profoundly Retarded Students, New Orleans, April 1975.

Williams, W., Hamre-Nietupski, S., Pumpian, I., McDaniel Marx, J., & Wheeler, J. Teaching social skills. In M.E. Snell (Ed.), *Systematic instruction of the moderately and severely handicapped.* Columbus, Ohio: Charles E. Merrill, 1978.

Wolfe, V.F., & Cuvo, A.J. Effects of within-stimulus and extra-stimulus prompting on letter discrimination by mentally retarded persons. *American Journal of Mental Deficiency,* 1978, *83,* 297–303.

Wright, E.C., Abbas, K.A., & Meredith, C. A study of the interactions between nursing staff and profoundly mentally retarded children. *British Journal of Mental Subnormality,* 1974, *20,* 14–17.

Yoder, P., & Forehand, R. Effects of modeling and verbal cues upon concept acquisition of nonretarded and retarded children. *American Journal of Mental Deficiency,* 1974, *78,* 566–570.

Zigler, E., & Balla, D.A. Impact of institutional experience on the behavior and development of retarded persons. *American Journal of Mental Deficiency,* 1977, *82,* 1–11.

Chapter 7

Motor Skills and Adaptations

Bonnie Utley
University of Kansas

PROBLEMS AND PAST PRACTICES

The problems that confront a teacher of severely and profoundly handicapped students with neuromuscular involvement fall into four categories. The first is the sometimes overwhelming magnitude of the handicapping conditions. Many students exhibit little or no voluntary movement, present combinations of sensory handicaps in addition to their motor and intellectual deficits, and may be fragile with regard to their health.

The second category of problems is the range of service delivery models in operation. A teacher's responsibilities may range from conducting a "holding area" for therapists to that of primary programmer with input from therapy consultants. The latter model is more desirable, being more efficient in terms of the student's time as well as resulting in more consistent programming. To function effectively in this capacity, however, the teacher must be familiar with the terminology and basic procedures of occupational and physical therapy.

The third category of problems relates to the theoretical model adopted by teachers of this population. It is not uncommon for educators to adopt theoretical models from other disciplines as the basis for educational services. An example of this is the impact of behavioral psychology within special education. A similar phenomenon has occurred with regard to services for severely and profoundly handicapped students with neuromuscular involvement. In this case, however, the theoretical models that underlie therapy models (such as neurodevelopmental treatment) lack empirical support. To compound the problem, many educators of this population find application of a treatment model incompatible with systematic instruction. Both models can (and must) exist together to meet the educational needs of this population.

The final category of problems relates to documentation of past practices. With the exception of Shane, Reynolds, and Geary (1977) and Banerdt and

Bricker (1978), there are few published studies that include data demonstrating the effectiveness of motor-related systematic instruction with this population.

The content of this chapter will address some of these problems by providing information on physical management, motor programming, and feeding techniques. Suggested methods of measurement are included to facilitate data collection documenting the effectiveness of systematic instruction within these content areas.

SUGGESTED METHODS

Physical Management

The excellent volume by Finnie (1975) remains the best source for clear, concise, and comprehensive information regarding general physical management of students with neuromuscular involvement. It is strongly recommended that the information in the chapters related to movement, principles of handling, carrying, and dressing be mastered, as they provide guidance for solving most of the practical problems (such as putting on shoes and socks) a teacher might encounter throughout the school day. Refer also to Utley, Holvoet, and Barnes (1977) for information regarding good body mechanics during performance of wheelchair transfers.

A number of preliminary definitions should be tendered here. *Tone* refers to the degree of tension in a muscle. *Hypertonia* is a condition that exists when there is excessive or high tone (increased tightness) present. *Hypotonia* is the condition where little or no muscle tone is evident.

Flexion refers to the bending of a joint and *extension* to the straightening of a joint. *Supine* refers to a postural position where one lays horizontally on the back with face upward. In the *prone* position, one lays horizontally on the stomach with face downward.

Midline positioning is placing the body so that the trunk, arms, and legs are aligned in a symmetrical posture. *Abduction* refers to the lateral movement of the limbs away from the midline of the body. *Adduction* is the lateral movement of the limbs toward the midline of the body.

Many handicapped individuals with neuromuscular deficits exhibit what are termed *primitive reflexes*. In the normal individual these reflexes appear typically early in life and then are integrated into normal movement patterns. Many of the motor techniques that are used to assist a severely or profoundly handicapped student in instructional settings (such as positioning and handling) must be designed so that these primitive reflexes are inhibited and other normal movement patterns are facilitated. Following is a brief description of some of these primitive reflexes.

- *Asymmetrical Tonic Neck Reflex (ATNR)*. Sometimes referred to as the "fencer" position, the reflex is apparent when the individual is lying supine with his or her head turned to one side. The extremities on that side of the body are in extension with the extremities of the opposite side of the body in flexion. This reflex may also be exhibited in the sitting position.
- *Symmetrical Tonic Neck Reflex (STNR)*. When the individual is in the prone position, the arms will extend and legs flex when his or her head is raised. However, simply flexing the neck will cause the opposite effect (flexion in the arms and extension in the legs).
- *Tonic Labyrinthine Neck Reflex*. When the individual is lying supine, the arms and legs show extensor tone. When the individual is lying prone, flexor tone of the extremities dominates.
- *Positive Supporting Reaction*. When held in a vertical position, placed on his or her balls of the feet upon a hard surface, and bounced several times, the individual exhibits increased extensor tone in the legs.
- *Neck Righting Reaction*. When the individual is lying supine and the head is passively turned to one side, the rest of the body turns as one unit.
- *Moro Reflex*. There are two phases to this reflex. In phase 1, upon sudden extension of the individual's head, there is extension of the arms away from the body and the hands open. In phase 2, the arms flex and gradually move toward the midline of the body with the hands closing.

Handling Techniques

Physical management of students with neuromuscular involvement requires a set of skills that are difficult to teach through written materials alone. The physical "give and take" necessary to control excessive (such as spastic) and/or fluctuating (as in athetosis) muscle tone requires sensitivity to minor tonal changes as well as the confidence to use firm support when necessary to "break up" abnormal patterns (as in hyperextension, where the student displays extension beyond that which is necessary to merely straighten a part of his or her body). Because of the difficulty in applying these principles it is recommended that persons completely unfamiliar with tone normalization activities avail themselves of the guidance of a therapist or skilled teacher/ trainer until mastery of these techniques is obtained.

Rotation can be either a handling technique to be used during lifts and carries, an antecedent condition to maximize performance in an instructional program, or a separate target behavior. It should be used for students with high or fluctuating tone. There is *trunk rotation* and *hip rotation*. Both decrease midline hypertonicity by producing movement at the waist. Both also provide relaxation.

Hip rotation can be either a target behavior in itself or a relaxation technique. The student is positioned on his or her back either on a partially deflated ball or a mat. A small pillow may be placed behind the neck to bring the chin slightly forward to the chest and limit the amount of extension induced by the supine position. The teacher flexes the student's hips and knees so an angle of approximately 45 degrees (or less) is formed at the hips. The teacher then grasps the student's legs above the knees in one of two ways. For the student with too much external rotation at the hips, the teacher's forearms should be outside the student's thighs with the teacher's fingers over the top of the student's thighs. A maximum separation of two to three inches between the thighs should be allowed (see Figure 7-1). For students whose legs pull tightly together (adductor spasticity), the opposite arm position should be used with the teacher's forearms inserted between the student's legs to provide more separation between the knees. After positioning the hands the teacher should gently move the child's hips together in a swivel motion in as wide an arc as the child's range of motion will allow. If the student's upper trunk moves with the swivel motion, the teacher can reduce the distance of the arc or, if the student is small, the teacher can attempt to control both legs with one hand and arm and place the other forearm across the student's upper chest to keep both shoulders flat on the supporting surface.

The above procedures should be continued from five to ten minutes. A simple measurement technique can be used before and after the procedures. Measurement consists of gently pushing the legs once to each side as far as they will go without resistance. A record can be made of whether or not both shoulders remain in contact with the supporting surface (a positive response) during these test trials. Measurement of approximately how far the lower knee is above the supporting surface before resistance is encountered can also be done. If hip rotation is a target behavior, the objective may be to have the lower knee touch the supporting surface following a ten-minute session.

Trunk rotation should be used during lifts and carries of small students as an antecedent relaxation technique, and as a target behavior in itself. To be incorporated into lifts and carries the following procedure should be utilized. When a student is lifted, there should be a slight twist at the waist so the hips and shoulders are oriented in slightly opposite directions. Trunk rotation can be incorporated into carries with the student in either a sitting or prone position (see Figure 7-2). The twist at the waist should be maintained if the prone carrying position is used and gentle shaking may also be added if tone increases. The above often results in spontaneous head lifting if the transitions are done carefully.

Figure 7-1 Positions for Hip Rotation

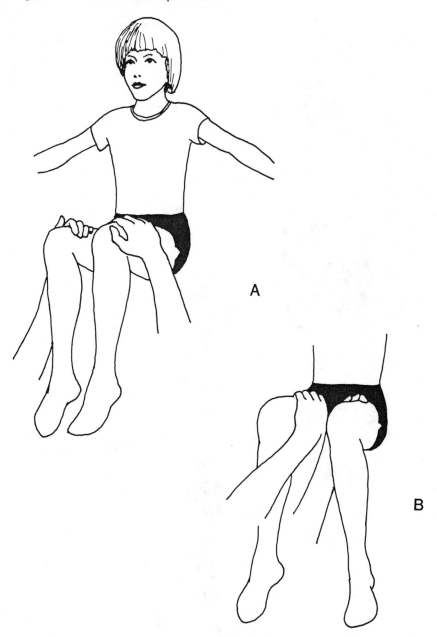

A. For students with too much external rotation at the hips. B. For students with adductor spasticity (the legs pull tightly together).

Figure 7-2 Trunk Rotation in Carrying

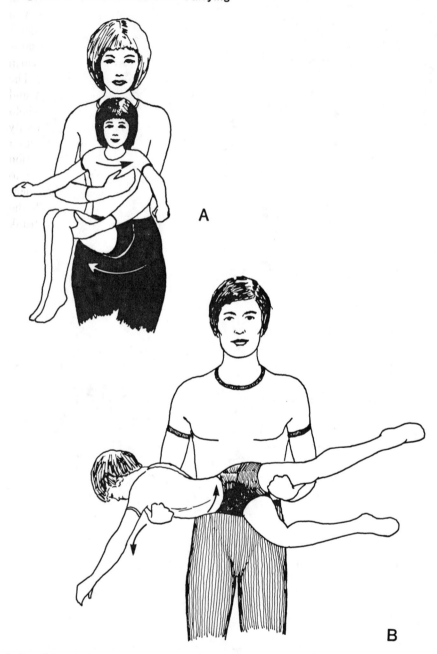

A. In a sitting position. B. In the prone position.

Trunk rotation can also be used in a sitting position for the purpose of relaxation or when trunk rotation is a target behavior. For small students a position astride one or both of the teacher's legs is used. For larger students both student and teacher may sit astride a barrel or roll facing in the same direction. In either case the teacher holds the student by placing one forearm across the student's upper chest and holding him or her near the armpit. The teacher's other forearm extends across the student's lower abdomen and extends over the student's hip bone (see Figure 7-3). The teacher should hold the student close to his or her body and both should be leaning slightly forward. The teacher then twists his or her body at the waist and provides a push in opposite directions at the student's hips and upper body. The direction of the push should alternate every ten to fifteen seconds or after resistance to the movement ceases. The following record can be made if a measurement system is desired. Before and after the session the teacher should provide the push at the shoulders only. The presence of a crease or "wrinkle" in the trunk

Figure 7-3 Trunk Rotation with the Student on the Teacher's Lap

at or slightly above the waist is considered a positive response, as the hips must remain oriented in a forward direction for the crease to appear. This measurement requires that the student's shirt be lifted slightly for ease of observation.

The final use of rotation as a handling technique is in a side-lying position for students who are too large to be easily accommodated in a sitting position. The student should be positioned in side-lying with good body alignment (see the following section). The teacher usually kneels behind the student's back and places one of his or her hands on the student's shoulders and the other on the student's hips. A gentle pushing and pulling movement is then provided with the shoulders and hips alternating in forward and backward directions. A measurement system procedure similar to the one just described can be used to monitor the effectiveness of this technique. A push or pull should be provided at the shoulders only with concomitant observation for a "crease" at the waist.

Another handling technique that normalizes tone and is useful therefore as an antecedent in certain instructional programs is inversion. *Inversion* refers to placement of a student with his or her head lower than the hips. The inverted position stimulates head lifting, strengthens a student's movements against gravity, and encourages extension of the arms and hands in parachute reactions (hands and arms extended downward).

Inversion is usually done either over the teacher's lap or over a beach ball or barrel. If the teacher's lap is used, the student should be positioned prone across the teacher's thighs. This is followed by extension of the teacher's leg nearest the student's head to ensure that the head is lower than the hips (see Figure 7-4). If a beach ball or barrel is used, the student should be placed in a prone position and then the barrel or ball should be rolled forward until it is possible for the student to reach a toy placed on the floor.

Positioning

Positioning, like handling, should be used as an antecedent event in programming for students with neuromuscular involvement. Too many classrooms are conducted according to a schedule which requires only that students be positioned with an attractive toy or mobile within reach. Although there are limited times during the school day when this arrangement is necessary (such as during staff lunch breaks), therapeutic positioning without systematic instruction is insufficient to meet the educational needs of these students. Positioning should be viewed instead as a facilitator to maximum participation in educational tasks. For organizational reasons, however, the remainder of this section will describe general principles of positioning followed by specific

Figure 7-4 The Inverted Position (Head Lower Than Hips)

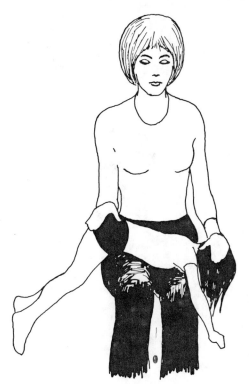

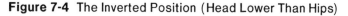

suggestions for each of the most common positions. Specific examples of positioning as an antecedent event are included in the next major section.

The goals of therapeutic positioning are good body alignment and normalization of muscle tone. Correct body alignment helps to lessen the devastating effects seen when certain muscle groups exert disproportionate force on a student's body. This results in spinal curvature and/or deformities at the joints. Normalization of muscle tone permits freedom from tightness (or stability for students with fluctuating tone) and the possibility for more normal movement.

The first step in achieving the goals described above is to observe each individual student in his or her typical position. The following abnormal patterns are commonly seen. In supine, the student's head and shoulders are pushed back into the supporting surface and the hips are extended. The legs are stiff and straight and held tightly together (so tightly that they may cross in a "scissor" pattern). Variations in this pattern may include emergence of an

Figure 7-5 Common Abnormal Patterns

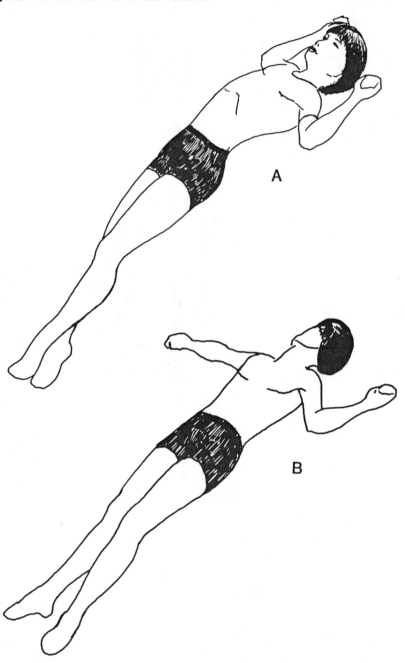

Figure 7-5 continued

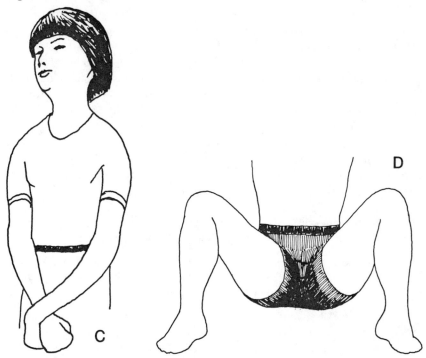

A. Head and shoulders pushed back into the supporting surface with extended hips and "scissored" legs. B. Asymmetrical tonic neck reflex (ATNR). C. Rounded shoulders with extended arms and fisted hands. D. Externally rotated hips with flexion at hips and knees.

asymmetrical tonic neck reflex (ATNR), where turning the head to one side causes extension of the arm and leg on the face side and flexion of the arm and leg on the back side of the head. Also possible is a position where the arms are extended with the shoulders rolled forward and hands tightly clenched. Another common deviation from correct body alignment is seen in the hip position of some students. These students show flexion at the hips and knees with external rotation at the hips. These abnormal patterns are illustrated in Figure 7-5.

Following observation of each student's typical posture, more normal tone can be achieved by *reversing* the student's abnormal patterns and/or movement. Students with extreme deviations in tone (very high or very low) will show little spontaneous movement. The goal for students with excessive tone is positioning that provides relaxation so more normal movement can be initiated. For students with low tone, stability and support should be provided at the shoulders, hips, and throughout the trunk as needed to give a secure base for spontaneous movement. For students who show almost continuous movement (often from one abnormal reflex to another), support and stability at the key points of head/neck, shoulders, and hips are required.

The final general consideration in therapeutic positioning is an analysis of the effects of gravity on a student's body. Despite the resistance encountered in handling students with abnormal tone, they are weak rather than strong in their ability to move against the force of gravity. Gravity, however, can be used to advantage through good positioning. Examples of how these general guidelines operate in various positions follow.

Prone positioning is beneficial for some students as it may encourage development of strength in the shoulder area and spontaneous head lifting. Proper prone positioning requires the following:

- The supporting surface must be of appropriate height. The student should be able to bear weight on either elbows or open hands.

- The student should be placed far enough forward on the supporting surface to allow for weight bearing on the upper extremities. The edge of the supporting surface should be at the student's armpits.

- Good body alignment can be promoted through the placement of long sandbags on both sides of the trunk. Sandbags may also help prevent the student from rolling off the wedge or roll if his or her tone increases.

- Many students show extreme extension in the prone position. This can be alleviated somewhat by correct positioning of the feet. A small roll or sandbag can be placed under the student's ankles to provide slight flexion at the knees. In addition to reducing extension, the roll allows the force of gravity to pull the student's feet into a more normal position and puts a slight and beneficial stretch on the heel chords. See Figure 7-6 for an illustration of prone positioning.

- For students who show extension in the prone position, the typical use of a wedge can be reversed. The student can be placed so that he or she bears weight on the elbows at the low end of the wedge. The student's hips are flexed at an angle less than 90 degrees so weight is also borne on the knees (refer to Figure 7–6 for an illustration). In addition to controlling extension, this use of a wedge may increase head lifting because of the inverted position as well as aid in postural drainage (drainage of congestion from the throat and chest area).

- Gradual transition into the prone position may reduce extension. It is often helpful to place the student on the wedge or roll in a side-lying position first. Relaxation is then induced by gentle shaking and trunk

Figure 7-6 Positioning in Prone

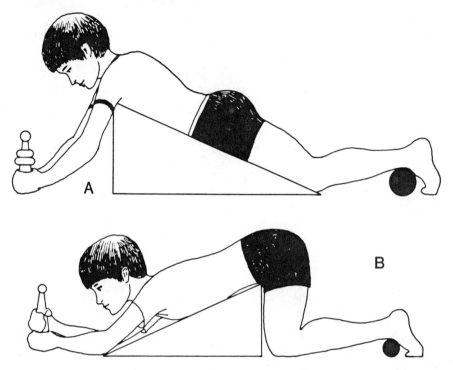

A. Typical use of a wedge. B. Wedge reversed to promote postural drainage, head lifting, and slight weight bearing on lower extremities.

rotation. The arms are gradually extended over the edge of the wedge as the body is rolled slowly over into prone.

Supine positioning is the least desirable position for therapeutic purposes as it is a typical position for many students and one in which little freedom of movement is possible. Supine positioning puts pressure on the back of the skull and may increase extension. The head may also deviate easily from midline, resulting in the appearance of an ATNR. Supine positioning can be used for short periods of the day, however, if the following precautions are taken:

- Flexion of the chin to the chest should be provided to lessen pressure of the skull against the supporting surface and increase the student's visual field.

- Small pillows can be placed under the student's shoulders if they are retracted (pushed back). Addition of the pillows increases the possibility for movement of the upper extremities and hand-to-hand contact.
- Flexion should be provided at the hips and knees and the feet should be as flat as possible on the supporting surface. This adaptation can be provided by placing large sandbags along the student's hips and ankles. Correct supine positioning is shown in Figure 7-7.

Positioning in side-lying is one of the most beneficial positions especially for students who exhibit an ATNR or who have flat chests. In side-lying, gravity prevents deviation of the head from midline (and subsequent emergence of the ATNR) as well as provides a pull to bring the rib cage into its more normal rounded position. The side-lying position promotes relaxation for students with high tone, allows eye-hand activities, and provides good alignment of the spine. The elements of good side-lying positioning are as follows·

- The student's head should be in alignment with the spine. This can be accomplished by use of a small pillow under the head if necessary. The head should also be flexed slightly forward to assist in maintenance of this position and promote visually directed upper extremity movement.
- The lower shoulder should be brought far enough forward to free the elbow from being trapped under the trunk. This allows better alignment of the spine, helps to decrease rolling out of the position, and allows two-handed activities.
- The hips, knees, and ankles should form 90-degree angles to promote relaxation and maintenance of the position.

Figure 7-7 Positioning in Supine

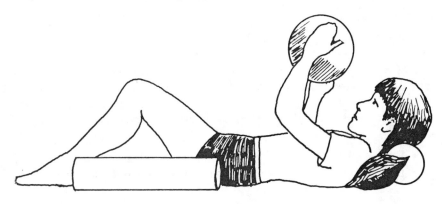

- A small pillow should be placed between the knees and ankles if they are extremely bony. If the student exhibits adductor spasticity (the legs pull tightly together), experimentation with the use of a cushion between the knees may be required. A soft pillow *may* stimulate more adduction and a harder substance (such as Styrofoam covered with cloth) may be used.

- As in prone positioning, the transition into side-lying should be gradual. Intermittent trunk rotation will promote relaxation and prolong the length of time the position is maintained.

The *sitting position* is beneficial for performance of preacademic, fine motor, and communication programming as it helps to provide free movement of the upper extremities. The availability of adapted wheelchairs has increased significantly in the past few years but certain guidelines remain regarding a correct sitting position. The most important guidelines are:

- The depth of the chair seat should be modified to ensure that the student is sitting well up on his or her buttocks rather than on the lumbar vertebrae. The knees and hips should form 90-degree angles and the feet should rest firmly on the floor or a footrest.

- For students with extreme extension, an angle of less than 90 degrees at the hips is often recommended, especially during feeding. With some students, however, the decreased angle at the hips allows the student enough leverage to push into extension with foot pressure on the supporting surface.

- The use of a vest or harness may be necessary for students with inadequate trunk stability. If a chest support is used, an attempt should be made to loosen the straps gradually over time to increase trunk strength.

- The recommended sitting positions for students with too much external rotation at the hips for on-floor sitting are long sitting and side sitting to alternate sides (see Figure 7-8).

- The recommended sitting positions for students with too much internal rotation at the hips and adductor spasticity for on-floor sitting are ring sitting, tailor (or Indian style) sitting, and side-sitting (see Figure 7-8).

- For students with low tone, sitting on a wooden box or stool of an appropriate height (feet flat on the floor) is recommended to increase trunk control (see Figure 7-8). Any of the other sitting positions are also appropriate for these students unless there is external rotation at the hips, in which case long-sitting and side-sitting to alternate sides are preferred.

Figure 7-8 Positioning in Sitting

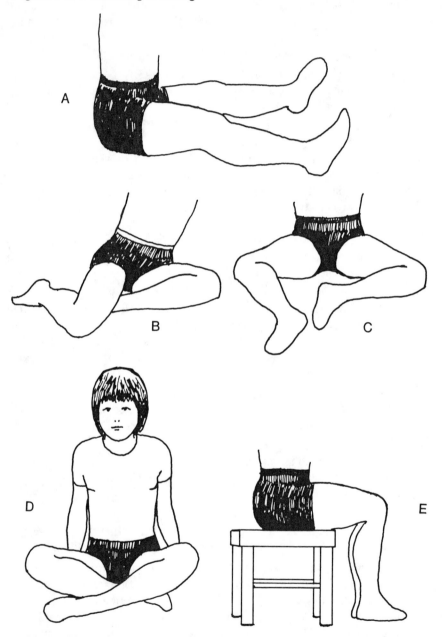

A. Long sitting. B. Side sitting. C. Ring (circle) sitting. D. Tailor (Indian style) sitting.
E. Sitting on a low stool.

- For students positioned in a corner chair, the same guidelines apply regarding seat depth and vests. An additional suggestion related to corner chairs is the use of dowel rods to assist in proper hip alignment. For students with external rotation at the hips, padded dowel rods can be placed on the outside of the legs to encourage long sitting and extension at both knees and hips. For students with adductor spasticity, the dowel rods should be placed between the legs to encourage more abduction (see Figure 7-9).

The availability of prone boards has greatly simplified and increased the use of the *standing position*. The benefits of standing are many, including improved bowel and bladder function, a decrease in flexion contractures (permanent shortening of a muscle-tendon unit) at the hips, knees, and ankles, and prevention of brittle long leg bones. The most important benefit of the standing position is a possible decrease in the incidence of hip dislocation. Measurement and fitting for a prone board is usually completed by a therapist

Figure 7-9 Use of Dowel Rods in a Corner Chair

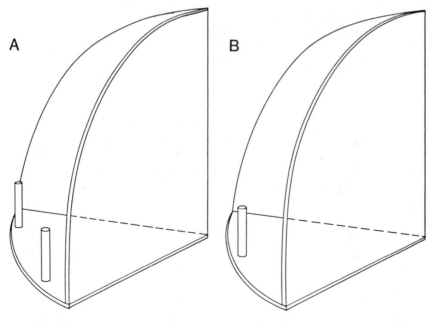

A. Dowels outside the legs to encourage long sitting (for students with too much external rotation at the hips). B. Dowel between the legs to separate legs held tightly together.

or an adaptive equipment salesperson. The following are some guidelines that govern positioning in standing.

- The legs should be separated slightly with the hips in alignment (as indicated by both feet pointing straight ahead).
- The knees should be flexed slightly.
- Both feet should be flat and parallel to one another.

These positioning guidelines are meant to be applied in a trial and error fashion. The distribution of tone and combination of abnormal reflex activity varies tremendously from student to student. Many of the techniques must be used in combination to meet the varied needs of this population. The presence of good body alignment and normalized muscle tone should be the final factor in determining whether a particular position or handling technique is appropriate for an individual student.

There are three other physical management skills that are extremely valuable in providing quality services to severely and profoundly handicapped students. The first two are co-contraction and joint approximation. The appropriate use of these techniques requires well-developed judgment regarding good body alignment. Refer to Buttram and Brown (1977) for information on these techniques as well as to a therapist for supervised practice in their application. The third physical management skill is the development of equilibrium and righting reactions. Refer to Bobath and Bobath (1972), Buttram and Brown (1977), and Johnson (1978) for theoretical information and illustrated instructions on the appropriate use of these techniques.

Motor Programming

This section is limited to suggested strategies for programming gross and fine motor development. Refer to Hamre-Nietupski, Stoll, Holtz, Fullerton, Ryan-Flottum, and Brown (1977); Reichle and Yoder (1979); Shane (1979); Sailor, Guess, Goetz, Schuler, Utley, and Baldwin (1980); Guess (1980); and Sternberg, Battle, and Hill (1980) for information regarding issues and strategies related to assessment and training of language/communication skills. Refer to Kahn (1978); Robinson and Robinson (1978); Switzky, Woolsey-Hill, and Quoss (1979); and Karlan (1981) for information regarding issues and strategies related to assessment and training of cognitive development.

Assessment

Assessment is one of the basics of program development. At this time, however, there are no completely satisfactory assessment models within the area of motor development for this population. Individual patterns of neuro-muscular involvement and the presence of sensory deficits make reliance on a single assessment instrument impossible. No clear resolution of the conflict between the developmental and functional/remedial models has yet been made. This is due, at least in part, to individual factors such as the student's age and his or her present and future home and school environments, which should determine priority skills for assessment and intervention. The presence of noncompliant behavior also complicates assessment because of the diffi-culty in discriminating which skills a student *will not* do from those he or she *cannot* do. The solution to this dilemma lies in synthesizing portions of a number of assessment models into one in which the following factors are considered:

- the student's age
- the student's present and future school and home environments
- parental priorities
- noncompliance and/or other behavior problems
- gross developmental level in all areas
- the presence of a functional operant response to be used in language/cognitive programming

Refer to York and Williams (1977); Guess, Horner, Utley, Holvoet, Maxon, Tucker, and Warren (1978); Bricker and Campbell (1980); and Umbreit (1980) for information that should contribute to the development of a functional, highly individualized assessment model.

Teaching Strategies

There are a number of systematic instructional strategies available to teachers of severely and profoundly handicapped students. Many of these are described in Falvey, Brown, Lyon, Baumgart, and Schroeder (1980) and Liberty, Haring, and Martin (1981). There is an additional strategy that is of particular use in programming skill acquisition for this population. The strategy requires both precise task analysis and systematic fading of prompts. There are two applications of this strategy. The first is used for training active motor responses (such as reaching). The motor response is task analyzed until the smallest final component of the behavior is determined. The student is then put through all earlier steps in the task analysis and only the final segment is required. An example is a program to teach the response of reaching toward and touching a toy. The student is positioned to promote maximum freedom of movement. The teacher grasps the student's dominant arm and provides upward support against gravity. The arm is then extended until contact with the toy is made. This is consequated enthusiastically. The teacher then extends the arm to the toy a second time but stops within one-half to one inch of contact. The student is required to extend his or her arm slightly to touch the toy in order to receive reinforcement. If a correct response is not made, the distance is shortened even further until an active, correct response is made. The amount of prompting decreases in one-half- to one-inch increments over a series of training sessions as the student improves.

There are two differences between the strategy just described and what is more commonly done. This strategy requires that each trial end with an active response on the part of the student rather than his or her being put through the correct response as a consequence for failure to perform correctly. The latter may result in the student receiving gradually increasing amounts of reinforcement for passive performance.

The second difference between this strategy and more typical programming is that the student has an opportunity to experience the correct response before any actual effort is required. For students with little voluntary movement, motivation, or contingency awareness, this practice trial may clarify the contingent relationship necessary for reinforcement to be forthcoming.

The second application of this strategy is in training behaviors that are static (that is, require the student to maintain a position). An example is in training balance in standing. If the goal is ten seconds of independent standing, the first step in the program consists of positioning the student in standing and providing support (downward pressure at the hips or shoulders) for nine to nine and one-half seconds. Support is lessened at that point and a record is made of whether the student maintains independent standing for one-half to one second. As that criterion is reached, support is provided less and less over a series of sessions (decreasing in one-second increments).

This strategy has been effective with a number of passive severely handicapped students. It requires careful measurement of student performance, however, to make decisions regarding when a change in the level of physical prompting is appropriate.

Measurement

Precise, daily measurement should accompany systematic instruction to give direction to the teacher regarding the success/failure of the procedures, for accountability reasons, and to reinforce the teacher by providing evidence of small improvements in behavior.

Two types of measurement are possible. The first is *direct* measurement of the behavior as it is occurring. Examples of direct measurement include *percent correct* or number correct (*frequency*) out of a set number of opportunities to respond, *duration,* counting the *number of prompts,* and recording the *levels of assistance* (verbal cue, gesture, etc.) required before the student makes a correct response. *Indirect* measurement is used when a particular technique is conducted for a specified time period and a record is made as to whether or not the technique produced the desired result (as with measurement of the presence or absence of a "crease" at the waist following trunk rotation). Examples of both types of measurement accompany the suggested gross and fine motor training strategies that follow.

Gross Motor: Head Control

Initial head control is typically taught in either (or both) the prone or supine positions. In the prone position, the student is placed over a wedge or roll and a noisemaker or attractive toy is used to encourage head lifting. In the supine position, the child is pulled to a sitting position and the presence or absence of head "lag" (head not lifted as trunk is raised) is noted. Both procedures have some merit, but more systematic instruction is needed for many students to acquire this skill. The following strategies have proven to be effective in the development of head control.

> *Head Control Strategy 1.* The student is placed in a prone position over a wedge or roll. His or her head is lifted gently into alignment with the spinal column with the teacher's less dominant hand. Control of the head is lessened gradually and replaced by gentle tapping of the student's forehead if the head begins to fall forward. Reinforcement in the form of verbal praise and/or a more tangible reward such as music (for example, a radio with the volume preset and controlled with an on/off switch) is used *only* for those segments of time during which the student exerts effort to maintain head erect behavior.

This strategy differs from more traditional methods because verbal encouragement and tangible items (potential reinforcers) are used only as consequent rather than as antecedent events (that is, the student receives attention when he or she is performing the behavior *not* prior to performing it). Another difference from the traditional strategy is that the student is provided with an opportunity to experience the "feel" of a correct response rather than having to experiment with other responses (such as head turning) that may be undesirable. Finally, it is easier to maintain a head lift than it is to lift the head from a lower position. The latter often results only in extension without true head lifting.

An appropriate measurement technique for this strategy is to count the number of times (out of ten, for example) that head lifting is maintained for more than three seconds following removal of support. As duration of head lifting consistently exceeds three seconds, another measure, such as mean duration of head lifting across ten opportunities, can be used.

Head Control Strategy 2. This strategy uses trunk rotation and side-sitting (see Figure 7-10). The height of the teacher's knee may be modified during this procedure as needed. If the student's head and neck hyperextend (that is, fall or extend backward to rest on his

---

Figure 7-10 Position for Head Control Strategy 2

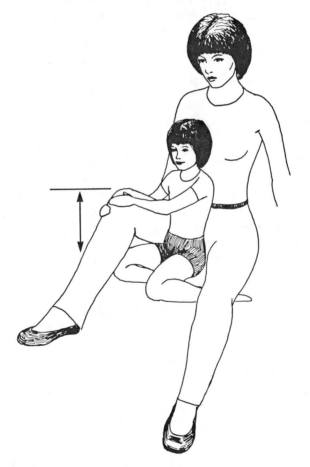

Trunk rotation and side sitting. Teacher should modify height of knee (indicated by arrow) to control position of head.

or her back), the teacher's knee should be lowered. If the student's head falls forward, the knee should be elevated slightly. If extreme extension occurs, the trainer's leg can be gently bounced to provide relaxation.

An appropriate measurement technique for this strategy is to measure total duration out of a ten-minute period in which head erect behavior occurred.

Gross Motor: Sitting

Traditional training in many of the gross motor milestones consists of placing the student in position (side-sitting, for example), withdrawing support, and measuring the duration of independent performance. It is not uncommon for the student to end a trial by falling over when his or her limit is reached; nor is it uncommon for reinforcement to be delivered after the student ceases independent performance. To correct the above misapplication of behavioral principles, a *changing criterion* (Hall & Box, 1975) should be used. Use of the changing criterion design first requires baseline measurement of the behavior until stable performance is documented. The mean performance should be determined and a level slightly above the mean should be the goal for the initial step of training. For example, if mean duration levels of sitting behavior across four days of baseline are 6, 5, 7, and 5 seconds, respectively, the mean is 4.6 seconds and an appropriate goal for training is 6 seconds. Each training trial for this step would consist of placing the child in the appropriate position, withdrawing support, and starting the stopwatch. Verbal and/or tangible reinforcement would be provided during the time the behavior is performed and cease if the student stops performing. When the goal of 6 seconds is reached, the trial would be *interrupted* by the teacher by reintroducing support and/or hugging the student, and the like. After an interval of rest the student would be repositioned and another trial would begin. As soon as the goal is met 80 percent or more of the trials in three out of five sessions, the next training step with a slightly higher criterion would begin.

Programming according to a changing criterion design prevents accidental reinforcement of the termination of the behavior and the punishing consequence of having the student fall when he or she tires. Collection of baseline data is critical to the success of this procedure as the training goals (especially the initial one) must be within the student's capability. The changing criterion design can be applied to training any of the motor milestones in which increased duration is the goal. This approach forms the basis for Sitting Strategy 1.

Sitting Strategy 1. The student is placed in a side-sitting position with some trunk rotation provided by a slight twist at the waist. His or her arms should be extended and weight bearing should occur on open hands. Placement of the hands in relation to the body should be adjusted until sitting balance is obtained in as upright a position as possible. The legs should be semiflexed at the hips and knees. When secure sitting balance is obtained, support is gradually withdrawn and timing of independent performance is begun. Reinforcement should accompany correct sitting behavior. When the goal is reached, the student's body should be supported, a brief rest period should be provided, and the trial should be repeated to the opposite side.

Measurement during the changing criterion design differs from baseline to training conditions. Baseline data are used to establish initial training goals and consist of mean duration of target behavior per session. Training steps consist of a preset goal, and a running record of each trial is made. The percentage of trials that meet or exceed the goal is computed. Changes in the criterion are made based on these data. A partially complete data sheet showing this progression is presented in Exhibit 7-1.

In programming for sitting or any of the other "static" motor milestones (kneeling, standing, etc.) it is important to program two other skills concurrently. The first is the set of *transition behaviors* that surrounds the milestone. In this case the transition behaviors are assuming side-sitting from side-lying

---

Exhibit 7-1 Partially Completed Data Sheet Showing Progression of Data for Changing Criterion Design

Student: __D. Miller__   Program: __Side-sitting (Propped both arms)__

Teacher: __K. Ferrel__   Next Program: __Side-sitting (Propped one arm)__

	Baseline				Training Step 1 Goal 6 Secs.					Training Step 2 Goal 8 Secs.					
Date:	8/24	8/25	8/26	8/28	8/31	9/1	9/2	9/3	9/4	9/7	9/8	9/10	9/11	9/14	9/15
Trial 1	7	5	7	4	5	5	6	6	6	6	9	5	8	8	10
Trial 2	5	4	8	6	6	4	5	5	6	8	10	9	8	7	9
Trial 3	6	6	5	4	7	7	5	7	7	9	8	10	11	10	8
Trial 4	5	4	7	6	8	6	7	8	8	8	8	8	6	9	11
Trial 5	7	6	8	5	6	7	6	6	7	6	6	6	7	8	9
x̄	6	5	7	5	80%	60%	60%	80%	100%	60%	80%	60%	60%	80%	100%

positions and moving from side-sitting to side-lying positions. Increasing duration of a behavior without training in transitional skills does little to increase the student's overall motor development and independence. The second related skill is *protective reactions* (that is, the ability to "catch" oneself if balance is lost) in that position. Protective reactions would be taught concurrently with the example outlined in Strategy 1 because they develop normally in conjunction with or just after propping in that position.

Sitting Strategy 2. The student is placed in a sitting position facing away from the teacher with his or her legs abducted over one or both of the trainer's thighs. The student's back should be within two to three inches of the teacher's trunk. The student's hips and knees should be flexed at angles of 90 degrees or less and the feet should rest firmly on the floor. Support (downward pressure) is initially given at the shoulders with the shoulders rounded slightly forward. When balance is obtained and the head is in alignment with the spine, support is moved (one hand at a time) from the shoulders down to the hip bones, where downward pressure is again applied. The teacher should gently bounce the student on his or her legs if extension begins. If extension is severe, the teacher should lean forward and push the student's trunk forward with his or her trunk (providing flexion at the hips) until extension subsides.

Gross Motor: Hands and Knees Position (All Fours)

The hands and knees position is beneficial for development of arm and shoulder strength and is necessary for the development of creeping.

All Fours Strategy 1. These procedures train the transition from side-sitting to the all fours position. The procedure begins with the student in side-sitting position with arms extended and weight bearing on open hands. The hand position should be at approximately a 45-degree angle to the student's midline. When the student is stable in this position the following instructional/task analysis is performed.

1. Gently move the student's hands two to three inches from his or her initial position away from the student.
2. Slide the underneath leg slightly back and away from the hands and move the top leg slightly forward.
3. Slip one hand under the student's lower hip and elevate the hips three to four inches.
4. Continue upward support of the hips but add a tapping movement, which is repeated two to three times.

5. Slide the underneath leg back and away from the hands and move the top leg slightly forward again, making sure that the hips and knees remain flexed at approximately 90 degrees.
6. Continue tapping the hips in an upward direction until weight is borne on the knees.
7. Make adjustments of body alignment until the legs are parallel and weight is borne on all four extremities.
8. Maintain this position for 20 to 30 seconds. Reinforce with music or an active toy.
9. Repeat the steps above in reverse order to return the student to the side-sitting position.

Measurement of this skill can consist of counting the number of voluntary adjustments the student makes to bear weight during performance of the analysis. The number of taps required before the student assumes the all fours position can also be counted.

All Fours Strategy 2. This strategy requires the use of an inflatable cylinder. The cylinder should be wide enough in diameter to fit underneath the student's trunk and provide slight support when he or she is in the all fours position. The procedure begins with the cylinder in place on the mat or floor and the student tall kneeling (trunk extended vertically) next to it with the teacher behind him or her. The teacher grasps the student's arms just below the shoulders and extends them (by shaking them gently if necessary) at an angle of approximately 45 degrees above shoulder level. The teacher then brings the student forward and down until weight is borne on open hands and the student is supported throughout the trunk by the cylinder. The position should be maintained for 20 to 30 seconds with reinforcement provided by music or an active toy. During this interval the teacher should produce downward pressure, alternating between pressure at the shoulders and hips.

Measurement should consist of recording whether or not the student maintains the position for the desired length of time. Phases of the program should be outlined, and inflation and downward pressure should both be faded over time.

Gross Motor: The Progression to Upright Posture

The following procedures outline the steps leading to upright posture. Before this progression is begun, the student should be able to tall kneel for short periods and have adequate protective reactions.

Strategy. The student should be in the all fours position with the teacher behind him or her. When stability is obtained on all fours (by providing short episodes of downward pressure at the shoulders and hips if necessary), the pelvis should be shifted slightly to the right side so weight is borne on the right knee. The left leg is placed in a squat position so that the left foot is flat on the floor. The teacher's left leg should be placed outside of the student's leg to provide support. The pelvis should be shifted to the left so weight is borne on that leg. A one- to two-second pause should occur to see if the right leg spontaneously adopts the squat position. If not, the right leg should be prompted into that position. Another pause of a few seconds should occur for balance to be obtained in the full squat position. To facilitate this the student's weight should be forward of the body axis. The teacher then either offers his or her hand for support at the upper extremities if the student has good voluntary grasp or provides support at the trunk just below the armpits. A slight lift is provided and the student should rise to standing.

Gross Motor: Simulated Standing

Many students are too involved to bear weight in the normal fashion. The benefits of weight bearing (particularly proper hip formation) can be provided by a simulated standing program.

Strategy. A large, heavy barrel is needed for this program. The barrel is preferable to a therapy ball because only front/back movement is needed. The student should be placed in a prone position over the top of the barrel with his or her arms extended or flexed so weight is borne on the elbows. The teacher kneels behind the student and separates the legs slightly (abduction) with external rotation at the hips. The feet are supported at the arches by having them rest in the palms of the teacher's hands. A 90-degree angle should be formed at the ankles. Relaxation is produced by slowly rolling the barrel forward and back. When the student is relaxed, he or she is rolled back toward the teacher until some of the student's body weight is borne on the teacher's hands. This position should be maintained for 20 to 30 seconds or until tone increases, in which case the barrel is rolled forward again and relaxation is provided. The barrel can be rolled far enough back to allow the student to bear weight on the floor if he or she is capable of that behavior. If this latter adaptation is used, the student's weight should be shifted gradually from the teacher's hands to the floor.

This procedure should be carried out for an eight- to ten-minute period. The total length of time the student bears weight should be recorded.

Gross Motor: Walking

Some severely or profoundly handicapped students are able to walk with support but lose their balance easily because of instability in the trunk. The following procedures are designed to increase trunk strength and balance but are carried out just prior to the time at which walking is required.

> *Strategy.* Place the student on a barrel so that his or her legs straddle it. The teacher straddles the barrel behind the student and places his or her hands on the student's hips to provide support. The barrel is rolled to the left approximately six to eight inches. The student should arch his or her trunk so that the shoulders move to the right. The arch should occur within five to ten seconds. The barrel is returned to its original position and upright alignment of the trunk should follow. The barrel is then rolled to the right six to eight inches and the student should arch his or her trunk again but with the shoulders moving to the left. The barrel is returned to its original position and the entire sequence is repeated five times.

Two measures of the effectiveness of this procedure are possible. The first is a record of whether the student arches within five to ten seconds of each shift in space. The second is a count of the number of times the student loses his or her balance while walking a certain distance (such as 30 feet) immediately following the procedures.

Fine Motor Development

Adequate fine motor performance requires that the student be positioned well to normalize tone as much as possible and to control reflex activity. Control of the hands is dependent on stability and control in the upper extremity joints closer to the trunk of the body (that is, the elbow and shoulder joints). Training fine motor behavior, therefore, should begin with gross arm movements and gradually move to more refined responses.

Fine Motor: Reaching

The student should be positioned with a table or wheelchair tray placed slightly above waist level. The teacher should face the student and cup one of his or her hands around the shoulder joint of the student's preferred upper extremity to provide stability and direct the arm toward midline. The teacher's hand should also provide a slight lift to offset the force of gravity and make arm movements easier. The teacher then positions his or her other hand (or toy, functional object, etc.) within one to two inches of the student's hand. The teacher cues the student to touch the stimulus and pauses. If the student touches the stimulus within five to ten seconds, he or she is reinforced. If he or she fails to respond correctly, the teacher should move the student's arm (at the shoulder) through the correct response, back to its original position, and then present the cue again. The student must make some small movement toward the stimulus at this point to be reinforced.

Measurement should be divided into phases according to the distance the student must move. A weighted scoring system can be used that gives the student two points for touching after the initial cue, one point after the prompt and cue have been presented again, and zero points if the student fails to respond. As the number of points earned is equal to or above 80 percent of the total points possible, the required distance should increase.

Fine Motor: Grasping

The same position as was described in the previous strategy is used. The student's preferred upper extremity should be flexed at the elbow and rest on the wheelchair tray or table. If the student has high tone, a crayon, pencil, or something similar should be inserted into a cone-shaped cylinder. This will assist in normalizing tone in the hand and arm. If the student has low tone, a soft material such as foam should cover the object to be held. The object is then inserted into the student's hand and the teacher should hold the student's hand around it for four to four-and-one-half seconds. The teacher's grasp loosens and the student should maintain the grasp for one-half to one second. The teacher should offer support again and put the student through a scribbling response as a consequence for grasping. The amount of teacher prompting should be systematically faded over time.

Measurement is again divided into phases dependent on the amount of teacher prompting. The level of prompting decreases in one-half to one-second increments over time as an 80 percent criterion at each level is reached.

Fine Motor: Release

The procedures to promote release occur in two stages. The first is slight extension at the elbow with simultaneous cueing to release. A pause of a few seconds is given. If extension at the elbow does not produce release, a second procedure should follow. This procedure requires gentle bending of the hand downward at the wrist joint to produce extension of the fingers and release.

Measurement of release can also be done with a weighted scoring system. The student can be given two points for releasing the object following extension at the elbow, one point after bending at the wrist, and zero points if the object must be removed manually.

Feeding Techniques

The poor coordination seen in students with neuromuscular involvement is not restricted to overall body patterns but is also seen in the oral musculature. Abnormal or primitive oral patterns require that systematic feeding techniques be used to ensure adequate intake of nutrients (both liquid and solid) during the six-hour school day.

The feeding responsibilities that an individual teacher has depend on the service delivery model in operation. A basic understanding of the feeding process, however, is necessary for all professionals who serve this population.

Assessment

The expertise of an occupational, physical, or speech therapist is critically important during feeding assessment. This is due to the many factors that need to be considered, including assessment of oral reflexes and oral hypersensitivity, responses to texture, and the like. The staffing available for services to physically handicapped students varies from program to program, but almost all programs have access to therapists for initial assessment. In those rare instances where consultant services are not available, the teacher should contact the nearest university medical center (or similar agency) for a comprehensive feeding evaluation.

Although feeding assessment should be completed by a therapist, teachers should know the areas to be assessed and be able to assist in the process (and periodic re-evaluation) if necessary. Refer to Farber (1974), Schmidt (1976), and Campbell (1979a) for assessment guidelines. In general the following areas should be evaluated:

- overall muscle tone
- abnormal or primitive total body reflexes
- gross motor developmental level
- abnormal or primitive oral reflexes
- feeding patterns (such as tongue movements)

Positioning for Feeding   .

During the feeding process the student should be seated upright with hips and knees at 90-degree angles and the feet flat. The head position is important in all therapeutic positioning because of the role it plays in controlling extensor tone and abnormal reflex activity. The head position becomes even more important during the feeding process because of the danger of choking and aspiration of food. The head must be in midline with slight flexion of the chin to the chest to promote an active swallow. For students who lack even minimal head control the correct head position should be provided by attachments on an adapted chair.

In some instances (for example, a very large student with a heavy head) positioning in a fully upright position can be difficult. A slight backward tilt of the supportive equipment may help to stabilize the head. If the tilted position is used, a small roll must be placed behind the student's neck to provide slight flexion of the chin to the chest. This is necessary to avoid the hazards of "bird feeding." Refer to Finnie (1975) for illustrated examples of positions that are appropriate for feeding infants and children.

Position of the Feeder

Three feeding positions are commonly seen. The first and most common position is face-to-face with the student. In the face-to-face position, jaw control (and/or manipulation of the oral musculature) is provided from the front (see Figure 7-11). This position is beneficial for feeding students who tend to extend. In this case, the face-to-face position permits the feeder to rest the side of his or her wrist and forearm of the hand providing jaw control on the student's sternum at midline. If extension begins, the feeder can put firm pressure on the sternum with his or her forearm in combination with gentle shaking from side to side to normalize tone. Pressure on the sternum tends to bring the student's chin down to his or her chest thereby interrupting the extension pattern. The face-to-face position also permits eye contact and is conducive to speech-building activities. The feeder should sit very close to the student, however, and maintain an upright sitting position to minimize strain on the lower back.

The second possible position for the feeder is next to the student, with jaw control provided from the side by the feeder's less preferred hand (see Figure 7-11). This position is *not* recommended for students with an ATNR unless the feeder's hand preference and student's ATNR side are such that the feeder can be positioned on the side *opposite* that of the student's predominant head turn. The side-by-side position is less conducive to social interaction during the feeding process, and the feeder may have difficulty seeing during use of the intervention strategies. It is, however, the preferred position for cup drinking.

The third position for the feeder is to sit directly behind the student with both feeder and student facing a mirror. Jaw control is provided from the side by the feeder's less preferred hand and intervention strategies and assistance

Figure 7-11 Positions for Providing Jaw Control

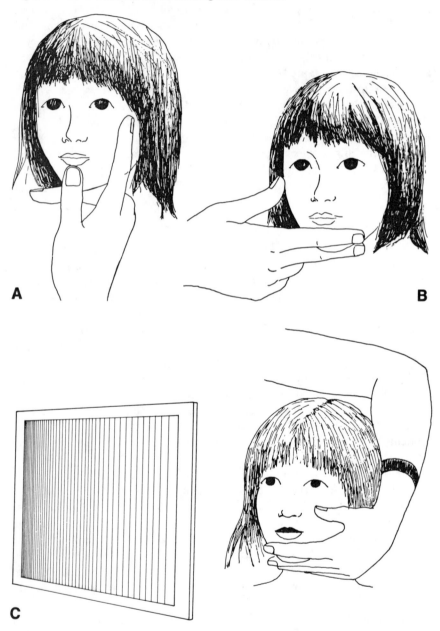

A. Jaw control from the front. B. Jaw control from the side. C. Jaw control from the back with both teacher and student facing a mirror.

in self-feeding are provided by the feeder's dominant hand (see Figure 7-11). This position is usually used for students who have head control and whose wheelchair or other positioning device does not obstruct the feeder's observation of the student in the mirror.

The food position should also be considered. The food should be placed within easy reach of the feeder so the spoon can be refilled without interruption of jaw control.

Intervention Strategies for Feeding Problems

This section describes specific intervention strategies for several of the most common feeding problems. Refer also to Mueller (1972, 1975); Farber (1974); Campbell (1979b); Utley, Holvoet, and Barnes (1977); Morris (1977); Connor, Williamson, and Siepp (1978); and Messina, Sternat, and Lyon (1978) for additional information regarding intervention strategies.

The importance of team service delivery cannot be overemphasized. Selection of priority target behaviors and appropriate intervention strategies should be a team process with input from a variety of professionals as well as parents.

Most students will present only a portion of the problems that these strategies are designed to remediate. Also, some of the strategies (such as correct spoon presentation) are appropriate interventions for a variety of feeding difficulties. Therefore, a combination of strategies appropriate for the problems presented by each individual student must be selected.

Precautions

There are a number of precautions that should be considered prior to and during the feeding process.

- The medical information available on each of the students should be scrutinized. Look for information regarding the presence of food allergies as well as any mention of anatomical deformities in the respiratory or digestive systems that could interfere with the feeding process.
- Each student should be assessed for the ability to breathe through his or her nose prior to implementation of any intervention strategies. This is done by holding a small mirror directly beneath the student's nostrils to see if two distinct "clouds" appear during exhalation of air. Jaw control should be used during this procedure if the student has a habitually open mouth. If clouding fails to occur the student should be examined by a physician to see if mouth breathing is a habit or whether there are anatomical reasons for failure to breathe through the nose.

For students who are habitual mouth breathers and for those with obvious colds and congestion, jaw control and other procedures that interfere with mouth breathing should be used only for 15 to 20 seconds.

- Many students respond to ingestion of dairy products with additional mucus production. For this reason, end each meal with a glass of water or tart juice to rinse milky residues left in the mouth.

- Students with inadequate lip closure and/or tongue thrust are messy to feed. Food is often expelled from the mouth and runs down the chin. Care must be taken to *blot* rather than wipe the facial area every three to four bites. A soft, absorbent terry cloth material should be used. Wiping the facial area may elicit oral reflex activity and mouth opening.

- Most students with feeding problems are given a diet of pureed foods. There is little support for this practice as most students are able to tolerate soft, lumpy foods. Increasing texture may in fact result in development of more mature feeding patterns. Another practice is that of combining all foods of a meal into a blender and mixing milk into all pureed foods. Both practices should be eliminated; the first because it is dehumanizing to eliminate variety from the student's diet, and the second because all foods become mucus producing following the addition of milk.

- In addition to increasing texture, an attempt should be made to control temperature of the food. Extremes in temperature should be avoided but electric warming bowls should be used when appropriate to maintain food at a palatable temperature during lengthy feeding sessions.

- The use of verbal instructions should be avoided during the initial stages of intervention in the feeding process. Many students respond to verbal instructions with increased tone as this is a side effect of increased effort. For example, refrain from saying "Open your mouth" to a student with clenched teeth. Instead, use one of the intervention strategies to open clenched teeth in conjunction with a description of the student's response to that strategy (such as "Good, your mouth is open now"). As the student gains voluntary control over his or her oral musculature and becomes familiar with the feelings associated with the verbal labels, the use of verbal instructions can be increased.

The following description is of two successful strategies that produce *mouth opening* in students with clenched teeth. Both utilize upward pressure on the lower jaw. Prior to their use, however, close observation is necessary to determine if the jaws are aligned as much as possible. If the jaws are not aligned (that is, if the teeth do not meet evenly and/or the lower jaw protrudes forward, to either side, or is retracted), gentle manipulation of the lower jaw to bring about proper alignment should be done before either strategy is used.

When proper alignment is observed, firm pressure upward is applied for 15 to 20 consecutive seconds; *or,* a series of three or four firm upward movements separated by a few seconds each should be used (see Figure 7-12 for position to provide upward pressure). This procedure is also helpful for releasing teeth clamped on a utensil because of a hyperactive bite reflex.

The spoon should be filled so the food is heaped in the first third of the bowl of the spoon. This will allow easy removal of food from the spoon. The filled spoon should be placed on the first third of the tongue. This is especially important for students with a hyperactive gag reflex. As the spoon is placed on the tongue, firm downward pressure is applied and maintained for three or four seconds to control tongue thrust and to encourage lip closure around the spoon for removal of the food.

The spoon should be removed horizontally *without* upward movement of the handle (this will prevent removal of food from the spoon by the student's teeth). If the student's lips do not spontaneously assist in food removal, a series of exercises should be completed prior to each of the first ten bites of every

---

Figure 7-12 Position of the Teacher's Hand to Provide Upward Pressure for Mouth Opening

meal. These prefeeding exercises are outlined in the section on lip closure. For the remainder of the meal (and for older students whose upper lip may be permanently retracted) the index finger of the hand providing jaw control can be used to pull the lip down over the spoon to remove the food (see Figure 7-13).

Following spoon removal, the mouth should close and remain closed until swallowing occurs. If the mouth does not close spontaneously (or if a tongue thrust is present), jaw control to close the mouth manually may be required until swallowing occurs. Mouth closure and swallowing should be an active process if possible. The appropriate use of jaw control requires a sensitive give-and-take to allow maximum independent normal mouth movement with quick closure to control tongue thrusting if necessary.

A technique that puts a stretch on the circular muscle around the mouth is effective for students with inadequate *lip closure*. The technique can be performed in one of two ways. The first uses the feeder's index and middle fingers, as shown in Figure 7-14, Part A. The second uses the fingertips of the feeder's index and middle fingers (see Figure 7-14, Part B). In both cases the

---

Figure 7-13 Use of the Teacher's Index Finger to Pull Upper Lip Down over Spoon to Remove Food

Figure 7-14 Placement of the Teacher's Fingers to Promote Lip Closure

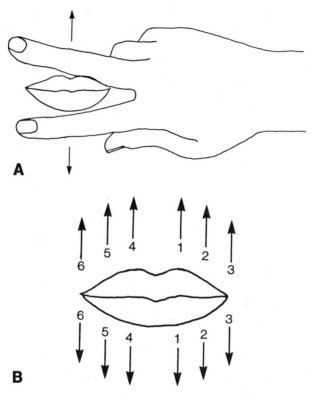

A. Index and middle fingers extended above and below the mouth with firm stretch applied in the directions indicated by the arrows. B. Numbered points indicate positions where firm stretch is applied in the direction of arrows with fingertips of teacher's index and middle fingers.

feeder should apply enough pressure to feel the student's gums and/or teeth through the student's face.

Following placement of the feeder's fingers in one of the two positions, a quick, firm stretch is applied. For the first position described above, the direction of the stretch is indicated by the arrows in the figure. The firm, quick stretch should be repeated three to four times in succession. For the second position, one quick stretch outward at each of the numbered points should be applied. The feeder should start at the midline of the lips and move first to one corner of the mouth and then to the other corner (that is, stretch at points 1, 2, and 3; then at points 4, 5, and 6). The entire sequence should be repeated three times.

One of the two applications of this technique should be used prior to *each* of the first ten bites of every meal to improve lip closure and active removal of food from the spoon. The procedure can also be used at various times throughout the school day to promote a more normal mouth position and to control drooling.

In relation to *swallowing,* the following procedure is recommended following removal of the spoon and mouth closure for students without an active swallow. The feeder's index finger should be placed midway between the upper lip and the nose (see Figure 7-15). Pressure should be applied in this position for up to 30 seconds or until a swallow occurs. The pressure should be firm enough for the feeder to feel the jaw and/or teeth through the face. This procedure should be used in conjunction with jaw control and is most effective if the chin is well flexed to the chest.

Many students lack free *movement of the tongue* in all directions (up, down, in, out, and to both sides). Two strategies are effective to encourage tongue movement.

The first requires the use of a thick, sticky substance, such as peanut butter, which should be placed at a number of locations in the mouth to encourage tongue movement. Placement should occur once at each of the following locations in succession: the roof of the mouth (just behind the upper front teeth), lower front teeth, left lower teeth, and right lower teeth. Approximately one minute should be allowed for the student to retrieve the substance at each location and coordinate a swallow.

Figure 7-15 Placement of the Teacher's Fingers to Encourage Swallowing

Inward pressure is applied with the index finger.

The second procedure uses a tongue blade covered with tape to prevent splintering. The tip of the tongue blade should be used to gently push the tongue to both sides and back into the mouth. The tongue will move in the direction *opposite* to the direction of the push following removal of the blade. The gentle push should be maintained for 2 to 3 seconds in each of the above directions in succession. The sequence should be repeated three times and is a beneficial prefeeding exercise.

Many students with neuromuscular involvement exhibit a *tongue thrust*. The presence of a tongue thrust causes extreme feeding difficulties and produces deformities in the teeth and jaws. Firm downward pressure on the tongue during presentation of the spoon is helpful in controlling the tongue thrust of many students. In extreme cases it may be necessary to replace use of a spoon with a taped tongue blade for presentation of food. The tongue blade is used to place food on the lower molars of either side. Manual rapid mouth closure should follow presentation of each bite and horizontal removal of the tongue blade.

A beneficial prefeeding exercise to aid in control of a tongue thrust is tongue walking (tongue walking also helps to reduce hyperactive bite and gag reflexes). Tongue walking requires firm pressure down on the midline of the tongue with a taped tongue blade or "swizzle stick." Downward pressure begins at the front of the tongue and moves in a series of one-quarter to one-half inch increments toward the back of the tongue. The tongue should be resting behind the lower teeth when the procedure is begun. Backward movement should cease either two-thirds of the way back on the tongue or as soon as the tongue begins to "hump" indicating elicitation of the gag reflex. Each series of movements should be accompanied by jaw control and end with mouth closure to promote an active swallow of the saliva that is produced by this procedure. Tongue walking should be repeated no more than two or three times in succession, as it is generally unpleasant for the student.

The final procedure related to tongue control is used to produce *retraction of the tongue*. It is appropriate for students with a tongue thrust or for those who exhibit nearly constant tongue protrusion. Flex the student's chin to the chest. Upward pressure is then applied with the tip of the feeder's index finger under the chin in the soft area inside the rim formed by the lower jawbone. (If front jaw control is being used, the second knuckle of the feeder's middle finger is used to apply the upward pressure). Simple upward pressure may be insufficient to produce tongue retraction in some students. In this case, the feeder's fingertip or knuckle should be vibrated rapidly to produce the desired result.

In terms of *normalization of oral sensitivity,* many students show extreme sensitivity to touch around the facial area. For these students it may be beneficial to carry out a series of prefeeding exercises. These procedures require firm jaw control from beginning to end to prevent avoidance of the procedures and to provide assistance in mouth closure and swallowing of accumulated saliva. The jaws should be held closed and in symmetry with the feeder's less preferred hand. The index finger of the other hand is inserted into the student's mouth, and the outer surface of the upper gums is stroked firmly two to three times from the molars forward to midline, first on one side and then on the other. Each sequence should be followed by removal of the feeder's finger and mouth closure to promote swallowing. The same steps should be followed with the outside surface of the lower gums. For students who have unrestricted hand-to-mouth movement, the student's index finger can be used for the stimulation. A second desensitization procedure is to gently brush the student's teeth with a soft toothbrush. This is also important for students who receive those anticonvulsant medications (for example, Dilantin) that result in excessive gum growth.

Many of the intervention strategies described above require manipulation of the student's oral musculature. The oral desensitization and tongue-walking procedures can be particularly aversive, although all of the strategies can be unpleasant because of their invasiveness. For this reason the procedures should be implemented with concern and sensitivity for the student's reactions, and use of these procedures should be introduced gradually.

Chewing has as prerequisites the inhibition of tongue thrusting and the development of tongue lateralization (side-to-side movements). The development of chewing can be encouraged through the use of two strategies that should be implemented in combination with one another.

The first strategy is to increase texture with the hope that chewing will develop spontaneously. The second strategy requires the use of strips of firm bread crusts, licorice whips, or any four- to six-inch strip of food that will provide resistance. One end of the food strip is inserted between the molars on either side of the student's mouth. Jaw control is used to produce firm mouth closure. A quick, firm stretch is applied to the other end of the food strip. Jaw control should lessen slightly at this point to allow spontaneous chewing to occur.

This procedure is remarkably effective in producing short periods of chewing behavior. There is, however, little generalization seen from the use of this procedure to spontaneous chewing of lumpy foods. For this reason, the above procedure should be used every few bites throughout each meal to increase carryover. Manipulation of the lower jaw in an up and down or rotary pattern is generally ineffective for producing the chewing behavior.

For *cup drinking,* proper presentation of liquids requires use of the following procedures. The student should be seated in a fully upright position. The feeder should sit or stand next to the student and provide jaw control from the side. The feeder's elbow and forearm should support the back of the student's neck to help ensure a good head position by providing some flexion of the student's chin to his or her chest.

The cup should be cut out and be presented so the lip of the cup rests gently on the student's lower lip (see Figure 7-16). The cup should *never* be presented so that it touches the student's teeth. Enough jaw control should be provided to almost completely close the student's mouth around the lip of the cup. The cup

---

Figure 7-16 Cup Drinking

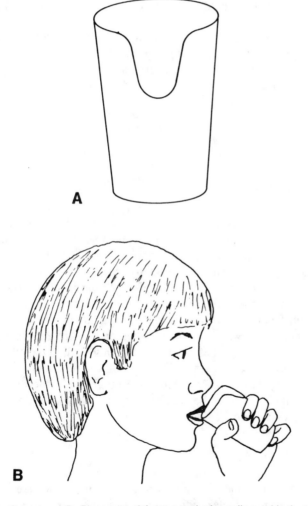

A. Cut out cup. B. Placement of the cup on the lower lip outside the teeth.

is then tipped slowly until a swallow of liquid runs into the student's mouth. The mouth is then closed completely (although the cup is *not* removed from between the student's lips) and a pause for swallowing is allowed. A second and third swallow of liquid are presented in this manner before the cup is removed. The above procedure is repeated several times in succession until adequate liquid is provided.

For students with poor lip closure, the stretching exercises around the mouth described earlier can be used prior to each presentation of the cup. For an older student with a permanently retracted upper lip, the index finger of the hand providing jaw control should be placed above the student's upper lip and downward pressure should be provided to form a seal around the edge of the cup and to prevent spillage.

There are four important behaviors necessary for successful *self-feeding*. It is not necessary for these behaviors to be performed independently prior to the development of self-feeding. If they are not in the student's repertoire, however, their function should be replaced through the use of adaptive equipment. These behaviors are

- head control
- trunk control/sitting balance
- grasping
- hand-to-mouth movement

The battle rages on as to when a severely or profoundly handicapped student with oral pathology should begin self-feeding. This is an issue because many of these handicapped students show a deterioration in their feeding patterns following the development of self-feeding. There are a number of factors to be considered in this decision, of which the most important are the student's age and motivation to self-feed. A compromise may be to begin training in self-feeding (if the student is motivated) in the later preschool years in combination with continued intervention on abnormal feeding patterns. Intervention strategies can be used during the first ten bites of every meal and self-feeding can be trained throughout the remainder of the meal. Refer to Banerdt and Bricker (1978) for an example of a self-feeding program and to Campbell (1979b) and Barnes, Murphy, Waldo, and Sailor (1979) for additional information on feeding equipment.

CONCLUSION

Severely and profoundly handicapped students with neuromuscular involvement present complex educational problems that are difficult to overcome. However, these members of society are capable of learning, given the right combination of conditions and teacher expertise. Recommendations for the future with this population include longitudinal studies to examine the effect of various methods of treatment, the development of new teaching strategies, and documentation of the use of systematic instruction through quality applied behavioral research.

REFERENCES

Banerdt, B., & Bricker, D. A training program for selected self-feeding skills for the motorically impaired. *AAESPH Review,* 1978, *3,* 222–230.

Barnes, K.J., Murphy, M., Waldo, L., & Sailor, W. Adaptive equipment for the severely multiply handicapped child. In R.L. York & E. Edgar (Eds.), *Teaching the severely handicapped* (Vol. IV). Columbus, Ohio: Special Press, 1979.

Bobath, K., & Bobath, B. Cerebral palsy. In P.H. Pearson & C.E. Williams (Eds.), *Physical therapy services in the developmental disabilities.* Springfield, Ill.: Charles C. Thomas, 1972.

Bricker, W.A., & Campbell, P.H. Interdisciplinary assessment and programming for multihandicapped students. In W. Sailor, B. Wilcox, & L. Brown (Eds.), *Methods of instruction for severely handicapped persons.* Baltimore: Paul H. Brookes, 1980.

Buttram, B., & Brown, G. *Developmental physical management of the multidisabled child.* Tuscaloosa: The University of Alabama, Area of Special Education, 1977.

Campbell, P.H. Assessing oral-motor skills in severely handicapped persons: An analysis of normal and abnormal patterns of movement. In R.L. York & E. Edgar (Eds.), *Teaching the severely handicapped* (Vol. IV). Columbus, Ohio: Special Press, 1979a.

Campbell, P.H. *Problem oriented approaches to feeding the handicapped child.* Reston, Va.: The Council for Exceptional Children, 1979b.

Connor, F.P., Williamson, G.G., & Siepp, J.M. *Program guide for infants and toddlers with neuromuscular and other developmental disabilities.* New York: Teachers College Press, 1978.

Falvey, M., Brown, L., Lyon, S., Baumgart, D., & Schroeder, J. Strategies for using cues and correction procedures. In W. Sailor, B. Wilcox, & L. Brown (Eds.), *Methods of instruction for severely handicapped persons.* Baltimore: Paul H. Brookes, 1980.

Farber, S.D. *Sensorimotor evaluation and treatment procedures for allied health personnel.* Indianapolis: Indiana-Purdue University at Indianapolis, School of Medicine, Division of Allied Health Services, 1974.

Finnie, N. (Ed.). *Handling the young cerebral palsied child at home.* New York: E.P. Dutton, 1975.

Guess, D. Methods in communication instruction for severely handicapped persons. In W. Sailor, B. Wilcox, & L. Brown (Eds.), *Methods of instruction for severely handicapped persons.* Baltimore: Paul H. Brookes, 1980.

Guess, D., Horner, R.D., Utley, B., Holvoet, J., Maxon, D., Tucker, D., & Warren, S. A functional curriculum sequencing model for teaching the severely handicapped. *AAESPH Review,* 1978, *3,* 202–216.

Hall, R.V., & Box, R. Changing criterion designs: An alternative applied behavior analysis procedure. In B. Etzel, J. LeBlanc, & D. Baer (Eds.), *New dimensions in behavioral research: Theory, methods, and application.* Hillsdale, N.J.: Lawrence Erlbaum Associates, 1975.

Hamre-Nietupski, S., Stoll, A., Holtz, K., Fullerton, P., Ryan-Flottum, M., & Brown, L. Curricular strategies for teaching selected non-verbal students. In L. Brown, J. Nietupski, S. Lyon, S. Hamre-Nietupski, T. Crowner, & L. Gruenewald (Eds.), *Curricular strategies for teaching functional object use, non-verbal communication, problem-solving, and mealtime skills to severely handicapped students* (Vol. III, Part I). Madison, Wisc.: Madison Metropolitan School District, 1977.

Johnson, J.L. Programming for early motor responses within the classroom. *AAESPH Review,* 1978, *3,* 4–15.

Kahn, J.V. Acceleration of object permanence with severely and profoundly retarded children. *AAESPH Review,* 1978, *3,* 15–23.

Karlan, G.R. The effects of preference for objects and repeated measures upon the assessed level of object permanence and means/end ability in severely handicapped students. *Journal of the Association for the Severely Handicapped,* 1981, *6,* 5–14.

Liberty, K., Haring, N.G., & Martin, M.M. Teaching new skills to the severely handicapped. *Journal of the Association for the Severely Handicapped,* 1981, *6,* 5–14.

Messina, R., Sternat, J., & Lyon, S. Curricular strategies for teaching selected mealtime skills to severely handicapped students with sensorimotor impairments. In L. Brown (Ed.), *Curricular strategies for teaching functional object use, nonverbal communication, problem solving, and mealtime skills to severely handicapped students.* Madison, Wisc.: Madison Metropolitan School District, Department of Specialized Services, 1978.

Morris, S.E. *Program guidelines for children with feeding problems.* Edison, N.J.: Childcraft Education Corporation, 1977.

Mueller, H. Facilitating feeding and pre-speech. In P.H. Pearson & C.E. Williams (Eds.), *Physical therapy services in the developmental disabilities.* Springfield, Ill.: Charles C. Thomas, 1972.

Mueller, H. Feeding. In N. Finnie (Ed.), *Handling the young cerebral palsied child at home.* New York: E.P. Dutton, 1975.

Reichle, J.E., & Yoder, D.E. Assessment and early stimulation of communication in the severely and profoundly mentally retarded. In R.L. York & E. Edgar (Eds.), *Teaching the severely handicapped* (Vol. IV). Columbus, Ohio: Special Press, 1979.

Robinson, C.C., & Robinson, J.H. Sensorimotor functions and cognitive development. In M.E. Snell (Ed.), *Systematic instruction of the moderately and severely handicapped.* Columbus, Ohio: Charles E. Merrill, 1978.

Sailor, W., Guess, D., Goetz, L., Schuler, A., Utley, B., & Baldwin, M. Language and the severely handicapped: Deciding what to teach to whom. In W. Sailor, B. Wilcox, & L. Brown (Eds.), *Methods of instruction for severely handicapped persons.* Baltimore: Paul H. Brookes, 1980.

Schmidt, P. Feeding assessment and therapy for the neurologically impaired. *AAESPH Review,* 1976, *1,* 19–27.

Shane, H.C. Approaches to communication training with the severely handicapped. In R.L. York & E. Edgar (Eds.), *Teaching the severely handicapped* (Vol. IV). Columbus, Ohio: Special Press, 1979.

Shane, H.C., Reynolds, A.T., & Geary, D. The elicitation of latent oral communicative potential in a severely handicapped adult: Procedures and implications. *AAESPH Review,* 1977, *2,* 202–209.

Sternberg, L., Battle, C., & Hill, J. Prelanguage communication programming for the severely and profoundly handicapped. *Journal of the Association for the Severely Handicapped,* 1980, *5,* 224–234.

Switzky, H.N., Woolsey-Hill, J., & Quoss, T. Habituation of visual fixation responses: An assessment tool to measure visual sensory-perceptual cognitive processes in nonverbal profoundly handicapped children in the classroom. *AAESPH Review, 1979, 4,* 136–148.

Umbreit, J. Effects of developmentally sequenced instruction on the rate of skill acquisition by severely handicapped persons. *Journal of the Association for the Severely Handicapped, 1980, 5,* 121–130.

Utley, B.L., Holvoet, J., & Barnes, K. Handling, positioning and feeding the severely handicapped. In E. Sontag, J. Smith, & N. Certo (Eds.), *Educational programming for the severely and profoundly handicapped.* Reston, Va.: The Council for Exceptional Children, 1977.

York, R., & Williams, W. Curricula and ongoing assessment for individualized programming in the classroom. In R. York, P. Thorpe, & R. Minisi (Eds.), *Education of the severely and profoundly retarded handicapped people.* Hightstown, N.J.: Northeast Regional Resource Center, 1977.

Communication Instruction*

Les Sternberg
Florida Atlantic University

PROBLEM

Although much has been written about language development theory (Chomsky, 1969; McNeill, 1970), assessment of language (Horstmeier & MacDonald, 1975b; Kirk, McCarthy, & Kirk, 1968; Lee, 1971), and language intervention programs and techniques (Gray & Ryan, 1973; Guess, Sailor, & Baer, 1974, 1976), there is little theoretical, assessment, and intervention information pertaining to prelanguage communication skills. The literature focuses narrowly on the area of communication/language. Communication is basically a process to exchange information, whereas language is a structure which one uses to communicate. The current trend seems to make communication synonymous with formal language structures (oral production, signs, symbols, codes, etc.). This is appropriate only if the human subjects under investigation are capable of dealing with a formalized structured language. For many severely and profoundly handicapped individuals, this synonymity is not warranted. Rather, one must begin dealing with communication as a separate entity from language.

PAST PRACTICES

According to Hollis, Carrier, and Spradlin (1976), all teachers of the handicapped must determine the disabled individual's functional receptive and expressive communication channels. For individuals who are severely or profoundly handicapped, this may involve starting at a point where the

---

*Sections of this chapter are reprinted or adapted from "Prelanguage communication programming for the severely and profoundly handicapped," by L. Sternberg, C. Battle, and J. Hill (*Journal of the Association for the Severely Handicapped*, 1980, *5*, 224–233), with permission from The Association for the Severely Handicapped.

meaning and uses of communication are developed and stimulated. For the individual who conceptually cannot separate himself or herself from the environment of objects and people, this may, in essence, mean activities directed toward controlling and affecting one's environment (Harris-Vanderheiden & Vanderheiden, 1977). It appears appropriate, then, to deal with communicative intentions rather than communication in isolation (Leonard, 1978). With the hypothesized relationship between normal cognitive development and linguistic development (Bates, Benigni, Bretherton, Camaioni, & Volterra, 1977), past techniques to foster communicative intentions have focused on the development of specific cognitive skills to effect communication change. Although this approach does merit attention, a more direct communication training procedure may be worthwhile.

SUGGESTED METHODS

The Van Dijk communication program (Van Dijk, 1965a,b) was originally designed for use with deaf/blind individuals. It is applicable to other severe and profound handicapping conditions, however, especially those accompanied by cognitive deficits. The goal of the Van Dijk program is to develop communicative intentions and communication procedures through conversation, using movement, signals, gestures, objects, pictures, signs, or speech. At the present time validation data on the use of the program with severely and profoundly handicapped children are being analyzed, and the results should be forthcoming.

Prelanguage Programming Concerns

In order to acquire language, a student must have some connection with the social world. It is probable that the asocial student can never fully participate in or appreciate communication, since communication is a social act. In order, therefore, to interface the social aspects with communicative behaviors, the student must realize a number of prelanguage communication accomplishments and concepts. The first of these is the student's awareness that he or she is separate from the environment. The individual must know the boundaries of self as well as the interfacing boundaries of the environment. We can recognize whether an individual has such knowledge by observing the way in which the individual manipulates objects. For example, if a severely or profoundly handicapped student immediately mouths objects, always manipulates objects close to the body, or never varies the manner of playing with the objects, then we may hypothesize that the student does not comprehend that the object is separate from himself or herself.

This perception of separation is necessary in order for the individual to acquire and display two prelanguage accomplishments: (1) that he or she can communicate, and (2) that there are things around him or her to communicate about and people with whom to communicate. Actively interacting with people and objects helps the student learn specific aspects related to the people and objects. Then as the student develops, he or she may learn that an aspect of an object, person, or event can represent that object, person, or event. Once the student knows that he or she can communicate, that there are things to communicate about, and that those things can be represented using body movements, the student may use idiosyncratic representations to think and to communicate. Eventually, these idiosyncratic representations may be replaced by conventional representations or language.

The major mission of the Van Dijk communication program is to help the prelanguage, noncommunicative individual develop communication and eventually language. This is accomplished by using a stage-to-stage procedure that employs movement by the student and the teacher to foster communication awareness.

The Van Dijk Program

The first major procedural stage of the Van Dijk communication program is termed *resonance*. At this stage the student learns that his or her movements can be used to affect another's behavior. Here, one responds to the student's movements as if they were communicative, thereby helping the student learn that his or her movements can effect change. Emphasis is placed on the development of a primary relationship between the teacher and student to provide the student with a connection to the outside world. The teacher's behavior is contingent upon the student's behavior. Initially, one starts with basic movement patterns of the student (such as rocking). If the student shows no consistent movement patterns, the teacher must help the student develop movements that can be used in a movement program. Such movements can usually be promoted through the use of shaping techniques and the application of other behavioral principles as a part of the student's regular physical education or physical therapy training. Starting with these nonthreatening movement patterns will help make the necessary later transition to altered body movements easier.

In the resonance stage it is mandatory that the teacher be in the same physical plane with the student (body-to-body). For example, if the student has been observed to rock, the teacher would rock with the student with the student's back against the teacher's chest. Later, after the student demonstrated success in the body-to-body plane, the teacher would proceed to the opposition plane (the teacher facing the student), but some physical contact would still be necessary.

In resonance, there is no separation in time or space. Receptive resonance is evident when the student shows awareness of the mutual movement (for example, by smiling or cooing). When the teacher and student move together, the teacher should stop and wait to see if the student provides a cue to the teacher to initiate the movement once again. The teacher can develop these expressive resonance cues (such as an intentional push backwards against the teacher's chest or patting the teacher's leg) initially by physical guidance and by following the cue with the desired movement.

Once this signal-to-movement connection has been established, the teacher may begin to create a more complete *movement dialogue*. Here, additional movements and cues are added and an order of movements is established to help the student build anticipation and memory. Generally, no extrinsic reinforcement is necessary, for movement itself is intrinsically reinforcing. Again, the purpose of this procedural stage is not to teach movements but rather to use movement to communicate.

The second stage of the Van Dijk communication program is termed *co-active movement*. At this level, the teacher and the student are separated in space but not in time. For example, the teacher may sit beside the student, remaining in close proximity. The teacher may initiate a familiar movement (with or without a corresponding cue) to determine the student's receptive co-active movement (that is, awareness of the mutual movement), or the student may use a signal to initiate a mutual move (an expressive co-active movement). The movement dialogue continues, but because of the separation in space, the student must observe the teacher as the teacher proceeds from one movement to another. Again, sequence and anticipation are developed by gradually building up sequences the student can perform with the teacher. Typically, gross motor movements are pursued before fine motor movements. Symmetrical movements (such as both limbs moving in the same directional plane at the same time) appear to be easier to duplicate than asymmetrical movements. Once the student can move through a variety of sequences with the adult, objects can be introduced into the movement sequences. For example, teacher and student might co-actively get blocks from a box, carry them to the table, and place the blocks on the table. Through this type of activity, the constructive use of objects and interactive play are stimulated. The student learns about objects in relation to his or her body and movements, thus helping the student use the body as a tool for exploring the world.

When the student can follow a series of co-active symmetrical and asymmetrical movements, *nonrepresentational reference* activities are initiated. The purposes of these activities are to build body image and to teach the student that the body can be represented. Initially, the teacher points out parts of his or her own body and encourages the student to duplicate the pointing that is being modeled. Once the student displays consistent nonrepresentational reference movements with the teacher as a model, the teacher may introduce a doll as a model. The doll-as-teacher model then shifts to a clay figure-as-doll model and finally to a paper and pencil or chalkboard stick figure representation of the body. Again, each model and the student are separated in space, but the model remains for the student to duplicate. The purposes of these activities are to develop body image, to teach pointing, and to help the student become aware that the body can be represented.

The third stage of Van Dijk's communication program is *deferred imitation*. Here, there is separation in both time and space. The teacher may display a certain movement pattern, stop the movement, and wait for the student to duplicate the pattern (receptive deferred imitation), or the student may initiate the same activity, providing the expressive cue (expressive deferred imitation). The key difference between co-active movement and deferred imitation, then, is that in deferred imitation whatever model is used is no longer available for the student to duplicate. For example, if one were using chalkboard stick figures as representation, the teacher would draw the stick figure model, ask the student to look at the model, erase the model, and ask the student to duplicate what he or she saw. In this situation, the student must defer movement until after the model is no longer available.

A communication device used throughout the co-active movement and deferred imitation stages is *anticipation shelves*. Typically, these are a series of connected cubicles, each cubicle representing a different activity during the school day. Within each cubicle will be placed an object the student will associate with the specific activity (a cup, for example, representing lunch). Just prior to each activity, the student is requested to get the appropriate object (initially this will be done through physical guidance), and then the student proceeds to the related activity. Once the student is finished with this activity, he or she is directed toward putting the object back onto the appropriate shelf or into a "finished box." During co-active movements, the major purpose of the shelf is to have the student associate the object with the physical movement toward the corresponding activity; in deferred imitation, the purpose is to have the student associate the object with the actual activity.

The pattern of using the anticipation shelves is consistently repeated, and the procedure helps the student structure the day, teaches the function of objects, and helps the student make transitions from one activity to another. Concrete to abstract representation is used with the anticipation shelves. One initially starts with objects, then proceeds to predrawn pictures or photographs of the objects, and finally arrives at graphic or line drawings of the objects. Again, before the student can use an abstract representational system (language), he or she must become aware that things can be represented.

Resonance, co-active movement, and deferred imitation should not be looked upon as procedures to be used in an isolated activity approach; they must be infused into a student's total program. For example, if the student is in the co-active communication level, everything that happens during the day should be done co-actively (washing hands, moving charts to a table, etc.). Given the supraordinate nature of communication, its relationship to other ecological events must be stressed.

As a result of a student's progression through deferred imitation, *natural gesture construction* will become evident. This phase serves as the transition from reference to representation. Here, the student learns that refined body movements can be used to communicate. This realization is necessary in order for the student to move from the concrete to the abstract, and to understand the future use of symbols and language. Natural gestures are, by definition, those that are self-developed. As such, they are not really amenable to procedural development. Initially, the gestures will represent what the student can do with the object (performative function, for example, a tearing motion for paper, a throwing motion for a ball) and proceed to what the object looks like (referential function, for example, a spherical hand motion for a ball). Again, it is extremely important that whatever natural gestures are constructed reflect a motor behavior the student has consistently exhibited. In the beginning of the natural gesture phase, the gestures are truly unique to the student and do not actually have meaning to anyone else. Therefore, the purpose of the initial natural gestures may be self-communication (that is, receptive and expressive communication *within* the individual). Later, these gestures will be based on request and then for the purpose of expressive (to other) communication.

Assessing the Student for Communication Programming

The stage-to-stage Van Dijk communication procedure represents the presymbolic levels of a systematic training approach for use with prelanguage individuals. As in all sequential training programs, it is necessary to determine where an individual falls within the sequence prior to any formal instruction. Miller (1974) supports an assessment procedure that includes measures of cognitive, receptive language, and expressive language behaviors as a necessary step prior to the implementation of any communication program. Given the relationship between cognition, communication, and language (Furth, 1970, 1971; Moorehead & Ingram, 1973; Cromer, 1974), determining in which Van Dijk stage an individual belongs will require an in-depth developmental assessment. Although Van Dijk's communication program represents *procedures* to be followed and as such should be used as a flexible tool for facilitating communication development in prelinguistic students, the obvious correlation between the discrete stages and theoretical levels of cognition (for example, Piaget's sensorimotor stages) cannot and should not be avoided.

A Communication Programming Inventory

The Appendix has been developed to give an indication to the teacher (or other communication facilitator) of the developmental level of functioning of a student in cognition, receptive communication, and expressive communication. Selected behaviors in each area have been gleaned from a number of sources dealing with developmental behaviors (*Callier-Azusa Scale*, Stillman, 1978; *Developmental Pinpoints*, Cohen, Gross, & Haring, 1976). These behaviors have been separated by area and developmental age ranges. An attempt has been made to avoid duplication of behaviors across different areas (for example, cognition and receptive communication), although it would not be unexpected to find these behaviors listed under different areas in other developmental scales or inventories. Numbers preceding behaviors indicate the relative ordinal position of that behavior within that level. Letters indicate different behaviors at the same basic position and do not presuppose any order of development.

To assess a student for communication programming, it is necessary that one who is familiar with the student provide the assessment information. However, it is not recommended that this information be based on material obtained from an interview. Rather, careful observation is required with the addition of anecdotal records (if appropriate). The following is a list of preferred strategies for conducting an assessment with this inventory:

- Become familiar with the selected behaviors sampled. This will require becoming aware of slight differences between similar behaviors at different developmental levels.
- Observe the student, preferably in different situations with different people. This observation should be conducted for no less than one week. This will give the opportunity for enough behaviors to be sampled and observed.
- Determine if behaviors observed are either person-specific or situation-specific. If the student exhibits an observed behavior only with a certain person present or only within a certain situation, then one should *not* conclude that that behavior is within the student's repertoire.
- Determine if behaviors observed occur only when certain artificial cues are given. For example, if the student exhibits a behavior only when a physical prompt is administered, then one should *not* conclude that that

behavior is within the student's repertoire. *Remember, however, that an artificial cue to one individual might be a natural cue to another* (for example, a deaf-blind student might need a tactual cue to respond; this may very well be that student's natural cue).

Completing the Inventory

Once the observation is concluded, the inventory should be completed. Each behavior listed in the Appendix can be rated in one of four ways. A *Yes* check indicates that the behavior is within the student's repertoire (that is, it occurs without the use of artificial prompts and occurs across different people and different situations). A *Pos* check indicates that the behavior is present but either occurs with the use of artificial prompts or is person or situation specific. A *No* check indicates that the student does not exhibit the behavior at the present time. However, it is possible that at some future time he or she might be able to exhibit that behavior. A *NA* check indicates that the student's handicapping condition precludes present *and* future exhibition of the behavior (a student who is born without eyes, for example, will not be able to visually track a moving object). *All behaviors on the inventory should be rated.*

It is important to note that items that are capable of adaptation ought to be adapted to the student's handicapping condition. For example, an item that stresses the use of a visual cue may be changed for a student who is blind. If the item were "recognizes object as same whether he or she sees part or all" (Cognition: 4–8 months), it would be appropriate to allow the blind student to touch only a part of a familiar toy and see whether he or she discards the toy or attempts to play with it without further tactual investigation. This type of adaptation is necessary for students with auditory and/or motor impairments as well. For each adaptation that the communication facilitator feels is justified, a notation of the type of adaptation should be made by the item.

Scoring and Interpreting

After checking all behaviors, add up the number of *Yes, Pos,* and *No* responses per level (such as Cognition: 0–1 month) to obtain the *Total # Score.* Determine the *% Yes Score* by dividing the *# Yes* by the *Total # Score* and multiplying the result by 100. This score is used to determine the approximate level of functioning of the student per area. To determine the functional level in each area, locate the *% Yes Score* that is at least 50 percent and that has the highest position within the developmental sequence. For example, if one obtained in the area of receptive communication a 0–1 month *% Yes Score* of 100 percent, a 1–4 month *% Yes Score* of 80 percent, and all following level *% Yes Scores* below 50 percent, the functional level of the student would be designated as 1–4 months. In the event that two sequential levels have *% Yes Scores* above and very close to 50 percent (and the following level *% Yes Scores* are below 50 percent), it would probably be wise to designate the lower level as the functioning level. Obviously, there may be children who do not exhibit scores that follow a simple or consistent sequence. It is advised that, if possible, another individual should conduct an independent observation of the student; later, both observations should be compared for consensus. If questions still exist, communication facilitator judgment should be used as the deciding factor.

Using Results for Communication Programming

Once levels of functioning are established in all areas, one can refer to Table 8-1, in which critical developmental levels have been associated with specific communication programming procedural levels. For example, if a student is functioning in cognition from 1–4 months, in reception communication from 4–8 months, and in expressive communication from 4–8 months, the student is probably ready for communication training at the final resonance level. As a rule of thumb, the student's obtained cognitive level ought to be used as the key indicator for initiation into any programming level.

Operationalizing Communication Programming

The following section is a delineation of programming strategies in relation to the procedural levels specified in Table 8-1. Each strategy is prefaced by the name of the procedural level, the general area of concern addressed by the strategy, and the specific objective of the strategy. All strategies are written from the perspective that the reader is the communication facilitator.

Procedural Level: Pre-Resonance
Area: Reaction Development
Objective: To make a consistent simple motor movement or vocal response
  Strategy: Place yourself in a position so that you may observe any subtle body or facial movement on the part of the student. If the student makes a *spontaneous* controlled movement (preferably not self-stimulatory), reinforce the student for that movement *while* the student is exhibiting the movement. This may be as gross as a limb movement or as fine as a facial twitch. If the preferred target behavior is a vocalization, follow the same reinforcement procedure. Physical guidance will most probably be necessary at this level.
  In the event that the student has the potential for an extremely limited behavioral repertoire (a student who is, for example, bedridden and quadraplegic), attempt to shape a facial twitch or movement by physically guiding

Table 8-1 Translating Assessed Levels into Procedural Levels

	Critical Developmental Levels (Months)		
	Cognition	Receptive Communication	Expressive Communication
PRE-RESONANCE			
Development through shaping of a motor or vocal response	`0 - 1	0 - 1	0 - 1
INITIAL RESONANCE			
Receptive: awareness			
Expressive: participation	0 - 1	1 - 4	1 - 4
FINAL RESONANCE			
Receptive: anticipation			
Expressive: use of gross to fine signals, vocalizations	1 - 4	4 - 8	4 - 8
INITIAL CO-ACTIVE MOVEMENT			
Receptive: gross motor/symmetrical movement imitation	4 - 8	4 - 8	4 - 8
Expressive: fine-motor signals, vocalizations			
FINAL CO-ACTIVE MOVEMENT			
Receptive: fine-motor/asymmetrical movement imitation	8 - 12	8 - 12	8 - 12
Expressive: signals: anticipation shelves (concrete)			
INITIAL DEFERRED IMITATION			
Receptive: movement imitation, non-representational reference (concrete)	8 - 12	12 - 18	12 - 18
Expressive: gestures for self-communication, signals: anticipation shelves (abstract)			
FINAL DEFERRED IMITATION			
Receptive: non-representational reference (abstract)	12 - 18	12 - 18	12 - 18
Expressive: gestures for communication			

Communication Procedural Levels

Communication Instruction

and manipulating the student's face into the preferred movement. Be extremely aware of the development of a more voluntary response on the part of the student. Again, reinforce *during* the behavior and gradually fade out physical assistance. The purpose of involvement at this level is twofold. In the case of a student who has unlimited potential for exhibiting different movements or vocalizations, the consistent movement or vocalization that is developed will be the one used to initiate movement communication. In the case of a student who has extremely limited potential for exhibiting different movements or vocalizations, the consistent behavior that is developed (such as a facial twitch) will be used as a later *signal* for communication.

Procedural Level: Initial Resonance
Area: Receptive Communication
Objective: To make a motor or vocal response that indicates awareness of resonance movement
   Strategy: Place yourself in a position so that you are in close physical contact with the student (for example, sitting on a mat with the student's back against your chest). In the event that your position prevents you from observing the student's face, it is probably best to place a full-length mirror in front of the student so that you may observe his or her reactions. Begin to move with the student, employing a movement that the student has in his or her behavioral repertoire (such as rocking). While moving, observe whether the student exhibits a behavior (smiling, furrowing the brow, cooing, etc.) that indicates he or she is aware of the movement. Stop the movement to determine whether the student's awareness behavior *changes* to indicate that he or she realizes the movement has terminated.
   If the student's behavioral repertoire is extremely limited (as with a bedridden quadraplegic), move the student carefully in a repetitious movement (for example, rolling back and forth on his or her side). If you are moving the student by pushing with your hands on his or her back, place a mirror in a position so that you can observe facial reactions (awareness). Stop the movement to determine if the awareness behavior *changes.*

Procedural Level: Initial Resonance
Area: Expressive Communication
Objective: To make more active participation movements during resonance communication
   Strategy: Place yourself in a position so that you are in close physical contact with the student (for example, sitting on a mat with the student facing you with his or her upper legs draped over your upper legs). Begin to move with the student, employing a movement that the student has in his or her behavioral repertoire (such as swaying). While moving, observe whether there

is a noticeable change in the level of participation of the student. For example, initial participation may be only a voluntary acceptance by the student of your guiding him or her into the movement. More active participation might be an increase in the rate of movement of the student, an introductory attempt at expressing his or her desire to continue.

Procedural Level: Final Resonance
Area: Receptive Communication
Objective: To make anticipatory responses during resonance communication
    Strategy: Place yourself in a position so that you are in close physical contact with the student (for example, sitting on a mat with the student's back against your chest). Begin to move with the student, employing a movement that the student has in his or her behavioral repertoire (such as rocking). Stop the movement. See whether the student, of his or her own volition, begins the movement. If the movement is begun by the student, follow the movement with your body. It is also possible that the student will begin an anticipatory movement once the position for resonance movement is assumed (for example, once both of you are sitting on the mat in close physical contact). In this case, make sure that your movement follows his or her movement immediately.
    Begin to introduce sequences of resonance movements (such as rocking, swaying, arms up/arms down). Make sure that you always follow the same sequence each time the exercise is conducted. After each separate movement type is completed (for example, swaying), pause in the sequence to determine whether the student makes an anticipatory response to the *next* movement in the sequence. If this response is given, make sure that your movement follows his or her movement immediately.
    In the case of a student with an extremely limited behavioral repertoire, anticipatory responses may be extremely difficult to observe. However, be aware of any signal that the student may begin to employ for both communication and anticipation (for example, similar to those established during pre-resonance training).

Procedural Level: Final Resonance
Area: Expressive Communication
Objective: To make gross to fine motor signals (and/or vocalizations) during resonance communication
    Strategy: Place yourself in a position so that you are in close physical contact with the student (for example, sitting on a mat with the student facing you with his or her upper legs draped over your upper legs). In the event that your position prevents you from observing the student's face, it is probably best to place a full-length mirror in front of the student so that you may observe his or her vocalizations or attempts at vocalization. Begin a movement

with the student. Stop the movement. If the student makes a gross body movement (such as rocking forward), follow this immediately with the corresponding movement (rocking). Stop the movement after a short duration. Wait for the *same* gross body movement and follow this *signal* immediately with the corresponding movement. In the event that the student makes some other movement (rocking backwards, swaying), do *not* follow the different signal with the movement. Rather, place the student's body in the appropriate signal position (pushing the student forward), and follow the signal immediately with the corresponding movement. Any appropriate vocalization (that is, non-self-stimulatory sound) or attempt at vocalization (such as mouth opening) can also be used as a signal for the movement.

Once the student shows a consistent gross body signal to start a movement, begin to shape a fine motor signal. For example, if a forward rocking movement is the signal, each time this signal is given make sure that the student at the same time produces a fine motor signal (such as grabbing your hand). This can be accomplished by physically guiding the student's hand onto your hand. After a period of time, begin to fade out the physical guidance. It will also be necessary to fade out the gross body signal and finally use only the fine motor signal as a cue for movement. Be extremely aware of the student's voluntary use of the signal as opposed to your continued cueing of the signal.

It is necessary to develop a number of signal-to-movement matches. If you are operating with fixed sequences of movement (such as rocking to swaying), begin to develop separate gross body signals and then separate fine motor signals in the manner described above. If vocalization or attempts at vocalization are used as signals, make sure that discrete signals are used (that is, different vocalizations for different movements).

In the case of a student with an extremely limited behavioral repertoire, begin to shape the student's facial movements as discrete signals for movements that you initiate and terminate with the student's body.

Procedural Level: Initial Co-Active Movement
Area: Receptive Communication
Objective: To imitate gross motor symmetrical movements during co-active exercises
Strategy: Place yourself in a position so that the student can observe your movements. Body-to-body physical contact is not necessary. Begin to exhibit gross motor movements that are symmetrical (for example, both arms extended to the side). If the student has been through resonance activities, you may wish to use movements that were utilized during that level. Indicate to the student that you want him or her to exhibit the same gross motor movement *while* you are exhibiting the movement. This can be accomplished

by showing the movement or position, and then, once again as he or she exhibits the movement or position, duplicate that movement or position with your body. Focus should be on the student's voluntary imitation of gross motor symmetrical movements or positions while the student observes a model performing the movement or assuming a position.

If the student is blind, make sure that as you perform a movement or assume a position you allow the student to touch your body (tactile receptive communication) to indicate what he or she is to imitate. Follow the procedure used above allowing the student to break during his or her imitation to continually touch your body to provide the current model cue for his or her movement or position.

Procedural Level: Initial Co-Active Movement
Area: Expressive Communication
Objective: To make fine motor signals (and/or vocalizations) during co-active exercises

Strategy: Place yourself in a position so that the student can observe your movements. Body-to-body physical contact is not necessary. Prior to your exhibiting a body movement, request that the student exhibit a fine motor signal (such as grasping your hand) or vocalization (or vocalization attempt). This request can be initiated by you shaping the signal and must be followed immediately by a movement. It is imperative that once the movement is stopped, the signal must be terminated. This will aid the student in understanding that the signal is used to *start* the movement, not to stop the movement. If the student has been involved in resonance activities, you may wish to use movements and signals that were utilized during that level. It is also appropriate to allow the student to exhibit the movement while you exhibit the movement, provided that the signal is employed each time to initiate the activity.

If the student is blind, make sure that as you perform a movement you allow the student to touch your body (tactile receptive communication) to indicate that his or her signal is being followed by your movement.

In the case of a student with an extremely limited behavioral repertoire, it will be necessary for you to follow programmed signals (on the part of the student) with your movements. For example, if the student has a certain facial twitch as a signal for rocking, you should wait for that signal (physical guidance will be necessary at first) and then rock with your body so that the student may observe you rocking.

Procedural Level: Final Co-Active Movement
Area: Receptive Communication
Objective: To imitate fine motor asymmetrical movements during co-active exercises

Strategy: Place yourself in a position so that the student can observe your movements. Body-to-body physical contact is not necessary. Begin to exhibit fine motor movements that are asymmetrical (for example, one hand slapping one knee). Indicate to the student that you want him or her to exhibit the same fine motor movement *while* you are exhibiting the movement. This can be accomplished by showing the movement or position to the student, physically guiding him or her into the same movement or position, and then, once again as he or she exhibits the movement or position, duplicating that movement or position with your body. Focus should be on the student's voluntary imitation of fine motor asymmetrical movements or positions *while* the student observes a model performing the movement or assuming the position.

If the student is blind, make sure that as you perform a movement or assume a position you allow the student to touch your body (tactile receptive communication) to indicate what he or she is to imitate. Follow the procedure used above allowing the student to break during his or her imitation to continually touch your body to provide the current model cue for his or her movement or position.

Procedural Level: Final Co-Active Movement
Area: Expressive Communication
Objective: To use objects to signal forthcoming activities
Strategy: Place, in reaching distance of the student, a set of horizontally connected cubicles (*anticipation shelves*), each cubicle large enough to hold objects that may be associated with a fixed sequence of activities conducted during the day (washcloth for washing, cup for feeding, etc.). There should be enough cubicles present to represent the major discrete activities of the day. Place in each cubicle a three-dimensional object that will be used in association with a specific activity. Before that activity is to be conducted, take the student to the shelf to obtain the object. With the object in the student's hand, take the student to the activity. The object would then be placed aside. Once the activity is terminated, have the student pick up the object and return it to the shelf or (preferably) to a separate dropoff container (a "finished box"). Every other activity in sequence should follow this pattern, with different objects associated with the remaining activities. Be aware of any anticipation responses on the part of the student (for example, if he or she begins to go to the shelf by himself or herself to obtain the object or to the appropriate activity area once the object is obtained). These anticipation responses should be developed by slowly fading out your physical guidance or assistance in using the shelf.

In the case of a student with an extremely limited behavioral repertoire, it will probably be necessary to shape an eye-attending or head-pointing response to the object on the shelf. The actual movement of the object to the activity will be your responsibility. However, anticipatory eye-attending or head-pointing responses should be encouraged.

Procedural Level: Initial Deferred Imitation
Area: Receptive Communication
Objective: To imitate body movements and sequences of body movements after a model has been given
   Strategy: Place yourself in a position so that the student may observe your movements. Tactile receptive communication may be necessary if the student is blind. Body-to-body physical contact is not necessary. Demonstrate any bodily movement or position to the student. Stop the demonstration and request the student to do what you did. Begin to build up to sequences of bodily movements and positions (for example, walking to crawling to sitting). Here, you model the entire sequence of movements or positions and then request the student to duplicate the sequence. Be extremely aware of any difficulty the student may encounter in remembering too many components of a sequence.
   It may be appropriate to conduct some sequences on a movement bench. Aside from the flexibility afforded a teacher in terms of the many different movements and positions that can be conducted on a bench, a bench also has more obvious starting and stopping points (that is, each end of the bench).

Procedural Level: Initial Deferred Imitation
Area: Receptive Communication
Objective: To point to various parts of his or her body after a concrete model has been given
   Strategy: Place yourself in a position so that the student may observe your movements. Body-to-body physical contact is not necessary. Begin to point to parts of your body (for example, nose, ear, mouth, arm, leg). Request the student to point to the same body part on his or her body. Initially, you may have to keep your model present while physically guiding the student to make the reference point on his or her own body. As the student shows consistent success, fade out the physical guidance and begin to ask the student to point to a specific body part *after* you have modeled the reference. For example, you should point to your nose, stop pointing, and ask the student to point to his or her nose (that is, do what I *did*). Emphasis should be placed on delaying (deferring) the student's imitation of *nonrepresentational reference* gestures.
   If the student is blind, allow the student to touch your body (tactile receptive communication) to indicate what he or she is to imitate.

Procedural Level: Initial Deferred Imitation
Area: Expressive Communication
Objective: To use abstract items to signal forthcoming activities

Strategy: Place, in reaching distance of the student, a set of horizontally connected cubicles (*anticipation shelves*), each cubicle large enough to hold pictures that may be associated with a fixed sequence of activities conducted during the day (a picture of a washcloth for washing, a picture of a cup for feeding, etc.). There should be enough cubicles present to represent the major discrete activities of the day. Place in each cubicle a picture that will be used in association with a specific activity. Selection of pictures may be based on objects that were used during an earlier use of anticipation shelves (final co-active movement level). Before the activity is to be conducted, the student must obtain the corresponding picture and take the picture to the activity. Once the activity is completed, the student must return the picture to the empty shelf or put the picture in a finished box or finished area. Every other activity in sequence should follow this pattern, with different pictures associated with the remaining activities.

Follow the use of pictures with large print cards, each card containing a word associated with the picture and/or activity (thus, in place of a picture of a washcloth is a *WASH* word card). Initially, these cards should be coupled with the pictures (that is, each time the student obtains the picture card, he or she also gets the word card). Slowly fade out the use of the picture card so that the student begins to rely increasingly on the more abstract representation.

As the shelves are used more often, begin to delay the onset of each activity until the student voluntarily obtains the abstract item and uses it to indicate to you that an activity should be forthcoming. For example, the student may obtain the picture or word card, come to you, and lead you to the activity area.

In the event that the student has an extremely limited behavioral repertoire, it will probably be necessary for the student to use an eye-attending or head-pointing response to the abstract items as a signal.

Procedural Level: Initial Deferred Imitation
Area: Expressive Communication
Objective: To develop natural gestures as a form of self-communication
Strategy: Observe the student's interaction with objects, people, and events. Pay close attention to any fine motor behavior that he or she exhibits whenever an interaction takes place. A student playing with a favorite toy may initially touch or grasp that toy in a certain way (for example, using a pincer grasp and rubbing his or her fingers together on a part of the toy). A student may rub his or her cheek each time feeding is to occur or run his or her fingers through his or her hair each time a certain person is present. These *natural gestures* are to be encouraged. Each time an object, person, or event that has an associated natural gesture is exposed to the student, the student should be requested to

use the gesture. Encouragement can initially take the form of physical guidance of the gesture.

At this level one should not automatically expect that the student will use his or her natural gestures expressively. That is, the student will not necessarily exhibit the gestures to you to obtain an object, person, or event. Rather, the student will exhibit the gestures when you request the student to do so.

Be keenly aware of situations where the student begins to use a gesture prior to playing with an object, interacting with a person, or participating in an activity, apparently for the purpose of self-communication. Also, at this level do not request that the student use a conventional word, sign, or symbol in association with his or her natural gestures. You may wish to associate these formal language signals with his or her gestures while you "converse" with the student, but it is only appropriate to request that the student use his or her own natural gestures.

Procedural Level: Final Deferred Imitation
Area: Receptive Communication
Objective: To point to various parts of his or her body after an abstract model has been given

Strategy: Take a doll and begin to manipulate different parts of its body in front of the student (for example, wagging its arms). Ask the student to duplicate the doll's movement with his or her own body. Initially, you may have to keep your model present while physically guiding the student to make the movement with his or her body. As the student shows consistent success, fade out the physical guidance and begin to ask the student to duplicate the doll's movements *after* you have modeled the movement with the doll.

Begin to point to different body parts of the doll (for example, nose, ear, mouth, arm, leg). Request the student to point to the same body part on his or her body. Attempt to delay (defer) the student's imitation by requesting that he or she not indicate the *nonrepresentational reference* gesture until you have completed your pointing gesture.

Follow the doll as a model with a picture of a person. Here, you would point out various parts of the person's body on the picture. The picture ought to be followed by the use of stick figures drawn on the blackboard. In this case, the stick figures can initially be drawn to show positions that the student must duplicate (for example, hand on head). Later, you should point to body parts on the stick figure that the student must point to on his or her body. Emphasis again should be placed on delaying (deferring) the student's imitation.

If the student is blind, allow the student to touch the doll (tactile receptive communication) to indicate what he or she is to imitate. With the stick figures, allow the student to grasp your hand as you draw the figures. This will aid him or her in duplicating positions indicated by the drawings.

Procedural Level: Final Deferred Imitation
Area: Expressive Communication
Objective: To use natural gestures as a form of communication
    Strategy: Request that the student use all of his or her own natural gestures when such use is appropriate (that is, when the student is beginning to interact with objects, people, or events). Begin to interrupt such interaction (once it has started) by requesting that the student exhibit the natural gesture associated with that object, person, or activity. This interruption is done for the purpose of showing the student that the natural gesture can stand on its own as a sign for the object, person, or activity and is not merely a signal for the beginning of an interaction activity. Continue this procedure until the student begins to use the natural gestures expressively. This will typically take the form of natural gesture requests on the part of the student (without cueing from you) to obtain specific objects, people, or activities. Once these requests become consistent, it is appropriate to pair each of the student's gestures with a formal language model (that is, a word, sign, or symbol). In this case, each time the student exhibited an expressive natural gesture, you would duplicate that gesture, and then model the formal language cue for that gesture. Encourage the student to then imitate the formal language cue.

The Transition to Formal Language Instruction

Once the handicapped student has demonstrated the ability of using his or her own natural gestures expressively, formal language cues may be associated with those gestures. The intent is to aid the student in making the transition from using "self-developed" communication symbols to employing "society-developed" language forms. A number of language intervention programs have been formulated to assist the student in developing formal language. From a theoretical point of view, debate has ensued for many years concerning the basis on which language is acquired. Thus, it is not surprising that each language training program operates from certain philosophical or theoretical bases. It is not the intent of this section to review issues imbedded in the debate or to make value judgments regarding the language intervention programs presented. Rather, the purpose is to give the communication facilitator various options regarding the training of language. For a review and discussion of issues pertaining to language training, refer to the work of McLean and Snyder-McLean (1978) and McLean, Yoder, and Schiefelbusch (1972).

Given the fact that various language training terms will be used to describe the instructional programs, it would be best to provide some definitions for those terms prior to the description and explanation of each program.

- In a *syntactic based program,* the word form and sequence or order of words (symbols) used to create complete thoughts (sentences) takes precedence in the language training process. In this type of program, the general purpose of training is to teach the student the basic rules of correct word usage (such as plurality) and combining words to form sentences.
- In a *semantic based program,* the emphasis is on the meaning of the word or sequence of words rather than on the correct word form or order of words.
- In a *developmentally based program,* the student's cognitive functioning level is used as a major index of what language programming techniques to employ.
- In a *behaviorally based program,* the presence or absence of a language behavior dictates what is to be taught and how it is to be taught, rather than the cognitive readiness of the individual to understand the language behavior.
- In an *isolated training program,* the paradigm is one in which the student is instructed in language for a specified (usually fixed) amount of time or trials per day.
- In an *integrated* (or ecological) *training program,* all natural environmental opportunities for language usage are employed for language training (social interactions, activities of daily living, etc.).

Language Intervention Programs

- *Functional Speech and Language Training for the Severely Handicapped* (Guess, Sailor, & Baer, 1976). This program is behaviorally based with training done in an isolated framework. Six basic language content areas are addressed in a step-by-step training sequence: persons and things (expressive use and receptive identification of label to object/person matches), actions with persons and things (expressive use and receptive identification of verb actions), possession (expressive use and receptive identification of possessive pronouns "my" and "your"), color (expressive use and receptive identification of colors), size (expressive use and receptive identification of "big" and "little"), and relation and location (expressive use and receptive identification of "on," "under," "inside," and "outside"). The intent of training is to assist the student in developing five concepts in relation to the content areas. The first is *reference,* whereby the student learns that specific sounds represent certain objects. In *control,* the student uses the sounds to obtain the objects. When the student begins to ask for the names of other objects, the student demonstrates *self-extended control.* The fourth concept is *integration,* where the student relies on his or her own memory to supply correct labels. In *reception,* the student understands questions that are asked and statements that are heard.

Each training session is separated into trials. The language trainer supplies a stimulus to the student (question, command, or object/action). A reinforcer follows a correct response with the anticipation that the student will move from more tangible reinforcers to naturally occurring social reinforcers. If a correct response is not forthcoming, the trainer is expected to use shaping techniques coupled with prompts and/or physical guidance. In certain instances, a second trainer acts as a model in the correction procedure. Aside from goal statements and procedures and instructions to follow for each training step, instructions are included for generalization training where applicable (that is, the use of parents and parent surrogates as trainers in other environments). Movement from one step to another is based on a pre-established criterion of either 80 percent correct responses within a training session or 12 consecutive correct responses within a training session. However, students who do not achieve criterion after 40 sessions are cleared to pursue the next step in the program.

There appears to be a much greater emphasis placed on syntactic than semantic aspects in this training program. Advanced training sequences require the student to use words expressively in the appropriate sequence (syntactic emphasis), whereas certain initial training endeavors allow the student to furnish nonordered responses. Given the overall intent of the training program (functional speech and language) and the general flow of the training sequences, the program should be considered syntactically based.

• *A Language Program for the Nonlanguage Child* (Gray & Ryan, 1973). This book describes in detail the basic underlying research and instructional model for the *Monterey Language Program* (Gray & Ryan, 1971). It is a behaviorally based program, syntactic in nature, and operates from an isolated training philosophy. The authors delineate the basic parameters of their training program as nine variables: response (specific expected student behaviors), stimulus (specific events that precede the response), reinforcer (tokens coupled with verbal praise following the correct response), criterion (10 to 20 successively correct responses, depending on the response required and the number of students in the language training group), reinforcement schedule (social reinforcement continues on a continuous schedule; tokens are faded), response mode (the description of the response: oral or nonoral), stimulus mode (the description of the stimulus: visual or aural), model (prompts that are used to assist the student in generating the correct response), and complexity (a description of the relationship between the model and the response). Five different models are used in the program: immediate complete (IC—the entire model of what the student is to say is given just prior to the expected response), delayed complete (DC—the entire model is given but the student must delay his or her response), immediate truncated (IT—a portion of the model is given just prior to the expected total response), delayed truncated (DT—a portion of the model is given and the student must delay his or her total response), and no model (N—the student is not given any model of what he or she is to say). The intent is to decrease the student's reliance on any type of model. In terms of complexity, each programming step is based on a certain number of response units (for example, number of words required in the response) coupled with a certain number of model units (for example, number of words used as prompts). This gives the language trainer an indication of the difficulty of the training step. All nine variables are used to describe each step or sequence in the training program.

The content of the training program is separated into three sections. The core section deals with identification and naming of nouns; the use of *is*; the use of singular and plural nouns in conjunction with correct present verb tenses; the use of the pronouns *he, she,* and *it*; and the use of the words *in, on,* and *the*. The secondary section deals with the use of *are*; the use of the pronouns *you, they,* and *we*; the distinction among *is, are,* and *am*; the distinction among noun, pronoun, and corresponding verb usage; and the use of singular and plural nouns in conjunction with correct past verb tenses. In the optional section, training sequences are directed toward the use of *was* and *were, does, do, did,* and *doing*; the rules of conjunction (*and*) and disjunction (*not*); future and perfect tenses; adjectives and possessives; the use of the words *this, that,* and *a*; and articulation. A total of 41 separate training sequences comprise the program.

Typically, there is a systematic order to the instructional variables as well as content. In each series of training steps, the movement is toward the use of no models, an increase in response length, a change to an intermittent type of reinforcement schedule, and a shift from the use of pictures and verbal statements as stimuli to only verbal questions as stimuli. The student is required to produce grammatically correct statements or (based on a number of interrogative-type training sequences) to produce grammatically correct questions.

Placement within the program sequences is accomplished by the use of the Programmed Conditioning for Language Test (PCLT) and the Criterion Test. The PCLT generates scores that help to determine the specific language training program or sequences that are necessary for the student. The

Criterion Test is merely a sampling of various programming steps within a targeted sequence. Based on performance on these items, the student is placed at the appropriate programming step.

If the student is experiencing difficulty in mastering a certain step, the language trainer is directed toward branching techniques. The first type of technique is the use of additional verbal instructions prior to the presentation of the model. If this is not successful, a second type of branching is required. In this type, the language trainer is referred to a branching index that lists alternative steps to employ for obtaining correct responses. A special branching index is also available if the student continues to respond incorrectly using the regular branching index. As a rule, special branching requires either a simplification of stimulus presentation or a reduction in the response requirements.

Two types of interventions are used to promote generalization and transfer. In the Spontaneous Language Record, the language trainer conducts a "show and tell" period during each training session. Here the intent is to have the student produce language forms that he or she has just learned by verbally reacting to the presentation of some object or picture. In the Initiate Home Carryover procedure, parents are requested to continue training procedures once the student has successfully mastered a program. Parents are given instructions related to the language behavior expected, instructional techniques to follow, and procedures for scoring responses.

• *Language Acquisition Program for the Retarded or Multiply Impaired* (Kent, 1974). This program is behaviorally based and training is done in an isolated fashion. Unlike the two preceding programs, it has a rather strong semantic basis to its content. Three major sections comprise the program. In the Preverbal Section, attending and motor imitation behaviors are taught. Key attending behaviors are sitting still, the absence of interfering behaviors, looking at objects, and pretrial eye contact with the language trainer. The purpose of motor imitation at the preverbal level is not to develop a generalized imitative repertoire. Rather, it is to train those motor responses (for example, pointing to an object or pointing to parts of the body) that will be required for successful performance in later parts of the program.

The Verbal-Receptive Section is divided into six phases. In the Basic Receptive Phase, the student is taught to point to body parts, room parts, and objects named, and to find named concealed objects hidden under a cloth. Also included are initial action requests in relation to body parts, room parts, and objects (for example, "Close your eyes," "Push the car," "Mop the floor"). In Receptive Expansion Phase I, the purpose is to expand the student's ability in performing the action requests of the Basic Receptive Phase. The student is also required to find concealed objects hidden in one of two boxes. In Receptive Expansion Phase II, the student is taught a number of skills: to distinguish between his or her body parts and another's body parts, to place objects in prepositional relationship to room parts (the concepts of in, on, and under), to give related objects on command (for example, "Give me the hat and the coat"), to find concealed pairs of objects, and to sort by color. In Receptive Expansion Phase III, the purposes are to have the student follow commands to move his or her body through space, to increase his or her receptive noun vocabulary, to sort by size (big and little), to find an object named, and to point to colors named. In Receptive Expansion Phases IV and V, the student is required to demonstrate increased facility with commands, new vocabulary, and number identification.

The Verbal-Expressive Section is comprised of five phases. The Vocal Imitation Phase involves training the student to imitate at least 10 of the 20 basic vocabulary words used in the Basic Receptive Phase. In the Basic Expressive Phase, the student is required to name the body parts, objects, and room parts that were used in the Basic Receptive Phase by responding to the questions "What is this?" or "What is in the box?". In the Expressive Expansion Phase I, the student must respond to more complex questions indicating correct possession (for example, "Whose nose is this?"), prepositional relationships (for example, "What is in the box?"), missing objects (for example, "What's gone?"), and relationships between objects and parts of the room (for example, "Where is the hat?"). Also included is training in the use of the words *push* and *throw* in order to make the language trainer comply with these requests. In Expressive Expansion Phase II, components of two types of noun phrases are taught: color + noun, and number + noun. Two-word noun phrases are also included in this phase: object + object, and object + room part (including appropriate preposition). In the Expressive Expansion Phase III, the student is expected to increase his or her noun and verb vocabulary, to produce phrases indicating color + noun, and to count the number of disappearing objects.

The principle of reinforcement theory defines the general method of the program. Primary reinforcers, such as food and/or tokens, are coupled with social praise to follow correct responses. In the expressive phases of the program, the student must request the reinforcer by name. Although an inventory is present to determine entry point into the total program, it is also appropriate to start each student at the very beginning (the Preverbal Section). The Initial Inventory, a randomized sequence of behaviors to be learned in each part of the program, is administered to determine which individual behaviors ought to be dealt with first. A test-teach paradigm is then employed as the student progresses through each program step. If the student is having some difficulty in performing a language behavior, prompts (gestures, modeling, physical guidance) are employed. However, credit for correct responses is given only for those appropriate responses following verbal instructions. The Final Inventory is administered when a major part of the program has been completed. This inventory indicates the success rate of the student on that part of the program just completed and also assesses the student's retention of language behaviors dealt with in earlier parts of the program. Data-recording procedures are outlined in addition to specified criterion levels of performance. Often, noncriterion tasks are interspersed among the criterion behaviors. These noncriterion tasks are used for facilitating generalization and retention and also for providing an introduction to content that will be presented in a later segment of the program.

• *Environmental Language Intervention Program* (Horstmeier & Mac-Donald, 1975a). This program is comprised of four major elements: the Environmental Prelanguage Battery (EPB), the Environmental Language Inventory (ELI), the Parent-Administered Communication Inventory (Oliver), and the Ready, Set, Go Talk to Me instructional program. The philosophical underpinnings of the program are represented by the cognitive school of thought and, as such, the program is developmental in nature. The emphasis in the entire program is on integrating the semantic aspects of language into the student's total environment. This integrated program approach stresses the social or interactive basis of language development. Regular scheduled training is recommended in conjunction with informal training to generalize all communication behaviors to new people and new situations.

The EPB assesses those prelinguistic skills that are deemed necessary for the development of spoken language. The target population for this battery is students who are functioning below or at the single-word level. The EPB assesses precommunication training behaviors (for example, attention to persons and objects, sitting still, and responding to a task), meaningful play, receptive language (identifying objects through the use of two-choice discrimination tasks, identifying pictures of objects and action, demonstrating verb actions, following directions), motor imitation, verbal imitation (of sounds and object names), and cued production (naming objects and actions in response to questions and commands). Typically, the examiner determines whether the student can perform the specific communication behavior. If the student gives no response or an incorrect response, the examiner attempts to train the response using various prompts. After training, the student is again assessed to determine if he or she has benefited from the training. Therefore, the examiner obtains additional information aside from the correctness of the response. Test levels are established with points designated for passing responses, emerging responses, or nonpassing responses. Two tests (repeating two-word phrases and responding to questions with word phrases) are included in the EPB as screening items for the Environmental Language Inventory.

The ELI assesses meaningful word phrases that typically comprise the initial sentences used by normally developing children. Three assessment modes are used: conversation, imitation, and play. Also determined are the length of utterance and the intelligibility of the utterance. In the conversation mode, a question or command is used to elicit a verbal response from the student. In the imitation mode, the examiner asks the student to repeat a word phrase. In the play mode, the student is observed with respect to his or her use of spontaneous language with prompts used only when dictated by the play situation.

The ELI assesses eight semantic-grammatical rules (that is, orders of words that connote a generalized meaning; for example, the rule sequence agent + action might be typified by the utterance "doll fall"). There are three stimuli presentations for each semantic-grammatical rule. Each stimulus presentation is comprised of a cue that is a demonstration of an environmental event providing meaning to the rule (showing the student that the doll falls), a conversational cue ("What is happening?"), and an imitative cue ("Say, 'doll fall.'"). The environmental event cue is first paired with the conversational cue, then with the imitative cue, and finally with the conversational cue once again. Data obtained from the administration of the ELI will enable the examiner to determine which semantic-grammatical rules are in need of training, what cues should be employed to stimulate the use of the rules, and what length of utterance should be the target.

The Oliver is comprised of five sections, each designed to answer questions related either directly or indirectly to the student's ability to communicate. The parent is asked to respond to a number of questions related to general information and history concerning the student and previously observed communication or communication-related behaviors. Also included are actual assessment tasks that the parent is asked to administer to determine more succinctly the communication performance level of the student.

Information from the EPB, ELI, and Oliver is used to place the student at an appropriate instructional level within the Ready, Set, Go Talk To Me instructional program. Given the basic integrated quality of the *Environmental Language Intervention Program,* the instructional program includes not only instructional procedures to follow but also suggestions as to how to apply the training objectives to other environments. This will hopefully allow the language behavior to come under more and more control from the natural environment. Training probes are used to determine if the student is benefiting from the training sessions. These probes are followed by carryover probes that require the student to apply his or her acquired language behavior to new, untrained objects, pictures, commands, and the like. Structured play situations are also outlined to assess the student's movement toward spontaneous language. Although operant procedures are recommended for language training, the purpose of the behavioral techniques is to foster a *class* of language behaviors (that is, semantic-grammatical rules) rather than individual language behaviors.

• *An Intervention Strategy for Language-Deficient Children* (Bricker, Ruder, & Vincent, 1976). This work represents a compilation of prior language training efforts with handicapped students (Bricker & Bricker, 1974). It is basically an outline or format of how language training should be accomplished. The program has a strong semantic emphasis, is developmental in nature, and operates from an integrated training paradigm. The major programmatic thread permeating the entire program is the language training lattice. The lattice is basically a programming decision-making tree that defines the movement of programming steps and concepts and the relationship between the steps and concepts.

The language training program is divided into two major sections. In Part I, which is comprised of 14 training phases, instruction begins with functional use of objects, proceeds to object/label associations and verbal imitations, and terminates with oral production of variants of the agent-action-object rule. Included in Part I is consideration of prerequisite behaviors for language training. Targeted are sitting quietly, eye attending to the teacher's face, and performing imitative behaviors. A later publication (Bricker & Dennison, 1978) delineates in more detail additional behaviors that are training prerequisites for language programming. In Part II, which is comprised of 29 training phases, emphasis is placed on the student's ability to change the agent-action-object statement according to a specified rule (for example, creating a question from a declarative statement) or to modify the agent-action-object statement without changing the intent of the statement (for example, adding an adjective to the object segment of the statement).

Each training phase of the language program describes individual components of the instructional paradigm. The setting for teaching is specified (such as a kitchen area or corner of the classroom), coupled with the environmental stimuli (objects, sounds, or words) to be used in training. It is recommended that baseline probes be administered prior to any training to determine the current functioning level of the student within that phase. If the student reaches criterion on the baseline probe, training is recommended in a following phase. Training techniques are outlined for each phase. Typically, physical guidance or modeling prompts are utilized. Once the student begins to display unprompted appropriate behavior, training probes should be administered. These are administered in the same fashion as the baseline probes and help to determine whether the student is learning the appropriate behavior. Also delineated in each phase are generalization training activities. These describe the environments to which extended training will be directed, the stimulus material that will be utilized, and the instructional and student response behavior that will be mandated. Procedures for data collection and data-collection targets (for example, frequency counts and duration measures) are also included in the training phases.

As with the Horstmeier and MacDonald program (1975a), behavioral strategies are employed throughout intervention. Again, the purpose of the use of operant techniques is not to develop isolated language or language-related behaviors. Rather, the behavioral techniques are used to assist the student in comprehending and producing semantic-grammatical language units.

Prelanguage Communication Skills versus Prelanguage Prerequisites

A number of the procedures in the language intervention programs that have been reviewed specify prelanguage prerequisite behaviors in order for language instruction to proceed. One should not confuse these prerequisites with the prelanguage communication skills that were described in the earlier portion of this chapter. Prelanguage communication skills are developed for the purpose of communication even in the absence of language. Prelanguage prerequisite behaviors (such as sitting still, eye attending to the language trainer) are developed in order that language training tasks will be more easily attended to and acquired by the student. Overlap between prelanguage communication skills and prelanguage prerequisite behaviors (for example, imitation) may cause some confusion. However, the purpose of the development of prelanguage communication skills *is* communication, whereas the purpose of the development of prelanguage prerequisites is to establish a specific behavioral repertoire.

Adaptations for Language Training

Deficits in the ability to use speech musculature for the production of oral language may preclude the suggested direct use of many of the aforementioned language training programs. However, adaptations of the required formal language output (such as signs and symbols) or response mode (such as pointing) may produce the desired results within the operational and theoretical framework of the language intervention procedure. For variants of formal language output, a number of manual communication systems may be used in place of oral response systems (Wilbur, 1976; Stokoe, 1960; Paget & Gorman, 1968; Gustason, Pfetzing, & Zawolkow, 1972; and Anthony, 1971). These communication alternatives differ in their language bases (for example, syntactic and semantic qualities) and their relationship to the English language. Although they are geared for the hearing impaired or deaf, other populations who experience difficulty in using the aural-oral modes of communication would benefit from their use as well.

Another type of formal language output is graphic communication. Clark and Woodcock (1976) delineate a number of graphic systems, with the *logographic system* representing an interesting alternative for use with the severely or profoundly handicapped student. In this system, symbols represent one or more words and may be pictorial or nonpictorial. An example of the pictorial logographic system is Bliss symbols (Bliss, 1965). Comprised of approximately 100 basic symbols, they convey words or ideas and are primarily used as an expressive language device for students unable to use the oral or manual communication modes. The *Non-Speech Language Initiation Program* (Carrier & Peak, 1975) represents a nonpictorial logographic system. Various shapes represent different words, and color cues dictate the proper placement of each word into a sentence. The program serves as an introduction into language for students who are unable to profit from aural training.

Consideration must also be given to alternative response modes, especially for students who are severely motorically impaired. Vanderheiden (1977) stresses the importance of using any formal language output in conjunction with a preferred means of *indication*. That is, for students who are unable to use an oral or gestural form of communication, a means of indicating an expressive language unit must be provided. Three types of indication are discussed. In *scanning,* choices are presented to the student and he or she must signal in some way (such as pointing or signaling "yes") the desired choice. This process may be used by even the most severely physically handicapped students. An example of using the scanning procedure would be when a communication board, comprised of a number of pictures, symbols, or words, serves as the choice board. The teacher can then point to each stimulus and wait for some affirmative response on the part of the student. Scanning can be rather slow as a method of indication but may represent the only possible mode of communication for the student. In *encoding,* the student must produce responses that depend on some pattern or code relationship to the desired output. For example, eye attending to different numerals that coincide with different words could produce a desired message. Encoding can be a more rapid method of indication than scanning but typically does require finer motor control and more specific motions. In *direct selection,* the student indicates the desired choice, without a request. This process ranges from direct gestures (where the student, for example, merely eye attends to what he or she desires in the immediate environment) to the use of communication boards (where the student's hand or head points to the language forms that will produce the desired message). Direct selection appears to be the most straightforward method of indication. However, it also requires the use of fine motor skills and increased range of motion.

Vanderheiden (1977) also describes levels of implementation of communication aids in relation to the methods of indication. The levels are hierarchical in terms of increased complexity of the aid and increased independence of communication for the student. Level I involves the use of unaided techniques, where the student can communicate only with a small number of people. Typically, the student must respond to questions but cannot ask questions of his or her own. The intent is to respond only to the student's basic needs. Level II involves the use of fundamental aids. These are basic methods or techniques of implementing the various types of indication. At this level, the communication facilitator is required to spend considerable time in decoding any messages produced by the student. Level III involves the use of simple electronic and mechanical aids. Here interpretation on the part of the communication facilitator is not necessary because the student is producing complete messages. At this level, communication with many more people is possible, although direct attention from the message receiver is required. Level IV involves the use of fully independent aids. These aids have some kind of printout or display. Attention on the part of the communication facilitator or message receiver is decreased to only the time it takes to read the message. Level V involves the use of fully independent and portable aids. This level of implementation creates the utmost communication independence for the student. Examples of Level II through Level V aids, both teacher-made and commercially available, are presented by Vanderheiden and Grilley (1977).

CONCLUSION

Communication skill deficits appear to represent the common thread of characteristics for severely and profoundly handicapped students. It seems logical that if appropriate communication skills were developed by the handicapped student instructional programming in all other content areas would be accomplished more effectively and efficaciously. Unfortunately, to merely state the proposition is not enough. Research must be conducted to determine not only the viability of specific communication programming techniques but also the relationship of those techniques to programming concerns and options in other content areas (activities of daily living, socialization, eating skills, etc.).

As stated in the beginning of this chapter, the focus of communication programming efforts, both in research and practice, has been in the area of language. This is indeed worthwhile for those individuals who will, at some point in time, be eligible for or benefit from some type of formal language training. However, there are many individuals coming into the education arena who at the present time should not be exposed to language intervention techniques. It may well be that future expectations for these students dictate the same apparent void of language content programming. This is not to say that *communication* programming must be avoided. On the contrary, the focus of the preliminary segment of this chapter on prelanguage communication skill development ought to give direction to those who are concerned with handicapped individuals who may never be capable of using formal language structures.

For many, the ultimate question pertaining to any type of programming or instructional effort is, of what benefit will the developed behaviors be to the student? Obviously, in the area of language, it is hoped that the newly acquired skills will be enriching. In the area of prelanguage communication programming (if this defines the highest level attainable by the student), the answer is not so readily forthcoming. It may well be that student-centered benefits are not the crucial area of concern. Rather, if in some way through elementary communication skills the student can impact the environment of his or her primary caretakers (for example, signaling immediately after soiling his or her diaper so that the cleanup process can be carried out more easily), the benefits derived will become basically for the change agents. In dealing with the severely and profoundly handicapped, therefore, improvement must be looked on from many standpoints.

REFERENCES

Anthony, D. *Signing essential English.* Anaheim, Calif.: Anaheim Union School District, Educational Services Division, 1971.

Bates, E., Benigni, L., Bretherton, I., Camaioni, L., & Volterra, V. From gesture to the first word: On cognitive and social prerequisites. In M. Lewis & L. Rosenblum (Eds.), *Interaction, conversation, and the development of language.* New York: John Wiley, 1977.

Bliss, C. *Semantography.* Sydney, Australia: Semantography Publications, 1965.

Bricker, D., & Dennison, L. Training prerequisites to verbal behavior. In M.E. Snell (Ed.), *Systematic instruction of the moderately and severely handicapped.* Columbus, Ohio: Charles E. Merrill, 1978.

Bricker, D., Ruder, K., & Vincent, L. An intervention strategy for language-deficient children. In N.G. Haring and R.L. Schiefelbusch (Eds.), *Teaching special children.* New York: McGraw-Hill, 1976.

Bricker, W., & Bricker, D. An early language training strategy. In R.L. Schiefelbusch and L.L. Lloyd (Eds.), *Language perspectives: Acquisition, retardation, and intervention.* Baltimore: University Park Press, 1974.

Carrier, J., & Peak, T. *Non-speech language initiation program.* Lawrence, Kans.: H & H Enterprises, 1975.

Chomsky, C. *The acquisition of syntax in children from five to ten.* Cambridge, Mass.: M.I.T. Press, 1969.

Clark, C., & Woodcock, R. Graphic systems of communication. In L. Lloyd (Ed.), *Communication assessment and intervention strategies*. Baltimore: University Park Press, 1976.

Cohen, M., Gross, P., & Haring, N.G. Developmental pinpoints. In N.G. Haring and L.J. Brown (Eds.), *Teaching the severely handicapped: Volume I*. New York: Grune & Stratton, 1976.

Cromer, R. Receptive language in the mentally retarded: Processes and diagnostic distinctions. In R.L. Schiefelbusch & L.L. Lloyd (Eds.), *Language perspectives: Acquisition, retardation, and intervention*. Baltimore: University Park Press, 1974.

Furth, H. On language and knowing in Piaget's developmental theory. *Human Development*, 1970, *13*, 241–257.

Furth, H. Linguistic deficiency and thinking: Research with deaf subjects, 1964–1969. *Psychological Bulletin*, 1971, *71*, 83.

Gray, B., & Ryan, B. *Programmed conditioning for language: Program book*. Monterey, Calif.: Monterey Learning Systems, 1971.

Gray, B., & Ryan, B. *A language program for the nonlanguage child*. Champaign, Ill.: Research Press, 1973.

Guess, D., Sailor, W., & Baer, D. To teach language to retarded children. In R.L. Schiefelbusch & L.L. Lloyd (Eds.), *Language perspectives: Acquisition, retardation, and intervention*. Baltimore: University Park Press, 1974.

Guess, D., Sailor, W., & Baer, D. *Functional speech and language training for the severely handicapped*. Lawrence, Kans.: H & H Enterprises, 1976.

Gustason, G., Pfetzing, D., & Zawolkow, E. *Signing exact English*. Rossmoor, Calif.: Modern Sign Press, 1972.

Harris-Vanderheiden, D., & Vanderheiden, G. Basic considerations in the development of communicative and interactive skills for non-vocal severely handicapped children. In E. Sontag, J. Smith, & N. Certo (Eds.), *Educational programming for the severely and profoundly handicapped*. Reston, Va.: The Council for Exceptional Children, 1977.

Hollis, J., Carrier, J., & Spradlin, J. An approach to remediation of communication and learning deficiencies. In L.L. Lloyd (Ed.), *Communication assessment and intervention strategies*. Baltimore: University Park Press, 1976.

Horstmeier, D., & MacDonald, J. *Environmental language intervention program*. Columbus, Ohio: Charles E. Merrill, 1975a.

Horstmeier, D., & MacDonald, J. *Environmental pre-language battery: A semantic-based assessment of prelanguage skills*. Columbus: The Ohio State University, Nisonger Center, 1975b.

Kent, L. *Language acquisition program for the retarded or multiply impaired*. Champaign, Ill.: Research Press, 1974.

Kirk, S., McCarthy, J., & Kirk, W. *Illinois Test of Psycholinguistic Abilities*. Urbana: University of Illinois Press, 1968.

Lee, L. *Northwestern Syntax Screening Test*. Evanston, Ill.: Northwestern University Press, 1971.

Leonard, L. Cognitive factors in early linguistic development. In R.L. Schiefelbusch (Ed.), *Bases of language intervention*. Baltimore: University Park Press, 1978.

McLean, J.E., & Snyder-McLean, L. *A transactional approach to early language training*. Columbus, Ohio: Charles E. Merrill, 1978.

McLean, J.E., Yoder, D.E., & Schiefelbusch, R.L. (Eds.), *Language intervention with the retarded*. Baltimore: University Park Press, 1972.

McNeill, D. The development of language. In P. Mussen (Ed.), *Carmichael's manual of child psychology.* New York: John Wiley, 1970.

Miller, J. *A developmental approach toward assessing communication behavior in children.* Madison: University of Wisconsin, Waisman Center on Mental Retardation and Human Development, 1974.

Moorehead, D., & Ingram, C. The development of base syntax in normal and deviant children. *Journal of Speech and Hearing Research,* 1973, *16,* 330–352.

Paget, R., & Gorman, P. *A systematic sign language.* London: National Institute for the Deaf, 1968.

Stillman, R. (Ed.). *The Callier-Azusa Scale.* Dallas: University of Texas at Dallas, Callier Center for Communication Disorders, 1978.

Stokoe, W. Sign language structure: An outline of the visual communication system of the American deaf. *Studies in Linguistics,* Occasional Papers No. 8, 1960.

Van Dijk, J. The first steps of the deaf/blind child towards language. *Proceedings of the conference on the deaf/blind, Refsnes, Denmark.* Boston: Perkins School for the Blind, 1965a.

Van Dijk, J. Motor development in the education of deaf/blind children. *Proceedings of the conference on the deaf/blind, Refsnes, Denmark.* Boston: Perkins School for the Blind, 1965b.

Vanderheiden, G. Providing the child with a means to indicate. In G. Vanderheiden & K. Grilley (Eds.), *Non-vocal communication techniques and aids for the severely physically handicapped.* Baltimore: University Park Press, 1977.

Vanderheiden, G., & Grilley, K. (Eds.). *Non-vocal communication techniques and aids for the severely physically handicapped.* Baltimore: University Park Press, 1977.

Wilbur, R. The linguistics of manual language and manual systems. In L. Lloyd (Ed.), *Communication assessment and intervention strategies.* Baltimore: University Park Press, 1976.

Chapter 9

Independent Living Skills*

Gary L. Adams
Florida Atlantic University

PROBLEM

The acquisition of independent living skills is important because it greatly improves the chances for severely and profoundly handicapped students becoming self-sufficient. Research on deinstitutionalized retarded clients shows that those with higher level of independent living skills did better in community settings (Gollay, Freedman, Wyngaarden, & Kurtz, 1978; Hull & Thompson, 1980; Schalock, Harper, & Genung, 1981; Sutter, Mayeda, Call, Yanagi, & Yee, 1980).

As little as 30 years ago it was thought that the acquisition of self-help and other independent living skills was next to impossible. Early research based on behavioral principles in the 1960s (see, for example, Bensberg, 1965) showed that handicapped individuals could gain self-help skills when properly instructed. Since that time, there have been many examples of programs to successfully instruct various independent living skills. Although the number of skills that have been researched has increased dramatically, there are still two major problems in this field. First, the number of independent living skill behaviors that have been researched is still fairly small. Second, some behaviors have several examples of successful training using multiple methods. Unfortunately, there have been few studies comparing the often conflicting procedures.

PAST PRACTICES AND SUGGESTED METHODS

Because of the limited amount of research, it is unreasonable to suggest methods except in a few skill fields where comparison studies have been

---

*Figures are reprinted from *Toilet training the retarded: A rapid program for day and nighttime independent toileting,* by R.M. Foxx and N.H. Azrin (Champaign, Ill.: Research Press, 1973), with permission from Research Press.

conducted. For this reason, past practices and suggested methods coverage have combined. This chapter will be limited to a discussion of empirical studies containing data on profoundly to moderately retarded or disturbed students. Descriptive programs (see, for example, Marchant, 1979; Spellman, DeBriere, Jarboe, Campbell, & Harris, 1978) have been excluded because, even though they may contain valuable information, they do not present data to prove that they work. Also, traditional academic programs have not been included for two reasons. First, classroom observations show that often too much time is spent on academic skills (possibly because school is thought of as a place for reading, writing, and arithmetic), instead of more important skills that are needed for independent living. Second, there is very little support that these skills can be acquired *and maintained over time.* For example, several reading programs have been implemented (Brown, Huppler, Pierce, York, & Sontag, 1974; Domnie & Brown, 1977; Nietupski, Williams, & York, 1976), but these studies do not show that the participating students maintain their skills after a period of time. This is not to say that severely and profoundly handicapped cannot learn these traditional academic skills. At this point in time, however, it would seem that training efforts should be spent on other endeavors. Academic skills will be mentioned in this chapter, but as a part of training an independent living skill (for example, using a calculator to make purchases at a store).

Toileting Skills

The acquisition of toileting skills is important for health and psychological reasons. Largo and Stutzle (1977a) conducted a large-scale longitudinal study to investigate the development of bowel and bladder control in nonhandicapped children during the first six years. The data on 320 Swiss children showed that most children had complete bowel control by three years of age and bladder control (day and night) by five to six years of age. In contrast, Azrin, Sneed, and Foxx (1973) and Sugaya (1967) found that approximately two-thirds of institutionalized severely and profoundly retarded clients are incontinent at night. The probability of their gaining in toileting skills without proper training is very low (Lohman, Eyman, & Lask, 1967).

Research on nonhandicapped children shows that early training (before the age of one) has only a short-term effect on bowel training (Largo & Stutzle, 1977b). Azrin and Foxx (1976), however, have shown that by using behavioral techniques it is possible to toilet train nonhandicapped two-year-olds in less than a day. Behaviors that are often characteristic of severely and profoundly handicapped individuals, such as the presence of brain damage or seizures, leg coordination problems, negativism, and emotionality are correlated with the lack of bowel control (Spencer, Temerlin, & Trousdale, 1968).

Low intelligence and a lengthy period of institutionalization (Lohman et al., 1967) as well as low support skills (zipping and buttoning, for example), seriously reduce the chances of quick training success with severely and profoundly handicapped individuals.

Systematic research on toilet training of severely and profoundly handicapped individuals is only fairly recent. In 1963, Ellis provided a theoretical behavioral model for toilet training. Early attempts to train severely and profoundly handicapped individuals, usually in institutional settings, used shaping techniques to get them to sit on commodes, and there were few attempts to teach self-initiated toileting. Dayan (1964) described a procedure of having attendants place 25 institutionalized students on commodes every two hours each day. Students were reinforced with edibles if they voided and ignored for nonresponding. Daya mentioned that the amount of soiled linen was halved, but no hard data on toileting success were provided. Baumeister and Klosowski (1965) attempted to train 11 subjects over a period of 70 days by isolating them on a separate ward with one trainer. Starting on the 49th day, the students were assimilated back into their normal ward. Although good success was shown in the isolated setting, the intervention effects were lost when the students returned to their natural setting.

Daytime Toilet Training

Current toilet training programs tend to be built around one of three approaches. The first is a schedule-based approach emphasizing shaping commode sitting behavior (see, for example, Fredericks, Baldwin, Grove, & Moore, 1975; Linford, Hipsher, & Silikovitz, 1972). Usually 15 to 30 days of baseline data are taken before the introduction of the intervention program. Based on the analysis of when the student tends to wet or soil his or her pants, the teacher begins by placing the student on the commode before that time period. Fredericks et al. (1975) have suggested that only a small time block at a convenient time be used at first. When the student voids consistently during that time period, further time periods are added until the training program lasts all day. Minimum prompts are used and data on the student's voiding are collected. Snell (1978) has noted that this schedule-based commode training lacks data showing that it results in self-initiated toilet training.

The second approach was developed around a device to help discriminate bladder tension (Mahoney, Van Wagenen, & Meyerson, 1971; Van Wagenen, Meyerson, Kerr, & Mahoney, 1969; Van Wagenen & Murdock, 1966). Van Wagenen et al. (1969) described a program in which a signaling device was connected to the genital area of severely and profoundly handicapped students. When urination occurred, the following procedure was used: (1) the teacher rapidly approached the student and said "No," which usually stopped the urine flow; (2) the teacher walked the student to the toilet; (3) the teacher placed the student in the correct stance; (4) urination was reinforced; and (5) with success, the signaling device was replaced by regular cotton briefs. Nine severely and profoundly handicapped students were successfully trained after an average of 12.5 sessions of three to four hours.

Mahoney et al. (1971) modified their signaling device so that the teacher could activate it by using an audio signal. First, each student was trained to go through the toileting behaviors of going to the bathroom using physical, verbal, and signaling device prompts. Then the physical and verbal prompts were faded. At this point, the amount of liquids was increased. If the teacher thought that the student was ready to urinate, the teacher would activate the signaling device. If the student urinated in the toilet, he was reinforced. "Accidents" were handled by shouting for the student to stop and go to the bathroom. Four of the five severely and profoundly handicapped students were trained in an average of 29 hours. Followup probes taken six weeks later, however, included only one student.

The third major approach was developed by Azrin and Foxx (Azrin & Foxx, 1971; Azrin, Sneed, & Foxx, 1973; Foxx & Azrin, 1973a; Foxx & Azrin, 1973b). They suggest a rapid training process with daily sessions lasting a minimum of four hours per day and not over three students being trained at a time. Two signaling devices are used in this program. One device is connected to snaps placed in the student's briefs and another device is connected to an insert that is placed in the toilet bowl. When urine or feces moisten the area between the snaps and thus make a circuit, a tone is produced by the signaling device. Figure 9-1 shows the two signaling devices.

Initially, training sessions begin at half-hour intervals. The teacher and the student who is wearing the signaling device sit near the toilet with the signaling device inserted in the bowl. The teacher gives the student liquids. Then the teacher follows the procedure as described in Exhibit 9-1. As Exhibit 9-1 shows, the student is reinforced for eliminating in the toilet. The teacher can tell that the student has eliminated in the toilet because of the tone from the toilet signaling device. If the student wets, the signaling device connected to the student's briefs is activated and the teacher initiates the correction procedure. First, the student must clean up the mess that he has made, and then he must practice the correct toileting behavior six times by going to the bathroom, pulling down his pants and briefs, sitting on the toilet, pulling up briefs and pants, and returning to the place where he wet.

When the student begins to self-initiate toileting, the teacher starts to gradually fade the intensive toileting process. The student's chair is moved further away from the toilet, he is placed on an intermittent reinforcement schedule, there are longer time periods between pants checks, the signaling

Figure 9-1 Signaling Devices for Toilet Training

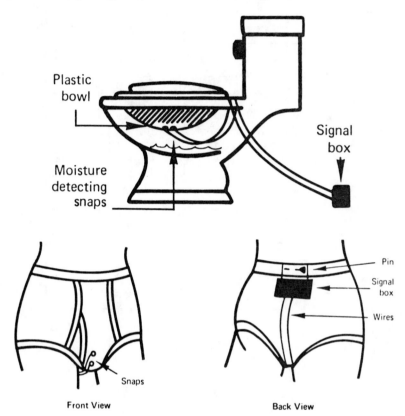

Plastic bowl

Moisture detecting snaps

Signal box

Pin

Signal box

Wires

Snaps

Front View

Back View

devices are removed, and the student must find the bathroom from various locations.

Comparative Research

Sadler and Merkert (1977) compared schedule-based training versus the Foxx and Azrin approach and found that the Foxx and Azrin approach was superior. Smith (1979) conducted the only comparison of Van Wagenen versus Foxx and Azrin approaches. In addition, he compared individualized versus group training. He found that individualized training was significantly more successful than group training. There was no significant difference, however, between the two toilet training approaches. The comparison may have been unfair to the Foxx and Azrin approach because the positive practice

Exhibit 9-1 Procedural Steps for Toilet Training

Start exactly on the half-hour, for example, 8:00 or 8:30

Starting Time _____ Resident's Name _____   Date _____

Check under the appropriate item when completed.
Repeat the following steps every half-hour until a self-initiation occurs.

	8:00	8:30	9:00	9:30	10:00	10:30	11:00	11:30	12:00	12:30	1:00	1:30	2:00	2:30	3:00	3:30	4:00	4:30
1. Gave as much fluid as resident would drink while seated in his chair.																		
Note number of cups of fluid consumed.																		
a. Waited about 1 minute.																		
2. Directed resident to toilet using the minimal possible prompt.																		
3. Directed resident to pull his pants down using the minimal possible prompt.																		
4. **If resident voided:**																		
a. Gave edibles and praise while he was seated, then directed him to stand.																		
b. Directed resident to flush toilet using the minimal possible prompt.																		
c. Note each time of voiding.																		
5. **If resident did not void** within 20 minutes of drinking the fluids, directed him to stand.																		
6. Directed resident to pull up his pants using the minimal possible prompt.																		
7. Directed resident to his chair using the minimal possible prompt.																		
8. Inspected resident for dry pants 5 minutes after he had been sitting and every 5 minutes thereafter; gave edible and praise if pants were dry.																		
9. **If accident occurred:**																		
a. Gave Brief Cleanliness Training and Positive Practice. (p. 48)																		
b. Note exact time of occurrence.																		

Continuously praise resident for being dry. When self-initiation occurs, start the self-initiation procedure. Give exact time of self-initiation _____ procedure, probably a key feature of the program, was not used. The trainers preferred the Foxx and Azrin approach.

Nighttime Toilet Training

Like daytime toilet training, some nighttime programs have been based on scheduled toileting (Fredericks et al., 1975). Again, there are no data to support this approach. Mowrer and Mowrer (1938) developed the earliest approach using a signaling device. The most popular device is now a "sandwich" pad: two pieces of foil that are connected to an audio device and a piece of fabric that is placed between the two pieces of foil. When the fabric is wet, a circuit is completed and the toilet training device is activated. This device is available at most department stores.

Foxx and Azrin (1973b) incorporated the use of the "sandwich" pad in their rapid toilet training approach. After the student had gained daytime toilet training, the nighttime toilet training was started. The sandwich pad was placed on the bed and the signaling device was placed in the toilet. The student was given fluids and taken to the toilet at hourly intervals. Successful elimination in the toilet was reinforced. If the student had an accident, the cleanliness training and positive practice were continued, as described earlier. When the student began to self-initiate, the use of the device and the intensive training procedure were faded out. Azrin, Sneed, and Foxx (1973) demonstrated that this approach can be used successfully.

Eating Behaviors

Research on training eating behaviors has included self-feeding using a spoon (Groves & Carroccio, 1971; Lemke & Mitchell, 1972; Zeiler & Jervey, 1968); using spoon, knife, and fork (Nelson, Cone, & Hanson, 1975; O'Brien & Azrin, 1972); and table manners (Barton, Guess, Garcia, & Baer, 1970; Henriksen & Doughty, 1967). Most of the research on training eating skills has used food as the natural reinforcer and has involved a timeout procedure in which inappropriate eating resulted in the student being halted from eating or being removed from the dining area. For example, Martin, McDonald, and Omichinski (1971) compared the use of social reinforcement and timeout on food slopping by four severely and profoundly handicapped students. They found that social reinforcement had little effect, but timeout was effective.

Prompt Procedures

Graduated guidance employing reversed chaining was used in several studies (O'Brien & Azrin, 1972; Zeiler & Jervey, 1968). In this method, the trainer physically guides the student through the steps of the program and then releases assistance at the last step (for example, spoon at lips). With success, the student is required to do an increasing number of steps until the student can do the behavior independently. Azrin and Armstrong (1973) demonstrated the success of a physical assistance fading strategy. At first, the teacher places his or her hand over the student's hand and guides the student through the eating process. When the student becomes consistent, the teacher moves his or her physical assistance upward while reducing the strength: the teacher starts at a hand-over-hand position, then moves to the forearm, then the elbow, then the shoulder, and finally the teacher just keeps light physical contact by touching the student's upper back.

Ecological Training

Richman, Sonderby, and Kahn (1980) focused on whether or not it was better to teach the students at the dining table, as was done in the majority of the studies, or to teach them during other times of the days using artificial food. Three students were trained to use fork skills at the dining table using real food. The other three students were trained for four three-minute sessions a day using the same prompting procedure, but using Styrofoam food. The teacher stopped the student's hand three inches from the mouth, took away the Styrofoam, and gave social praise. The results indicated that the effects of the training using artificial food generalized to the dining room setting. Also, followup probes after training indicated better maintenance by members of the group who practiced using artificial food.

Intensive Training

Rather than using the students' eating cycle of three meals a day, Azrin and Armstrong (1973) used an intensive "mini-meal" approach. The students were trained hourly using small portions of food. Initially, two teachers were used: one for directing the student's arm and the other to focus on lap, hand, and/or head problems. The student was given constant attention during this program and errors were corrected. The results showed that the 11 students were trained within 12 days. The average number of eating errors went from 83 percent during baseline to an average of 6 percent during the followup probes taken up to 28 weeks later. The success of this approach was replicated in a study by Stimbert, Minor, and McCoy (1977).

Associated Problems

One of the problems in teaching eating behavior is that of speed of food intake. Favell, McGimsey, and Jones (1980) found that over one-fourth of the students surveyed in one institution ate rapidly. A meal that would normally be consumed in 15 to 20 minutes would be consumed in 1 to 3 minutes by rapid eaters. To solve this problem, they reinforced short pauses between bites and then shaped longer pauses. This was done by telling the student to wait and then by reinforcing the student with bites of a favorite food. This approach reduced the eating speed to a normal level.

Proof of maintenance of eating skills after the intervention phase of training has been lacking in most of the studies. In a study by Albin (1977), a maintenance phase was included after the initial eating training program, and there was evidence that the training program resulted in a decrease in inappropriate eating behaviors. A sign showing the behavioral techniques (reprimand and timeout) was posted for staff during the maintenance phase. The improved behavior maintained and continued, as shown in the followup probes taken in another setting six and eighteen months later.

Dressing and Grooming Behaviors

Research has shown that many of the training techniques that were used to train eating skills (for example, graduated guidance) can be used to train dressing skills (Azrin, Schaeffer, & Wesolowski, 1976; Martin, Kehoe, Bird, Jensen, & Darbyshire, 1971; Minge & Ball, 1967), hand and face washing (Treffry, Martin, Samels, & Watson, 1970), toothbrushing (Abramson & Wunderlich, 1972; Horner & Keilitz, 1975; Wehman, 1974), and use of sanitary napkins by menstruating retarded females (Hamilton, Allen, Stephens, & Davall, 1969). All of the studies showed successful skill training. Unfortunately, most of these studies lacked rigorous experimental control so that the validation of the training techniques that were used is hard to evaluate (Wehman, 1979; Westling & Murden, 1978).

With the exception of the dressing program of Azrin et al. (1976), most of the studies involved a fairly high number of daily training sessions. Like the rapid training programs by Azrin in feeding (Azrin & Armstrong, 1973) and toileting (Foxx & Azrin, 1973b), the rapid dressing program used long training sessions (three-hour sessions) with intensive reinforced practice. Oversized clothing was used to ensure initial success. In an average of twelve hours, the four students in this study gained dressing skills.When compared with previous research, this result is impressive, but it should be remembered that the students were selected because of their potential for training success. Also, the dressing skills involved only slip-on garments without fasteners.

Doleys, Stacy, and Knowles (1981) used a token reinforcement system to increase the performance of the following grooming skills: bathing, brushing teeth, washing hair, shaving, wearing clean clothes, and dressing appropriately. The seven mentally retarded students in this study had been deinstitutionalized and the goal was to achieve appearance more appropriate by community standards. The grooming behaviors improved when token reinforcers were given, but this study lacked followup probes to indicate that the improved behavior was maintained.

Maintenance

Several strategies have been used to maintain already trained grooming skills. Thinesen and Bryan (1981) used sequential pictorial cues to maintain grooming skills. The three students in this study had acquired the eight targeted grooming skills, but they did not perform them unless supervised. Students were trained to use a photograph sequence book that contained eight pages (three photographs depicting one of the eight target behaviors and a picture of an edible reinforcer on each page). The students were then expected to do each of the behaviors independently and they received verbal praise and an edible item for each grooming behavior performed correctly. When the performance was consistently high, the use of the picture book was faded by removing one page at a time from the book. Followup probes taken up to 16 weeks later showed maintenance of grooming behavior well above the baseline levels.

Clothes Selection

Although most training curricula have the basic dressing programs (such as buttoning, zipping, and snapping), there is almost no research on programs for training students to look appropriate in public. Severely and profoundly handicapped students with shirttails out and mismatched colors and patterns bring attention to themselves. Nutter and Reid (1978) in an ingenious study taught five severely and profoundly retarded women to wear clothing in color combinations in agreement with local norms. Over 600 women were observed to evaluate which types of clothing, colors, and color patterns (solid versus nonsolid) were prevalent. A body puzzle with attachable clothing pieces was used for training. The puzzle was used instead of real clothing to make training faster and to allow for more training trials. After the students mastered the puzzle, actual garments were used in training with a puzzle-to-garments match being required. The results of this training showed that the students were able to correctly select clothing for the puzzle and select five coordinated outfits from a clothing rack. Four of the five students maintained performance in followup probes that were taken eight to fourteen months later.

Home Living Skills Training

There have been only a few studies showing successful home living skills training of severely and profoundly handicapped students. Some studies have used mildly handicapped students (for example, teaching housekeeping skills by Bauman and Iwata, 1977), but only a few researchers (for example, Cuvo, Matson, and Wehman) have conducted multiple studies on a severely and profoundly handicapped population.

Meal Preparation

Although there have been several meal preparation programs created (see, for example, Kahan, 1974; Spellman et al., 1978; Yates, 1972), there have been very few empirical studies showing programs that are effective. One of the main problems is that severely and profoundly handicapped students cannot read cookbooks. The alternative is to use picture based cookbooks. Although lacking in experimental control, a study by Robinson-Wilson (1977) showed that three severely and profoundly handicapped students could learn to cook a hot dog, make Jell-O, and make hot chocolate by following pictorial instruction. Her data indicated that after the first skill was trained, subsequent recipes were learned faster. Also, there was generalization across recipes taught.

Matson (1979) explained a program to train meal preparation skills to 21 severely and moderately retarded adults. A group training procedure with four to six students per group was used to train 21 behaviors. The average percentage of correct responses on the behaviors prior to training was 52 percent. In the instructional procedure, the teacher modeled the target behavior step by step. Then one of the students was asked to perform the behavior. The teacher used minimal prompting. After the demonstration, the other students were asked questions about the task. Correct answers were reinforced and uncorrected answers were given a "No" response followed by the correct answer. The average number of trials per behavior was 4.5 to reach the criterion of 90 percent correct. Matson reported that informal reports after training showed maintenance and generalization of the meal preparation skills. Unfortunately, it is hard to evaluate the effectiveness of this study because it, like the previous study, lacked experimental control.

A multiple baseline across behaviors design was used in a study by Schleien, Ash, Kiernan, and Wehman (1981). In this study, a profoundly retarded woman was taught to boil (an egg), broil (a muffin with cheese on top), and bake (a TV dinner). Baseline data showed a general low level of performance on all three tasks. The student was trained four to five times a week for approximately 15 minutes per session. The results showed that, even though the student had seizures that interfered with some training sessions, the number of sessions needed to acquire each of the three skills ranged from only 23 to 46 sessions. Weekly probes showed that the behaviors did maintain. Also, probes using the action verbs (boil, broil, and bake) were taken to evaluate generalization to another community facility, to the home setting, and across other materials and foods. Overall, generalization was shown.

Johnson and Cuvo (1981) taught four retarded adults to boil, bake, and broil. It should be noted that only one of the four students was below the mildly retarded range and that all of the students possessed the following prerequisite behaviors: could open packaged and canned food items, could pour liquids, and could identify cooking materials and numbers. Six tasks using three cooking modes were selected: boiling (egg, vegetables), baking (cornbread, biscuits), and broiling (hot dog, English muffin). Pictorial recipes were developed for each of these cooking tasks. A design including a multiple baseline across students and behaviors was used. The teachers employed a less to more restrictive prompt sequence (no help, verbal instruction, verbal instruction + visual cue, verbal instruction + modeling, and verbal instruction + physical guidance). Correct responses were reinforced by verbal praise on a variable-ratio schedule by the teacher, praise from training staff members, verbal and graphic feedback for response accuracy, and consumables (eating the cooked food).

The results showed that it took an average of four to six sessions to learn each cooking skill. For three of the four students, the learning of one cooking behavior generalized to other cooking behaviors. Followup probes taken seven to eleven days after the acquisition phase showed 82 percent to 100 percent maintenance and only a few sessions were needed to return each student to the training criterion level. The average cost per student to train all six cooking behaviors was only $46.47. Also, two of the four students began cooking in their home setting.

Bathroom Cleaning Skills

Although originally designed as a validation of training a vocational skill, a study by Cuvo, Leaf, and Borakove (1978) represents the only empirical study on training bathroom cleaning skills. Six tasks were selected: (1) cleaning a mirror; (2) cleaning a sink; (3) cleaning a urinal; (4) cleaning a toilet; (5) returning equipment, emptying a wastebasket, sweeping the floor; and (6) mopping the floor. As with other research by Cuvo, the task analysis went through a sophisticated process. The school janitor and a retarded student with cleaning skills were observed and videotaped. Students in a graduate course on job restructuring modified the task analysis. Then the task analysis was piloted on retarded students who were not involved in the study.

Training occurred in a bathroom that had been used by 70 handicapped students. Two prompt sequences were used in training. A more-to-less restrictive prompt sequence was used for 20 steps identified as difficult and a less-to-more restrictive prompt sequence was used on the other 161 steps. The teacher gave M & M's and social praise on a variable-ratio basis: 62 percent of the responses on the first session, twice during the second session, and once on subsequent sessions. After one subtask was trained, maintenance probes were taken to ensure consistent performance while another subtask was being trained.

All students reached a 90 percent no-help criterion in nine days (an average of 2.67 hours). Also, the cleaning behavior generalized to another bathroom both immediately after instruction in the training bathroom and two weeks after the end of the program. This study demonstrated effective training with generalization.

Laundry Skills

The only research on training laundry skills has been conducted by Cuvo, Jacobi, and Sipko (1981). Four moderately and one mildly retarded student were instructed for one session per day (average session of 13.5 minutes) to sort, wash, and dry clothing. The task analysis for these behaviors was developed after watching school personnel and adults at laundromats. A videotape of the program was made based on the task analysis and then experts in special education, home economics, and rehabilitation critiqued it. During baseline the average percentage of correct responses by the five students was 30 percent for sorting, 22 percent for washing, and 19 percent for drying.

Unlike most studies that use one prompt sequence, three prompt sequences were used: one based on more-to-less restrictive prompts and two based on less-to-more restrictive prompts. Changes in prompt sequences were made based on student progress. Training time was reduced by not actually running the washer and dryer. Laundry procedures were simulated by placing a piece of cellophane in the detergent dispenser and lint in the dryer. At the end of each session, students were given feedback by showing them the graphs of their progress. If the performance was superior to the previous session, verbal praise was given. A 90 percent criterion for the three subtasks was required.

The average time to teach the sorting, washing, and drying subtasks was about three hours, at an average cost of $12.65. When compared with the cost of sending the laundry to a commercial laundry service, the expenditure for training (excluding testing) could be recovered in approximately one month.

Clothes Mending

Cronin and Cuvo (1979) have conducted the only study on clothes mending with severely and profoundly handicapped students. Five moderately retarded students were trained to perform three handsewing tasks: repairing a hem, sewing on a button, and mending seams. The task analyses were created after observing experts and nonexperts doing the three tasks. The 58 steps in the three task analyses comprised the Sewing Skills Test. None of the five students scored above 35 percent correct during baseline on any of the three tasks.

The students were trained to select the correct color of thread and button against three distractors. The following prompt sequence was used: no help, verbal instruction, verbal instruction and modeling, verbal instruction and physical guidance, and verbal instruction and visual cue (a stitch line or button placement was marked on the fabric). The criterion to move to a more restrictive prompt was a five-second delay without trainee self-initiation. Every fourth correct response was praised. The order of training for the three skills was counterbalanced with a 100 percent criterion, with no help on a skill required before going to another skill.

The results of this study showed that there was some generalization across skills (for example, the student's seam mending score improved even though the training task was to repair a hem). One week after the initial acquisition of all three skills, two students required retraining sessions (one student required one session and the other student required two sessions). All five students demonstrated 100 percent maintenance during the two-week followup probe. The cost of training these three skills was small—an average of $19.94.

Safety Training

Knowing when and how to respond to emergencies is important. Matson (1980a) taught severely and profoundly handicapped students how to respond to a fire emergency, bandage a cut, and assist someone who is having a seizure. In the first experiment in the study, students were instructed in a classroom setting where the teacher described the steps in the task analysis and then the students were asked to describe how to react if a fire were to occur. The teacher and peers reinforced correct responses. When the student could verbally describe all of the behaviors twice, the student was asked to observe the teacher demonstrating the correct behavior using cardboard figures. Then the student imitated the teacher's performance and was given verbal or physical prompts, if necessary. The instructional program lasted slightly over two weeks. Followup probes taken seven months after the termination of the instructional program showed significant improvement in performance (the ability to describe the fire escape process). In the second experiment, the students learned to bandage a cut and respond to a seizuring person. Besides a classroom training phase, as was used in the earlier study, role playing in the living environment was conducted. The author noted that the active role playing improved the chances of maintenance of the skill. Followup probes taken one month after intervention showed a high level of maintenance.

Telephone Training

There has been very little research on teaching severely and profoundly handicapped students to use a telephone. Leff (1974, 1975) described adaptive devices to aid in teaching telephone dialing. One aid was a cover with large numbers that was placed over the dial. For students who still had trouble, color inserts were placed over the numbers on the dial and then the student matched to a color sequence. Another aid allowed for one digit of the telephone number to be viewed individually. Leff reported a 90 percent success rate in teaching dialing through the use of these devices.

In a classroom setting, Risley and Cuvo (1980) taught three students to make emergency telephone calls to the police, the fire department, and a doctor. The task analysis was created by viewing a retarded student with telephoning skills, receiving advice (from a telephone consultant and fire and police departments), and watching a training film on telephone dialing. The student had to make the decision as to who to call, find the number in the directory, dial the telephone number, and provide the necessary information. Each student was presented with an emergency situation (for example, a picture of a fire) and was prompted through the training sequence, the prompt becoming more restrictive if necessary. Students role played telephoning by dialing the correct number on a disconnected telephone and then the teacher on another disconnected telephone asked for information. The results of this study showed that the students were not only able to learn the telephoning process for the targeted emergency, but also generalized the skill to the other two emergency situations. It took only an average of six sessions to train correct performance on all three types of emergency calls. The cost of this training for the three students was $10.94, $14.20, and $15.81.

Smith and Meyers (1979) compared individualized versus group training of telephone skills on 60 profoundly to moderately retarded students. Also, they compared different types of prompts: verbal explanation, model, verbal explanation and model, and a control situation. The teacher in the conditions involving verbal explanation covered the functions of the telephone, whereas the students in the control situation received an irrelevant lecture. Students were tested after each of the two instructional sessions and during two followup probes two weeks and three months later. The results showed no significant differences between the prompt groups. It appears that practice, even without formal training (the control group), results in improvements of telephoning skills. Also, there was no difference in acquisition rates between individual and group training. The authors suggest that for economic reasons it may be advantageous to use a group training structure.

Beyond the problem of a general lack of telephone training studies, there is a need to demonstrate that severely and profoundly handicapped students can learn to generalize skills beyond a classroom role-playing situation. Using a telephone requires many judgments (for example, looking up a telephone number, dialing on rotary and push-button telephones, knowing when to hang up if no one answers, and giving information). Further research is needed to demonstrate that this population can independently display this skill.

Economic Skills Training

Coin Equivalence

Research has shown that retarded persons who have been deinstitutionalized have trouble managing money (Aanes & Moen, 1976; Bell, 1976; Edgerton, 1967; McCarver & Craig, 1974). One of the skills needed to assist in functioning independently is the ability to use coins in combinations to make a purchase. Trace, Cuvo, and Criswell (1977) used a coin machine that provided feedback (a "happy face" and M & M's) to teach handicapped students coin equivalence. Nickels, dimes, and quarters were used to train 37 possible coin combinations. The stages of training went from nickel to quarter combinations to reach a $.50 total. After the teacher modeled a correct coin combination, the student was allowed to respond. The results of this study showed that students who received training were able to learn coin equivalence in an average of 9.43 sessions (three hours and eight minutes). Also, there was substantial maintenance as shown in followup probes one week and one month later. Students in the control group did not make progress in the same time period.

One precautionary note should be made. It is unclear how many of the students in this study were severely and profoundly handicapped—at least one student was moderately retarded. Also, each of the students was able to count by ones and fives to one hundred, name coins (penny, nickel, dime, quarter, and half dollar), and sum ten-coin combinations. Such skills may require extensive training before the initiation of this program.

Coin Computation

Cuvo, Veitch, Trace, and Konke (1978) taught three handicapped students to make coin computations. Prerequisite skills for inclusion in this study were being able to name five coins, sum combinations of coins, read simulated price tags, and demonstrate coin equivalence skills. It should be noted that this requirement eliminated a sizable percentage of the possible student participants.

The task was to be able to compute the difference between an item priced at less than a dollar and a specific amount of money given to the student. Four response classes were taught in succession: $.01 to $.04, $.05 to $.09, $.10 to $.45, and $.11 to $.49. The goal was to have the students use the fewest number of coins. A two-trial instruction format was used. During the first trial, the teacher modeled the correct behavior. The student was shown a stimulus card with a price tag and told the cost of the item. The teacher stated the name of coins as they were presented in descending order. Then the teacher stated the correct amount of change and the process of using the fewest number of coins. After the modeling trial, the next trial and further trials used verbal instruction without modeling. When the student responded correctly 90 percent of the trials, he or she went to the next response class. Reviews were conducted to ensure against losing previous response classes.

Training to criterion on all four response classes took between seven to twenty hours. The initial acquisition maintained for the three students as shown by followup probes taken two weeks after training. The generalization across response classes (the effect of learning one response class on other response classes) varied across students. Further research on currency to see if the training generalizes to real item and money situations is needed.

Travel Training

Pedestrian Skills Training

There have been few studies in which the goal has been teaching pedestrian skills to severely and profoundly handicapped students. Previous research by Page, Iwata, and Neef (1976) has indicated that pedestrian skills can be trained through classroom instruction. This research, however, involved mildly retarded students. Matson (1980b) used institutionalized severely and moderately retarded students in a study comparing three conditions: classroom training using a model intersection, independence training (instruction on sign recognition and practice using a mock intersection), and a control group. Proper sidewalk behavior, recognition of an intersection, and crossing the street were three components to the pedestrian training program. The classroom training condition was designed to approximate the Page et al. (1976) procedures. Daily 30-minute sessions contained trials in which the instructor told the student to move a model figure along the model of a street to the intersection. The student was required to verbally describe what he or she was doing (for example, "I'm walking to a corner crossing"). Also, the student had to answer questions that matched steps on the task analysis. Correct responses were socially reinforced, and incorrect responses resulted in the student repeating the step correctly.

Independence training was started with training of common pedestrian signs. Then training at a mock intersection was conducted in groups of three. The training procedure was similar to the group using the model, except feedback and reinforcement by peers were given at the end of the session. Like the previous condition, training lasted for three months even though students may have reached criterion.

Progress was assessed by having staff who were unaware of the experimental conditions evaluate the percentage of the steps on the task analysis each student could perform. The assessment was taken at baseline and three weeks after the completion of the intervention programs. Students in the classroom and independence training groups did significantly better than students in the control group, which did not receive any training. Students in the independence training, however, did significantly better than those in the classroom training. For safety reasons, the instructional training program is a promising approach to training pedestrian skills to severely and profoundly handicapped students.

Bus-Riding Training

In our mobile society, the ability to go to places such as work, movies, and friends' homes may involve problems of transportation. Walking long distances is unreasonable. Driving a car is probably an unreasonable goal for most severely and profoundly handicapped students, and transportation by taxi is expensive and unavailable in some locations. Several researchers (Coon, Vogelsberg, & Williams, 1981; Neef, Iwata, & Page, 1978; Sowers, Rusch, & Hudson, 1979) have shown that bus riding is an alternative for severely and profoundly handicapped students.

Neef, Iwata, and Page (1978) were able to teach bus-riding skills to seven handicapped students. Five of the students were taught in the classroom. The classroom training required that the students respond correctly in three situations: (1) training on a model that simulated a bus stop area, (2) answering questions about a slide sequence showing instances and noninstances of bus riding to designated places, and (3) role playing a bus ride on a simulated bus. During the model training, the teacher gave the student a doll and the student followed the teacher's instructions and verbalized the actions while manipulating the doll. For comparison, two students were trained using an in vivo procedure. Training occurred in the natural setting (bus stop locations or buses). The teacher followed the student and gave either contingent praise or corrective feedback.

Both the classroom and the in vivo procedure were effective in teaching bus-riding behavior. Probes taken as long as one year later showed continued maintenance for both groups. Also, generalization to another bus was demonstrated. Because of equal levels of success, a main factor is cost. The average cost of training per student was $126.00 for students in the in vivo group and only $33.60 for students in the classroom group. Thus, the classroom training procedure appears to be more cost efficient.

Using a single subject design, Coon, Vogelsberg, and Williams (1981) attempted by using a classroom instruction procedure to train bus riding. A simulated bus with seats and a coin box were created. Cards containing bus route names were to be matched to bus stop signs. Although rapid progress was demonstrated in classroom performance, generalization to the natural settings showed little improvement. When instruction was shifted to the natural setting, the student-acquired bus-riding behavior generalized and was maintained.

Although at first glance the results of this study seem to contradict the Neef et al. study (1978), it must be remembered that there was a difference in classroom instruction procedures. The Neef et al. procedure may have been superior, and thus resulted in better transfer to the natural setting.

Combined Bus Riding and Purchasing

Marholin, O'Toole, Touchette, Berger, and Doyle (1979) conducted a study combining bus-travel training and purchasing items at a store and fast-food restaurant. A multiple baseline design across four subjects was used. After baseline, the trainers in the intervention program used a variety of techniques: graduated prompting, contingent reinforcement, corrective feedback, practice, modeling, and timeout. At the end of the intervention period, a transfer test was given to evaluate if the students could perform the bus riding and purchasing in a different restaurant and store.

The results of this study are somewhat hard to interpret because of very short baselines. At best, only two of the four students made clinically significant improvements on both bus-riding and purchasing tasks. The trend lines for the other two students during intervention did not seem to change significantly from baseline, and their performance leveled off at a two-thirds correct level. As the authors noted, part of the problem may be due to the lack of prerequisite skills (for example, money computation for purchases). Also, transfer to another setting was shown, but it must be remembered that the trainer continued to use the intervention procedure during the transfer test.

Leisure Skills

The majority of severely and profoundly handicapped students do not know how to use leisure time. Most mentally retarded persons spend their free time involved in isolated activities away from a social group (Gozali & Charney, 1972; Katz & Yekutiel, 1974). This is supported by Bjannes and Butler (1974), who found that only 3 percent of the free time of retarded clients was spent in goal-directed leisure activities. Reid, Willis, Jarman, and Brown (1978) conducted a study to discover the effects of providing the opportunity for voluntary use of leisure activities. Institutionalized severely and profoundly handicapped students were placed in a leisure room with things like games and books. When compared with the ward setting, the percentage of desirable behavior displayed increased dramatically. The leisure activities were made available in the ward setting, but the percentage of desirable behavior decreased in that setting. The conclusions, based on observational data, student verbal preference, and observations by a Human Rights Committee, were all in favor of making available activities in a separate setting.

Adkins and Matson (1980) showed that merely making activities available is not enough. They had staff members suggest that six severely and profoundly handicapped students use the available leisure activities (making potholders, drawing, and playing with puzzles), but the students did not participate. Then the staff members trained the students to make potholders as a leisure skill. During this intervention phase, the students began to draw and put puzzles together. Followup probes taken immediately after intervention and six weeks later showed continued participation with all three leisure activities.

Schleien, Kiernan, and Wehman (1981) demonstrated that severely and profoundly handicapped students can learn leisure skills. After baseline, six moderately retarded students were involved in an instructional program that included presenting age-appropriate materials, leisure counseling, and reinforcement of appropriate behavior. The results showed that the percentage of time showing high quality leisure behavior increased and the inappropriate social behavior decreased during the leisure skills intervention program.

Research has shown that some particular leisure skills can be trained. Marchant and Wehman (1979), for example, taught four students to play three lotto table games. Horst, Wehman, Hill, and Bailey (1981) taught severely and profoundly handicapped students to use a Frisbee, operate a cassette recorder, and play an electronic bowling game. This study shows the possibility of teaching age-appropriate leisure skills, rather than teaching toy play that would not match the students' chronological ages.

Matson and Marchetti (1980) compared five procedures to train the use of a stereo record player as a leisure behavior. One group received independence training in which the trainer modeled the correct behavior, then physically guided the student, and finally asked the student to perform the behavior independently. Not every student received training each day. Students in the traditional classroom training group were individually singled out and asked about different aspects of stereo operation. Another group of students received alternating days of independence training and traditional classroom instruction. The other two groups acted as control groups. Students in the three active intervention groups did significantly better than students in the control groups. The independence training was the superior procedure, as shown at posttest and followup probes two weeks after training.

CONCLUSION

Early research in teaching independent living skills focused primarily on self-help skills. In the past few years, the focus has changed to other, and more sophisticated, skills. Also, the quality of the research has improved. There is now support that some behaviors previously believed to be impossible to learn have been acquired and maintained by severely and profoundly handicapped students. It must be remembered, however, that when the target behaviors that have empirical evidence of being teachable are compared with lists of target behaviors (test items) on adaptive behavior tests, it is evident that educators are really only in the infancy stage of instruction in independent living skills for the severely and profoundly handicapped. At all cost, there must be a continuation of effort coupled with the necessary research validation.

REFERENCES

Aanes, D., & Moen, M. Adaptive behavior changes of group home residents. *Mental Retardation*, 1976, *14*(4), 36–40.

Abramson, E.E., & Wunderlich, R.A. Dental hygiene training for retardates: An application of behavioral techniques. *Mental Retardation*, 1972, *10*(3), 6–8.

Adkins, J., & Matson, J.L. Teaching institutionalized mentally retarded adults socially appropriate leisure skills. *Mental Retardation*, 1980, *18*, 249–252.

Albin, J. Some variables influencing the maintenance of acquired self-feeding behavior in profoundly retarded children. *Mental Retardation*, 1977, *15*(5), 49–52.

Azrin, N.H., & Armstrong, P.M. The "mini-meal"—A method for teaching eating skills to the profoundly retarded. *Mental Retardation*, 1973, *11*(1), 9–11.

Azrin, N.H., & Foxx, R.M. A rapid method of toilet training the institutionalized retarded. *Journal of Applied Behavior Analysis*, 1971, *4*, 89–99.

Azrin, N.H., & Foxx, R.M. *Toilet training in less than a day.* New York: Pocket Books, 1976.

Azrin, N.H., Schaeffer, R.M., & Wesolowski, M.D. A rapid method of teaching profoundly retarded persons to dress by a reinforcement-guidance method. *Mental Retardation*, 1976, *14*(6), 29–33.

Azrin, N.H., Sneed, T.J., & Foxx, R.M. Dry bed: A rapid method of eliminating bedwetting (enuresis) of the retarded. *Behaviour Research and Therapy*, 1973, *11*, 427–434.

Barton, E.S., Guess, D., Garcia, E., & Baer, D. Improvements of retardates' mealtime behaviors by timeout procedures using the multiple baseline technique. *Journal of Applied Behavior Analysis*, 1970, *3*, 77–84.

Bauman, K.E., & Iwata, B.A. Maintenance of independent housekeeping skills using scheduling plus self-recording procedures. *Behavior Therapy*, 1977, *8*, 554–560.

Baumeister, A.A., & Klosowski, R. An attempt to group toilet train severely retarded patients. *Mental Retardation*, 1965, *3*(6), 24–26.

Bell, N.J. IQ as a factor in community lifestyle of previously institutionalized retardates. *Mental Retardation,* 1976, *14*(3), 29–33.

Bensberg, G.J., Jr. (Ed.). *Teaching the mentally retarded.* Atlanta: Southern Regional Education Board, 1965.

Bjannes, A.T., & Butler, E.W. Environment variation in community care facilities for mentally retarded persons. *American Journal of Mental Deficiency,* 1974, *78,* 429–439.

Brown, L., Huppler, B., Pierce, L., York, R., & Sontag, E. Teaching trainable level retarded students to read unconjugated action verbs. *Journal of Special Education,* 1974, *8,* 51–56.

Coon, M.E., Vogelsberg, R.T., & Williams, W. Effects of classroom public transportation instruction on generalization to the natural environment. *Journal of The Association for the Severely Handicapped,* 1981, *6,* 46–53.

Cronin, K.A., & Cuvo, A.J. Teaching mending skills to mentally retarded adolescents. *Journal of Applied Behavior Analysis,* 1979, *12,* 401–406.

Cuvo, A.J., Jacobi, L., & Sipko, R. Teaching laundry skills to mentally retarded students. *Education and Training of the Mentally Retarded,* 1981, *16,* 54–64.

Cuvo, A.J., Leaf, R.B., & Borakove, L.S. Teaching janitorial skills to the mentally retarded: Acquisition, generalization, and maintenance. *Journal of Applied Behavior Analysis,* 1978, *11,* 345–355.

Cuvo, A.J., Veitch, V.D., Trace, M.W., & Konke, J.L. Teaching change computation to the mentally retarded. *Behavior Modification,* 1978, *2,* 531–548.

Dayan, M. Toilet training retarded children in a state residential institution. *Mental Retardation,* 1964, *2*(2), 116–117.

Doleys, D.M., Stacy, D., & Knowles, S. Modification of grooming behavior in adult retarded: Token reinforcement in a community-based program. *Behavior Modification,* 1981, *5,* 119–128.

Domnie, M. & Brown, L. Teaching severely handicapped students reading skills requiring printed answers to who, what, and where questions. *Education and Training of the Mentally Retarded,* 1977, *12,* 324–331.

Edgerton, R.B. *The cloak of competence: Stigma in the lives of the mentally retarded.* Berkeley: University of California Press, 1967.

Ellis, N.R. Toilet training the severely defective patient: An S-R reinforcement analysis. *American Journal of Mental Deficiency,* 1963, *68,* 98–103.

Favell, J.E., McGimsey, J.F., & Jones, M.L. Rapid eating in the retarded: Reduction by nonaversive procedures. *Behavior Modification,* 1980, *4,* 481–492.

Foxx, R.M., & Azrin, N.H. Dry pants: A rapid method of toilet training children. *Behaviour Research and Therapy,* 1973a, *11,* 435–442.

Foxx, R.M., & Azrin, N.H. *Toilet training the retarded: A rapid program for day and nighttime independent toileting.* Champaign, Ill.: Research Press, 1973b.

Fredericks, H.B., Baldwin, V.L., Grove, D.N., & Moore, W.G. *Toilet training the handicapped child.* Monmouth, Oreg.: Instructional Development, 1975.

Gollay, E., Freedman, R., Wyngaarden, M., & Kurtz, N.R. *Coming back: The community experiences of deinstitutionalized mentally retarded people.* Cambridge, Mass.: Abt Books, 1978.

Gozali, J., & Charney, B. Agenda for the '70's: Full social integration of the retarded. *Mental Retardation,* 1972, *10*(6), 20–21.

Groves, I., & Carroccio, D. A self-feeding program for the severely and profoundly mentally retarded. *Mental Retardation,* 1971, *9*(3), 10–12.

Hamilton, J., Allen, P., Stephens, L., & Davall, E. Training mentally retarded females to use sanitary napkins. *Mental Retardation*, 1969, *7*(1), 40–43.

Henriksen, K., & Doughty, R. Decelerating undesired mealtime behavior in a group of profoundly retarded boys. *American Journal of Mental Deficiency*, 1967, *72*, 40–44.

Horner, R.D., & Keilitz, I. Training mentally retarded adolescents to brush their teeth. *Journal of Applied Behavior Analysis*, 1975, *8*, 301–309.

Horst, G., Wehman, P., Hill, J.W., & Bailey, C. Developing age-appropriate leisure skills in severely handicapped adolescents. *Teaching Exceptional Children*, 1981, *14*(1), 11–16.

Hull, J.T., & Thompson, J.C. Predicting adaptive functioning of mentally retarded persons in community settings. *American Journal of Mental Deficiency*, 1980, *85*, 253–261.

Johnson, B.F., & Cuvo, A.J. Teaching mentally retarded adults to cook. *Behavior Modification*, 1981, *5*, 187–202.

Kahan, E.H. *Cooking activities for the retarded child*. Nashville, Tenn.: Abingdon, 1974.

Katz, S., & Yekutiel, E. Leisure time problems of mentally retarded graduates of training programs. *Mental Retardation*, 1974, *12*(3), 54–57.

Largo, R.H., & Stutzle, W. Longitudinal study of bowel and bladder control by day and at night in the first six years of life: I. Epidemiology and interactions between bowel and bladder control. *Developmental Medicine and Child Neurology*, 1977a, *19*, 598–606.

Largo, R.H., & Stutzle, W. Longitudinal study of bowel and bladder control by day and at night in the first six years of life: II. The role of potty training and the child's initiative. *Developmental Medicine and Child Neurology*, 1977b, *19*, 607–613.

Leff, R.B. Teaching the TMR to dial the telephone. *Mental Retardation*, 1974, *12*(2), 12–13.

Leff, R.B. Teaching TMR children and adults to dial the telephone. *Mental Retardation*, 1975, *13*(3), 9–12.

Lemke, H., & Mitchell, R.D. Controlling the behavior of a profoundly retarded child. *American Journal of Occupational Therapy*, 1972, *26*(5), 261–264.

Linford, M.D., Hipsher, L.W., & Silikovitz, R.G. *Systematic instruction for retarded children: The Illinois program. Part III: Self-help instruction*. Danville, Ill.: Interstate Printers, 1972.

Lohman, W., Eyman, R., & Lask, E. Toilet training. *American Journal of Mental Deficiency*, 1967, *71*, 551–557.

Mahoney, K., Van Wagenen, R.K., & Meyerson, L. Toilet training of normal and retarded children. *Journal of Applied Behavior Analysis*, 1971, *4*, 173–181.

Marchant, J.A. Teaching games and hobbies. In P. Wehman (Ed.), *Recreation programming for developmentally disabled persons*. Baltimore: University Park Press, 1979.

Marchant, J., & Wehman, P. Teaching table games to severely retarded children. *Mental Retardation*, 1979, *17*, 150–152.

Marholin, D., O'Toole, K.M., Touchette, P.E., Berger, P.L., & Doyle, D.A. "I'll have a Big Mac, large fries, large coke, and apple pie" . . . or teaching adaptive community skills. *Behavior Therapy*, 1979, *10*, 236–248.

Martin, G.L., Kehoe, B., Bird, E., Jensen, V., & Darbyshire, M. Operant conditioning in dressing behavior of severely retarded girls. *Mental Retardation*, 1971, *9*(3), 27–30.

Martin, G.L., McDonald, S., & Omichinski, M. An operant analysis of response interactions during meals with severely retarded children. *American Journal of Mental Deficiency*, 1971, *76*, 68–75.

Matson, J.L. A field tested system of training meal preparation skills to the retarded. *British Journal of Mental Subnormality*, 1979, *25*, 14–18.

Matson, J.L. Preventing home accidents: A training program for the retarded. *Behavior Modification,* 1980a, *4,* 397–410.

Matson, J.L. A controlled group study of pedestrian-skill training for the mentally retarded. *Behaviour Research and Therapy,* 1980b, *18,* 99–106.

Matson, J.L., & Marchetti, A. A comparison of leisure skills training procedures for the mentally retarded. *Applied Research in Mental Retardation,* 1980, *1,* 113–122.

McCarver, R.B., & Craig, E.M. Placement of the retarded in the community: Prognosis and outcome. In N.R. Ellis (Ed.), *International review of research in mental retardation* (Vol. 7). New York: Academic, 1974.

Minge, M.R., & Ball, T.S. Teaching self-help skills to profoundly retarded patients. *American Journal of Mental Deficiency,* 1967, *71,* 864–868.

Mowrer, O.H., & Mowrer, W.M. Enuresis: A method for its study and treatment. *American Journal of Orthopsychiatry,* 1938, *8,* 436–459.

Neef, N.A., Iwata, B.A., & Page, T.J. Public transportation training: In vivo versus classroom instruction. *Journal of Applied Behavior Analysis,* 1978, *11,* 331–344.

Nelson, G.L., Cone, J.D., & Hanson, C.R. Training correct utensil use in retarded children: Modeling vs. physical guidance. *American Journal of Mental Deficiency,* 1975, *80,* 114–122.

Nietupski, J., Williams, W., & York, R. Teaching selected phonic word analysis reading and spelling skills to moderately and severely handicapped students. In F. Johnson, J. Nietupski, L. Brown, & T. Crowner (Eds.), *Papers and programs related to teaching reading skills to severely handicapped students. Vol. VI, Part 2.* Madison, Wis.: Madison Metropolitan School District, 1976.

Nutter, D., & Reid, D.H. Teaching retarded women a clothing selection skill using community norms. *Journal of Applied Behavior Analysis,* 1978, *11,* 475–488.

O'Brien, F., & Azrin, N.H. Developing proper mealtime behaviors of the institutionalized retarded. *Journal of Applied Behavior Analysis,* 1972, *5,* 389–399.

Page, T.J., Iwata, B.A., & Neef, N.A. Teaching pedestrian skills to retarded persons: Generalization from the classroom norms. *Journal of Applied Behavior Analysis,* 1976, *9,* 433–444.

Reid, D.H., Willis, B.S., Jarman, P.H., & Brown, K.M. Increasing leisure activity of physically disabled retarded persons through resource availability. *AAESPH Review,* 1978, *3,* 78–93.

Richman, J.S., Sonderby, T., & Kahn, J.V. Prerequisite vs. in vivo acquisition of self-feeding skill. *Behaviour Research and Therapy,* 1980, *18,* 327–332.

Risley, R., & Cuvo, A.J. Training mentally retarded adults to make emergency telephone calls. *Behavior Modification,* 1980, *4,* 513–525.

Robinson-Wilson, M.A. Picture recipe cards as an approach to teaching severely and profoundly retarded adults to cook. *Education and Training of the Mentally Retarded,* 1977, *12,* 69–73.

Sadler, O.W., & Merkert, F. Evaluating the Foxx and Azrin toilet training program for retarded children in a day training center. *Behavior Therapy,* 1977, *8,* 499–500.

Schalock, R.L., Harper, R.S., & Genung, T. Community integration of mentally retarded adults: Community placement and program success. *American Journal of Mental Deficiency,* 1981, *85,* 478–488.

Schleien, S.J., Ash, T., Kiernan, J., & Wehman, P. Developing independent cooking skills in a profoundly retarded woman. *Journal of The Association for the Severely Handicapped,* 1981, *6,* 23–29.

Schleien, S.J., Kiernan, J., & Wehman, P. Evaluation of an age-appropriate leisure skills program for moderately retarded adults. *Education and Training of the Mentally Retarded,* 1981, *16,* 13–19.

Smith, M., & Meyers, A. Telephone training for retarded adults: Group and individual demonstrations with and without verbal instruction. *American Journal of Mental Deficiency,* 1979, *83,* 581–587.

Smith, P.S. A comparison of different methods of toilet training the mentally handicapped. *Behaviour Research and Therapy,* 1979, *17,* 33–43.

Snell, M.E. Self-care skills. In M.E. Snell (Ed.), *Systematic instruction of the moderately and severely handicapped.* Columbus, Ohio: Charles E. Merrill, 1978.

Sowers, J., Rusch, F., & Hudson, C. Training a severely retarded young adult to ride the city bus to and from work. *AAESPH Review,* 1979, *4,* 15–22.

Spellman, C., DeBriere, T., Jarboe, D., Campbell, S., & Harris, C. Pictorial instruction: Training daily living skills. In M.E. Snell (Ed.), *Systematic instruction of the moderately and severely handicapped.* Columbus, Ohio: Charles E. Merrill, 1978.

Spencer, R.L., Temerlin, M.K., & Trousdale, W.W. Some correlates of bowel control in the profoundly retarded. *American Journal of Mental Deficiency,* 1968, *72,* 879–882.

Stimbert, V.E., Minor, J.W., & McCoy, J.F. Intensive feeding training with retarded children. *Behavior Modification,* 1977, *1,* 517–530.

Sugaya, K. Survey of the enuresis problem in an institution for the mentally retarded with emphasis on the clinical psychological aspects. *Japanese Journal of Child Psychiatry,* 1967, *8,* 142–150.

Sutter, P., Mayeda, T., Call, T., Yanagi, G., & Yee, S. Comparison of successful and unsuccessful community-placed mentally retarded persons. *American Journal of Mental Deficiency,* 1980, *85,* 262–267.

Thinesen, P.J., & Bryan, A.J. The use of sequential pictorial cues in the initiation and maintenance of grooming behavior with mentally retarded adults. *Mental Retardation,* 1981, *19,* 246–250.

Trace, M.W., Cuvo, A.J., & Criswell, J.L. Teaching coin equivalence to the mentally retarded. *Journal of Applied Behavior Analysis,* 1977, *10,* 85–92.

Treffry, D., Martin, G., Samels, J., & Watson, C. Operant conditioning of grooming behavior of severely retarded girls. *Mental Retardation,* 1970, *8*(4), 29–33.

Van Wagenen, R.K., Meyerson, L., Kerr, N.J., & Mahoney, K. Field trials of a new procedure for toilet training. *Journal of Experimental Child Psychology,* 1969, *8,* 147–159.

Van Wagenen, R.K., & Murdock, E.E. A transistorized signal-package for toilet training of infants. *Journal of Experimental Child Psychology,* 1966, *3,* 312–314.

Wehman, P.H. Effects of token reinforcement on maintaining oral hygiene skills in geriatric retarded women. *Training School Bulletin,* 1974, *71*(1), 39–40.

Wehman, P. *Curriculum design for the severely and profoundly handicapped.* New York: Human Services Press, 1979.

Westling, D.L., & Murden, L. Self-help skills training: A review of operant studies. *Journal of Special Education,* 1978, *12,* 253–283.

Yates, J. *Look and cook.* Seattle, Wash.: Bernie Straub Publishing Co., 1972.

Zeiler, M.D., & Jervey, S.S. Development of behavior: Self-feeding. *Journal of Consulting & Clinical Psychology,* 1968, *32,* 164–168.

Chapter 10

Vocational Training

Janet W. Hill
Virginia Commonwealth University

PROBLEM

The appropriateness of early and comprehensive vocational training for the population of severely and profoundly handicapped students addressed in this text is still seriously questioned by many educators and parents alike. Even at present, a vocational program may simply not exist within the educational plan for many of the more severely handicapped, nor are special educators prepared for the vocational needs of these students (Snell, 1978). In fact, because of the magnitude of student needs, many teachers and administrators are reluctant to relinquish small portions of valuable school time strictly for vocational training (Wehman & Bates, 1978; Lynch & Singer, 1980). It is ironic in this day of zero exclusion from schools and our struggle to provide appropriate educational services to all handicapped that the vocational expectations for this group are often so low that vocational training is considered a waste of time. Although curriculum development has surged in nearly all other areas, there remains a paucity of information on basic vocational directions for individuals who are the most significantly handicapped. It is these individuals who undoubtedly most need early and sustained vocational training if they are to become vocationally integrated in some form in their community (Snell, 1978).

Low expectations of vocational potential for the severely handicapped have not been formed from demonstrations that have proved it is impossible to train this population. On the contrary, it has been repeatedly demonstrated that this population can achieve successful performance levels in the acquisition of complex tasks. From a practitioner's point of reference, there exist two concrete problems of application that have contributed to the proliferation of ideas of low expectations and lack of growth in the field of vocational education for these students. The first is the basic inadequacy of our vocational service delivery system to all handicapped persons in this country.

This system effectively functions as a bottleneck in which less handicapped individuals find great difficulty, for a variety of reasons, in achieving the final transition to competitive employment and independence. Thus, there is currently no potential outlet for severely handicapped workers even if they have received the rigorous training they would require. The second problem is that nonhandicapped people in general have definite preconceived notions regarding skill levels required in a remunerative situation. Severely and profoundly handicapped individuals are viewed as so different from the norm or from the average paid worker that functioning in the world of work seems almost ludicrous. Therefore, the more severely handicapped often lack vocational credibility and because their potential contributions are viewed as inconsequential, many educators/rehabilitators believe training emphasis should be placed elsewhere.

Inadequacies in Vocational Service Delivery

In order to discuss appropriate vocational needs for the more severely handicapped, one must examine the problems in vocational service delivery to those persons who are less severely handicapped. It is important to understand advancements in the vocational habilitation for the moderately and mildly handicapped, for it is these efforts that may relieve the "bottleneck" inhibiting vocational developments for the severely and profoundly handicapped.

The development of the sheltered workshop was the first real commitment to vocational training for the handicapped in general (Hansen, 1980). This type of workshop was an innovation that evolved largely through pressure exerted by parent groups as well as the rehabilitation needs of war veterans. The original intent was to create a short-term training unit aimed at intensive preparation of individuals in order to return them to the real work force in the community (Hansen, 1980; Bellamy, Sheehan, Horner, & Boles, 1980; Flexer & Martin, 1978).

The continuum of services was theoretically as follows:

School
Home ⟶ Sheltered ⟶ Competitive
Unemployment Workshop Employment

While the severely handicapped are often denied entry to such programs since it is assumed they lack competitive employment potential (Cortazzo, 1972), the more mildly handicapped today still have great difficulty getting out of such programs (Hansen, 1980). The problems in achieving that final transition to competitive employment have occurred from the lack of refined training technologies and from the traditional pressure of parents in the programs who often encouraged long-term placement in programs rather than intensive short-term training (Nelson, 1971). Of equal impact have been our social, welfare, and public assistance programs, which have often served as financial disincentives for individuals to try to work and for programs that try to prepare persons for work (Bellamy et al., 1980).

In the late 1950s, the work activities center concept was developed in order to deal with the individual excluded from the rapidly expanding sheltered workshop programs. Thus, another level was formed in the continuum of vocational services for those persons who seemed to lack vocational potential. The continuum now included another element:

School	Adult			
Home	→ Work	→	Sheltered	→ Competitive
Unemployment	Activities		Workshops	Employment

Theoretically, transition through the continuum was intended. Today, however, stilted upward movement is often the reality. The work activities centers often serve as a terminal placement for many handicapped people. These activities centers have grown at incredible rates over the last 20 years, as have sheltered workshops. Surveys show that activities centers, often not geared toward preparation for eventual employment, have shown far greater growth than workshops (Whitehead, 1979; Bellamy et al., 1980). Thus, a bottleneck in the service delivery system was formed and remains today, trapping the more severely handicapped at the lower end of the continuum.

Given this bleak view of the success rate in adult services with persons who are moderately and mildly handicapped, strong efforts to develop rigorous school-age vocational programs for the severely and profoundly handicapped are often scoffed at and ultimately thwarted. However, although a great many policy changes are needed on the state and federal levels to support the development of adult programs aimed at enabling persons the greatest amount of vocational independence possible (Bellamy et al., 1980), educators of the more severely handicapped can and must exert pressure for change. Special educators are perhaps best equipped to design, develop, and implement exemplary programs demonstrating the vocational potential of these students. Such programs would effectively apply upward pressure for transition on the community based programs and hopefully help to relieve the current bottleneck of services (Lynch & Singer, 1980; Gold, 1973).

Recent Innovations Improving Service Delivery

There have been recent advancements in the field involving creative programming alternatives that effectively *work around* a stagnant system. The most important of these are efforts to place moderately and severely handicapped persons directly in competitive employment without transition through a sheltered workshop. Many investigators around the country have found that by using appropriate behavioral technologies and a direct on-the-job training approach many persons previously thought to have little vocational potential can be employed and maintain a job (Levy, 1980; Rusch & Mithaug, 1980; Larson & Edwards, 1980; Wehman & Hill, M., 1980; Wehman & Hill, 1979). Individuals placed in competitive employment in this manner often require a network of support (Belmore & Brown, 1978) as well as an initially high expenditure of staff time; however, this model has repeatedly been proven successful and cost effective (Wehman & Hill, M., 1980; Schneider, Rusch, Henderson, & Geske, 1981; Levy, 1980).

Although this model as well as other solutions (for example, enclaves in private industry) may help relieve the bottleneck in the vocational service delivery system and free up placement openings in sheltered programs for the severely handicapped, it should be noted that long-term employment in a sheltered workshop may not be the most desirable goal for the more severely handicapped. The sheltered workshop model has many drawbacks, the most detrimental being its isolation of individuals from community access to nonhandicapped persons. Levy (1980) warns that currently ". . . not only do these programs fail in their attempts to realize maximum vocational potential for their clients, but in many cases, they actually create debilitating factors, such as new inappropriate behaviors, which even further hinder the clients" (p. 74).

Although in the near future a more comprehensive range of adult vocational services may be available to the severely handicapped, the quality of these services will need much improvement over services now delivered in sheltered workshops. The model that may develop to serve the more severely handicapped will probably include longer-term sheltered or semisheltered employment (Levy, 1980; Bellamy et al., 1980); however, the essential ingredient for improved services will be the integration of handicapped and nonhandicapped workers together in some form. Creative alternatives will need to be developed experimenting with nonhandicapped workers as models, enclaves of the severely handicapped in industry, enclaves of the nonhandicapped in sheltered workshops, mixed work crews, etc. Again, educators cannot simply wait for these models to be developed in the community adult services network. Instead, work should begin in middle and secondary education to provide vocational training for severely and profoundly handicapped students, including as many interactions with nonhandicapped persons and as much generalization training in nonhandicapped settings as possible.

Lack of Vocational Credibility

The second major problem already mentioned which has hampered greater development in the vocational area for the more severely handicapped is the commonly held attitude that these individuals are so vastly deficient compared with the average paid worker that it would be literally impossible to prepare them for any type of consequential work (Hansen, 1980). This attitude is reinforced by the fact that the more handicapped an individual is, the greater is the requirement for increased staff, materials, financial expenditure, and elaborate interventions in order to effect behavioral change (Bellamy et al., 1980). In the past " ... it was easier, and still is, to discount the severely handicapped person's chances of learning anything useful and to move on to the lower risk clients" (Flexer & Martin, 1978, p. 422). Financial reasons as well as taking the easiest options first have compelled educators/ rehabilitators and even researchers to expend their energies with individuals who are less handicapped.

Changing Attitudes

The prevalence of negative assessments of vocational potential is still quite evident in schools and adult services today. However, several positive arguments are currently being put forth by innovators and these will, hopefully, assist in changing the vocational image of the severely and profoundly handicapped.

They Can Learn

The strongest argument for improving vocational services is based on the many successful demonstrations involving training of these persons. The training of the severely and profoundly handicapped has truly seen a turnabout in this century from bedlam to bicycle brake assembly (see below). The last decade has been a period of experimentation and application with greatly encouraging results. Investigators have consistently found that given adherence to systematic training procedures, severely handicapped individuals show the ability to learn complex vocational tasks (Bellamy, Peterson, & Close, 1975; Bellamy, Horner, & Inman, 1979; Gold, 1976; Karan, Wehman, Renzaglia, & Schultz, 1976; Flexer & Martin, 1978). In view of the short history of education of the severely and profoundly handicapped, these demonstrations of vocational potential, with a relatively untrained population, are quite remarkable. They should also be a source of optimism for those involved in training with the next generation of students who will have received early and continued education.

They Have a Right to Learn

Even in view of these demonstrations many skeptics maintain that vocational training for the more severely handicapped is inappropriate because these persons will never achieve complete vocational independence. However, given this country's commitment to the work ethic and our society's values stressing the desirability of working, the advocate for vocational services can clearly argue that every individual, no matter how handicapped, has the right to the option of work (Bellamy et al., 1980). In addition, legislation in the form of the Rehabilitation Act of 1973, especially Section 504, legally validates these arguments and eventually programs will be confronted with the *illegalities* of withholding vocational services to the severely handicapped (Laski, 1979).

To fully implement and deliver these withheld services, our preconceived definitions of what constitutes consequential work, how and where it is performed, and what degree and type of support can be supplied will have to be adjusted. If success is to be attained, it is certain that creatively different and nontraditional work alternatives will be needed for this group of people.

They Need to Learn

Some may still argue that it is unethical to force such low functioning persons to perform work. Is this itself ethical? The affirmative answer to a question such as this one truly must be based on the acceptance of the concept of normalization (Wolfensberger, 1972). By denying individuals the option to perform work, one is denying a very basic element of normal life styles (Terkel, 1972). Many innovators believe work can actually assist in a process of normalization (Brolin, 1976; Wehman, 1981). Through participation in work activities we clearly increase the likelihood of acceptance of handicapped people by the nonhandicapped community (Gold, 1973; Terkel, 1972). Admittedly, the work of the more severely handicapped may have less consequence than that of others, but perhaps the goal of work ultimately becomes a vehicle by which one can live as normal a life as possible.

Finally, skeptics further insist that the severely handicapped more critically need training in other areas such as self-help, language, motor development, etc., and vocational training should be considered as secondary. This argument reflects the current simplistic approach to teaching often used by educators of this group. For them each curricular area must have a separate time period if learning is to occur. It is such an approach that undoubtedly has contributed to the artificiality in training and lack of generalization in learning (Falvey, Brown, Lyon, Baumgart, & Schroeder, 1980). Bellamy et al. (1980) note that this problem continues also into adult services, where there is a lack of clearly specified program models that combine work training *concurrently* with other needed services. Because of the magnitude of student needs, more complex training approaches aimed at simultaneous skill development in more than one area must be established. Fortunately, the vocational area provides an excellent arena within which to establish such procedures, since to demonstrate even partial vocational proficiency, the student must practice and apply skills from nearly all other curricular areas. For example, to function successfully in a simulated workshop setting, the student must acquire certain communication, motor, self-help, and social skills, as well as necessary vocational skills.

PAST PRACTICES

A considerable body of evidence regarding the potential and the rights of the severely and profoundly handicapped to vocational training has accumulated. Demonstrations of successful systemwide programs have been reported (Bellamy et al., 1975; Bellamy et al., 1979; Gold, 1973; Karan et al., 1976; Larson & Edwards, 1980; Lynch & Singer, 1980). The following questions then arise: Why can't the average school or community services system take such information and implement appropriate programs? Why have many community vocational programs for even higher functioning persons failed in the past?

Failures in the practical application of vocational training stem from many of the problems already discussed, especially those involving lack of administrative commitment because of estimates of high risk/low return (Gold, 1973) and other general low expectations for skill development in handicapped populations. In addition, Whitehead (1979) points out that innovators involved in exemplary programs must devise better methods of helping to replicate these successful programs under normal staffing and funding conditions.

Two other past practices that have led to failure must be mentioned and have strong implications for future directions in constructing vocational programs for lower functioning persons. First, in the past and unfortunately still today, many school or community based vocational programs for handicapped people have been conducted in settings isolated from the real world and teaching skills that are so artificial as to have no true relevance in the world of work. Therefore, generalization of learning and later transition to less restrictive vocational situations is limited. Second, it is apparent that the key to effective behavior change in the severely handicapped is largely dependent on staff skill (Bellamy et al., 1980). Unfortunately, until only recently the multidisciplinary skill requirements of the trainer/habilitator were neither well defined nor attainable, given the focus of current personnel preparation programs. In the past, teachers charged with vocational training had little knowledge or experience in training vocational behaviors and could not respond appropriately to the vocational needs of severely or profoundly handicapped individuals.

Isolated Settings/Artificial Skills Development

Often programs have been developed without input or focus from already existing community programs or local private industry. Neither trainers nor participants were exposed to realistic expectations found in real work in the community; thus, student objectives were developed arbitrarily or perhaps selected from outdated career education curriculum guides. This type of isolation does a disservice not only to the trainees but also the community itself, which will one day be charged with responsibility for these persons. Repeatedly, it has been found that without transitional planning for the handicapped and direct communication among community agencies, vocational failure is the result (Hansen & Haring, 1980; Vogelsberg, Williams, & Friedl, 1980; Lynch & Singer, 1980; Brown, Pumpian, Baumgart, Van Deventer, Ford, Nisbet, Schroeder, & Gruenewald, 1981).

The failures of the past lend support to current trends of early and sustained generalization training in a variety of community settings (Falvey et al., 1980) and a community integrative approach (Wehman & Hill, J., 1980) allowing for skill development directly in community settings. Among the many important advantages of training in real settings for the vocational educator is the assurance that student objectives reflect realistic work expectations. Clearly, if the vocational success rate is to be improved, " . . . educators must move out from the confines of the school building and open lines of communication with those who recruit, employ, and train workers" (Gold & Pomerantz, 1978, p. 434).

Educator/Habilitator Skills

It was not until the results of recent innovative programs were gathered that the degree of skill required for a successful trainer was realized (Bellamy et al., 1980; Wehman & Hill, 1979; Lynch & Singer, 1980). Clearly the special educator involved in transitional vocational training for the more severely handicapped must be equipped with some sophisticated skills in some rather distinct areas. Some of these are systematic assessment and training, applied behavior analysis, and public relations with business, services agencies, and parents. We also know that this individual must carefully arrange the learning environment if behavior change is to occur. Finally, this person needs a great deal of common sense and a keen awareness of the production realities and worker expectations in business and industry. Although such an array of skills appears overwhelming for one person, given the development of good personnel preparation programs and the utilization of resource persons within a transdisciplinary approach, this trainer can and does exist. Lynch and Singer (1980) note, however, that there are severe shortages of teachers with the dual emphasis needed; that is, special education and vocational education. Hopefully, with greater practical information on program development, improved personnel preparation programs will emerge.

SUGGESTED METHODS

The curriculum guidelines presented below will describe methods of early and sustained vocational training for persons considered severely or profoundly handicapped. Vocational training is advocated for nearly all persons regardless of the severity of their handicap; however, adjustments in what is considered consequential work may be required.

General Program Development

The acceptance of the principle that all individuals, no matter how handicapped, deserve the option of work and work training leads educators to some heretofore unresolved problems. These include the very basic issues of what, when, and how to teach these persons vocational skills and how to convince society to accept them in the work world. The sequence for program development given in Figure 10-1 specifies the necessary steps in implementation.

Define Vocational Commitment

Program development must begin with a statement or commitment that the general goal of the program is to prepare all students/clients for the less restrictive vocational environment. This goal also assumes the philosophy that some type of vocational expectations should be generated for *all* students. It does not ensure that all related persons and agencies will be convinced that the students in question have vocational potential. It simply means that the goal of the program is clearly identified and should be apparent to all others having dealings with the program (other agencies, parents, administrators, teachers, more advanced programs, etc.). Identifying program commitment and conveying it to others set the goal of the program. Reaching that goal may then be approached through the remaining steps in the program sequence.

Assess Community Resources

Recently, greater emphasis has been placed on assessment of the requirements and resources specific to a community prior to program development in many curricular areas. For example, before developing a leisure skills training program, the programmer must closely examine leisure behavior alternatives and resources available in a given community in order that the students may

Figure 10-1 Sequence of Program Development

Define Vocational Commitment

Assess Community Resources

Determine Model of Transitional Services

Design and Implement Program Levels or Phases

Utilization of Community Resources

Evaluate Student Progress and Community
Receptivity/Acceptance

Modify Program Based on Evaluative Data

---

actually get the opportunity to use the skills they are being taught. This type of planning is especially critical in vocational program development because in order to be vocationally successful the student must "graduate" and exhibit skills in either some type of public program or a community job.

Public program resources that are available in most communities may include the following: state rehabilitation programs, mental health/mental retardation services, workshop programs, public school vocational education, the National Association for Retarded Citizens (NARC), state employment commissions, the National Alliance of Business, and similar agencies. The resources they may offer as well as specific information regarding entry level requirements to their programs should be determined early in program development. In addition, communication with these public agencies is essential to ease the transition in the future.

The community job market is also considered a program resource for several reasons. First, assessment of the job market defines the type of nonsheltered jobs the program should be emphasizing in training because of job availability. Second, community jobs may serve as less restrictive nonpaid or paid training environments for students who are still in school.

Examination of the job market shows the type of specific work or employment available in a given community. For instance, it would be inappropriate to stress horticultural training in an urban area that cannot accommodate a greater number of greenhouse workers. This appears to be a most obvious consideration in program development; however, many schools or service agencies overlook this point and determine arbitrarily or expediently what the content of the program will include without an examination of the community job market.

If a community is rich in certain types of jobs or industry, creativity must be exercised to determine how such jobs or parts of jobs can be completed by the more severely handicapped. Prosthetic aids or adaptive equipment could change a seemingly impossible job into one that could be easily accomplished by a severely handicapped person. High school industrial arts programs may even serve as a resource for constructing the adaptive equipment.

Once community resources are identified and contacted, programmers may then give some thought as to how they can be utilized by the program for a variety of purposes, such as generalization environments, additional funds, staff inservice, interactions with the nonhandicapped work world, and the like.

Determine Model of Transitional Services

After a realistic examination of community resources, the programmer then has the rare opportunity to be idealistic by conceiving the program's theoretical model of transition or continuum of services. This model should be based on current community resources *and* optimistic projections for services in the future. We should not develop programs based on what is actually available at present for severely and profoundly handicapped adults (Bellamy et al., 1980) because, as noted earlier, very little is currently available. Thus, we should at least begin with an ideal plan of vocational transition from which to direct realistic efforts. An example of such a transitional plan may be found in Figure 10-2. This plan includes two program alternatives for students: training for eventual placement in "modified sheltered employment" and training for competitive service type jobs (food service or janitorial work). The sheltered and competitive tracks are flexible, however, and students can receive placement and trial periods in both throughout their habilitation. Figure 10-2 depicts the program's "four phase transitional plan," which includes structuring the student's exposure to increasing vocational require-

Figure 10-2 Model of Transitional Plan

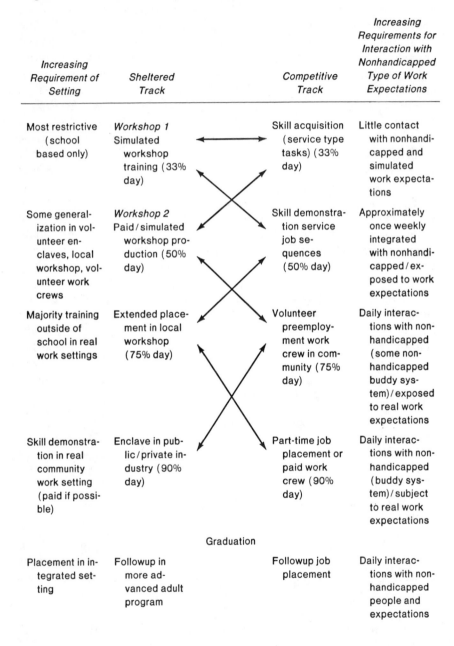

Increasing Requirement of Setting	Sheltered Track		Competitive Track	Increasing Requirements for Interaction with Nonhandicapped Type of Work Expectations
Most restrictive (school based only)	Workshop 1 Simulated workshop training (33% day)		Skill acquisition (service type tasks) (33% day)	Little contact with nonhandicapped and simulated work expectations
Some generalization in volunteer enclaves, local workshop, volunteer work crews	Workshop 2 Paid/simulated workshop production (50% day)		Skill demonstration service job sequences (50% day)	Approximately once weekly integrated with nonhandicapped/exposed to work expectations
Majority training outside of school in real work settings	Extended placement in local workshop (75% day)		Volunteer preemployment work crew in community (75% day)	Daily interactions with nonhandicapped (some nonhandicapped buddy system)/exposed to real work expectations
Skill demonstration in real community work setting (paid if possible)	Enclave in public/private industry (90% day)		Part-time job placement or paid work crew (90% day)	Daily interactions with nonhandicapped (buddy system)/subject to real work expectations
		Graduation		
Placement in integrated setting	Followup in more advanced adult program		Followup job placement	Daily interactions with nonhandicapped people and expectations

ments in several areas. The two middle columns of Figure 10-2 show basic programming for students in either or both tracks (sheltered or competitive). Sheltered trainees move from short simulated training in school, to paid longer training, to trials in the real sheltered workshop, and finally to trial placement in private industry enclaves. Students receiving preparation for competitive employment begin by simple acquisition training in service type tasks (for example, sanitizing toilets), then move to longer periods of simulated skill, demonstration, to volunteer or paid work crews, and finally to part-time job placement while still in school.

The left column of the figure shows the increasing requirements of the training setting. Here, as a student progresses, he or she moves from a highly restrictive school-only setting to the least restrictive vocational settings in jobs or enclaves. These less restrictive settings are in industry enclaves for the sheltered track students and actual part-time job placement for the competitive tracks. An *enclave* here refers to placement of a group of handicapped workers in regular industry with, perhaps, additional staff, training, equipment, and support. The right column shows the program's gradually increasing requirements for interactions or exposure to nonhandicapped persons and real work expectations found in jobs or more advanced programs.

This model indicates that if training takes place only in the restrictive school setting, few interactions with nonhandicapped individuals can occur *and* work expectations can only be simulated by teacher personnel who probably know very little of production or service type job requirements. The model views exposure to these requirements as something that could occur early in training, not broached suddenly later in life. Finally, the transitional plan also details the amount of training time needed each day under each phase shown in the middle columns. The requirements would naturally vary according to the age of the student, with secondary students committing far greater amounts of time than middle school students.

Design and Implement Program Levels or Phases

The next step in program development is often the most difficult. Given staff, funding, and time constraints, program design and actual implementation can be extremely complicated. Designs of effective vocational programs vary greatly from program to program, as do the training content, training approach, task selection, and other elements. There are, however, certain characteristics of appropriate vocational programming which can be delineated.

Although not necessarily in priority order, critical vocational program characteristics to consider when designing and implementing program levels include the following:

- transitional planning
- utilization of systematic training procedures
- generalization training
- parent involvement
- more complex program models combining work training concurrently with other needed training
- age-appropriate handling of the following variables: physical environment, training content, task selection, staff/student attitudes, and daily time commitment to training

Transitional planning, as described earlier, must form the basis of a vocational program. This means that school and community habilitation agencies must coordinate and interact on a continuous basis to ensure that upon graduation a student does not return home to lifelong nonproductivity and isolation. Many investigators agree that transitional planning should not simply involve the last two years of school but rather transdisciplinary planning should be directed toward the entire life span of the handicapped, starting with early school years to adulthood (Brown et al., 1981).

Systematic training procedures must be utilized (Bellamy et al., 1980; Lynch & Singer, 1980). Under this broad procedural category, the use of applied behavioral analysis would be the most important tool of the trainer. In a later section, systematic training procedures will be discussed in greater detail.

Early and sustained generalization training in less restrictive settings with different vocational trainers and on many different tasks and jobs is also essential for effective programming with the more severely handicapped. An indirect effect of generalization training is refinement of staff expectations and student potentials in regard to actual vocational settings.

Parent involvement is crucial to the success of a vocational program for severely and profoundly handicapped individuals. Many parents have extremely low vocational expectations for their children, which may have been instilled early by well-meaning professionals. Parents also have strong concerns regarding cessation of public assistance payments for the disabled if their child is shown to have vocational potential. Although funds could not be denied based on the mere demonstration of vocational potential, often parents are confused and fearful about this issue. This is understandable considering the incredible financial expense involved in maintaining a severely or profoundly handicapped person in the home. Because of these and other factors, parents, if not involved, can actually thwart a vocational program and inhibit the vocational transitions of their child. Continuous parent involvement and education is, therefore, very important.

Advocates of vocational training accept the fact that severely and profoundly handicapped individuals have vast and diverse training needs and that only one of these needs is vocational skill development. However, vocational advocates contend that more complex program models could be developed and interfaced with work training. In other words, language training does not have to occur during a language period, hygiene training during self-help period, etc. Instead, appropriate objectives in other curricular areas could be formulated and addressed based on the functional needs identified during the vocational training period in segregated and integrated community settings.

A vocational program, perhaps more than any other training area, should appear as chronologically age-appropriate as possible, regardless of the functioning level of the students. Even with profoundly retarded middle school students functioning cognitively at the five-month level, the vocational training program should look and feel like a place where young people are learning how to work. Particular attention should be given to the establishment of a correct physical environment. Staff visits to more advanced vocational settings should help with creating an appropriate atmosphere. The vocational training should be in an area separate from the other training activity areas. A separate "workshop," or at least a separate work area, will provide environmental cues that prompt work behavior. The area itself should be free of toys, gadgets, and classroom type bulletin board decorations. The reason for such austerity is to demonstrate clearly to all who enter that this training area reflects a serious commitment to a program goal involving in a very real sense the futures of the students. It also helps teachers, aides, and students develop an appropriate perspective regarding vocational training.

Instead of spending funds on expensive vocational kits or gathering up as many little colored blocks and pegboards as possible, attempts should be made to secure real or simulated materials of jobs or tasks that exist in the local community. Contract or salvage work from the local workshop can be simulated as closely as possible, or workshops may donate defective parts of the real jobs in order that these tasks can be acquired and practiced. Whenever possible, one should obtain real work or jobs the students can perform on a volunteer basis initially. The first commitment to real work is critically important to the program because it exposes students *and* staff to work expectations that are considerably different from those of make-work or simulated work. To ensure greater exposure and refinement of student objectives, efforts to perform the work in a host company within a type of enclave or more advanced program should be a prime goal of the vocational training effort.

Staff and students should take the training seriously even if initial efforts appear futile, as is often the case with the more severely handicapped. In the work setting the relationship should no longer be teacher/student, but rather supervisor/worker. Teachers obviously are largely responsible for shaping their own behavior toward students first. If much student hand holding, coddling, or hugging is exhibited toward adolescent or adult students, the teacher may first need to modify his or her own behavior.

The appropriate amount of time committed to daily vocational training can vary greatly according to student age and other program requirements. Increasing time commitments are needed as a student progresses into the secondary level and in age toward graduation. Figure 10-3 illustrates increases in vocational training time in a school system from elementary school levels through middle and secondary and finally to adult programs. The figure shows that when one begins in the secondary level program, vocational training should optimally consist of two hours advancing to three hours per day or, on the lower end, at least one full hour advancing to two hours per day by the time the student reaches 17 years of age. It is important to note that this model of increasing vocational emphasis supports the contention that other

Figure 10-3 Time Commitment to Vocational Training

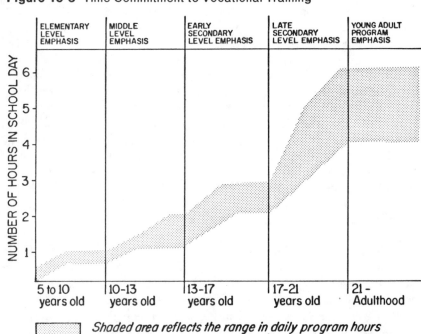

Shaded area reflects the range in daily program hours committed to vocational training (top shaded edge shows optimum daily hours / lower edge shows bare minimum appropriate.)

curricular areas, such as motor, hygiene, communication, or social objectives, can be approached simultaneously with structured vocational training.

The amount of time committed to any given activity often reflects the general emphasis of the program. If, for example, whole days of vocational programming are suspended several times a month to permit older students to attend puppet shows or basketball games, the program appears quite committed to recreational activities and less to the need for vocational preparation that approaches real work conditions as much as possible.

Utilization of Community Resources

After program levels or phases have been developed, students should begin to gain access to some of the vocational community resources that the programmer has identified and made arrangements with. Advantages that accrue from such an effort are (1) the acquisition of less restrictive community settings for generalization training, (2) the development of modeling situations where nonhandicapped workers/peers serve as models in the segregated or community settings, and (3) the procurement of "real" contract/salvage work that students may perform in either type setting.

Evaluate Student Progress and Community Receptivity/Acceptance

Planning for evaluation is a necessary step in program development and should include evaluation not only of student progress but also of the effectiveness of the program, especially in the eyes of the community and community vocational habilitators. Evaluation of student progress should include assessment of student acquisition and production rates on work tasks. Other, less obvious, areas of student evaluation are degree of work endurance, appropriateness of behavior/attitudes while working, work quality, speed of applying skills, and generalization of critical nonvocational skills.

One way of evaluating program effectiveness can be by determining the number of students who achieve entrance into the next less restrictive vocational environment upon graduation. Community acceptance of a program is also an indicator of effectiveness. Therefore, one should survey community consumers and community vocational habilitators for data related to social validation of the content and direction of the program (Rusch, 1979).

Modify Program Based on Evaluation Data

The final step in program development involves the maintenance of program flexibilty that allows for modifications when necessary. Modifications may be needed based on evaluative data or when a new vocational resource becomes available. As a program's reputation and the degree of community acceptance grow, many changes in the program will and must occur.

Development of Program Components

This section returns to a more complete analysis of the design and implementation phase of the sequence of program development just discussed.

Assessment

In a curricular area, two types of assessment usually occur. First, *global assessment* is performed utilizing standardized or informal testing devices. With the severely and profoundly handicapped population, this global testing yields little more than areas of greatest deficit or greatest strength. Therefore, a second type of assessment is always required for appropriate formulation of the training plan. This is designated as *detailed assessment.* In the vocational arena, task analysis is the most widely used detailed assessment (Flexer & Martin, 1978).

It is well known that traditional psychological testing is biased against persons who are more severely handicapped (Snell, 1978). Such testing tends to yield highly negative estimates of behavior and obscures individual differences within the group. In general, the results of the test serve very little purpose for the programmer. The same is true of traditional vocational evaluation devices used by rehabilitators or vocational educators. In addition to the use of standardized tests, traditional vocational evaluation utilizes brief, structured, and direct observation periods in the form of "work samples." Although this should be commended, the observational periods are often so short (for example, 50 minutes) that the learning capacity of a severely handicapped individual cannot be adequately examined (Revel & Wehman, 1978).

One global assessment device that is now frequently used by educators is the *Prevocational Assessment and Curriculum Guide* (Mithaug, Mar, & Stewart, 1978). It provides information comparing student behavior with behavior requirements in sheltered workshops, work activities centers, etc. This device may be useful to illustrate pretest/posttest gains or for more definitive program decisions (Wehman, 1981). Unfortunately, parts of the device may not be useful or appropriate with the more profoundly handicapped.

Given the dearth of appropriate global assessment instruments that can be used with the severely and profoundly handicapped, the importance of detailed assessment is underscored. Before discussing the parts of a comprehensive detailed assessment, two characteristics that facilitate more appropriate assessment should be emphasized. First, all detailed assessment should take an ecological approach. That is, a student should be assessed with regard to what skills will consistently be needed in his or her future vocational environment, not in comparison with all appropriate vocational skills. Therefore, the environments or proposed environments the student will one day enter must be analyzed and assessment guidelines should be derived from these analyses. Second, vocational assessment for severely and profoundly handicapped individuals must be comprised of direct observation over long periods of time. Assessment for this population is not accomplished over a five- or ten-day evaluation period but rather must be considered as an ongoing process.

Task analysis helps us to determine whether or not an individual knows how to perform a task thoroughly, correctly, and consistently. This is undoubtedly the most useful information discussed thus far in assessment; however, it should be noted that other vocational information is also needed in order to make programming decisions. This other needed vocational information is often more difficult to observe and quantify. For instance, although task analysis assesses whether or not an individual has acquired a task or task step, it does not show how fast he or she performs it, the quality of his or her work, how long he or she can work, how he or she behaves while working, or the appropriateness of his or her social contacts. These skills are equally important for vocational development; therefore, a longitudinal comprehensive vocational assessment should include information on the following domains: (1) acquisition of vocational skills, (2) production rates or proficiency of skills, (3) quality of work, (4) endurance in work, (5) work compliance, (6) social survival skills, and (7) student interest.

A technique to assess each area should be developed utilizing behavior observation and on-the-job training, rather than tests. Greater detail regarding what is included in each assessment area and certain assessment suggestions are given in Table 10-1. The assessment content shown in Table 10-1 is for a student who is to be placed in preparation for sheltered employment. An illustration of comprehensive vocational assessment is provided showing examples of behavior that should be assessed and suggested methods of assessment within seven behavior domains. Utilizing the same behavioral domains, the assessment could also be geared for an individual potentially entering competitive employment.

Parent involvement in the assessment process cannot be overlooked. Moreover, surveying parent interest in vocational training for the student or discussing assessment data is important to help parents raise their vocational expectations and develop more realistic ones for their son or daughter.

Curriculum Sequence

The training sequence of any vocational program will include a series of work tasks the student must learn to perform as well as related behaviors that

Table 10-1 Comprehensive Vocational Assessment for Sheltered Preparation

Vocational Behavior Domains ⟶	Acquisition of Skills	Production of Skills	Quality of Work	Endurance of Work	Work Compliance	Social Survival Skills	Student Interest
Examples of Behaviors	a) The number of simulated/real tasks acquired. b) How long to criterion.	Number of work units completed within time constraint a) During baseline vs. intervention; b) During increasingly longer work periods; c) With less supervision, etc.	a) Number of errors; b) Number of below quality pieces (e.g., smudged, torn, loose, etc.).	a) Length of work period maintaining criterion prior to reinforcement delivery (e.g., works to criterion for 30 minutes for token delivery). b) Length of total work day while maintaining adequate on-task behavior.	Behavior attitudes while working such as: 1) Cooperativeness; 2) Eagerness to work; 3) Treatment of work materials; 4) Arriving/leaving on time.	Appropriate social behaviors while at work such as: 1) Greeting Supervisor; 2) Occasionally smiling; 3) Appearance/hygiene; 4) Behavior at breaktime.	Biweekly basis student selects which type of work he or she wants to do.
Suggested Methods of Assessment	a) Task analysis.	Rate data — Units completed / # of minutes a) Compare rate to sheltered or factory "standard."	Frequency count or spot check (e.g., every 10 units).	a) Probe increments in uninterrupted work periods while maintaining criterion. b) Probe longer work day by time sampling on- and off-task behavior under longer hours.	a) Contriving daily situation where appropriate behaviors can be readily displayed. Count appropriate behaviors. b) Count or sample exhibitions of specific inappropriate behavior for student(s).	a) Contriving daily situations for displaying appropriate behaviors, count behaviors; b) Count/sample when student does not perform behaviors.	a) Note selection patterns over time. b) Examine consistent differences in speed and quality on different tasks.

are also critical to vocational success. Appropriate identification of behaviors in both areas will now be discussed and an illustrative curriculum sequence given. The curriculum sequence of a vocational training program should be based on the ecological analysis of the community, its employment resources, and more advanced vocational programs available to students. Training programs are directed toward developing those skills needed in the potential work environments that have been inventoried. Thus, ultimately the commu-

---

Exhibit 10-1 Work Tasks and Critical Related Behaviors for Sheltered Preparation

---

Work Tasks*

1. Hospital Kit Assembly (Conveyer belt).

2. Many billing jobs (including envelope stuffing, labeling, sealing).

3. Drill Bit Packaging (12 drill bits to a pre-gummed envelope and sealing).

4. Ball point pen assembly.

5. Mailing jobs (including folding newsletters, stapling, collating).

6. Boiler drain assembly (more complex assembly job).

Critical Related Behaviors*

o Must work at 15% of standard production rate.

o Must remain on-task 80% of the time.

o Must work continuously for 90 minutes before break.

o Must have an 8% error rate or lower.

o Must be cooperative (e.g., no back talk).

o Must want to work.

o Must be able to get around safely in shop.

o Must keep a good appearance.

o Must communicate basic needs for toilet, food, etc.

* Local adult programs socially validate the consistent need for these behaviors.

nity job assessment leads to a list of *work tasks* that are specific and relevant to the community. These tasks may range from simple mailing jobs, such as attaching labels, to complex industrial jobs, such as wiring electronic circuit boards.

With work tasks in hand, the educator must now consider what other vocational behavior domains should be addressed during training. The job of the vocational teacher is not complete unless objectives in relation to other skills such as work habits, work behaviors, and attitudes are met in conjunction with performance of tasks of an occupation (Flexer & Martin, 1978). Again, vocational training of the severely handicapped should not be considered simply as a demonstration in acquisition of complex tasks but rather as a process to develop a competent worker across many behavioral domains. Therefore, all of the related behavioral assessment domains become program areas. In actual practice, then, assessment items and curriculum are developed simultaneously. An illustrative list of work tasks and critical related behaviors are given in Exhibits 10-1 and 10-2. Exhibit 10-1 includes work tasks and related behaviors for sheltered training content and possible contract jobs that could be obtained. Exhibit 10-2 shows potential jobs found in a competitive vein from a large local cafeteria system with corresponding work tasks and general related behaviors. These include very simple jobs with which a training program may begin based on results of that community's job assessment.

Social Validation of Content

During the community job assessment, attempts should be made to socially validate (Rusch, 1979) the relevance and appropriateness of assessment items and training goals in all of the behavioral domains selected. Consumers, employers, supervisors of adult programs, etc., can all provide information on what tasks and vocationally related behaviors are consistently needed in the more advanced and available vocational environments. This provides the program with focus for skill selection out of the literally hundreds of skills that are related to work. Social validation of training content ensures appropriate emphasis and most effective use of training time.

The Comprehensive Nature of Vocational Training

It is advisable that program objectives in all areas be addressed through an on-the-job training approach rather than through artificially engineered activities in an isolated classroom setting. The use of career work sheets, work learning kits, vocational games, or other indirect methods of teaching are unnecessary and may impede the speed with which real work behaviors are acquired. Instead, the challenge to the vocational teacher is to first teach

Exhibit 10-2 Work Tasks and Critical Related Behaviors for Competitive Employment

Work Tasks   Work Skills

1) Busing Dining Hall   a) Clear tables of trays, paper
                                           plates, cups, etc. and
                                           wipe down
                                        b) Break down trays
                                        c) Clean ash trays
                                        d) Sanitize tables, chairs
                                        e) Rearrange chairs and items on
                                           tables

                                        f) Sweeping

2) Scrubbing Pots/Washing   a) Prepare pots, dishes and sinks
   Dishes/Prepare Items for   for wash
   Dish Machine   b) Wash dishes
                                        c) Scrub pots
                                        d) Clean sinks
                                        e) Put items away

3) Clean Floors/Wipe Down   a) Sweep specified area
   Equipment (Look Busy)   b) Prepare cleaning solution
                                        c) Industrial mopping
                                        d) Put items away
                                        e) Look busy by wiping down
                                           equipment

4) Cleaning Rest Rooms   a) Clean sinks
                                        b) Clean toilets
                                        c) Clean mirrors
                                        d) Sweep
                                        e) Mop
                                        f) Empty trash

Critical Related Behaviors*

o Work at rates comparable to nonhandicapped employees
o Must be cooperative
o Must communicate basic needs
o Must be neat and clean
o Should be friendly but not overly so
o Should have good attendance
o Must be compliant when assigned job
o Must protect self from dangers

* Local food service/janitorial employment programs socially validate
  the consistent need for these behaviors

students to perform work tasks and while students are working, related vocational behaviors (work habits, attitudes, rates, etc.) are approached. This type of teaching avoids the great difficulties severely handicapped students have in generalizing skills learned in an artificial manner and setting to the natural environment.

There are many ways of structuring training to enhance generalizability. Horner and Bellamy (1978) suggest that vocational programs identify the "concepts" (stimulus characteristics) and the "operations" (response sets) that are most used throughout the variety of jobs and work tasks in a community. The training content then would include teaching more and more complex concepts and operations, rather than focusing on any particular work task. For example, one would identify and teach operations such as tool use, basic assembly, and the like. Although this is a most valid approach, lower functioning and younger students may require training toward development of even more basic worker characteristics that are often lacking in the more severely handicapped (for example, attending to task). All work tasks and related behaviors selected are arranged in hierarchical order based on complexity and time study data. Hierarchies are then divided again into skill levels that emphasize the development of specific worker characteristics. Table 10-2 provides an example of vocational behaviors related to worker characteristics.

Most profoundly handicapped persons exhibit limited attending behaviors particularly to situations and materials as unfamiliar as those involving work. These persons have no experience with the reinforcement contingencies that can and should occur in a work situation; therefore, *Level I: Developing Attention to Task* defines the first sequence of vocational training that would be used to gain the student's attention and deliver reinforcement for these behaviors.

Level I work tasks differ from those that follow in that some of the tasks do not actually occur in the community. They are, rather, expressly designed to gain student attention. In essence, Level I work tasks are those that help to develop prerequisite skills for later levels. The *work routine sequence* is a program to condition and increase responding to simple one-step commands regarding work. The program is designed for individuals exhibiting very little work behavior in general and it relies heavily on the use of tangible reinforcers to condition and shape responses. *Large hospital kit assembly* is a work task adapted (that is, using larger materials) from a real community job of placing an item in a plastic tub as it passes the worker on a conveyer belt. It is a simple task to begin work training and a conveyer belt can be simulated to provide a natural discriminative stimulus for the response of dropping an item in the tub. *Co-worker alerting* is one of the few tasks that students with little or no motor movement can perform in the work arena. It requires that the students be equipped with some type of buzzer that they can readily activate (head-operated, snap-on, etc.). Next, students learn to attend to the work of a fellow student involved in some production task. When the fellow student goes off-task or stops working, the "alerter" signals the co-worker to get back to work with the buzzer. Other similar alerting tasks can be signaling break times, the need for more materials, and the like. *Simple envelope stuffing* includes use of small envelopes and stiff, small cards to be stuffed. Quality is less of an issue in this task than simply attending to the sequence of the task, completing that sequence, and receiving reinforcement for doing so. Work tasks in the competitive vein are very limited at this level; however, Table 10-2 provides one possible example, wiping down equipment. This is a useful task to gain student attention.

Production rate is not emphasized in Level I. However, endurance (percentage of time displaying on-task behavior) is considered an important factor. Quality of work with very low functioning or young students often begins with teaching students not to place work materials in their mouth. This is an appropriate objective to target in any curriculum area. It can be easily approached in the vocational area by teaching students that they are not paid for mouthed or wet materials.

Level I compliance includes staying in a seat or assigned area and exhibiting zero refusal-to-work responses. The social/survival objectives are specified in order to establish attending skills with respect to supervisors' facial area, looking at materials while working, and following simple directions quickly. At this level, one would aim to eradicate aggressive, highly disruptive behavior and to reduce stereotypic behavior while working.

In *Level II: Understanding Production,* the student finally is required to complete simple work units within a designated time constraint. The student is taught this worker characteristic through the delivery or withholding of reinforcement if the target number of units is completed or not completed within the time period. The students learn many new concepts through this changing criterion approach, including simple aspects of time, speed of work, and often something about disappointment when they fail to "beat the clock."

Work tasks for this level involve the production of tangible, countable units. An examination of the sheltered work tasks selected for production shows that there are few ways to make mistakes in this type of production. Again, the emphasis is on helping the students to understand that work must be completed within some time limit in order for them to receive reinforcement. Competitive vein work tasks at Level II are also simple, requiring the completion of a viable, tangible work unit such as breaking down a tray. This job requires removing and sorting silverware and removing plate, cup, and

Table 10-2 Worker Characteristics and Vocational Goals

Examples Of
Level I Goals
Worker Characteristic: Attention to Task

Work Tasks (Appendix A)	Production Rate	Endurance Rate	Quality Rate	Compliance Skills	Social Skills
Sheltered Preparation					
1. Work Routine Sequence	No Production Emphasis Level I	Displays On-Task Behavior (80% of sample) up to 30 min. period	o Zero mouthing responses	o Zero out-of-seat responses	o Attends to supervisor's face 80% of trials.
2. Large Hospital Kit Assembly			o No destruction of materials	o Zero "refusals" to work	o Attends to materials 80% of trials.
3. Co-worker Alerting					o Zero aggressive or highly disruptive behaviors.
4. Simple Envelope Stuffing					o Follows one-step instruction within 10 seconds.
Competitive Job Preparation					
e.g., Wiping Down Equipment					o Shows fewer (_%) stereo-typic responses during 1:1 training

Examples of
Level II Goals
Worker Characteristics: Understanding Production

Work Tasks	Production Rate	Endurance Rate	Quality Rate	Compliance Skills	Social Skills
Sheltered Preparation	Sheltered: changing criterion building to 5% of standard production rate	o Displays on-task behavior for 70% of designated work period (length of work period depends on age and ability)	o Displays appropriate use of materials	o Begins work independently or within 5 seconds of prompt	o Checks appearance prior to entry (simple level: shirt tucked, hair smooth, etc.).
1. Sealing Gummed Envelopes					
2. Regular Envelope			o Displays 15% or less error rate	o Acknowledges assignment (nods, smiles, or verbal response) 100% of trials	o Greets supervisor upon entry to work area (smile, wave, verbal, etc.).
3. Attaching mailing labels				o Initiates contact with supervisor when in need of more materials within 60 seconds	o Communicates need for bathroom use (sign, picture card, verbal).
4. Simple Assembly (e.g., curtain pulley)	Competitive: changing criterion building to 50% of speed of nonhandicapped worker			o Goes directly to assigned work station	o Exhibits zero stereotypic responses during all 1:1 training session.
Competitive Job Preparation					
1. Sanitizing tables					
2. Clearing tables					
3. Breaking down trays					
4. Cleaning ash trays					

Table 10-2 continued

Examples of
Level III Goals
Worker Characteristic: Working Under Delayed Reinforcement

Work Tasks	Production Rate	Endurance Rate	Quality Rate	Compliance Skills	Social Skills
Sheltered Preparation					
1. Collating (2-6 pages)	Changing criterion approach building to 10% of standard production rate	o Displays on-task behavior for 75% of designated work period	o Complete 80% neat clean units	o When asked to perform extra work, accepts appropriately 100% of trials. (Displays zero groans, complaints, etc.).	o Checks appearance prior to entry (complex level - clean hands, zipper up, buttons done, etc.).
2. Folding in half (newsletters)					
3. Regular envelope sealing		o Displays works continuously for 60 min. before break	o Displays less than 10% error rate	o Displays appropriate behavior while working (e.g., responds appropriately when supervisor checks work, shows good posture while working, works quietly, etc.)	o Greets supervisor and at least one co-worker (only once).
4. Stapling					
5. Placing 12 drill bits in jig (component of drill bit assembly)					
6. Ball point pen assembly				o Stays at work station until told to leave	o Takes breaks and returns at appropriate times.
Competitive Job Preparation					o Displays appropriate behavior at breaks - 70% of samples.
1. Use/operate dish machine					
2. Sweeping an area					
3. Industrial mopping					
4. Scrubbing pots					
5. Prepare sinks					
6. Clean sinks/toilets					
7. Clean windows/mirrors					
8. Collect/empty trash					

Examples of
Level IV Goals
Worker Characteristic: Self-Initiation of Work

Work Tasks	Production Rate	Endurance Rate	Quality Rate	Compliance Skills	Social Skills
Sheltered Preparation	Changing criterion approach building to at least 15% of standard production rate	o Displays on-task behavior for 80% of designated work period.	o Completes 90% neat/clean units	o Continuous work during disruptions 100% of trials (e.g., visitors, accidents, etc.).	o Communicates basic needs (toilet, pain, sickness, etc.).
1. Folding letters in thirds					
2. Collating (6 or more pages)		o Works continuously for 90 minutes before break.		o Volunteers for jobs 80% of trials.	o Dresses appropriately for work
3. Boiler drain assembly				o Appears at work station without prompting.	o Avoids danger 100% of trials.
4. Packing drill bits				o Exhibits pride in work by reaching criteria for 'worker of the month.'	
5. Other complex assemblies					
Competitive Preparation					
1. Bus Dining Hall					
2. Scrub Pots/Dish Machine Operator					
3. Clean floors					
4. Clean Restrooms					

dirty napkin from the tray. All Level II competitive work tasks stress the completion of a tangible unit within some time frame.

Naturally, since this level approaches understanding of production, one must begin to compare the production rates of students with those of regular workers (the *standard production rate*). In this sequence, the goal of Level II is to help the student exhibit at least 5 percent of the standard production rate on the work tasks. The standard production rate on any task is determined by performing time studies to see how fast the average individual produces units or performs tasks (Flexer & Martin, 1978). This can be accomplished by having three colleagues perform a task for an equal time period and averaging their production rate. In this level, the teacher would then require students to perform to at least 5 percent standard rate for two out of four tasks before moving on to Level III. Production requirements for competitive work tasks should be higher than 5 percent of standard.

Endurance rates are increased with gradual increments in the length of the work period. In Level II, observations through time sampling should show students on-task for 70 percent of samples throughout the longer work periods. Quality objectives in Level II include appropriate use of materials (no slamming, throwing, etc.) and an error rate (mistakes, omissions, loose parts) that is no more than 15 percent of the completed units.

Level II compliance goals include simple behaviors such as starting work immediately after prompt delivery; acknowledging a work assignment with a nod, smile, verbal response, etc.; initiating contact with a supervisor when more materials are needed; and going to the correct work station appropriately. Social skills of Level II include beginning a simple self-check of appearance, greeting one's supervisor upon entry, communicating the need for the bathroom appropriately, and exhibiting no stereotypic responses when the supervisor is providing one-to-one training. Many of the compliance and social behavior objectives are isolated to help students develop behaviors as a part of their work repertoire that will help them make a good impression on others, particularly future supervisors. It has been shown that these behaviors will greatly facilitate maintenance in sheltered employment (Mithaug, Hagmeier, & Haring, 1977).

The worker characteristic stressed in *Level III: Working under Delayed Reinforcement* involves producing more units and working for longer periods of time before reinforcement is received. This is a critical characteristic of a good worker within a sheltered program since less staff and resources are usually available within such programs. Persons who achieve competitive employment must also work under more natural schedules of reinforcement. Tasks and objectives of Level III, then, are designed specifically to help thin the schedules.

All work tasks of Level III are slightly more complex, more time consuming, and require more attention to quality factors than do those of Level II. Production rate requirements at Level III include accelerating the worker to approximately 10 percent of standard production rate. Individual production rates should be established for students who exceed these levels prior to training. The 10 percent figure represents only a minimum production rate requirement.

Endurance in Level III includes gradually increasing the length of the workday while examining and maintaining on-task student behavior for at least 75 percent of the work samples. Randomly reinforcing on-task workers may be an effective training technique in this area. Level III also requires that students work for at least 60 minutes prior to a bonafide break. Of course, within that 60 minutes reinforcement can be given. Tokens can be delivered and exchanged, and several shorter uninterrupted work periods can be established (for example, 10 minutes before token delivery).

Quality goals within Level III include close examination of the cleanliness and neatness of the work. Students should be taught to produce clean work and maintain a neat station. Reinforcement can be withheld or aversive consequences applied for lack of quality. Error rates, as previously defined, must also be held below 10 percent of total production.

Behavioral objectives within the compliance and social skills areas become gradually more complex and the teacher must create or contrive situations on a regular basis in order to approach such objectives in a systematic way. An example of a compliance objective for Level III is "accepts extra work appropriately." To help the student develop this behavior the teacher must on a regular basis assign the student extra work near the end of a work period and monitor the response. If the student's response is inappropriate, the student must be taught to respond appropriately and be reinforced for doing so. Regular practice with situations such as these is important yet nearly always neglected in a training program. Social skills in Level III also include what to do with free time at break and appropriate interaction skills that should be displayed with co-workers. Again, these are often neglected in vocational training programs.

Very basic vocational training programs with severely and profoundly handicapped must also include attention to the development of self-initiated behavior (Kazdin, 1971; Wehman & McLaughlin, 1980). Many severely handicapped students can perform work tasks under close supervision and through external control; however, they would exhibit little or no behavior if left alone. Specific program emphasis must be given to self-initiation of work behavior, self-reinforcement techniques, development of pride in work, minor competitive behavior among workers, and other related work characteristics. The training content of *Level IV: Self-Initiation of Work* provides increases in task complexity and requirements for related vocational behaviors. In order to acquire skills related to these more advanced objectives the student must naturally be exhibiting more self-initiated behavior because the external control of staff is not increased and tasks are more time consuming. Other specific interventions must be included in Level IV programming to facilitate self-initiation to work. Such techniques may include systematically reducing supervisor prompting by utilizing self-payment/self-reinforcement (Wehman & McLaughlin, 1980), encouraging competition among workers, encouraging and reinforcing pride in work, and using redundant cues to help visually represent necessary performance criteria (Renzaglia, Wehman, Schultz, & Karan, 1978).

Work tasks at Level IV include any complex assembly task as well as certain paper tasks that do not appear complex but in practice are quite difficult. For instance, simply folding a letter in thirds is a very time consuming and difficult task for the more severely handicapped largely because of the quality requirements for appropriate proportions. The work tasks listed for competitive job preparation at this level include self-initiation of many smaller jobs that comprise each work task listed. For instance, busing a dining hall includes clearing tables, breaking down trays, cleaning ashtrays, sanitizing, etc. Therefore, a good deal of self-direction and initiation is needed at this level.

Production requirements at this level rise to the requirements found in the local sheltered workshop. In the example presented, the local workshop requires workers to produce on the average at 15 percent of standard production rate. Endurance objectives at Level IV continue to rise, with students exhibiting 80 percent on-task behavior during sampling taken throughout longer and longer work periods. In addition, students must work for 90-minute periods before a regular break time. Quality levels include neat and clean work and an error rate of no more than 10 percent of a student's total production. Compliance and social skills at Level IV include shaping independently more self-initiated interactions with the supervisor and the development of other needed behaviors.

The social survival skills requirements of Level IV should directly reflect the entry level social requirements of the next program or job the student will enter. From the extensive surveying of sheltered employment programs done by Mithaug et al. (1977), specific social skill requirements can be gleaned. For example, we know communicating basic needs of hunger and pain is considered a prerequisite social skill for entry into many sheltered workshops.

This section has provided guidelines for selecting training content and designing a curriculum sequence in a hierarchical order from simple behaviors to far more complex vocational behaviors. This sequence has included simple sheltered type work tasks and a very basic sequence of work tasks for competitive service jobs. For additional information on training for competitive employment, refer to Rusch and Mithaug (1980) and Hill, Wehman, and Kochany (1979). The related work behaviors that are suggested can be adapted for students in sheltered workshops.

Basic Instructional Techniques

Work training can be divided readily into two instructional phases: an *acquisition phase,* where the student learns the skill, and a *production phase,* where the student adequately performs the skill to a certain standard based on speed, quality, endurance, etc. (Wehman & McLaughlin, 1980). The acquisition phase of vocational training includes much the same planning and training techniques used in all other curricular areas. In vocational acquisition, as in all other types of acquisition training, equal attention must be given to two types of instructional manipulations: manipulation of the antecedents of a response (for example, prompting, fading, and chaining strategies) and manipulation of the consequences of a response (for example, reinforcement schedules).

The production phase of vocational training requires optimal performance of an already acquired skill or behavior. Here, the emphasis is not on how to elicit learning through antecedent manipulation but on how to strengthen and increase the response. Therefore, greater attention must be paid to what occurs after a response is made, that is, the consequences of a response.

Schedules of Reinforcement

A schedule of reinforcement involves the relationship between the response and the reinforcer. Two dimensions of scheduling must be considered in order to accelerate the occurrence of a response. These are *time* and *number.* The time dimension refers to the time between the response and the delivery of reinforcement. The number dimension refers to the number of responses necessary to produce or earn reinforcement. For instance, the most simple schedule of reinforcement is continuous reinforcement in which the reinforcer is delivered immediately and only one response is required for reinforcement to be delivered. In the following schedules, time and number dimensions are manipulated in more complex ways to bring about increases in the production rates of vocational behaviors. The implementation of these schedules in social skills training is considered in Chapter 5.

A *Differential Reinforcement of High Rate Responding (DRH) Schedule* involves systematic reinforcement delivery to an individual for having a particular rate or higher of performance. A DRH schedule of reinforcement is a basic component of any production training program since its purpose is to shape or accelerate responding. It allows the teacher to manipulate the amount of work or number of units a student must complete and the time it takes to complete the work by defining systematic opportunities to deliver or withhold reinforcement accordingly. Two examples will be given to demonstrate the utility of this schedule in a work context.

In a sheltered preparation program, following the acquisition of a work task such as ball point pen assembly, the teacher would first examine the student's production rate during a baseline period. The student would be asked to begin work and the total time of the work period and the number of pens produced during the period would be recorded. No further prompts would be given in order that the teacher could examine the student's independent behavior without intervention. If after three days the student produced zero pens and consistently left his or her seat after six minutes into each work period, the teacher would know that the initial DRH schedule should include relatively low requirements in time and number. Thus, because the initial schedule of reinforcement must directly reflect the baseline rate of responding, the teacher might establish several five-minute work periods in which the student would have to produce only one ball point pen to receive a highly desired and visible item. As the student's production rate reached this criterion and he or she received approximately 90 percent of available rewards over several consecutive sessions, the schedule would be gradually accelerated. For example, depending on probe data, DRH acceleration could proceed as follows: Phase I—1 pen in 5 minutes; Phase II—2 pens in 8 minutes; Phase III—3 pens in 10 minutes; Phase IV—4 pens in 10 minutes; Phase V—6 pens in 15 minutes; and so on.

A DRH schedule of reinforcement can also be used with work tasks preparing students for competitive employment. For example, a task such as sweeping can be accelerated through this schedule. If a student's baseline rate showed that it took 40 minutes to independently complete sweeping of the cafeteria floor, a strong reinforcer could be shown to the student and the criterion of completing the floor could be raised to 35 minutes in order that the reinforcer could be received. Again, the schedule could be gradually accelerated to some final standard. Time studies should be done to ensure that superhuman performance is not being required.

In its purest form, a DRH schedule allows for delivery of reinforcement when a criterion is met. If it is not met, the teacher provides no punishment but simply begins the session again with the same criterion. In a well-conceived production training program, a DRH schedule should always be in effect. If some inappropriate or interfering behavior occurs during work training, one of the following three schedules can be used in conjunction with the DRH schedule.

A *Differential Reinforcement of Incompatible Behavior (DRI) Schedule* requires the sometimes difficult identification of an appropriate behavior that is incompatible with a behavior defined as a problem in the work setting. For instance, if a student's out-of-seat behavior is considered a problem to the teacher, an incompatible response must be selected that can be reinforced, thereby reducing the problem behavior. The obvious incompatible behavior to an out-of-seat response is an in-seat response. Another example is to reinforce a student for raising his or her hand before speaking as an incompatible response to talking out in a work setting.

A DRI schedule to reduce inappropriate behavior can readily be used in conjunction with a DRH schedule to accelerate work behavior. For example, a criterion for reinforcement for a student may be to remain in his or her seat for 10 minutes and produce five ball point pens. Reinforcement would not be delivered unless the student satisfied the criterion of both the DRI and the DRH schedules.

The *Differential Reinforcement of Low Rate Responding (DRL) Schedule* is useful when one does not wish to eliminate an inappropriate behavior completely, but rather to decrease it significantly (for example, behaviors such as talking out in the work setting, eating too quickly, and the like). This schedule is also appropriate when the behavior appears so habitually that reduction is the only realistic alternative. Here, after examining the baseline data, a criterion level of responding (that is, inappropriate responding) is determined at slightly lower than the baseline rate. For example, if in baseline the student exhibited an average of 20 talking-out responses in five minutes during work periods, the initial DRL schedule for reinforcement would be that 15 or fewer talkouts during each five-minute work period would produce reinforcement. If, however, 16 talkouts were counted in five minutes, no reinforcement would be delivered and the session would be started again. DRL schedules can also be used in conjunction with DRH schedules to increase work production and reduce inappropriate behavior simultaneously. Once the student begins to learn the relationship between his or her behavior and the reward, the level of responding during the timed interval can be lowered still more and finally lowered to an acceptable level (such as one or no talk-outs in 15 minutes).

The *Differential Reinforcement of Other Behavior (DRO) Schedule* represents a process by which reinforcement is delivered if the response (that is, the inappropriate response) does not occur for a preselected length of time. The length of time is determined by examining the baseline data. For instance, if in baseline one finds that a student is emitting an inappropriate response once every five minutes, the initial DRO schedule of reinforcement could be for zero responses to occur in five minutes in order that reinforcement could be delivered. A kitchen timer could be set for five minutes and if no responses had been counted when the bell rang, reinforcement would be delivered to the student.

A DRO schedule always means that no (zero) responses can occur within a given time interval. It should be obvious, however, that if in baseline an average of 20 responses occur within five minutes, the initial schedule of reinforcement cannot be zero responses in five minutes. In this case, the initial response requirement of zero responses in five minutes is far too great to ensure success. Thus, the initial schedule of reinforcement must directly reflect the baseline rate of responding. In the example of a baseline rate of 20 responses in five minutes, the student is actually emitting one response every 15 seconds; therefore, an appropriate initial DRO schedule of reinforcement would be every 15 seconds if no responses were counted. This schedule would then be quickly accelerated to 30 seconds, once the student had learned the value of the reinforcer and the relationship between his or her behavior and the reinforcer. The DRO schedule is then accelerated until an acceptable level is reached and maintained.

It should be apparent that accuracy in measuring response occurrence is crucial to the success of a DRO schedule. If the initial schedule of reinforcement is too great, the reinforcer will simply hold little value. During each timed interval, the teacher prompts "other" behavior, which, in this case, is work production. At the end of an interval, if no inappropriate responses occur, the teacher delivers the reinforcers and resets the timer. If the response does occur during the interval, the reinforcer is not delivered and the session is started again. One may also wish to include timeout periods, mild punishment, and other devices if the response does occur. DRO schedules show clear utility in eliminating an interfering behavior during work periods. If DRO scheduling is used in conjunction with the DRH schedule to accelerate work rate, inappropriate behavior is eliminated while simultaneously the student's work production rate is increased.

Table 10-3 identifies common problem behaviors or interfering behavior often seen in work training. Student-centered objectives in the second column are aimed at eliminating the problem behavior and increasing work behavior. In the third column, three strategies utilizing the schedules of reinforcement discussed above are given. It is advisable always to first try the most positive instructional technique (that is, the first strategy next to each objective). If ineffective, mild negative consequences can be attempted, as suggested in the second and third strategies.

Monitoring System for Production Rate

The simplest and most frequently used data system in a vocational training program is one in which the number of units or the amount of work completed

Table 10-3 Student Objectives and Suggested Strategies for the Elimination of Problem Behaviors in a Work Setting

Common Problem Behavior	Example Objective(s)	Examples of Strategies
Works Slowly (Low Production)	Will produce ___ units per minute for ___ minute work periods over three consecutive sessions or Will work ___ % more rapidly than baseline data over three consecutive sessions.	(All initial schedules based on rate of production in baseline phase) DRH – Select gradually increased criterion over baseline to be produced within time period. If at end of period, target criterion of work completed, deliver reinforcement. If not, begin session again. DRH with response cost – same as above; however, if target criterion of work not completed at end of interval, take back one token or other reinforcer already given to student. DRH with time out – use same DRH procedures above; however, if work criterion not met, time student out for 2 minutes (i.e., away from teacher, other students).
Refuses to Work	Will produce one unit independently in ___ minutes over 3 consecutive sessions. (accelerate gradually with success).	DRI – Incompatible behavior – Producing one work unit (e.g., a ball point pen). Prompt work behavior; show strong reinforcer. If student completes unit, deliver reinforcer. Accelerate requirements gradually. DRI – with time out – Same as above; however, if student refuses to produce unit within work period include a brief time out period. Begin session again. DRI with positive practice – same as DRI procedure above; however, if student refuses to produce unit within work period, physically guide him through the production task repeatedly (e.g., 20 times).

Table 10-3 continued

Common Problem Behavior	Example Objective(s)	Examples of Strategies
Exhibits off-task behavior after only a few minutes of work.	Will gradually increase production output to a final criterion of ___ % of standard production rate and work continuously for 30 minutes over 3 consecutive session, e.g. Interim criterion are: 5 units 5/min. 8 units/8 min. 15 units/10 min. 30 units/20 min. 50 units/25 min. 60 units/30 min.	DRH - After examining baseline data, select appropriate initial criterion, just above baseline, to be completed within a specific time period. If met, deliver reinforcement. Begin session again. DRH with verbal reprimand. Same as above; however, add verbal reprimand if student does not reach criterion. DRH with Response Cost - Same DRH procedures above; however, if student does not reach target criterion, take back one previously earned token or other reinforcer.
Does not work unless constantly prompted.	Will produce units to ___ criteria with no more than ___ teacher prompts per 30-minute work period over 3 consecutive sessions.	DRH - In addition to production baseline data, have aide take baseline on number of prompts teacher gives to student - (1) Select target number of work units to be completed within specific work period which is slightly above baseline production performance. (2) Determine the number of prompts to be given which is slightly below baseline of needed teacher prompts. If at the end of the work period student has completed target for work units given only the reduced number of prompts, deliver reward. If not, start session again. DRH with time out - Same as above; however, include brief time out period if student does not complete target with reduced prompts. DRH with Response cost - Same DRH procedures; however, take back one token or other reinforcer for not reaching criterion.

Examples of Interfering Behaviors	Vocational Objective(s)	Suggested Strategies
Frequently out-of-seat	Will produce units to ____ criteria and display continual in-seat behavior throughout ____ minutes work period over 3 consecutive days.	DRH/DRI - Examination of baseline data on production and out-of-seat behavior should help establish initial in-seat target which is sufficiently brief that success is likely. Student should display in-seat target of ____ minutes and appropriate production criterion to receive reinforcement. If not, start session again. DRH/DRI with response cost - Same as above; however, response cost (returning one previously earned token) should be instituted if student gets out of seat. DRH/DRI with time out - Same as above; however, include a brief time out period if student leaves his seat.
Emits continual loud noise during work periods.	Will produce units to ____ criterion and emit ____ % fewer noisemaking responses during ____ minute work period over 3 consecutive sessions. (DRL programs) (2) Emit zero noise-making responses ...(DRO Program)	DRH/DRL - Examination of production baseline and noisemaking baseline should identify a number of noisemaking responses which is slightly less than the average number emitted during baseline. Explain contingency to student; start work period. Tally in view of student the number of noises emitted. Warn student when he nears "noise" criterion. If at the end of the interval, student did not exceed number of permitted noises, deliver reinforcer. If too many noises were counted start session again. Gradually require that fewer and fewer noises be emitted. DRH/DRL with response cost - Same as above, but if student exceeds noise criterion take back one previously earned token. DRH/DRO from baseline data, select an initial work period which is sufficiently brief in that zero noisemaking is likely to occur. If at end of interval, zero noises are counted, deliver reinforcement. Gradually increase time period.

Table 10-3 continued

Examples of Interfering Behaviors	Vocational Objective(s)	Suggested Strategies
Exhibits mouthing of self or materials.	Produces ___ units per minute and exhibits zero mouthing responses in ___ minute work period over 3 consecutive days.	DRH/DRO – Examination of baseline data on production and mouthing should help to establish an initial time constraint which is sufficiently brief that no mouthing responses are likely to occur. Prompt work production during this period. If at end of interval, work target is reached and zero mouthing has occurred, deliver reinforcer. If not, start session again. Accelerate length of work period with zero mouthing gradually. DRH/DRO – with response cost – Same as above; however, if mouthing response occurs take back one token or other reinforcer. DRH/DRO with verbal reprimand – Same as above; however, if mouthing occurs stop session and deliver sharp verbal reprimand.

within a recorded time period is monitored. This yields rate data on student production. Rate assessments are computed by dividing the total number of work units (for example, pens assembled) or amount of work completed (for example, tables cleaned) by the total number of minutes the individual worked. This gives the teacher an evaluation based on standard measurement rate per minute. When using rate per minute data, the length of the work period can vary without distorting the production data. In addition, examining student progress through rate data is particularly useful with the more severely handicapped since even small increments can be discerned through this sensitive measure. Figure 10-4 is a graphic display of rate data pertaining to an assembly task.

CONCLUSION

This chapter has considered a major inequity of our educational system, which in effect denies the right of vocational training to those students who most need it: the severely and profoundly handicapped. The reasons for this denial do not involve inability on the part of severely handicapped students to learn vocational skills but rather point out the lack of currently available vocational transitions for severely handicapped adults. Past practices have repeatedly shown successful demonstrations of the ability of the severely handicapped to perform complex vocational tasks. However, successful or

---

Figure 10-4 Graphic Illustration of Monitoring of Rate Data

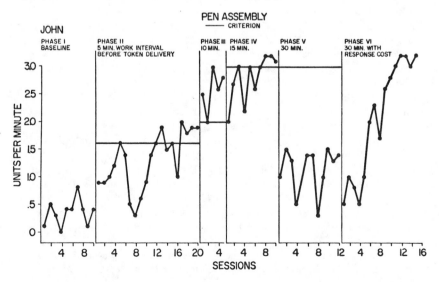

even adequate vocational programs for this group do not generally exist in the average community. Segregated settings breeding artificiality in training, as well as the scarcity of appropriate personnel preparation programs for vocational teachers, are all contributors to the failures of training programs that do exist.

A detailed sequence of program development was presented based on the rationale that our society has a commitment to provide the option of vocational training to all students regardless of the severity of handicap. Vocational training geared toward the next more advanced transition and the provision of early and sustained opportunities to interact in the nonhandicapped work world were stressed. Finally, an illustrative curriculum sequence provided an example of appropriate vocational training content and basic instructional strategies utilizing schedules of reinforcements. It is hoped that the content of this chapter may provide some guidelines for improving the present vocational training inequity that exists with the severely and profoundly handicapped.

REFERENCES

Bellamy, T., Horner, R., & Inman, D. *Vocational habilitation of severely retarded adults: A direct service technology.* Baltimore: University Park Press, 1979.

Bellamy, T., Peterson, L., & Close, D. Habilitation of the severely and profoundly retarded: Illustrations of competence. *Education and Training of the Mentally Retarded,* 1975, *10,* 174–186.

Bellamy, T., Sheehan, M., Horner, R., & Boles, S. Community programs for severely handicapped adults: An analysis. *Journal of The Association for the Severely Handicapped,* 1980, *5*(4), 307-324.

Belmore, K.J., & Brown, L. A job skill inventory strategy designed for severely handicapped potential workers. In N. Haring & D. Bricker (Eds.), *Teaching the severely handicapped, Volume III.* Columbus, Ohio: Special Press, 1978.

Brolin, D.E. *Vocational preparation of retarded citizens.* Columbus, Ohio: Charles E. Merrill, 1976.

Brown, L., Pumpian, I., Baumgart, D., Van Deventer, P., Ford, A., Nisbet, J., Schroeder, J., & Gruenewald, L. Longitudinal transition plans in programs for severely handicapped students. *Exceptional Children,* 1981, *47*(8), 624–630.

Cortazzo, A. *Activity centers for retarded adults.* Washington, D.C.: President's Committee on Mental Retardation, 1972.

Falvey, M., Brown, L., Lyon, S., Baumgart, D., & Schroeder, J. Strategies for using cues and correction procedures. In W. Sailor, B. Wilcox, & L. Brown (Eds.), *Methods of instruction for severely handicapped students.* Baltimore: Paul H. Brookes, 1980.

Flexer, R., & Martin, A. Sheltered workshops and vocational training settings. In M.E. Snell (Ed.), *Systematic instruction of the moderately and severely handicapped.* Columbus, Ohio: Charles E. Merrill, 1978.

Gold, M. Research on the vocational habilitation of the retarded: The present, the future. In N. Ellis (Ed.), *International review of research in mental retardation (Volume 6).* New York: Academic, 1973.

Gold, M. Task analysis of a complex assembly task by the retarded blind. *Exceptional Children,* 1976, *42,* 78–84.

Gold, M., & Pomerantz, D. Issues in prevocational training. In M.E. Snell (Ed.), *Systematic instruction of the moderately and severely handicapped.* Columbus, Ohio: Charles E. Merrill, 1978.

Hansen, C.L. History of vocational habilitation of the handicapped. In C.L. Hansen & N.G. Haring (Eds.), *Expanding opportunities: Vocational education for the handicapped.* Washington, D.C.: United States Department of Education, Office of Special Education and Rehabilitation Services, 1980.

Hansen, C.L., & Haring, N.G. Perspectives on vocational education and rehabilitation for the handicapped. In C.L. Hansen and N.G. Haring (Eds.), *Expanding opportunities: Vocational education for the handicapped.* Washington, D.C.: United States Department of Education, Office of Special Education and Rehabilitation Services, 1980.

Hill, J., Wehman, P., & Kochany, L. Development of a community based pre-employment program. *Rehabilitation Literature,* 1979, *40*(11–12), 330–335.

Horner, R., & Bellamy, T. A conceptual analysis of vocational training. In M.E. Snell (Ed.), *Systematic instruction of the moderately and severely handicapped.* Columbus, Ohio: Charles E. Merrill, 1978.

Karan, O., Wehman, P., Renzaglia, A., & Schultz, R. (Eds.). *Habilitation practices with the severely and developmentally disabled: Volume one.* Madison: University of Wisconsin, Waisman Center on Mental Retardation, 1976.

Kazdin, A.E. Toward a client administered token reinforcement program. *Education and Training of the Mentally Retarded,* 1971, *8,* 4–11.

Larson, K., & Edwards, J. Community based vocational training and placement for the severely handicapped. In C.L. Hansen and N.G. Haring (Eds.), *Expanding opportunities: Vocational education for the handicapped.* Washington, D.C.: United States Department of Education, Office of Special Education and Rehabilitation Services, 1980.

Laski, F.J. Legal strategies to secure entitlement to services for severely handicapped persons. In T. Bellamy, G. O'Connor, & O.C. Karan (Eds.), *Vocational rehabilitation of the severely handicapped: Contemporary service strategies.* Baltimore: University Park Press, 1979.

Levy, S. The debilitating effects of the habilitation process. In C.L. Hansen and N.G. Haring (Eds.), *Expanding opportunities: Vocational education for the handicapped.* Washington, D.C.: United States Department of Education, Office of Special Education and Rehabilitation Services, 1980.

Lynch, A., & Singer, T. Vocational programming for the severe and profound in the public schools. In C.L. Hansen and N.G. Haring (Eds.), *Expanding opportunities: Vocational education for the handicapped.* Washington, D.C.: United States Department of Education, Office of Special Education and Rehabilitation Services, 1980.

Mithaug, D.E., Hagmeier, L.D., & Haring, N.G. The relationship between training activities and job placement in vocational education of the severely handicapped. *AAESPH Review,* 1977, *2,* 89–109.

Mithaug, D., Mar, D., & Stewart, O. *Prevocational assessment and curriculum guide.* Seattle: Exceptional Education Press, 1978.

Nelson, N. *Workshops for the handicapped in the United States: An historical and developmental perspective.* Springfield, Ill.: Charles C Thomas, 1971.

Renzaglia, A., Wehman, P., Schultz, R., & Karan, O. Use of cue redundancy and positive reinforcement to accelerate production in two profoundly retarded workers. *British Journal of Social and Clinical Psychology,* 1978, *17,* 183–187.

Revel, G., & Wehman, P. Vocational evaluation of severely and profoundly retarded clients. *Rehabilitation Literature,* 1978, *39*(8), 226–231.

Rusch, F.R. Toward the validation of social vocational survival skills. *Mental Retardation,* 1979, *17*(3), 143–145.

Rusch, F.R., & Mithaug, D.E. *Vocational training for mentally retarded adults.* Champaign, Ill.: Research Press, 1980.

Schneider, K., Rusch, F., Henderson, R., & Geske, T. *Competitive employment for mentally retarded persons: Costs versus benefits.* Manuscript submitted for publication, 1981.

Snell, M.E. (Ed.). *Systematic instruction of the moderately and severely handicapped.* Columbus, Ohio: Charles E. Merrill, 1978.

Terkel, S. *Working.* New York: Pantheon, 1972.

Vogelsberg, R., Williams, W., & Friedl, M. Facilitating systems change for the severely handicapped: Secondary and adult services. *Journal of the Association for the Severely Handicapped,* 1980, 5(1), 73–85.

Wehman, P. *Competitive employment.* Baltimore: Paul H. Brookes, 1981.

Wehman, P., & Bates, P. Education curriculum for severely and profoundly handicapped persons: A review. *Rehabilitation Literature,* 1978, *39*(1), 2–14.

Wehman, P., & Hill, J. *Vocational training and placement of severely disabled persons: Project employability, Volume I.* Richmond: Virginia Commonwealth University, 1979.

Wehman, P., & Hill, J. *Vocational training and placement of severely disabled persons, Volume II.* Richmond: Virginia Commonwealth University, 1980.

Wehman, P., & Hill, M. *Instructional programming for severely handicapped youth.* Richmond: Virginia Commonwealth University, 1980.

Wehman, P., & McLaughlin, P.J. *Vocational curriculum for developmentally disabled persons.* Baltimore: University Park Press, 1980.

Whitehead, C. Sheltered workshops in the decade ahead: Work and wages or welfare. In T. Bellamy, G. O'Connor and O.C. Karan (Eds.), *Vocational rehabilitation for developmentally disabled persons: Contemporary service strategies.* Baltimore: University Park Press, 1979.

Wolfensberger, W. (Ed.). *The principle of normalization in human services.* Downsview, Toronto, Canada: National Institute on Mental Retardation, York University Campus, 1972.

Part VI

Summary

Future Directions in the Education of Severely and Profoundly Handicapped Students

Les Sternberg and Gary L. Adams

A paradigm used as a framework to structure the content of this book was the umbrella model. Four areas were identified as crucial for understanding educational aspects pertaining to the severely and profoundly handicapped. They were environmental concerns, assessment procedures, management techniques, and curricular components. Although an attempt has been made throughout to address current issues or problems related to each of these areas, future directions have much to do with the ultimate outcome for the severely and profoundly handicapped student, in terms of both education and later life styles. The following sections of this chapter delineate future directions that educators must take in order that the goal of appropriate and effective education for all severely and profoundly handicapped students can be achieved.

A FUTURE LOOK AT THE ENVIRONMENT

What is the appropriate instructional setting is one of the predominant issues related to educating severely and profoundly handicapped students. In the past the institution represented the educational arena. Over the past few decades, *mainstreaming* (placing students in the least restrictive environment) and *normalization* (creating environments and behaviors that more closely approximate "normal" expectations) have had a strong impact on the selection of instructional sites for severely and profoundly handicapped students. Unfortunately, too often school administrators have misinterpreted mainstreaming and normalization as meaning merely the attempt to place severely and profoundly handicapped students with students of the same chronological age. Given the common presence of physical impairments in more severely disabled students, the administrative alternative has been to place them in segregated schools (centers) and away from the regular public

315

schools, a practice that falls far short of the intent of mainstreaming or normalization.

Some public school districts have realized that severely and profoundly handicapped students can be integrated into neighborhood schools. There is, however, more than the issue of physical setting that needs to be considered. Before the handicapped students are placed into a self-contained classroom in the neighborhood school setting, the regular school teachers, the nonhandicapped students, and the parents and families of the handicapped and regular school children must be prepared for the integration efforts. An orientation program may calm many of the initial fears of the participants.

In regard to the handicapped student's home environment, it is imperative that the family receive formal training in order that a carryover of the student's in-school program may be accomplished. This is not to say that educators must somehow create a formal parent/sibling-as-teacher. Rather, educators must begin to understand the day-to-day constraints placed on the family of a severely or profoundly handicapped individual and be able to suggest ways in which carryover education can be infused into the at-home environment—without violating the life styles of the family members. Of equal importance is the necessity for developing coordinated respite care programs to afford family members the opportunity of some relief from those day-to-day trials and tribulations that the families of severely and profoundly handicapped students encounter.

The teacher of severely and profoundly handicapped students is the key person in dictating whether success will be achieved in the formal instructional setting. Unfortunately, preservice and inservice education with this population has been lacking. Several authors have noted the high level of teaching expertise that is needed (see, for example, Smith & Smith, 1978; Sontag, Burke, & York, 1973), but at this time universities and colleges have not provided much assistance. Most universities have not developed training programs for teachers of the severely and profoundly handicapped, or the programs directed toward these students are so new that there are currently not enough trained teachers to fill the pressing demand. Some universities or college training programs have attempted to bridge the educational gap by either offering isolated introductory courses or infusing some content pertaining to severely and profoundly handicapped students into existing coursework dealing with mildly/moderately impaired students. Comprehensive and coordinated training is necessary, with instruction conducted by professors who have expertise in the field of training severely and profoundly handicapped students. Colleges and universities must not be tempted to fill the teacher shortage by creating courses and having professors who have experience only with mildly/moderately students teach classes about severely and profoundly handicapped students.

Given the present training situation at colleges and universities, program administrators in public schools are faced with a difficult dilemma. Most of their teachers are either recent graduates or teachers of mildly handicapped students who have been transferred. These teachers are not trained with the population that they must serve and their expectations for student growth may be completely unrealistic. Such conditions tend to lead to high teacher turnover rates. Unfortunately, most inservice efforts have not helped this situation. Too often, program administrators have offered one-day workshops as the solution. The result is that teachers receive multiple workshops on one topic (language training, for example) and no training on other topics. Further confusion is generated by multiple workshops given by presenters who have very different training approaches. This piecemeal approach to inservice training is expensive, and the teachers still do not have the skills they need. Program administrators must create comprehensive inservice training.

A FUTURE LOOK AT ASSESSMENT

For mildly and moderately handicapped students, assessment usually has involved obtaining results from standardized academic achievement tests (for example, the *Wide Range Achievement Test* and the *Stanford Achievement Test*) in conjunction with results of other norm-referenced tests purporting to measure various constructs (intelligence, aptitude, abilities, etc.). The stress on academic skills and the comparatively high performance level of these tests make them inappropriate for severely and profoundly handicapped students. Instead, tests of adaptive behavior are typically used. These tests usually have one of two formats: descriptive or prescriptive. Descriptive tests, such as the *Adaptive Behavior Scale* (Lambert, Windmiller, Cole, & Figueroa, 1975), focus on screening. Prescriptive tests, such as the *Camelot Behavioral Checklist* (Foster, 1974), use a test/teach/test format.

Most of the adaptive behavior tests are fraught with problems. Some simply do not include behaviors at the lower end of the behavioral spectrum. Many of the test items are not in small increments and not stated as behavioral objectives. Many of the test developers have relied on an unproven assumption regarding the sequence of items. Often the order of items has been based on the developmental sequence of normal children. One of the problems with this approach is that there are discrepancies across lists of developmental sequences. A behavior (for example, lifts head while sitting) may be at one age level on one particular test and at a different age level on another test. Aside from this problem, there is the related assumption that severely and profoundly handicapped students should be trained in the same sequence as that in which the average normal child acquires behaviors. An example of this problem is explained by Williams, Hamre-Nietupski, Pumpian, McDaniel

Marks, and Wheeler (1978). They state that the teacher should not spend time training at only the lower levels of social behavior and stressing isolated play when the student can be instructed at higher levels of social interaction at the same time. A rigid reliance on this developmental model may actually slow down student progress. Research on this assessment assumption needs to be conducted.

One unenviable characteristic of the vast majority of these tests is that they lack the acceptable minimum standards of test construction. A survey of adaptive behavior tests conducted by Walls, Werner, and Bacon (1976) shows that less than 25 percent of the tests provided reliability or validity information. Tests with high reliability and validity, such as the *Behavior Inventory for Rating the Retarded* (Sparrow & Cicchetti, 1978), the *Empirically Based Training Assessment* (Adams, 1981), and the *Quantitative Assessment of Motor and Sensory/Motor Acquisition in Handicapped and Nonhandicapped Infants and Young Children* (Guess, Rues, Warren, Lyon, & Janssen, 1981), are some of the notable exceptions. Test users must begin to expect the same type of standards for test construction for adaptive behavior tests as they do with other types of tests.

Another basic problem in assessing severely and profoundly handicapped students is how to generate accurate expectations. Without some idea of what to expect in terms of growth, educators will be very hard pressed to delineate appropriate goals and objectives. Questions will arise as to whether one should expect normality or whether one should gear programming toward more attainable but less "noble" goals. Many might argue that to specify expectations for a severely or profoundly handicapped student would necessarily place limits on the student's program. However, to not generate some idea of expectations may lead to something much worse: the establishment of a program that has realism for the community but not for the student, or the establishment of a program that develops piecemeal skills having no coordination with any functional aspect of behavior to which those skills might contribute.

Severely and profoundly handicapped students typically require considerable modification in their instructional programming. These modifications may require physical adaptations (such as the use of prosthetic devices and positioning), an adaptation of prompts (for example, the use of modeling in place of verbal cues), and/or an adaptation of responses (for example, a motor response instead of a verbal response). It stands to reason that if adaptations are required in instruction, the same may be true in assessment (Duncan, Sbardellati, Maheady, & Sainato, 1981). This type of assessment format is called *interaction analysis*. Instead of using a yes/no format to assess if the student can perform the behavior in its entirety, the behavior (test item) is broken down into multiple prompt, response, and physical adaptation modes to see if the student succeeds with the modification. If adaptations do not produce successful behavioral outputs, additional assessment information can be obtained by monitoring the student's success in a test/teach/test paradigm. Here, data pertaining to the ability to profit from instruction (that is, learning potential) are obtained. This interactive learning potential assessment of the student could provide invaluable information related not only to expectations of growth but also to preferred instructional techniques. If this type of assessment paradigm were used on a longitudinal basis, further information could be gleaned pertaining to intervention efficiency. That is, given an initial assessment of the student that delineated effective physical adaptations, prompts, and responses, any intervention done over time could be compared with any prior period of intervention. Attainment records could be obtained and compared to determine if a "growth rate" had either sustained itself, accelerated, or decelerated.

A FUTURE LOOK AT BEHAVIOR MANAGEMENT

Examples of successful behavioral interventions on severely and profoundly handicapped students using applied behavior analysis techniques are numerous (see, for example, Azrin & Foxx, 1971; Hamilton, Stephens, & Allen, 1967; Tate & Baroff, 1966). The success of the majority of the techniques has been due to the use of consequent behavior modification. Unfortunately, this success has somehow detoured our concern away from two related problems: how the student will generalize the changed behavior to new situations and how to teach the student to control his or her behavior without a teacher (or other change agent) being physically near. It appears as if these problems can be addressed by future research directed toward a number of areas. First, there must be an increased emphasis on the use and control of antecedent events. Many of the aberrant behaviors exhibited by severely or profoundly handicapped students are due to poor environmental structuring. For example, in many classrooms the teacher and aide conduct one-to-one training while the other students are left to exhibit maladaptive behaviors. Then the teacher complains about the number of students who are displaying stereotypic, ritualistic, or other inappropriate behaviors. Research of classroom structures that coordinate social skills with other types of skill training programs, such as self-help skills, is needed.

An increased emphasis on the use and control of antecedent events can also lead to the development of two necessary skills: the ability to control one's behavior without the necessity of the teacher (or other change agent) being present (self-control) and the ability to exhibit such control regardless of multiple conditions the student might encounter (generalization). This requires that those interested in behavior change implement behavior change from an ecological perspective. There is no reason why a social skills curriculum cannot be developed as we have developed curricula in other skill areas. Within this curriculum, specific social behaviors would be pinpointed (for example, standing at the appropriate physical distance while communicating). After this objective is reached, a strategy of internally cueing the behavior needs to be developed so that the student exhibits the behavior not only in one environment but also in other appropriate settings. The internal cueing strategy may be difficult to create because of the cognitive deficits of some severely or profoundly handicapped students. This approach toward self-control and generalization, however, forces change agents into designing behavioral interventions aimed at a more functional result than merely increasing or decreasing the frequency or rate of a specific behavior.

A FUTURE LOOK AT CURRICULUM

The topic of curriculum for severely and profoundly handicapped students invariably leads to arguments about curriculum models (for example, developmental versus future independent living skills) and instructional techniques (for example, backward versus forward chaining or the use of different prompt sequences). The issue of which curriculum model to use will partially depend on the characteristics of the student. It is difficult, for instance, to use a future independent living skills model for a one-year-old profoundly retarded child with gross physical impairments because the skills that the child will need in life (survival skills) may be hard to estimate. On the other hand, it would be inappropriate to have an 18-year-old severely retarded student with few physical impairments rolling a ball for the developmental reason of purposeful interaction with objects. Especially when the student is nearing the end of a school career, teachers must emphasize (if appropriate) future out-of-school survival skills. The argument about which curriculum model is best may be a waste of time because often the proponents are talking about two different types of students. What appears to be needed is a melding of the supposedly conflicting models: a continuum of model emphases. In this system, all developmental considerations would precede all future needs considerations within a pre-established sequence. When a student could change from a developmental to a future needs emphasis would depend solely on that student's characteristics. Most likely, this transition would take place during some critical period based on future expectations of that student. The expectations would be generated from assessment information that would help pinpoint the probability and level of future potential independent behavior.

The arguments about which instructional technique to use may be almost as fruitless as those arguments concerning curricular models. Neither side in the techniques debate has a strong case because the empirical research is simply not there. A complete review of the literature shows an embarrassingly small number of studies involving the analysis of instructional techniques (see, for example, Adams, Matlock, & Tallon, 1981; Close, Irvin, Prehm, & Taylor, 1978; Nelson, Cone, & Hanson, 1975). Obviously, much more research is needed.

Beyond the problem of not suggesting validated instructional techniques, curriculum authors have limited their scope of task analyses to a narrow range of behaviors. Within this narrow range, there are task analyses of many irrelevant skills. A look at the table of contents of most curricula for severely and profoundly handicapped students proves this point. A large percentage of the analyses are of pseudoacademic tasks (such as putting pegs in a pegboard) that have little utility in the students' lives. Also, the task-analyzed behaviors are taught in isolation, rather than in natural sequences. For example, almost every curriculum contains a shirt-buttoning task analysis, but there are few curricula containing a task analysis for tucking in the shirt after it is buttoned.

A major reason for using a task analysis approach is to make the instructional process more specific; yet most available task analyses are too general. The result is that the teacher must make major modifications. The excuse that is given is that the severely and profoundly handicapped population is heterogeneous and it is hard to write a specific task analysis to fit everyone's needs. The real problem is that with few exceptions (see, for example, Tawney, Knapp, O'Reilly, & Pratt, 1979) curriculum authors have not taken the time to really analyze the steps in the target behavior. This problem suggests another needed improvement in the quality of curricula. Validation data on task analyses are almost nonexistent. Curriculum authors used face validity, thinking that if one constructs a logical sequence of steps leading to the attainment of a terminal behavior, then it is an effective task analysis. This assumption must be proven by data being collected on how long it takes to move across the steps in the task analysis.

Another related question involved with implementation of curricula is, at what age should formal education begin and terminate for the severely and profoundly handicapped? Although many states now mandate education for the handicapped from age three, this may be too late. The severely and profoundly handicapped can typically be identified as handicapped long before age three because of the presence of obvious clinical symptoms (for example, profound delay in the attainment of developmental milestones, severe sensory impairment, absence of basic survival skills). If a parent or caretaker is not exposed to appropriate training regarding how to effect change with the child, the child's pattern of growth becomes syndrome based. For example, a profoundly handicapped child who shows no apparent awareness of the environment may continue to show this deficit only because the parent or caretaker believes the behavior should continue because the behavior is typical of the child. The first problem inherent in this situation is that once deficited behavior is allowed to occur, it may become habitual. The second problem is that once a deficit habit is developed and you wish to teach a more appropriate behavior, you are forced to deal with two competing behaviors. This can take an inordinate amount of instructional time, a situation that could have been easily avoided if comprehensive instructional services were available from birth.

The expansion of program offerings should also apply to the time period after which formal education is customarily terminated (in many states, 21 years of age). For those severely or profoundly handicapped individuals who are capable of some type of vocational placement, ongoing educational services appear to be a necessity. One cannot assume that by the "magic" age of 21 years all necessary vocational behaviors will be learned and applied. Obviously, there will be many profoundly handicapped individuals who will not be capable of benefiting from vocational programming, in either a sheltered workshop or competitive employment site. Assessed expectations again can dictate to what extent extended educational opportunities ought to be offered. Unfortunately, at the present time different agencies control different age spans of the handicapped student. In most cases, the educational agency dictates the parameters of the student's education for students up to the age of 21 years. After 21 years of age, other agencies (if willing to deal with the severely and profoundly handicapped) take over responsibilities (for example, Vocational Rehabilitation, Mental Health/Mental Retardation, Developmental Disabilities). Continuity of educational services may very well be lost during the transition.

It is imperative that different agencies responsible for certain program aspects begin to rethink their instructional emphases (in terms of both content offered and age restrictions). Whether one type of agency assumes ultimate programmatic control remains to be seen. It is apparent, however, that the "sacred turf phenomenon" that defines the current operational focus of different agencies must be dealt with if viable programs for the severely and profoundly handicapped are to be realized and continued.

CONCLUSION

The intent of this chapter was to delineate future directions in the education of severely and profoundly handicapped students. A main theme permeating the different topics is the need for more empirical research. This is not to say that teachers and researchers have been lazy. On the contrary, the amount of research done in the fairly young history of the systematic instruction of severely and profoundly handicapped students is impressive. We simply hope that future directions will provide the necessary continuation of efforts.

REFERENCES

Adams, G.L. Empirically based training assessment. Unpublished manuscript, 1981.

Adams, G.L., Matlock, B.L., & Tallon, R. Analysis of social praise given during the correction procedure of skill training. *American Journal of Mental Deficiency*, 1981, *85*, 652–654.

Azrin, N.H., & Foxx, R.M. A rapid method of toilet training the institutionalized retarded. *Journal of Applied Behavior Analysis*, 1971, *4*, 89–99.

Close, D.W., Irvin, L.K., Prehm, H.J., & Taylor, V.E. Systematic correction procedures in vocational skill training of severely retarded individuals. *American Journal of Mental Deficiency*, 1978, *83*, 270–275.

Duncan, D., Sbardellati, E., Maheady, L., & Sainato, D. Nondiscriminatory assessment of severely physically handicapped individuals. *Journal of The Association for the Severely Handicapped*, 1981, *6*(2), 17–22.

Foster, R.W. *Camelot Behavioral Checklist*. Lawrence, Kans.: Camelot Behavioral Systems, 1974.

Guess, D., Rues, J., Warren, S., Lyon, S., & Janssen, C. *Quantitative assessment of motor and sensory/motor acquisition in handicapped and nonhandicapped infants and young children. Volume II: Interobserver reliability results for the procedures*. Lawrence, Kans.: Early Childhood Institute, 1981.

Hamilton, J., Stephens, L., & Allen, P. Controlling aggressive and destructive behavior in severely retarded institutionalized residents. *American Journal of Mental Deficiency*, 1967, *7*, 852–856.

Lambert, N., Windmiller, M., Cole, L., & Figueroa, R. *AAMD Adaptive Behavior Scale, Public School Version (1974 rev.)*. Washington, D.C.: American Association of Mental Deficiency, 1975.

Nelson, G.L., Cone, J.D., & Hanson, C.R. Training correct utensil use in retarded children: Modeling vs. physical guidance. *American Journal of Mental Deficiency*, 1975, *80*, 114–122.

Smith, D.D., & Smith, J.O. Trends. In M.E. Snell (Ed.), *Systematic instruction of the moderately and severely handicapped*. Columbus, Ohio: Charles E. Merrill, 1978.

Sontag, E., Burke, P., & York, R. Considerations for serving the severely handicapped in the public schools. *Education and Training of the Mentally Retarded*, 1973, *82*, 20–26.

Sparrow, S.S., & Cicchetti, D.V. Behavior rating inventory for moderately, severely, and profoundly retarded persons. *American Journal of Mental Deficiency*, 1978, *82*, 365–374.

Tate, B.G., & Baroff, G.S. Aversive control of self-injurious behavior in a psychotic boy. *Behaviour Research and Therapy*, 1966, *4*, 281–287.

Tawney, J.W., Knapp, D.S., O'Reilly, C.D., & Pratt, S.S. *Programmed environments curriculum*. Columbus, Ohio: Charles E. Merrill, 1979.

Walls, R.T., Werner, T.J., & Bacon, A. *Behavior checklists*. Morgantown, W.Va.: West Virginia University Research and Training Center, 1976.

Williams, W., Hamre-Nietupski, S., Pumpian, I., McDaniel Marks, J., & Wheeler, J. Teaching social skills. In M.E. Snell (Ed.), *Systematic instruction of the moderately and severely handicapped*. Columbus, Ohio: Charles E. Merrill, 1978.

Communication Programming Inventory

COMMUNICATION PROGRAMMING INVENTORY

AREA: COGNITION

LEVEL		BEHAVIORS	RATING

RATING

Y P N N
E O O A
S S

0 – 1 Month

1a. Reflexive behavior predominates (e.g., sucking, grasping, crying, body and head movements). _ _ _ _

b. Movement present but not in response to external stimulation. _ _ _ _

c. Not responsive to the environment. _ _ _ _

*2a. Objects evoke undifferentiated reflexive responses. _ _ _ _

*b. Behavior changes when stimulated (aurally, visually, or tactually). _ _ _ _

Total # Score   + +   / = ___

% Yes Score   = ___

1 – 4 Months

1a. Repeats bodily movements; self-stimulation of body. _ _ _ _

b. Anticipates familiar event when body placed in certain position (e.g., placement in slight reclining position for feeding leads consistently to an increase in movement). _ _ _ _

c. Looks at spot where moving object or person last seen. _ _ _ _

d. Moves head and eyes toward a sound in front of him/her which is coming from left or right (eye-ear coordination). _ _ _ _

e. Eyes follow moving objects. _ _ _ _

f. Sucks thumb (hand-mouth coordination). _ _ _ _

2a. Recognizes a familiar object or the beginning of a familiar activity (e.g., student produces the same type of sound or movement when confronted with familiar object or activity). _ _ _ _

b. Shows preliminary object discrimination (e.g., quiets when given certain blanket but not when other objects are given). _ _ _ _

3. Unintentionally commits behavior(s) with object(s) and then repeats the behavior(s) on the object(s) (e.g., accidentally pushes object off table, continues to push other objects off table). _ _ _ _

Total # Score   + +   / = ___

% Yes Score   = ___

* If YES, credit previous 1a, 1b, and 1c as YES.

COMMUNICATION PROGRAMMING INVENTORY

AREA: COGNITION

LEVEL	BEHAVIORS	RATING

RATING: YES PROS NO NA

4 – 8 Months

1a. Reaches persistently for objects or persons. ___ ___ ___ ___

b. Grasps and manipulates all objects s/he can reach. ___ ___ ___ ___

c. Recognizes familiar people (e.g., produces the same type of sound or movement when confronted with a familiar person). ___ ___ ___ ___

2a. Performs one and then another behavior with objects, chaining these behaviors in a similar sequence with all objects (e.g., shakes and then mouths objects). ___ ___ ___ ___

b. Recognizes self in mirror. ___ ___ ___ ___

3a. Turns back to where an object is after losing contact to attend to another object or activity. ___ ___ ___ ___

b. Recognizes object as same whether s/he sees part or all (e.g., grabs partially hidden toy). ___ ___ ___ ___

c. Explores new objects by visual, aural, and/or tactual means. ___ ___ ___ ___

d. Performs specific actions on specific familiar objects (e.g., squeaky toy is squeaked). ___ ___ ___ ___

e. Anticipates positions objects will pass through while they are moving (e.g., looks for objects in places where s/he predicts they have fallen). ___ ___ ___ ___

Total # Score ___ + ___ + ___ / ___ = ___

% Yes Score = ___

8 – 12 Months

1a. Searches for objects that disappear but not always in places where they are viewed to disappear; no comprehension of visible sequential displacement (e.g., s/he may look for an object that was hidden in the first hiding place although s/he saw that it was moved from that place to a second hiding place). ___ ___ ___ ___

b. Uses two typical behaviors in sequence to intentionally obtain an object or achieve a goal (e.g., pushing aside one object to pick up another object). ___ ___ ___ ___

c. Realizes that objects can cause action (e.g., another person shakes toy, the student grabs that person's hand to lead it to the toy to reproduce the action). ___ ___ ___ ___

COMMUNICATION PROGRAMMING INVENTORY

AREA: COGNITION

LEVEL   BEHAVIORS   RATING

Y	P	N	N
E	O	O	A
S	S		

8 – 12 Months

2a. Recognizes size differences of objects (e.g., handing the
student a large object produces a wide arm grasp; a smaller
object, vice versa).   ___ ___ ___ ___

 b. Has preliminary shape constancy (e.g., given round blocks
and shape formboard with only round holes, student places
round blocks into the round holes).   ___ ___ ___ ___

                                               Total # Score   + + / = ___

                                                 % Yes Score   = ___

1a. Looks for object in the place where s/he saw it disappear;
comprehension of visible sequential displacement (e.g., after
seeing an object hidden in one place and then another, the
student searches for the object in the last hiding place).   ___ ___ ___ ___

 b. Plays with objects in new ways, emphasizing the special
visual, auditory, and/or tactual characteristics of the
objects (e.g., rubs a rubber doll against his/her cheek).   ___ ___ ___ ___

2a. Spontaneously scribbles with pencils, pens, crayons, etc.   ___ ___ ___ ___

 b. Shows, without a request, clothing and/or toys to familiar
person.   ___ ___ ___ ___

12 – 18 Months

3a. Functionally uses a variety of common objects other than
those customarily used for feeding and dressing (e.g., uses
a comb to comb his/her hair).   ___ ___ ___ ___

 b. Locates objects in the place where they are customarily
stored.   ___ ___ ___ ___

 c. Experiments through trial-and-error to find new ways to
solve problems (e.g., tries to reach toy on shelf by jump-
ing up and down).   ___ ___ ___ ___

 d. Places round and square blocks in formboard (given a formboard with round and square holes).   ___ ___ ___ ___

 e. Begins to understand the use of household objects.   ___ ___ ___ ___

 f. Engages in imaginary play using objects in their customary
fashion (e.g., uses a spoon to feed a doll).   ___ ___ ___ ___

                                               Total # Score   + + / = ___

                                                 % Yes Score   = ___

COMMUNICATION PROGRAMMING INVENTORY

AREA: COGNITION

LEVEL	BEHAVIORS	RATING YES	POS	NO	NA
18 - 24 Months	1a. Solves practical problems without first engaging in trial-and-error behaviors (e.g., reaches toy on shelf by immediately getting a chair on which s/he can stand).	___	___	___	___
	b. Plays by using objects to represent other objects (e.g., uses a bowl as a steering wheel).	___	___	___	___
	c. Reproduces activities which normally occur in a different situation (e.g., pretends to make a bed in an area that is not for sleeping).	___	___	___	___
	d. Understands that a picture can represent a real object if the picture is the same size and color as the object.	___	___	___	___
	2a. Locates object where s/he left it after a protracted period of time (object is not customarily kept in that place).	___	___	___	___
	b. Knows that a picture represents a real object even though the picture is a different size and/or color than the real object.	___	___	___	___
	c. Recognizes differences in sizes of a set of objects (color and shape are the same) with which s/he plays frequently (e.g., stacking rings done correctly).	___	___	___	___
	d. Finds objects that are hidden by invisible displacement; has object permanence (e.g., teacher's hand closed around thimble; hand under blanket; thimble released; hand withdrawn; student locates thimble under blanket).	___	___	___	___
	e. Finds objects that are hidden by invisible sequential displacement (same as above, but sequential hiding places where the student first searches for the object in the last hiding place).	___	___	___	___

Total # Score + + / = ____

% Yes Score = ____

COMMUNICATION PROGRAMMING INVENTORY

AREA: RECEPTIVE COMMUNICATION

LEVEL	BEHAVIORS	RATING

RATING columns: Y E S / P O S / N O / N A

0 - 1 Month

1a. Shows startle response to loud, sudden noises. ___ ___ ___ ___

b. Stops movement in response to emitted noise (bell, rattle, noisemaker). ___ ___ ___ ___

2a. Responds to tactile or kinesthetic stimulation. ___ ___ ___ ___

b. Stops movement in response to voice. ___ ___ ___ ___

c. Stops whimpering in response to friendly voice. ___ ___ ___ ___

Total # Score ___ + ___ + ___ / ___ = ___

% Yes Score = ___

1 - 4 Months

1a. Exhibits gross body movement as attention to voices. ___ ___ ___ ___

b. Looks toward speaker (head movement and/or eye movement) and responds by smiling. ___ ___ ___ ___

c. Moves eyes toward source of noise. ___ ___ ___ ___

d. Participates in familiar motion or movement after another has started the motion; physical contact necessary (e.g., student usually sways; teacher sways with student while in close physical contact; student freely participates in movement). ___ ___ ___ ___

2a. Participates in another's modification of his/her movement after another provides physical cue (e.g., using physical guidance to assist the student through a new movement, the student more actively cooperates and participates). ___ ___ ___ ___

b. Localizes speaker with eyes. ___ ___ ___ ___

c. Watches lips and mouth of speaker. ___ ___ ___ ___

3a. Searches for speaker. ___ ___ ___ ___

b. Responds to angry voice by furrowing the brow or frowning. ___ ___ ___ ___

c. Raises arm to be picked up in response to outreached arms of another. ___ ___ ___ ___

Total # Score ___ + ___ + ___ / ___ = ___

% Yes Score = ___

COMMUNICATION PROGRAMMING INVENTORY

AREA: RECEPTIVE COMMUNICATION

LEVEL   BEHAVIORS   RATING

Y P N N
E O O A
S S

4 – 8 Months

1a. Responds to own name.   ___ ___ ___ ___

 b. Stops crying when someone talks to him/her.   ___ ___ ___ ___

2a. Exhibits appropriate behavior to one or more tactile signals
    (e.g., tugging the student's arm leads to approach behavior). ___ ___ ___ ___

 b. Begins the next movement in a routine sequence of movements
    (e.g., when accustomed to rocking and then swaying, student
    begins to sway after rocking stopped).   ___ ___ ___ ___

 c. Briefly continues new movement when another changes one of
    his/her habitual movements; physical contact is necessary
    (e.g., student waves arms horizontally; teacher physically
    guides student to wave arms vertically; student continues
    to wave arms vertically).   ___ ___ ___ ___

 d. Responds with appropriate bodily movements to "come," "up,"
    "bye-bye," etc.   ___ ___ ___ ___

 e. Imitates familiar movements and/or sounds being produced by
    another (must see movement or hear sounds s/he is producing). ___ ___ ___ ___

 f. Responds to angry tone by crying.   ___ ___ ___ ___

3a. Turns head to familiar word.   ___ ___ ___ ___

 b. Stops activity when name is called.   ___ ___ ___ ___

 c. Responds to gestural games (e.g., peek-a-boo produces smile). ___ ___ ___ ___

 d. Stops movement to the word <u>no</u>.   ___ ___ ___ ___

                                               Total # Score   ___ + ___ + ___ / ___ = ___

                                               % Yes Score   = ___

8 – 12 Months

1a. Exhibits appropriate behaviors when commanded by gesture
    (e.g., teacher motions through gesture for student to sit
    down, student sits down).   ___ ___ ___ ___

 b. Imitates speech noises (e.g., smacking lips).   ___ ___ ___ ___

2a. Anticipates a routine event from cues (e.g., shown an object
    that is being associated with an activity, the student goes
    to the activity).   ___ ___ ___ ___

COMMUNICATION PROGRAMMING INVENTORY

AREA: RECEPTIVE COMMUNICATION

LEVEL		BEHAVIORS	RATING

RATING columns: YES, POS, NOO, NA

8 - 12 Months

b. Gives toys or other objects on verbal request.

c. While another is moving or vocalizing, student copies the different movements or vocalizations; physical contact is not necessary (movements or vocalizations must be in student's behavioral repertoire).

3a. Interacts with an appropriate object when a gesture is made by another indicating how the student uses the object; the object must be present (e.g., making comb motion through hair, student touches comb that is present).

b. Attends to object, person, or event being pointed to.

c. Responds to rhythmic music by body or hand movements.

d. After another completes simple movement, student imitates movement; position cue must be given; movement must be in student's behavioral repertoire.

e. Enjoys rhymes and simple songs.

f. Complies with certain actions to verbal requests (e.g., opens mouth when asked).

Total # Score   +   +   / = ___

% Yes Score   = ___

12 - 18 Months

1a. Interacts with an appropriate object when a gesture is made by another indicating how the student uses the object; the object is not present (e.g., making a writing motion, student goes and obtains a crayon).

b. After another has finished performing a simple movement, gesture, or vocalization, the student imitates; movement, gesture or vocalization is in student's repertoire; no position cue is necessary.

2a. Exhibits appropriate behaviors to a few simple one-word commands communicated in formal language (e.g., "come," "sit," "eat").

b. Identifies familiar objects when those objects are referred to by the use of formal language (e.g., "cup," "shoe").

c. Responds to inhibitory words communicated in formal language (e.g., "stop," "wait").

COMMUNICATION PROGRAMMING INVENTORY

AREA: RECEPTIVE COMMUNICATION

LEVEL	BEHAVIORS	RATING

		Y E S	P O S	N O	N A
	d. After another has finished performing <u>new</u> (to the student) simple movements, gestures, or vocalizations, the student imitates.	—	—	—	—
	3a. Exhibits appropriate behavior to two or three word commands or requests; action-object variety (e.g., "give shirt").	—	—	—	—
	b. Points to familiar persons, animals, toys on request.	—	—	—	—
12 - 18 Months	c. Understands correspondence between parts of a three-dimensional model and parts of his/her body (e.g., points to his/her body parts which are being pointed to on a doll).	—	—	—	—
	4a. Recognizes names of various parts of the body.	—	—	—	—
	b. Imitates a <u>new sequence</u> of behaviors when each behavior within the sequence is part of the student's repertoire.	—	—	—	—
	5a. Identifies any one object from a picture.	—	—	—	—
	b. Carries out two-step directions with familiar object (e.g., "put the ball in the can and in the box").	—	—	—	—

Total # Score   + +   / = ___

% Yes Score   = ___

		Y E S	P O S	N O	N A
	1a. Carries out two-stage related commands stated in formal language (e.g., "get the ball and go out the door").	—	—	—	—
	b. Responds appropriately to "what" and "where" questions.	—	—	—	—
18 - 24 Months	c. Demonstrates understanding of distinction in pronouns (e.g., "give it to her" versus "give it to me").	—	—	—	—
	2a. Carries out three-step directions with familiar object (e.g., "put the crayon on the table, in the drawer, and on the chair").	—	—	—	—
	b. Imitates activity or behavior sequence after a considerable amount of time.	—	—	—	—
	c. Imitates two and three word sentences.	—	—	—	—

COMMUNICATION PROGRAMMING INVENTORY

AREA: RECEPTIVE COMMUNICATION

LEVEL   BEHAVIORS   RATING

		Y E S	P O S	N O	N A
18 – 24 Months	3a. Points to two objects given three choices.	__	__	__	__
	b. Matches familiar objects.	__	__	__	__
	c. Understands concept of more.	__	__	__	__

Total # Score   +   +   / = ___

% Yes Score   = ___

COMMUNICATION PROGRAMMING INVENTORY

AREA: EXPRESSIVE COMMUNICATION

LEVEL	BEHAVIORS	RATING

| | | Y P N N
E O O A
S S |

0 - 1 Month

1a. Turns eyes to person's face (not prompted). ___ ___ ___

b. Displays frequent crying. ___ ___ ___

*2a. Fixes eyes on person's face (not prompted). ___ ___ ___

*b. Vocalizes (other than crying). ___ ___ ___

*c. Cries when hungry or uncomfortable. ___ ___ ___

Total # Score + + / = ____

% Yes Score = ____

1 - 4 Months

1a. Smiles as familiar person talks. ___ ___ ___

b. Smiles spontaneously. ___ ___ ___

c. Makes single vowel-like sounds (e.g., "an," "en," "un"). ___ ___ ___

d. Vocalizes when spoken to (non-speech vocal noises resembling speech sounds). ___ ___ ___

2. Cries with changes in pitch. ___ ___ ___

3a. Signals by movement or vocalization to continue an activity; physical contact is necessary (e.g., student rocks with teacher in close physical contact; teacher stops movement; student signals to start movement again). ___ ___ ___

b. Laughs during play with objects. ___ ___ ___

c. Babbles using a series of syllables. ___ ___ ___

Total # Score + + / = ____

% Yes Score = ____

* If YES, credit previous 1b as YES.

COMMUNICATION PROGRAMMING INVENTORY

AREA: EXPRESSIVE COMMUNICATION

LEVEL   BEHAVIORS   RATING

Y P N N
E O O A
S S

4 – 8 Months

1a. Uses movement or vocal signals in <u>several</u> activities to
indicate to another to continue the activity (e.g., student
may use multiple oral and/or motor signals to continue a
movement).   __ __ __ __

b. Laughs aloud spontaneously.   __ __ __ __

2. Makes spontaneous vocal sounds for socialization purposes
(e.g., growls, grunts).   __ __ __ __

3. Vocalizes single syllable (e.g., "da," "ba").   __ __ __ __

4a. Makes polysyllabic vowel sounds (e.g., "ga-ma").   __ __ __ __

b. Vocalizes with intonational pattern changes (pitch changes). __ __ __ __

c. Uses some gestural language (e.g., shaking head appropriately for "no").   __ __ __ __

Total # Score + + / = ___

% Yes Score   = ___

8 – 12 Months

1a. Uses simple gestures or vocalizations (not crying) to express wants or needs; the gestures or vocalizations are
started by the student (e.g., although the request "what
do you want?" is <u>not</u> given, student pulls another to door
to leave the room).   __ __ __ __

b. Seizes noisemaker in hand and imitates noisemaker's action.   __ __ __ __

c. Shouts to attract attention.   __ __ __ __

d. Babbles repeating syllables in a string (e.g., "ma-ma-ma").   __ __ __ __

2a. Says first words often (e.g., "da-da").   __ __ __ __

b. Uses echolalic <u>syllable</u> speech.   __ __ __ __

3a. Says one word (or short syllable) consistently to designate
an object.   __ __ __ __

b. Initiates speech-gesture games like "pat-a-cake" or "peek-a-
boo."   __ __ __ __

Total # Score + + / = ___

% Yes Score   = ___

COMMUNICATION PROGRAMMING INVENTORY

AREA: EXPRESSIVE COMMUNICATION

LEVEL	BEHAVIORS	RATING: YES	POS	NO	NA
12 - 18 Months	1a. Has one or more gestures or vocalizations meaningful to him/her and others but only used in specific context (e.g., uses a bathroom gesture only at home).	___	___	___	___
	b. Offers objects to another.	___	___	___	___
	2a. Uses gestures when asking for or identifying objects; the gesture indicates how the student uses the object (e.g., sticks two fingers in mouth indicating that s/he wants a "security" blanket).	___	___	___	___
	b. Points to make another attend to something.	___	___	___	___
	3a. Spontaneously uses one or two words which stand for a variety of related objects, activities, and feelings; used in new and appropriate situations (e.g., uses a word for bathroom when s/he uses the bathroom, when s/he sees another using the bathroom, when s/he visits a new bathroom area).	___	___	___	___
	b. Uses gesture, word, sign, or point to request aid in getting something.	___	___	___	___
	c. Uses gesture, specific vocalizations, or signs to represent objects or activities (object must be within student's perceptual field).	___	___	___	___
	d. Uses gesture, word, sign, or point to obtain interaction with another person.	___	___	___	___
	4a. Has vocabulary of at least four to six spontaneously used words (often indicating immediate wants and needs).	___	___	___	___
	b. Vocalizes in protest.	___	___	___	___
	Total # Score	+	+		/ = ___
	% Yes Score				= ___
18 - 24 Months	1a. Has vocabulary of at least ten spontaneously and appropriately used words.	___	___	___	___
	b. Begins using words rather than gestures to express wants and needs.	___	___	___	___
	c. Makes one word responses using initial consonant with vowel but not final consonant.	___	___	___	___

COMMUNICATION PROGRAMMING INVENTORY

AREA: EXPRESSIVE COMMUNICATION

LEVEL	BEHAVIORS	RATING: YES	POS	NO	NA
18 - 24 Months	2. Uses gestures, vocalizations, or signs to represent objects or activities (object need not be within student's perceptual field).	___	___	___	___
	3a. Uses successive single words or signs to describe the same object or event (e.g., "ball" then "red").	___	___	___	___
	b. Shows interest in learning new words.	___	___	___	___
	c. Combines two different words in speech to form short phrase/ sentence (e.g., "go bye-bye").	___	___	___	___
	4. Uses expressive vocabulary of at least 15 words.	___	___	___	___
	5a. Uses "me," "you," refers to self by name.	___	___	___	___
	b. Asks for water when thirsty (formal language).	___	___	___	___
	c. Asks for food when hungry (formal language).	___	___	___	___
	6a. Has oral language of 50 spontaneously and appropriately used words.	___	___	___	___
	b. Combines two words in form: modifier-object (e.g., "pretty ball"), object-modifier (e.g., "ball pretty"), action-object (e.g., "go car"), object-object (e.g., "Tommy bike").	___	___	___	___
	c. Uses "no" to indicate refusal.	___	___	___	___
	d. Begins to use "no," "not" in combination with other words (e.g., "no milk").	___	___	___	___
	e. Names familiar picture cards.	___	___	___	___

Total # Score + + / = ____

% Yes Score = ____

Author Index

A

Aanes, D., 258, 263
Abbas, K.A., 148, 161
Abeson, A., 22, 25
Abramson, E.E., 141, 156, 251, 263
Adams, G.L., 71, 92, 97, 98, 129, 142, 143, 148, 150, 156, 158, 318, 321, 323
Adkins, J.A., 129, 131, 155, 159, 262, 263
Aeschleman, S.R., 29, 42
Albin, J., 251, 263
Allen, K.E., 125, 130
Allen, P., 141, 158, 251, 265, 319, 323
Alpern, M.A., 148, 159
Altman, R., 141, 156
Anthony, D., 236, 239
Arick, J.R., 141, 157
Armstrong, M., 125, 132
Armstrong, P.M., 147, 157, 250, 251, 263
Ash, T., 253, 266
Ayllon, T., 99, 129
Azrin, N.H., 99, 102, 104, 105, 109, 129, 130, 131, 132, 140, 147, 157, 158, 160, 243, 244, 246, 249, 250, 251, 263, 264, 266, 319, 323

B

Bacon, A., 318, 323
Baer, D.M., 116, 129, 209, 228, 240, 249, 263
Bailey, C., 262, 265
Bailey, J.S., 148, 158, 159
Baker, B.L., 27, 28, 41
Baldwin, A.L., 40, 41
Baldwin, J., 29, 42
Baldwin, M., 180, 206
Baldwin, V.L., 245, 264
Ball, T.S., 140, 159, 251, 266
Balla, D.A., 140, 143, 161
Balthazar, E., 58, 92
Bandura, A., 100, 129
Banerdt, B., 163, 204, 205
Barclay, C., 140, 158
Barlow, D.H., 115, 130
Barnes, K.J., 164, 195, 204, 205, 207
Baroff, G.S., 319, 323
Barton, E.S., 249, 263
Bassinger, J.F., 29, 43
Bates, E., 210, 239
Bates, P., 269, 312
Battle, C., 180, 206, 209
Bauman, K.E., 253, 263
Baumeister, A., 114, 129, 136, 157, 245, 263
Baumgart, D., 181, 205, 274, 276, 310
Bayley, N., 51, 92
Becker, W.C., 125, 132
Bell, N.J., 258, 264
Bellack, A.S., 155, 157
Bellamy, T., 270, 271, 272, 273, 274, 275, 276, 279, 282, 292, 310, 311
Belmore, K.J., 272, 310

Benigni, L., 210, 239
Bensberg, G.T., 243, 264
Bereiter, C., 27, 41
Berger, P.L., 261, 265
Berkson, G., 103, 129, 147, 157
Bigler, J., 129, 130
Birch, J.W., 14, 25
Bird, E., 251, 265
Bjannes, A.T., 261, 264
Blanchard, K., 15, 25
Bliss, C., 237, 239
Bobath, B., 180, 205
Bobath, K., 180, 205
Boles, S., 270, 310
Bolick, N., 22, 25
Bolstad, O.D., 155, 157
Boozer, H., 148, 160
Borakave, L.S., 254, 264
Bornstein, M.R., 155, 157
Box, R., 185, 205
Brandl, C., 143, 158
Branston, M., 13, 25
Brantley, J.C., 149, 160
Breese, F.H., 40, 41
Bretherton, I., 210, 239
Bricker, D.D., 28, 41, 135, 158, 164, 204, 205, 235, 239
Bricker, W.A., 28, 41, 181, 205, 235, 239
Brigance, A., 61, 66, 92
Brolin, D.E., 274, 310
Brooks, P., 114, 129, 136, 157
Brophy, J.E., 27, 42
Brown, F., 147, 157, 159
Brown, G., 180, 205
Brown, K.M., 148, 159, 261, 266
Brown, L., 13, 25, 136, 143, 151, 157, 158, 161, 180, 181, 205, 206, 244, 264, 272, 274, 276, 282, 310
Bry, P.M., 140, 157
Bryan, A.J., 252, 267
Bucher, B., 102, 129
Buell, J.S., 125, 130
Bugle, C., 109, 131
Burello, L.C., 14, 25

Burg, M.N., 148, 157
Burke, P.J., 13, 16, 20, 25, 26, 316, 323
Burleigh, R.A., 140, 157
Butler, E.W., 261, 264
Buttram, B., 180, 205

C

Cain, L., 67, 93
Call, T., 243, 267
Camaioni, L., 210, 239
Campbell, A.A., 28, 42, 75, 93
Campbell, D.T., 114, 129
Campbell, P.H., 181, 192, 195, 204, 205
Campbell, S., 244, 267
Caponigri, V., 109, 132
Carey, R.G., 102, 129
Carney, I., 129, 130
Carrier, J., 209, 237, 239, 240
Carroccio, D., 249, 264
Cataldo, M.F., 128, 131
Cattell, P., 51, 93
Certo, N., 151, 161
Chardos, S., 140, 161
Charney, B., 261, 264
Chasey, W.C., 147, 157
Chomsky, C., 209, 239
Cicchetti, D.V., 49, 93, 318, 323
Clark, C., 237, 239
Cleland, C.C., 141, 156
Clobuciar, G., 129, 130
Close, D.W., 140, 141, 157, 273, 310, 321, 323
Cohen, M.A., 149, 157, 215, 240
Cohen, S., 31, 42
Cole, L., 317, 323
Cone, J., 48, 93, 111, 131, 140, 160, 249, 266, 321, 323
Connor, F.P., 195, 205
Coon, M.E., 260, 261, 264
Cooper, J.O., 144, 157
Cordua, G., 125, 130, 143, 159

Corley, E., 129, 130
Cortazzo, A., 270, 310
Craig, E.M., 258, 266
Crist, K., 142, 161
Criswell, J.L., 258, 267
Cromer, R., 214, 240
Cronin, K.A., 151, 157, 255, 264
Culbertson, J., 15, 25
Cushing, P.J., 128, 131
Cuvo, A.J., 141, 151, 157, 159, 161,
254, 255, 257, 258, 264, 265, 266,
267

D

Davall, E., 251, 264
Darbyshire, M., 251, 265
Davenport, R.K., 103, 129, 147, 157
Dayan, M., 245, 264
Deaton, S.L., 29, 42
DeBriere, T., 244, 267
Denhoff, E., 27, 42
Dennison, L., 235, 239
Dent, H., 147, 157
Desmond, E.F., 102, 131
Devine, V.T., 98, 131
Distefano, M.K., 143, 158
Doke, L.A., 102, 130
Doleys, D.M., 251, 264
Doll, E., 83, 93
Domnie, M., 244, 264
Donaldson, R.M., 29, 42
Dorsey, M.F., 128, 130
Doughty, R., 249, 265
Doyle, D.A., 261, 265
Duncan, D., 318, 323
Duvall, E., 141, 158

E

Edgerton, R.B., 258, 264
Edwards, J., 272, 275, 311
Egel, A.L., 153, 158

Ellis, N.R., 143, 158, 245, 264
Ellis, W.D., 139, 141, 161
Elzey, F., 67, 93
Engelmann, S., 27, 41
Epstein, L.H., 102, 104, 130
Erickson, L.M., 140, 159
Eyman, R., 244, 265

F

Falvey, M., 181, 205, 274, 276, 310
Farber, S.D., 192, 195, 205
Favell, James E., 147, 158, 250, 264
Favell, Judith E., 147, 158
Ferrara, D.M., 31, 42
Ferrari, M., 152, 158
Fiegenbaum, E., 102, 132
Figueroa, R., 317, 323
Finnie, N., 164, 193, 205
Fleisher, L., 129, 130
Flexer, R., 270, 273, 286, 290, 298, 310
Flynn, J.R., 22, 25
Ford, A., 276, 310
Forehand, R., 141, 161
Foshee, T.J., 148, 159
Foster, R., 53, 70, 72, 93, 149, 150,
158, 160, 317, 323
Foxx, R.M., 102, 103, 104, 105, 129,
130, 140, 147, 157, 158, 243, 244,
246, 249, 251, 263, 264, 319, 323
Fredericks, H.B., 29, 42, 245, 249, 264
Freedman, R., 243, 264
Friedl, M., 276, 312
Fullerton, P., 180, 206
Furth, H., 214, 240

G

Gacka, R., 22, 25
Garcia, E., 249, 263
Gardner, W.I., 143, 158
Garton, H., 15, 25
Geary, D., 163, 206
Genung, T., 243, 266

Gerken, K.C., 18, 25
Geske, T., 272, 312
Glendenning, N., 142, 158
Goetz, L., 180, 206
Gold, M., 140, 151, 158, 271, 273, 274, 275, 276, 310, 311
Goldstein, S., 28, 43
Gollay, E., 243, 264
Gordon, I., 31, 42
Gorman, P., 236, 241
Gottlieb, J., 21, 25
Gozali, J., 261, 264
Grant, L., 142, 161
Gray, B., 209, 229, 240
Gray, R.M., 143, 158
Greene, B.F., 148, 158
Greene, M., 9
Greenwood, J., 15, 25
Grigsby, C., 15, 25
Grilley, K., 238, 241
Gross, P.J., 149, 157, 215, 240
Grove, D.A., 29, 42
Grove, D.N., 245, 264
Groves, I., 249, 264
Gruenewald, L.A., 13, 25, 276, 310
Guess, D., 103, 130, 147, 157, 159, 180, 181, 205, 206, 209, 228, 240, 249, 263, 318, 323
Guralnick, M.J., 98, 130, 143, 158
Gustason, G., 236, 240

H

Hagmeier, L.D., 298, 311
Hake, D.F., 102, 132
Hall, R.V., 185, 205
Hamilton, J., 141, 158, 251, 265, 319, 323
Hamre-Nietupski, S., 13, 21, 22, 25, 26, 136, 155, 157, 161, 180, 206, 317, 323
Hansen, C.L., 270, 273, 276, 311
Hanson, A., 153, 160
Hanson, C.R., 111, 131, 140, 160, 249, 266, 321, 323

Haring, N.G., 5, 9, 29, 42, 135, 144, 149, 154, 157, 158, 181, 206, 215, 240, 276, 298, 311
Harper, R.S., 243, 266
Harris, C., 244, 267
Harris, F.R., 125, 130
Harris, S.L., 152, 158
Harris-Vanderheiden, D., 210, 240
Hart, B.M., 123, 125, 130, 146, 158
Harter, S., 143, 158
Hass, J., 22, 25
Hawkins, R., 48, 93
Hayden, A.H., 29, 42
Hayden, M., 125, 130, 143, 159
Haynes, V.B., 27, 42
Heifetz, L.J., 27, 28, 41
Henderson, R., 272, 312
Henderson, S., 139, 159
Henriksen, K., 249, 265
Herbert, E.W., 125, 130, 143, 159
Hersen, M., 115, 130, 155, 157
Hersey, P., 15, 25
Hill, J., 180, 206, 209, 262, 265, 272, 276, 301, 311, 312
Hill, M., 272, 312
Hipsher, L.W., 245, 265
Hodgins, A.S., 27, 42
Hogg, J., 136, 159
Hollis, J., 209, 240
Holtz, K., 180, 206
Holvoet, J., 147, 157, 159, 164, 181, 195, 205, 207
Hops, H., 102, 132
Horner, R.D., 140, 141, 159, 181, 205, 251, 265, 270, 273, 292, 310, 311
Horst, G., 262, 265
Horstmeier, D., 209, 233, 236, 240
Howe, C.E., 15, 17, 23, 24, 25
Huber, H., 28, 42
Hudson, C., 260, 267
Hull, J.T., 243, 265
Hundert, J., 102, 130
Huppler, B., 244, 264
Hyman, I., 27, 42

I

Ingram, C., 214, 241
Inman, D., 273, 310
Ironsmith, M., 155, 160
Irvin, L.K., 140, 141, 157, 321, 323
Iwata, B.A., 102, 128, 130, 131, 148,
    159, 253, 259, 260, 263, 266

J

Jackson, C., 125, 130, 143, 159
Jacobi, L., 151, 157, 255, 264
Janssen, C., 318, 323
Jarboe, D., 244, 267
Jarman, P.H., 261, 266
Jenkins, S., 27, 28, 30, 31, 39, 42
Jensen, V., 251, 265
Jervey, S.S., 249, 267
Johnson, B.F., 151, 159, 254, 265
Johnson, J., 13, 25, 180, 206
Johnson, R., 147, 157
Johnson, S.M., 155, 157
Jones, M.L., 250, 264
Justen, J.E., 4, 5, 9

K

Kahan, E.H., 253, 265
Kahn, J.V., 180, 206, 250, 266
Kalhorn, J., 40, 41
Kaplan, S.J., 104, 129
Karan, O., 273, 275, 300, 311
Karlan, G.R., 180, 206
Karnes, M.B., 27, 42
Kasteler, J.M., 143, 158
Katz, S., 261, 265
Kazdin, A.E., 98, 100, 103, 130, 139,
    140, 159, 299, 311
Kean, J., 27, 42
Kehoe, B., 251, 265
Keilitz, I., 140, 141, 159, 251, 265
Kellogg, J.S., 141, 160
Kent, L., 231, 240

Kerr, N.J., 245, 267
Kiernan, J., 253, 262, 266
Kirk, S., 209, 240
Kirk, W., 209, 240
Klinge, V., 104, 130
Klosowski, R., 245, 263
Knapp, D.S., 150, 160, 321, 323
Knowles, S., 251, 264
Kochany, L., 301, 311
Koegel, R.L., 147, 159
Konke, J.L., 258, 264
Koop, S., 143, 159
Kozloff, M.A., 103, 130
Kravik, M.A., 98, 130, 143, 158
Krug, D.A., 141, 157
Kurtz, N.R., 243, 264

L

Lambert, N., 317, 323
Landau, S.E., 18, 25
Langworthy, R., 153, 160
Largo, R.H., 244, 265
Larson, K., 272, 275, 311
Lask, E., 244, 265
Laski, F.J., 274, 311
Lattimore, J., 148, 157
Leaf, R.B., 254, 264
Lee, L., 209, 240
Leff, R.B., 257, 265
Leland, H., 53, 93, 149, 160
LeLaurin, K., 148, 159
Lemke, H., 140, 159, 249, 265
Lent, J.R., 99, 130, 140, 142, 159
Leonard, L., 210, 240
Levey, R., 148, 158
Levine, S., 67, 93
Levitt, E., 31, 42
Levy, S., 272, 311
Liberty, K.A., 153, 154, 158, 161, 181,
    206
Linford, M.D., 245, 265
Litrownik, A., 103, 131
Little, T.L., 28, 42, 75, 9ɔ
Locke, B., 98, 130

Lohman, W., 244, 245, 265
Lovaas, O.I., 103, 128, 131
Lovitt, T., 149, 159
Lutzker, J.R., 105, 131
Lynch, A., 269, 271, 275, 276, 282, 311
Lynch, F., 28, 42
Lyon, S., 181, 195, 205, 206, 274, 310, 318, 323

M

MacDonald, J., 209, 233, 236, 240
Maheady, L., 318, 323
Mahoney, K., 245, 246, 265, 267
Mann, R., 103, 131
Mar, D., 286, 311
Marchant, J., 244, 262, 265
Marchetti, A., 155, 159, 262, 266
Marholin, D., 140, 157, 261, 265
Martin, A., 270, 273, 286, 290, 298, 310
Martin, E.D., 105, 130
Martin, G., 143, 159, 249, 251, 265, 267
Martin, M.M., 181, 206
Matlock, B.L., 321, 323
Matson, J.L., 129, 131, 155, 159, 253, 256, 259, 262, 263, 265, 266
Maurer, S., 20, 26
Maxon, D., 181, 205
Mayeda, T., 243, 267
Mayer, G.R., 101, 121, 131
McCarthy, J., 209, 240
McCarver, R.B., 258, 266, 317
McCoy, J.E., 250, 267
McDaniel, Marx J., 155, 161, 317, 323
McDonald, M., 139, 159
McDonald, S., 249, 265
McGimsey, J.F., 147, 158, 250, 264
McGregor, D., 14, 25
McLaughlin, P.J., 299, 300, 301, 312
McLean, J.E., 227, 240
McNeill, D., 209, 240
McReynolds, L.V., 143, 159
McSween, T.E. 102, 128, 130, 131

Mees, H., 125, 132
Mercurio, S.R., 109, 132
Meredith, C., 148, 161
Merkert, F., 247, 266
Messina, R., 195, 206
Meyers, A., 257, 267
Meyerson, L., 245, 265, 267
Miller, J., 214, 241
Minge, M.R., 140, 159, 251, 266
Minor, J.W., 250, 267
Mitchell, R.D., 140, 159, 249, 265
Mithaug, D.E., 272, 286, 298, 300, 301, 311, 312
Mix, B., 79, 82, 93
Moen, M., 258, 263
Moore, J., 153, 160
Moore, W.G., 245, 264
Moorehead, D., 214, 241
Morris, N., 148, 160
Morris, S.E., 195, 206
Morrison, D.C., 143, 161
Morton, K., 31, 42
Mowrer, O.H., 249, 266
Mowrer, W.M., 249, 266
Mueller, H., 195, 206
Mulligan, M., 147, 157, 159
Murden, L., 251, 267
Murdock, E.E., 245, 267
Murphy, M., 204, 205
Myers, S., 104, 130

N

National Association for Retarded Citizens, 106, 131
National Association of State Directors of Special Education, 17, 25
Nawas, M.M., 140, 157
Neef, N.A., 259, 260, 261, 266
Nelson, G.L., 111, 131, 140, 160, 249, 266, 321, 323
Nelson, N., 271, 311
Nihira, K., 53, 93, 149, 160
Nietupski, J., 21, 22, 25, 26, 136, 157, 244, 266

Nisbet, J., 276, 310
Noll, M.B., 102, 131
Nutter, D., 252, 266

O

O'Brien, F., 109, 131, 140, 160, 249, 266
O'Leary, K.D., 98, 131, 155, 160
Omichinski, M., 249, 265
Ong, P., 128, 130
O'Reilly, C.D., 150, 160, 321, 323
O'Toole, K.M., 261, 265
Ottman, R.A., 21, 25

P

Page, T.J., 259, 260, 266
Paget, R., 236, 241
Pany, D., 129, 130
Panyan, M., 148, 160
Parrish, V., 27, 29, 43
Peak, T., 237, 239
Pendergrass, V.E., 112, 131
Peterson, L., 273, 310
Peterson, R.G., 143, 161
Pfetzing, D., 236, 240
Phillips, E.L., 102, 131
Pierce, L., 244, 264
Pinkston, E., 125, 130, 143, 159
Pinkston, S., 125, 130, 143, 159
Polvinale, R.A., 105, 131
Pomerantz, D.J., 151, 158, 276, 311
Pommer, D.A., 148, 160
Popovich, D., 139, 150, 160
Poulos, R.W., 98, 131
Pratt, S.S., 150, 160, 321, 323
Prehm, H.J., 140, 141, 157, 321, 323
Pumpian, I., 155, 161, 276, 310, 317, 323

Q

Quick, A.D., 28, 42, 75, 93
Quoss, T., 180, 207

R

Reichle, J.E., 180, 206
Reid, D.H., 148, 157, 252, 261, 266
Renzaglia, A., 273, 300, 311
Revel, G., 286, 312
Reynolds, A.T., 163, 206
Reynolds, M.C., 14, 25
Richman, J.S., 250, 266
Rimell, P., 148, 153, 156, 160
Rimmer, B., 102, 130
Rincover, A., 147, 159
Risley, T.R., 103, 116, 123, 125, 129, 130, 131, 132, 146, 148, 158, 159
Risley, R., 257, 266
Roberts, P., 102, 131
Robinson, C.C., 180, 206
Robinson, J.H., 180, 206
Robinson-Wilson, M.A., 253, 266
Rogers, P., 15, 16, 18, 19, 21, 25
Roos, P., 31, 42
Rosenthal, T.L., 141, 160
Roszkowski, M., 84, 93
Ruder, K., 235, 239
Rues, J., 318, 323
Rusch, F., 260, 267, 272, 290, 301, 312
Russo, D.C., 128, 131
Rutherford, G., 103, 130
Ryan, B., 209, 229, 240
Ryan-Flottum, M., 180, 206

S

Sadler, O.W., 247, 266
Sage, D.D., 14, 25
Sage, H.M., 154, 160
Sailor, W., 79, 82, 93, 180, 204, 205, 206, 209, 228, 240
Sainato, D., 318, 323
Sajwaj, T.E., 102, 125, 130, 143, 159
Salvia, J., 51, 93
Samels, J., 251, 267
Sanford, A., 74, 93
Saunders, M.K., 23, 25
Sbardellati, E., 318, 323

Schaeffer, B., 103, 131
Schaeffer, R.M., 147, 157, 251, 263
Schalock, R.L., 243, 266
Schiefelbusch, R.L., 227, 240
Schleien, S.J., 253, 262, 266
Schmidt, P., 192, 206
Schneider, K., 272, 312
Schreibman, L., 141, 160
Schroeder, J., 181, 205, 274, 276, 310
Schuler, A., 180, 206
Schultz, J., 31, 42
Schultz, R., 273, 300, 311
Sedlak, R., 6, 9
Shane, H.C., 163, 180, 206
Shearer, D.E., 28, 42
Shearer, M.S., 28, 42
Shehan, M., 270, 310
Shellhaas, M., 53, 93, 149, 160
Sienicki, D.A., 142, 161
Siepp, J.M., 195, 205
Silikovitz, R.G., 245, 265
Simmons, J.Q., 103, 128, 131
Simpson, R.L., 102, 131
Singer, T., 269, 271, 275, 276, 282, 311
Sipko, R., 151, 157, 255, 264
Slocumb, P., 58, 93
Smith, D.D., 21, 24, 25, 99, 131, 151,
    160, 316, 323
Smith, J.O., 21, 24, 25, 151, 160, 316,
    323
Smith, M., 257, 267
Smith, P.J., 143, 160
Smith, P.S., 247, 267
Sneed, T.J., 244, 246, 249, 263
Snell, M.E., 99, 131, 141, 160, 245,
    267, 269, 286, 312
Snyder-McLean, L., 227, 240
Somerton-Fair, E., 77, 80, 93
Sonderby, T., 250, 266
Sontag, E., 13, 16, 20, 25, 26, 244, 264,
    316, 323
Sorrel, S., 102, 130
Sowers, J., 260, 267
Sparrow, S.S., 49, 93, 318, 323
Spellman, C., 244, 253, 267
Spencer, R.L., 244, 267

Spradlin, J.E., 209, 240
Stacy, D., 251, 264
Staff of the Training Research Infant
    and Child Center, 139, 150, 160
Stagg, M.M., 153, 160
Stainback, S., 20, 26
Stainback, W., 20, 26
Stanley, J.C., 114, 129
Stephens, L., 141, 158, 251, 264, 319,
    323
Stephens, W.B., 27, 28, 31, 39, 42
Sternat, J., 195, 206
Sternberg, L., 6, 9, 27, 28, 39, 42, 142,
    158, 180, 206, 209
Stetson, F.E., 13, 16, 26
Stewart, O., 286, 311
Stillman, R., 68, 93, 215, 241
Stimbert, V.E., 250, 267
Stokoe, W., 236, 241
Stoll, A., 180, 206
Stoneburner, R.L., 27, 42
Streedbeck, D, 148, 160
Strickland, B., 28, 43, 149, 160
Striefel, S., 140, 160
Stutzle, W, 244, 265
Sugaya, K., 244, 267
Sultana, Q., 23, 25
Sulthons, E., 143, 159
Sulzer-Azaroff, B., 101, 121, 131
Sundeen, D.A., 22, 25
Sutter, P., 243, 267
Switzky, H.N., 180, 207

T

Talkington, L., 141, 156
Tallon, R.J., 148, 156, 321, 323
Tanner, B.A., 128, 131
Tate, B.G., 319, 323
Tawney, J.W., 29, 42, 150, 151, 160,
    321, 323
Taylor, R.L., 58, 89, 93, 97
Taylor, V.E., 140, 141, 157, 321, 323
Teaching Research Staff, 98, 132, 136,
    139, 148, 150, 153, 160

Temerlin, M.K., 244, 267
Terkel, S., 274, 312
Teska, J.A., 27, 42
The American National Standards
  Institute, 16, 26
Thinesen, P.J., 252, 267
Thomas, D.R., 125, 132
Thompson, J.C., 243, 265
Thrasher, P., 104, 130
Touchette, P.E., 261, 265
Trace, M.W., 258, 264, 267
Tramontana, J., 143, 160
Treffry, D., 251, 267
Trott, M.C., 147, 160
Trousdale, W.W., 244, 267
Tucker, D., 181, 205
Turkewitz, H., 155, 160
Turnbull, A.P., 23, 26, 28, 43, 149,
  160
Turner, K., 77, 80, 93
Turner, P., 129, 130

U

Umbreit, J., 181, 207
United States Architectural and
  Transportation Barriers Compliance
  Board, 16, 26
Utley, B., 164, 180, 181, 195, 205, 206,
  207

V

Van Deventer, P., 276, 310
Van Dijk, J., 210, 241
Van Wagenen, R.K., 245, 265, 267
Vanderheiden, G., 210, 237, 238, 240,
  241
Vanderpoel, S.J., 141, 161
VanHaecke, D., 153, 160
Veitch, V.D., 258, 264
Vincent, L., 235, 239
Vogelsberg, T., 260, 261, 264, 276, 312
Volterra, V., 210, 239

Vukelich, R., 102, 132
Vulpé, S., 85, 88, 93

W

Wabash Center for the Mentally
  Handicapped, 136, 161
Wahler, R.G., 143, 161
Waldo, L., 204, 205
Walker, H.M., 101, 102, 132
Walls, R.T., 139, 141, 142, 161, 318,
  323
Warren, S.A., 58, 93
Warren, S.F., 181, 205, 318, 323
Waters, L.G., 18, 26
Watson, C., 251, 267
Watson, L.S., 29, 43
Weber, M., 14, 26
Webster, D.R., 104, 132
Wehman, P., 156, 161, 251, 253, 262,
  265, 266, 267, 269, 272, 273, 274,
  276, 286, 299, 300, 301, 311, 312
Welch, C., 15, 25
Werner, T.J., 318, 323
Wesolowski, M.D., 104, 105, 129, 147,
  157, 251, 263
Westling, D.L., 251, 267
Wetherby, B., 140, 160
Wheeler, J., 155, 161, 318, 323
White, O.R., 144, 153, 154, 158, 161
Whitehead, C., 271, 275, 312
Whitman, T.L., 109, 132, 140, 161
Wiegerink, R., 27, 29, 43
Wilbur, R., 236, 241
Wilcox, B., 13, 20, 25, 26, 129, 130
Williams, W., 151, 155, 161, 180, 207,
  244, 260, 261, 264, 266, 276, 312,
  317, 323
Williamson, G.G., 195, 205
Willis, B.S., 148, 158, 261, 266
Windmiller, M., 317, 323
Winkel, G.H., 143, 161
Wolf, M.M., 103, 116, 125, 129, 130,
  131, 132
Wolfe, V.F., 141, 161

Wolfensberger, W., 274, 312
Woodcock, R., 237, 239
Woolsey-Hill, J., 180, 207
Wollersheim, J.P., 27, 42
Wright, E.C., 148, 161
Wunderlich, R.A., 141, 156, 251, 263
Wyngaarden, M., 243, 264

Y

Yanagi, G., 243, 267
Yates, J., 253, 267
Yee, S., 243, 267
Yekutiel, E., 261, 265
Yoder, D.E., 180, 206, 227, 240

Yoder, P., 141, 161
York, R., 13, 16, 20, 25, 26, 181, 207, 244, 264, 266, 316, 323
Ysseldyke, J., 51, 93
Yu, D., 143, 159

Z

Zakaras, M., 140, 161
Zane, T, 139, 141, 161
Zawolkow, E., 236, 240
Zeeck, J., 153, 160
Zeiler, M., 128, 131, 249, 267
Zeiss, R.A., 129, 131
Zigler, E., 140, 143, 158, 161

Subject Index

A

AAMD. *See* American Association on Mental Deficiency
Abduction, 164
Aberrant behavior, 57
Aberrations in chromosomes, 3
Ability to learn, 273
Absorption of cost, 19
Academic skills, 73
    standardized achievement tests of, 317
Acceptance
    by community, 285
    by nonhandicapped students, 21
Accessibility of program and services, 15
Achievement tests, 317
Acquisition phase of vocational training, 301
Activity areas, 148
Adaptations
    environmental, 122-123
    for language training, 236-238
    physical, 318
    social, 59
    of test items, 51-52
Adaptive Behavior Scale, (ABS), AAMD, 53, 90, 92, 149, 317
Adaptive behavior tests, 51, 53, 150, 317, 318

Adduction, 164
Adjustment problems in family, 27
Administrative table of organization, 17
Administrative theory, 14-15
Administrators, 13, 14, 15
Adversary role of administrator, 15
Advisory board, 19
Advocate role of administrator, 15
Affection, 98
Age
    chronological, 5, 135, 136
    developmental, 5
    developmental functioning, 135
    equivalents for, 48
    and formal education, 321, 322
Age-appropriate design of vocational program, 283
Alternate form reliability of tests, 49
Alternative behavior reinforcement, 101, 126
Alt-R. *See* Reinforcement of alternative behavior
American Association on Mental Deficiency (AAMD), 53, 90, 92, 149, 317
American National Standards Specifications for Making Buildings and Facilities Accessible to and Usable by the Physically Handicapped, 16

349

American National Standards
Institute, The, 16
Analysis
antecedent, 123
behavior, 319
interaction, 318
task, 52, 137, 151, 155, 286, 321
Antecedent analysis, 123
Antecedent events use and control,
319
Anticipation shelves, 213
Antisocial behavior, 56
Approval through facial expressions,
98
Architectural barrier removal, 15-16
Artificial reinforcers, 155
Artificial skills development, 276
Assessment, 4, 6, 47-93, 317-319
See also Evaluation
auxiliary, 91
for communication programming,
214-217
community job, 290
community resource, 277-279
detailed, 286
environmental, 87
global, 286
needs, 18
vocational skills, 286-287
Assistance, 140, 142
Assistant Superintendent for Special
Education, 17
Association for the Severely
Handicapped, 153
Attendance, 30
Attending behaviors, 292
training in, 103
Auditory skills, 78
Autistic students, 147
Auxiliary assessment, 91
Auxiliary programming, 91
Aversive procedures, 127-128

B

Backup reinforcers, 99, 100

Backward chaining, 138, 320
*Balthazar Scales of Adaptive
Behavior* (BSAB), 58, 90
Barriers
architectural, 15-16
between parents and educators, 28
Baseline, 153
behavior, 106-122
multiple, 116, 117, 119, 120
Basic functions, 85
Basic math, 63
Basic senses, 85
Bathing skills, 78
Bathroom cleaning skills, 254-255
Bayley Scales of Infant Development,
51
BCP. *See Behavioral Characteristics
Progression*
Bedrest overcorrection, 104
*Behavioral Characteristics
Progression* (BCP), 60
Behaviorally based language program,
228, 229, 231
Behavioral model for toilet training,
245
Behavioral psychology, 163
Behavior Characteristics Progression,
90, 91
*Behavior Inventory for Rating the
Retarded*, 318
Behaviors, 4
aberrant, 57
adaptive tests of, 51, 53, 150, 317,
318
alternative, 101
analysis of, 319
antisocial, 56
attending, 103, 292
changes in, 144-146
checklists for, 51
complex, 135
control of, 6
correct, 140
descriptions of, 3
destructive, 56
disruptive, 104

dressing, 251-252
eating, 84, 249-251
economic, 70
fine motor, 63, 74, 76, 78, 86
grooming, 251-252
gross motor, 63, 74, 76, 78, 85
growth in, 135
guidelines in, 106
hierarchical nature of growth in, 135
language. *See* Language
management of, 95-129, 319-320
measurement of changes in, 144-146
multiple baseline across, 116
observation of, 287
organization of, 86
preambulatory, 63
prelanguage prerequisite, 236
rebellious, 56
self-abusive, 3, 57
self-initiated, 299, 300
self-stimulatory, 103-104
sexually aberrant, 57
social, 70
stereotyped, 56
target, 106-122, 321
topographically dissimilar, 103
topographically similar, 103
untrustworthy, 56
violent, 56
vocational, 70
Between-group differences, 3
Boulder Training Model, 153
Boundaries of environment and self, 210
Bribing, 98
Brigance Diagnostic Inventory of Early Development, 61, 91, 92
BSAB. *See Balthazar Scales of Adaptive Behavior*
Bureaucratic model, 14
Burello and Sage's theory, 14, 15
Bus travel, 17, 260-261

C

Cain-Levine Social Competency Scale, 67, 90
Callier-Azusa Scale, 68, 90
Camelot Behavioral Checklist, 70, 89, 150, 317
Capacity of current operation, 16
Car pooling, 17
Categorical labeling of students, 3
Categories of handicapping condition, 4
Cattell Infant Intelligence Test, 51
Center-based training model of parent training, 29
Chaining, 137-139
backward, 138, 320
forward, 138, 320
reverse, 138
Change agent role of administrator, 15
Change in behavior, 144-146
Change in criterion design, 119
Checklists for behavior, 51
Chewing, 202
Chromosomal aberrations, 3
Chronological age, 5, 135, 136
Classification, 3, 4, 90
educational, 3
etiological, 3
Classroom involvement model of parent training, 29
Cleaning skills, 254-255
Closure of lips, 204
Clothes
mending of, 255-256
selection of, 252
Co-active movement, 212, 214, 221-224
Cognition, 69, 74, 86
Coin computation, 258-259
Collection of data, 48, 108, 110, 111, 152
Committee on Legal and Ethical Protection, NARC, 106, 127, 128
Committee on oversight, 106

Communication, 67, 69, 70, 78, 81, 84
    See also Language; Speech
    co-active, 214
    expressive, 219-221, 222, 223-226, 227
    graphic, 237
    instruction in, 209-241
    logographic, 237
    manual, 236
    nonverbal, 48
    prelanguage, 236
    receptive, 219, 220, 222-223, 224, 226-227
    speech therapist, 47
Communication program
    assessment for, 214-217
    inventory for, 215-216, 325-337
    operationalizing of, 217-227
    Van Dijk, 210, 211-214
Community job market, 279
    assessment of, 290
Community receptivity/acceptance
    evaluation, 285
Community resources
    assessment of, 277-279
    utilization of, 285
Competencies, 4
Complex behavior, 135
Compliance training, 128
Comprehension, 63
Comprehensive Development Scale, 91
Comprehensive nature of vocational training, 290-301
Computation of coins, 258-259
Concepts, 86
Conditioned reinforcers, 99
Conduct. See Behaviors
Consent, 23
Consistency of tests, 49
Constraints in environment, 6
Construct validity, 49
Content
    language, 228
    social validation of, 290

validity of, 49, 290
Contingent education procedures, 126-127
Contingent observation, 126
Continuous group training model of parent training, 28
Continuous Record for Educational-Developmental Gain, 77, 91
Continuous reinforcement, 301
Control, 229
    antecedent event, 319
    behavior, 6
    jaw, 202
    self-extended, 229
Correct behavior modeling, 140
Correlation coefficients, 49
Cost
    absorption of, 19
    of response, 101-102
Credibility, vocational, 272-273
Criterion, 229
    changing, 119
    of ultimate functioning model, 136-137
Criterion-referenced tests, 48, 52, 53, 60, 61, 68, 71, 74, 75, 77, 85
Criterion-related validity, 49
Criterion Test, 230, 231
Cues
    environmental, 136
    verbal, 51, 142
Cup drinking, 202
Current operation capacity, 16
Curriculum, 320-322
    design of, 6
    development of, 135-156
    field-tested, 151
    implementation of, 135-156
    Curriculum Assessment Guide, 77, 91
Custodial mentally retarded, 3

D

Daily living
    activities in, 87

skills in, 69
Data
  base of, 18
  collection of. *See* Data collection
  evaluation of across multiple time
    periods, 122-123
Data-based training decisions, 153
Data collection, 48, 152
  for duration measure, 110
  for event sampling, 108
  for time sampling, 111
Daytime toilet training, 245-249
Deferred imitation, 213, 224-227
Delayed complete model, 230
Delayed truncated model, 230
Delivery of services, 18
  models of, 163
  in vocational area, 270-272
Derived scores, 48, 52
Descriptive tests, 48, 317
Design
  age-appropriate, 283
  baseline, 116
  criterion, 119
  curriculum, 6
  environmental, 15
  evaluation of, 106-122
  multielement, 121
  multiple baseline, 116
  reversal, 114, 115
  single subject, 114
Descriptive tests, 53
Destructive behavior, 56
Detailed assessment, 286
Determination
  of educational objectives, 90-91
  of interrater reliability, 112-113
Development
  age of, 135
  artificial skill, 276
  curriculum, 135-136
  language, 56, 74
  level of, 135
  motor, 69
  perceptual, 69
  physical, 55, 70

reaction, 217-219
scales of, 51
severe discrepancy in, 5
skill, 6, 276
social, 69
Developmental age, 5
Developmentally based language
  program, 228
Developmental model, 4, 135-136
Developmental Pinpoints, 149
Developmental program, 223, 235
*Developmental Skill Assessment
  Record,* 76, 91
Developmental taxonomies, 78-79, 91
Diagnosis, 18
  medical, 47
Dialogue, 212
Differences between groups, 3
Differential reinforcement, 101
  of high rates (DRH), 302
  of incompatible behavior (DRI),
    303
  of low rates (DRL), 101
  of other behavior (DRO), 101,
    126, 303-304
Direct selection, 237
Disapproval, 104
Discrepancy in development, 5
Disruptive behavior, 104
Dissimilar behavior, 103
Dissimilar overcorrection, 102
Documentation, 124, 163
Domestic activity, 56
Dressing, 78, 84, 251-252
Dressing Scale, 58
DRH. *See* Differential reinforcement
  of high rates
Drinking
  cup, 202
  skills in, 78
Drivers training, 17
DRL. *See* Differential reinforcement
  of low rates
DRO. *See* Differential reinforcement
  of other behavior
Due process, 22-24

Duration measure, 109
  data collection sheet for, 110
Duties at home, 70

E

Eating, 78, 84, 204, 249-251
Eating Scale, 58
EBJA. *See Empirically Based
  Training Assessment*
Eccentric habits, 57
Ecological language training
  program, 228
Ecological training, 250
Ecological validity, 114
Economic activity, 55
Economic behavior, 70
Economic skills training, 258-259
Edible items as reinforcers, 98, 103,
  143, 153, 155
Education
  formal, 321, 322
  inservice, 20, 22
  preservice, 20, 22
  umbrella model of, 6-9
Educational administrators, 14
Educational classifications, 3
Educational fines, 127
Educational leaders, 14
Educational needs, 4
Educational objectives determination,
  90-91
Educational program
  evaluation of, 92
  implementation of, 91-92
Educational self-contained structures,
  5
Educational setting, 146
Educators
  barrier between parents and, 28
  regular, 21-22
  skills of, 276-277
ELI. *See* Environmental Language
  Inventory
Emergencies, 256

*Empirically Based Training
  Assessment* (EBJA), 71, 91, 150,
  318
Empirical sequencing, 149
Encoding, 237
Endurance, 293, 299
  rates of, 298
Environment, 11-41, 315-317
  adaptations of, 122-123
  assessment of, 87
  boundaries of, 210
  constraints in, 6
  cues in, 136
  design of, 15
  home, 316
  least restrictive, 22-24
  structure of, 146-149, 319
*Environmental Language Intervention
  Program*, 233, 234
Environmental Language Inventory
  (ELI), 233, 234
Environmental Prelanguage Battery
  (EPB), 233, 234
EPB. *See* Environmental
  Prelanguage Battery
Etiological classifications, 3
Evaluation
  See also Assessment
  of community receptivity/
    acceptance, 285
  of data across multiple time
    periods, 122-123
  design, 106-122
  educational program, 92
  home training session, 39
  home visit, 37
  independent, 23
  nondiscriminatory, 50
  parent, 37
  parent trainer, 37
  preplacement, 23
  in vocational training, 285
Event sampling, 107-109
Exclusion principle, 4
Expectations, 4, 318
  of vocational potential, 269

Expressions of approval, 98
Expressive communication, 219-221, 222, 223-226, 227, 237
Expressive language, 237
Extension of muscle, 164
Extinction, 125, 126
Extrapolation of test scores, 52

F

Facial expressions of approval, 98
Facilities
  location of, 16
  physical, 15
  usability of, 15
Fading, 139
Family adjustment problems, 27
Family training, 316
Feeding. *See* Eating
Fels Parent Behavior Rating Scale, 40
Field-tested curriculum, 151
Fine motor skills, 63, 74, 76, 78, 86
Fines, 127
Fixed-interval schedule of reinforcement, 123
Fixed-ratio schedule of reinforcement, 124
Flexion, 164
Food intake speed, 250
Formal education, age for, 321, 322
Formal language instruction, 227-228
Forward chaining, 138, 320
Functional independence scales, 58-59
Functional Speech and Language Training for the Severely Handicapped, 228
Functioning
  basic, 85
  developmental, 135
  independent, 55
  level of, 4, 135
  targeted independent, 136
  ultimate, 136-137
Funds for transportation, 17

G

General comprehension, 63
Generalization, 154-156, 231, 282, 319
Generalized conditioned reinforcer, 99
General knowledge, 63
Gestural prompts, 140, 142
Gesture construction, 214
Global assessment, 286
Goals
  See also Objectives
  multidisciplinary team, 18
  vocational, 294-297
Grade equivalents, 48
Grandma's rule, 100
Graphic communication, 237
Grooming behaviors, 251-252
Gross motor skills, 63, 74, 76, 78, 85
Group differences, 3
Group instruction, 147
Group meetings, 37, 38
Group similarities, 3
Group training models, 28
Growth in behavior, 135
Guidance, physical, 141
Guidebook to: The Minimum Federal Guidelines and Requirements for Accessible Design, The, 16
Guidelines for behavior, 106

H

Habits, 56, 57
Handicapped, defined, 4
Handicapping condition categories, 4
Hersey and Blanchard's situational leadership theory, 15
Hierarchical nature of behavioral growth, 135
History of administrative theory, 14
Home, 6
  duties at, 70
  environment at, 316

Home intervention model, 28
Home living skills, 73
  training in, 253-256
Home training session evaluation, 39
Home visits, 34-35, 37
  evaluation of, 37
  record of, 40
Hugs, 98
Hygiene skills, 78
Hyperactive tendencies, 57
Hypertonia, 164
Hypotonia, 164

I

Identification of planning target, 18
IEP. *See* Individualized education
  program
Imitation, 213, 224-227
Immediate complete model, 230
Immediate truncated model, 230
Implementation
  of curriculum, 135-156
  of educational program, 91-92, 149-152
  of IEP, 149-152
  of instruction, 137-146
Inappropriate interpersonal
  mannerisms, 56
Independence, 58-59
Independence-training procedure, 155
Independent evaluation, 23
Independent functioning, 55
  targeted, 136
Independent living skills, 73, 243-267
Independent travel, 70
Individual instruction, 147
Individualization of students, 3
Individualized education program
  (IEP), 36
  planning for meeting, 37
  selection and implementation of,
    149-152
Individualized home intervention
  model of parent training, 28
Individual Prescriptive Planning

Sheet, 79, 91
Infant scales, 50, 51
Information. *See* Data
Informed consent, 23
Initiate Home Carryover procedure,
  231
Initiative, 67
In-school attendance, 30
Inservice training, 20, 22
Institutions, 13
Instruction, 18
  activities in, 16
  communication, 209-241
  formal language, 227-228
  group, 147
  implementation of, 137-146
  individual, 147
  language, 227-228
  modification in, 318
  motor-related systematic, 164
  physical adaptations in, 318
  process of, 152-154
  systematic, 164
Intake of food, 250
Integrated (ecological) language
  training program, 228
Integrated instructional model, 6
Integrated program approach, 233
Integrated training, 235
Integration, 229
Intelligence quotient, 3
Intelligence scales for infants, 50
Intensive training, 250
Interaction
  analysis of, 318
  parent-to-parent, 28
  staff-student, 148
Interagency provisions, 19
Internal consistency of tests, 49
Interpersonal mannerisms, 56
Inter-program responsibilities, 19
Interrater reliability, 107, 112-113
Interval
  fixed, 123
  variable, 124
Interval time sampling, 112

Intervention programs
  language, 228-236
  validation of, 113-122
*Intervention Strategy for Language-
  Deficient Children, An,* 235
Instructional models, 6
Involvement
  classroom, 29
  multidisciplinary, 17-19
  parent, 27-43, 282, 287
Isolated language training program,
  228
Isolated settings, 276
Isolated training, 5, 229, 231

J

Jaw control, 202
Job market, 279
  assessment of, 290
Job training. *See* Vocational training

K

Knowledge, 63

L

Labeling, 4, 90
  categorical, 3
Language, 63, 69, 73, 76, 86
  See also Communication; Speech
  development of, 56, 74
  expressive, 237
  formal instruction in, 227-228
  sign, 51
*Language Acquisition Program for
  the Retarded or Multiply Impaired,*
  231
Language content areas, 228
*Language Program for the
  Nonlanguage Child, A,* 229
Language training, 228-236

adaptations for, 236-238
LAP. *See Learning Accomplishment
  Profile*
Laundry skills, 255
Layout, 146
Leadership
  Hersey and Blanchard's situational
    theory of, 15
  power struggle for by team
    members, 18
Learned responses, 98
Learning
  ability for, 273
  environment for, 146-149
  need for, 274-275
  right to, 273-274
  structure of environment for,
    146-149
Learning Accomplishment Profile
  (LAP), 74, 91
Least restrictive environment, 22-24
Legal rights of students, 23
Leisure skills, 261-263
Lip closure, 204
Living skills
  home, 253-256
  independent, 243-267
Location of facilities, 16
Locomotion, 84
Logographic communication system,
  237
Low expectations of vocational
  potential, 269

M

Mainstreaming, 315
Maintenance training, 154-156
Management, 6
  behavior, 95-129, 319-320
  physical, 164-180
Mandatory in-school attendance, 30
Manipulation of objects, 210
Mannerisms, 56
Manual communication systems, 236

Manuscript writing, 63
Math, 63
McGregor's Theory X and Theory Y
  motivational theory, 14
Meal preparation, 253-254
Measurement
  of behavioral change, 144-146
  duration, 109, 110
Medical diagnosis, 47
Medications, 57
Meetings
  group, 37, 38
  IEP planning, 37
MEMPHIS Comprehensive
  Developmental Scale, 75
Mending of clothes, 255-256
Midline positioning, 164
Minivans, 17
Modeling of correct behavior, 140,
  141
Modification in instructional
  programming, 318
Momentary time sampling, 109
Monitoring system for production
  rate, 304, 309
Monterey Language Program, 229
Motivational theory, 14
Motor-related systematic instruction,
  164
Motor skills, 73, 81, 163-207
  development of, 69
  fine, 63, 74, 76, 78, 86
  gross, 63, 74, 76, 78, 85
  preambulatory, 63
Movement
  co-active, 212, 221-224
  as reinforcement, 212
Movement dialogue, 212
Multidisciplinary team, 17-19, 47
  goals and objectives of, 18
Multielement design, 121
Multiple baseline, 116, 117, 119, 120
Multiple time periods for evaluation
  of data, 122-123
Muscle extension, 164
Muscle tone, 164

N

NARC. See National Association for
  Retarded Citizens
Nasal hygiene skills, 78
National Association for Retarded
  Citizens (NARC), 106
National Association of State
  Directors of Special Education, 17
Natural gesture construction, 214
Nature of population, 15
Needs
  assessment of, 18
  educational, 4
  for learning, 274-275
  parent training, 33
  staffing, 17-19
Negative reinforcement, 128
Neuromuscular deficits, 163, 164
Nighttime toilet training, 249
No-model concept, 230
Nondiscriminatory evaluation, 50
Nonhandicapped students, 21-22
Nonpictorial logographic system, 237
Nonrepresentational reference
  activities, 212
Non-Speech Language Initiation
  Program, 237
Nonverbal communication system, 48
Normalization, 315
Norm-referenced tests, 48, 49, 51, 52,
  53, 58, 67, 70, 79, 83, 92
Notification, 23
Number dimension in reinforcement
  schedule, 301
Numbers, 56
  skills in, 70

O

Objectives
  See also Goals
  determination of, 90-91
  of multidisciplinary team, 18
Object manipulation, 210

Observation
  behavior, 287
  contingent, 126
  of skills, 79
  strategies for, 79, 106, 107
Observer drift, 107
Occupation, 84
Occupational therapy, 163
Odd mannerisms, 56
On-the-job training, 272, 287, 290
Operationalizing of communication
  programming, 217-227
Orla hygiene skills, 78
Organization
  administrative table of, 17
  of behavior, 86
  teaching table of, 17
Overcorrection, 102-105, 127
  bedrest, 104
  topographically dissimilar, 102
  topographically similar, 102
Oversight committee, 106

P

Pain application, 103
Paired reinforcement, 143
Parent-Administered Communication
  Inventory, 233
Parent-as-parent trainer model of
  parent training, 30, 31-32
  validation of, 39-41
Parents, 150
  barrier between educators and, 28
  consent of, 23
  evaluation by, 37
  interactions among, 28
  involvement of, 27-43, 282, 287
  training of. *See* Parent training
  in vocational training, 282
Parent trainer evaluation, 37
Parent training, 27-43
  center-based training model of, 29
  classroom involvement model of,
    29

continuous group training model
  of, 28
individualized home intervention
  model of, 28
needs survey for, 33
parent-as-parent trainer model of,
  30, 39-41
restrictive group training model of,
  28
telecommunication training model
  of, 29
PCLT. *See* Programmed
  Conditioning for Language Test
Pedestrian skills training, 259-260
Pennsylvania Training Model, 77,
  91, 92
Percentiles, 48
Perception of separation, 211
Perceptual-cognitive skills, 76, 78
Perceptual development, 69
Performance levels, 4
Performance role of administrator, 15
Personal-social skills, 76
Physical adaptations in instructional
  programming, 318
Physical assistance, 140-142,
Physical development, 55, 70
Physical facilities, 15
Physical guidance, 141
Physical layout of educational setting,
  146
Physical management, 164-180
Physical prompts, 51, 141
Physical therapy, 47, 163
Physicians, 47
Pictorial logographic system, 237
PL 93-112, 15
PL 94-142, 13, 15, 16, 18, 22, 23, 24,
  27, 50, 51, 52
Placement, 22-24, 90
Planning
  identification of target for, 18
  IEP, 37
  transitional, 282
Population
  defining of, 3-5

nature of, 15
standardization, 48, 49
Positioning, 164
Positive practice, 102, 103, 104, 105
Positive reinforcement, 104, 105,
  123-126
  removal of, 125-126
Potential, 269
Power struggle for leadership of
  team, 18
Practice, 102, 103, 104, 105
Praise, 98, 99, 103, 143, 155, 232
Preambulatory behaviors, 63
Preferences in reinforcers, 153
Prelanguage accomplishments, 211
Prelanguage prerequisite behaviors
  vs. prelanguage communication
  skills, 236
Prelanguage programming, 210-211
Premack principle, 100
Preparation of staff, 20-21
Preplacement evaluation, 23
Prerequisite behaviors for
  prelanguage, 236
Pre-resonance level, 217-219
Prescriptive tests, 48, 53, 317
Preservice training, 20, 22
Pre-speech, 63
*Prevocational Assessment and
  Curriculum Guide,* 286
Primary reinforcers, 98, 143, 232
Primitive reflexes, 164
Private institutions, 13
Procedure specification, 19
Production phase of vocational
  training, 301
Production rates, 293, 298, 301
  monitoring system for, 304, 309
  standard, 298
Professional and Support Staff Needs
  Assessment Survey, 21
Profoundly handicapped, defined, 4
Program data base, 18
Programmed Conditioning for
  Language Test (PCLT), 230
Progress in vocational training, 285

Project MEMPHIS, 75, 91, 92
Project MORE, 140
Prompts, 139-141, 249
  gestural, 140, 142
  physical, 51, 141
  restrictive, 142
  sequences of, 140, 142, 320
  verbal, 140, 141
  within-stimulus, 141
Prone position, 164
Prorating of tests scores, 52
Psychological disturbances, 57
Psychologists, 18, 48
Psychology, 163
Psychometric descriptions, 3
Public school administrators, 13
Punishment, 128
Purchasing skills, 261

Q

Quality of work, 293, 299
*Quantitative Assessment of Motor
  and Sensory/Motor Acquisition in
  Handicapped and Nonhandicapped
  Infants and Young Children,* 318

R

Raw scores, 48
Reaction development, 217-219
Readiness, 63
Reading, 63
Ready, Set, Go Talk to Me
  instructional program, 233, 234
Rebellious behavior, 56
Reception, 229
Receptive communication, 219, 220,
  222-223, 224, 226-227
Receptive resonance, 212
Receptivity of community, 285
Records of home visits, 4
Reference activities, 212
Reference in content, 229

Referral process, 32
Regular educators, 21-22
Rehabilitation Act of 1973, 274
Reinforcement, 97, 143-144, 229
    artificial, 155
    backup, 99, 100
    conditioned, 99
    continuous, 301
    defined, 98
    differential, 101
    edible, 103, 143, 153, 155
    edible items as, 98
    generalized conditioned, 99
    movement as, 212
    negative, 128
    paired, 143
    positive. *See* Positive reinforcement
    preferences in, 153
    primary, 98, 143, 232
    response-based, 123, 124
    sampling of, 98
    schedules of. *See* Reinforcement
        schedules
    smiles as, 98
    social, 98, 99, 143, 153
    theory of, 232
    time-based, 123, 124
    token, 99, 100
    withholding of, 125
Reinforcement of alternative behavior
    (Alt-R), 101, 126
Reinforcement schedules, 123, 229,
    301-308
    DRH, 101, 301, 302
    DRL, 101, 303
    DRO, 101, 126, 303-304
    fixed-interval, 123
    fixed-ratio, 124
    number dimension in, 301
    time dimension in, 301
    variable-interval, 124
    variable-ratio, 124
Relaxation, 104
Reliability
    interrater, 107, 112-113
    test-retest, 49

of tests, 48, 49
Removal of positive reinforcement,
    125-126
Resonance, 212
    level of, 219-221
    receptive, 212
    in Van Dijk communication
        program, 211
Resources in community, 277-279,
    285
Response, 229
    cost of, 101-102
    to emergencies, 256
    learned, 98
    reinforcement based on, 123, 124
Response-fair tests, 51, 52
Responsibility, 56, 70
    inter-program, 19
Restitution, 102, 103
Restrictive group training model of
    parent training, 28
Restrictive prompt, 142
Reversal design, 114, 115
Reverse chaining, 138
Rewards, 97, 98
Rights of students, 23, 273, 274

S

Safety training, 256-257
Sampling
    event, 107-109
    interval time, 112
    momentary time, 109
    reinforcer, 98
    standardization, 52
    time, 109, 111, 112
Scaled scores, 48
Scales
    See also Tests
    adaptive behavior, 51, 53, 150
    development, 51
    functional independence, 58-59
    infant, 50, 51
    social adaptation, 59

Scanning, 237
Schedules
  of reinforcement. *See*
    Reinforcement schedules
  staff, 147-148
  student, 147-148
School administrator, 13
School psychologist, 18
School setting, 6
Scores
  derived, 48, 52
  extrapolation ot, 52
  prorating of, 52
  raw, 48
  scaled, 48
Screening, 89
Selection
  of clothes, 252
  direct, 237
  of IEP, 149-152
  of tests, 89
Self-abusive behavior, 3, 57
Self-contained classrooms, 13
Self-contained educational structures,
  5
Self-control, 229, 319
  techniques for, 155
Self-direction, 56, 84, 300
Self-feeding, 204
Self-help skills, 60, 63, 67, 70, 73, 74,
  81, 83, 84
Self-initiation, 299, 300
Self-stimulatory behavior, 103-104
Semantic based language program,
  228, 231, 235
Senses, 85
  stimuli of, 153
Sensory skills, 73
Separation perception, 211
Sequencing, 149
Services
  See also specific services
  accessibility of, 15
  delivery of, 18, 163, 270-272
  transitional, 279-281
  vocational, 270-272

Setting
  home, 6
  isolated, 276
  physical layout of, 146
  school, 6
Severe developmental discrepancy, 5
Severely handicapped, defined, 4
Sexually aberrant behavior, 57
Shaping, 137-139
  techniques for, 245
Sheltered program, 302
Sheltered workshop, 270, 272, 300
Shelves, 213
Sign language, 51
Similarities within groups, 3
Single subject designs, 114
Situational leadership theory, 15
Skills
  academic. *See* Academic skills
  artificial development of, 276
  auditory, 78
  bathing, 78
  bathroom cleaning, 254-255
  cognitive, 69, 74, 86
  communication. *See*
    Communication
  daily living, 69
  development of, 6, 276
  dressing, 78, 84, 251-252
  drinking, 78
  economic, 258-259
  educator/habilitator, 276-277
  feeding, 78
  fine motor, 63, 74, 76, 78, 86
  gross motor, 63, 74, 76, 78, 85
  home living, 73, 253-256
  independent functioning, 136
  independent living, 73, 243-267
  language. *See* Language
  laundry, 255
  leisure, 261-263
  motor. *See* Motor skills
  nasal hygiene, 78
  numerical, 70
  observation of, 79, 91
  oral hygiene, 78

pedestrian, 259-260
perceptual-cognitive, 76, 78
personal-social, 76
preambulatory motor, 63
prelanguage communication, 236
purchasing, 261
self-help, 60, 63, 67, 70, 73, 74, 81,
   83, 84
sensory, 73
social, 67, 73, 74, 78, 81, 97-132
tactile, 78
toileting, 78, 244-249
undressing, 78
visual, 78
vocational, 286-287
washing, 78
Smiles as reinforcers, 98
Social adaptation scales, 59
Social behaviors, 70
Social development, 69
Social disapproval, 104
Social interaction skills, 78
Socialization, 56, 84
Social praise, 98, 99, 103, 143, 155,
   232
Social reinforcers, 98, 99, 143, 153
Social skils, 67, 73, 74, 81, 97-132
Social system theory, 14
Social validation of content, 290
Social workers, 48
Specification of procedures, 19
Specific concepts, 86
Speech, 63
   See also Communication;
      Language
communication therapist, 47
Split-half reliability of tests, 49
Spontaneous Language Record, 231
Staff
   needs for, 17-19
   preparation of, 20-21
   schedules of, 147-148
   student interaction with, 148
Standardization population, 48, 49
Standardization procedures, 52
Standardization sample, 52

Standardized academic achievement
   tests, 317
Standard production rate, 298
Stanines, 48
State institutions, 13
Stereotyped behavior, 56
Stimulus, 229
   sensory, 153
Strengths, 4, 48
Structure
   environmental, 146-149, 319
   learning environment, 146-149
   self-contained educational, 5
Student progress evaluation, 285
Subject designs, 114
Supine position, 164
Survey of parent training needs, 33
Syntactic based language program,
   228, 229
Systematic application of pain, 103
Systematic instruction, 164
Systematic training procedures, 282

T

Table of organization, 17
Tactile skills, 78
Taking a frequency, 107
TARC Assessment System, 79, 89
Target behavior
   defined, 106-122
   steps in, 321
Targeted independent functioning
   skills, 136
Target for planning, 18
Target population defining, 3-5
Task analysis, 52, 137, 151, 155, 286,
   287, 321
Taxicabs, 17
Teacher training, 317
Teaching Research Infant and Child
   Center, 150
Teaching Research Model, 153
Teaching table of organization, 17
Team, 17-19, 47

power struggle for leadership of, 18
Telecommunication training model
    of parent training, 29
Telephone training, 257-258
Test item adaptation, 51-52
Test-retest reliability of tests, 48, 49
Tests
    See also Scales; specific tests
    academic, 317
    achievement, 317
    adaptive behavior, 51, 53, 150, 317,
        318
    criterion-referenced, 48, 52, 53, 60,
        61, 68, 71, 74, 75, 77, 85
    descriptive, 48, 53, 317
    design of for severely and
        profoundly handicapped
        individuals, 52
    extrapolation of scores on, 52
    internal consistency of, 49
    norm-referenced, 48, 49, 51, 52, 53,
        58, 67, 70, 79, 83, 92
    prescriptive, 48, 53, 317
    prorating of scores on, 52
    reliability of, 48, 49
    response-fair, 51, 52
    selection of, 89
    standardized academic achievement,
        317
    test-retest reliability of, 49
    validity of, 49
Theoretical models, 163
Theory X and Theory Y motivational
    theory, 14
Therapists, 47
Therapy, 163
Time-based reinforcement, 123, 124
Time concepts, 56
Time dimension in reinforcement
    schedule, 301
Timeout, 102, 104, 105, 126, 127
Time periods, 122-123
Time sampling
    data collection sheet for, 111
    interval, 112
    momentary, 109

Toileting Scales, 59
Toilet training, 78, 244-245
    behavioral model for, 245
    daytime, 245-249
    nighttime, 249
Token economies, 101, 127
Token reinforcement, 99, 100
Tone of muscles, 164
Topographically dissimilar behavior,
    103
Topographically dissimilar
    overcorrection, 102
Topographically similar behavior, 103
Topographically similar
    overcorrection, 102
Total individualization of students, 3
Traditional administrative theories, 14
Training, 147
    attention, 103
    bus-riding, 260-261
    center-based, 29
    compliance, 128
    continuous group, 28
    data-based, 153
    daytime toilet, 245-249
    driver, 17
    ecological, 250
    economic skills, 258-259
    family, 316
    generalization, 282
    home, 39
    home living skills, 253-256
    independence, 155
    inservice, 20, 22
    integrated, 235
    intensive, 250
    isolated, 5, 229, 231
    job. See Vocational training
    language. See Language training
    maintenance, 154-156
    needs survey for, 33
    nighttime toilet, 249
    on-the-job, 272, 287, 290
    parent. See Parent training
    pedestrian skills, 259-260
    preservice, 20, 22

restrictive group, 28
safety, 256-257
social skills, 97-132
systematic, 282
teacher 317
telecommunication, 29
telephone, 257-258
toilet. *See* Toilet training
travel, 259-261
vocational. *See* Vocational training
work. *See* Vocational training
Transfer, 231
Transitional services, 279-281, 282
Transportation, 16-17
funds for, 17
Transportation of the Handicapped: A Survey of State Education Agency Transportation Directors, 17
Travel
bus, 17, 260-261
independent, 70
training in, 259-261
Treatment models, 163
Tutors, 21

U

Ultimate functioning, 136-137
Umbrella model of education, 6-9
Unacceptable habits, 56, 57
Unadaptive Self-Directed Behavior, 59
Undressing skills, 78
United States Architectural and Transportation Barriers Compliance Board, 16
Untrustworthy behavior, 56
Usability of facilities, 15
Utilization of community resources, 285

V

Validation
construct, 49
content, 49

criterion-related, 49
ecological, 114
of intervention programs, 113-122
of parent-as-parent trainer model of parent training, 39-41
social, 290
of tests, 49
Van Dijk communication program, 211-214
Variable-interval schedule of reinforcement, 124
Variable-ratio schedule of reinforcement, 124
Verbal cues, 51, 142
Verbal prompts, 140, 141
Vertical umbrella model, 6, 7
Vineland Social Maturity Scale (VSMS), 83, 90, 92
Violent behavior, 56
Visibility of severely and profoundly handicapped, 22
Visits. *See* Home visits
Visual skills, 78
Vocal habits, 56
Vocational activity, 56
Vocational behavior, 70
Vocational credibility, 272-273
Vocational goals, 294-297
Vocational potential, 269
Vocational skills assessment, 286-287
Vocational training, 269-312
acquisition phase of, 301
age-appropriate design of, 283
comprehensive nature of, 290-301
delivery of, 270-272
evaluation of student progress in, 285
parent involvement in, 282
production phase of, 301
VSMS. *See Vineland Social Maturity Scale*
Vulpe Assessment Battery, 85, 91

W

Washing skills, 78

Weaknesses, 4, 48
Weber's bureaucratic model, 14
Withdrawal, 56
Withholding reinforcement, 125
Within-group similarities, 3
Within-stimulus prompts, 141
Worker characteristics, 294-297
Work quality, 293, 299
Workshops, 270, 272, 300

Work training. *See* Vocational
  training
Writing, 63
Written notification, 23

Z

Zero reject, 13, 22